I0005900

THE GLOSSARY OF
FINANCIAL
MANAGEMENT

Compiled & Edited By:
Nikita Iyer

Rhythm

Independent
Publication

THE GLOSSARY OF FINANCIAL MANAGEMENT

Compiled & Edited By:
Nikita Iyer

Copyright ©2023, All rights reserved.

ISBN:9798862339154

9798862339154

Published by:

Rhythm Independent Publication,

Jinkethimmanahalli, Varanasi, Bengaluru, Karnataka, India - 560036

For all types of correspondence, send your mails to the provided address above.

The information presented herein has been collated from a diverse range of sources, comprehensive perspective on the subject matter.

All rights reserved. No part of this publication may be reproduced, distributed, or transmitted in by any means, including photocopying, recording, or other electronic or mechanical methods, prior written permission of the publisher except in the case of brief quotations embodied in crit and certain other noncommercial uses permitted by copyright law.

Abnormal Profit

Abnormal profit, also known as supernormal profit, is a concept in financial management that refers to the excess profit earned by a business entity over the normal profit or the minimum level of profit required to cover all costs, including both explicit and implicit costs. It is the difference between total revenue and total cost, including both explicit and implicit costs. When a business earns abnormal profit, it means that it is generating more revenue than necessary to cover its costs and is earning a higher level of profit than what would be considered as normal in a competitive market. This can occur due to various factors, such as monopoly power, technological innovation, brand recognition, or unique market positioning.

Abnormal Return

Abnormal return, in the context of financial management, refers to the difference between the actual return on an investment and the expected return based on the overall market performance or a benchmark. It is a measure used to evaluate the performance of investments, such as stocks, bonds, or portfolios, by comparing their returns to what would be considered normal or expected. The expected return is usually calculated using various statistical methods, such as historical performance, market trends, or economic factors. It represents the return that an investor can reasonably expect to earn based on the risk and return characteristics associated with the investment. Abnormal return is often used in the field of finance to assess the effectiveness of investment strategies or to evaluate the performance of fund managers. It helps determine whether an investment has outperformed or underperformed the market or a specific benchmark. Positive abnormal return indicates that the investment has generated higher returns compared to what would be expected, indicating superior performance. This can be a result of various factors such as exceptional management decisions, favorable market conditions, or unique market insights. On the other hand, negative abnormal return suggests that the investment has underperformed, failing to meet expectations. This can be due to poor management decisions, adverse market conditions, or unforeseen events. Abnormal return is often used in conjunction with other performance metrics and ratios, such as alpha, beta, standard deviation, and Sharpe ratio, to provide a more comprehensive analysis of an investment's performance. It helps investors understand the risk and return trade-offs associated with their investments and make informed decisions. Overall, abnormal return provides valuable insights into the relative performance of investments and helps investors identify opportunities for maximizing returns or avoiding underperforming investments.

Absolute Return

Absolute return refers to the measure of the overall return on an investment or a portfolio over a specific period of time. It is a financial management concept used to evaluate the performance of an investment strategy, fund, or portfolio by comparing the actual return achieved to a benchmark or a target return. Unlike relative return, which measures the performance of an investment against a specific market index or a peer group, absolute return evaluates the investment's performance in isolation.

Accelerated Depreciation

Accelerated Depreciation is a method of depreciation that allows companies to recover the cost of an asset at a faster rate than traditional straight-line depreciation. This method benefits companies by reducing their taxable income in the earlier years of an asset's life, providing them with a larger tax shield and increased cash flow. In accelerated depreciation, the cost of the asset is allocated over its useful life, but the depreciation expense is front-loaded to the earlier years. This means that more depreciation expense is recognized in the early years of the asset's life and less in the later years. This contrasts with straight-line depreciation, where the same

1

amount of depreciation expense is recognized in each year of the asset's life. The main advantage of accelerated depreciation is the tax savings it provides to companies. By recognizing higher depreciation expense in the early years, companies can lower their taxable income and therefore reduce their tax liability. This can result in a significant cash flow benefit, as companies may be able to defer taxes or even receive tax refunds. Additionally, accelerated depreciation can help companies to minimize the overall cost of an asset by providing a faster recovery of its initial cost. There are different methods of accelerated depreciation, such as the declining balance method and the sum-of-the-years'-digits method. The declining balance method allows for a higher depreciation expense in the early years, gradually decreasing over time, while the sum-of-the-years'-digits method also front-loads depreciation expense but in a more gradual manner. These methods are commonly used for assets that are expected to be more valuable or productive in their earlier years. While accelerated depreciation provides immediate tax benefits, it does result in lower depreciation expenses in the later years of an asset's life. This can impact financial statements by reducing the asset's carrying value and potentially leading to a higher gain or loss upon disposal. Therefore, it is essential for companies to carefully consider the trade-off between tax savings and long-term financial implications when deciding to use accelerated depreciation.

Accounting Equation

The accounting equation is a fundamental concept in financial management that represents the fundamental relationship between a company's assets, liabilities, and owner's equity. It can be expressed as Assets = Liabilities + Owner's Equity. Assets refer to all the resources that a company owns or controls, which can include cash, inventory, property, equipment, and investments. These assets represent the economic value of the company and are used to generate revenue. Liabilities, on the other hand, represent the company's obligations or debts to external parties, such as loans, accounts payable, and accrued expenses. Owner's equity, also known as shareholders' equity or net worth, represents the residual interest in the assets of a company after deducting liabilities. In simple terms, it is the ownership or claim that the owners have on the company's assets. The accounting equation is based on the principle of double-entry bookkeeping, which states that for every transaction, there must be an equal debit and credit. This means that any increase in assets must be balanced by either an increase in liabilities or owner's equity, and vice versa. For example, if a company borrows money from a bank (increase in assets), it must also record a liability (increase in liabilities) to reflect the loan and maintain the equilibrium of the accounting equation. The accounting equation is a useful tool for financial management as it provides a snapshot of a company's financial position at any given time. By analyzing the equation, managers, investors, and creditors can assess the company's liquidity, solvency, and overall financial health. A company with a strong balance sheet will have a higher level of assets compared to its liabilities and a healthy level of owner's equity. On the other hand, a company with a weak balance sheet may have high levels of debt and low owner's equity, indicating financial instability. In conclusion, the accounting equation represents the fundamental relationship between a company's assets, liabilities, and owner's equity. It serves as a foundation for financial management and helps evaluate a company's financial position. By understanding and analyzing the equation, financial managers can make informed decisions regarding the allocation of resources and long-term financial strategies.

Accounts Payable Aging

Accounts Payable Aging refers to a financial management tool that monitors and categorizes the outstanding liabilities or debts owed by a company to its suppliers or vendors. It helps the management in tracking and managing the payment obligations of the company in an organized manner. The purpose of Accounts Payable Aging is to provide an overview of the company's current financial obligations and their due dates. This tool allows the management to analyze and understand the payment patterns, assess the liquidity position, and determine the company's ability to meet its short-term obligations. By categorizing the outstanding payments based on their due dates, such as 30 days, 60 days, 90 days, etc., it enables the management to identify the overdue payments and take appropriate actions to avoid any negative implications.

Accounts Payable Turnover

The Accounts Payable Turnover ratio is a financial management metric used to measure how efficiently a company pays off its suppliers and vendors. It indicates the number of times a company pays off its accounts payable during a specific period. This ratio is calculated by dividing the average accounts payable by the total purchases made on credit during the same period. The formula for Accounts Payable Turnover is: Accounts Payable Turnover = Total Purchases on Credit / Average Accounts Payable A high turnover ratio suggests that a company is paying off its suppliers quickly, which is generally considered a positive indicator of financial health and efficiency. On the other hand, a low turnover ratio may indicate that a company is delaying payments to its suppliers, which could be a sign of financial distress or poor cash flow management. It is important to note that a high turnover ratio can also indicate aggressive cash management or negotiation with suppliers to optimize working capital. Therefore, it is crucial to analyze the turnover ratio in conjunction with other financial ratios and industry benchmarks to gain a comprehensive understanding of a company's financial position. Additionally, changes in the turnover ratio over time can provide insights into a company's financial trends. A decreasing turnover ratio may suggest that a company is taking longer to pay off its suppliers, while an increasing ratio may indicate improved financial management and stronger supplier relationships. In conclusion, the Accounts Payable Turnover ratio is a useful financial metric that helps assess a company's efficiency in managing its accounts payable. It provides insights into how quickly a company pays off its suppliers and can be used to identify potential risks or opportunities in cash flow management.

Accounts Payable

Accounts payable is a term used in financial management to refer to the outstanding bills and obligations of a company that are yet to be paid to its creditors and suppliers. It represents the short-term liabilities of a business and is recorded on the balance sheet as a current liability. When a company purchases goods or services on credit, it incurs an accounts payable. These payables are essentially promises to pay a specific amount to the creditor in the future. They arise from various business transactions, such as the purchase of inventory, raw materials, equipment, utilities, or professional services. Accounts payable play a crucial role in the cash flow management of a company. Proper management of payables is important to maintain the financial health and stability of the organization. Effective management involves monitoring the payment terms, negotiating favorable terms with suppliers, and ensuring timely payment to avoid penalties or strained relationships with creditors. Accounts payable are typically recorded in an accounts payable ledger or system. This ledger keeps track of the amounts owed, due dates, payment terms, and other relevant information. The accounts payable department is responsible for the accurate and timely recording of payables, verification of invoices, and processing of payments. Managing accounts payable involves several key activities. This includes carefully reviewing and approving invoices, verifying the accuracy of the billings and payment terms, matching invoices with purchase orders and receiving reports, and reconciling any discrepancies. It also involves maintaining good communication with suppliers to address any concerns or issues that may arise. The management of accounts payable also aims to optimize cash flow and working capital. Delaying payment of payables within the agreed terms can help free up cash and improve liquidity. However, this should be balanced with maintaining good relationships with suppliers and avoiding any negative impacts on the business. In summary, accounts payable refer to the outstanding bills and obligations of a company that are yet to be paid to its creditors and suppliers. Effective management of payables is crucial for maintaining financial stability, cash flow, and strong supplier relationships.

Accounts Receivable Aging

Accounts Receivable Aging refers to a financial management technique used to categorize and analyze the outstanding invoices of a company. It provides a snapshot of the amounts that customers owe the business and the length of time the invoices have been overdue. This analysis helps in assessing the creditworthiness of customers and the effectiveness of the company's credit and collections policies. The Accounts Receivable Aging report is typically divided into various time periods, such as 30 days, 60 days, 90 days, and over 90 days. The report classifies each outstanding invoice based on the number of days it is past due. The purpose of this classification is to identify potential issues with collection efforts and to manage cash flow effectively.

3

Accounts Receivable Turnover

The Accounts Receivable Turnover is a financial management ratio that measures the efficiency of a company in collecting its accounts receivable. It indicates the number of times a company can turn over its accounts receivable during a specific period. The formula for calculating Accounts Receivable Turnover is: Accounts Receivable Turnover = Net Credit Sales / Average Accounts Receivable This ratio is important for financial managers and investors as it can provide insight into a company's liquidity, credit policies, and collection efficiency. A high turnover ratio indicates that a company is collecting its accounts receivable quickly, which is a positive sign as it signifies good cash flow. On the other hand, a low turnover ratio may indicate potential issues with collection efficiency or credit policies. It is important to note that the interpretation of the Accounts Receivable Turnover ratio depends on the industry and business model of the company. Some industries, such as retail, typically have higher turnover ratios due to faster inventory turnover and shorter credit terms. In contrast, industries with longer credit terms, such as manufacturing or distribution, may have lower turnover ratios. Financial managers can utilize the Accounts Receivable Turnover ratio to assess the effectiveness of credit policies and collection procedures. By monitoring changes in the ratio over time, they can identify trends and make necessary adjustments to improve cash flow and liquidity. Additionally, investors can use this ratio to evaluate a company's ability to manage its receivables efficiently and to generate cash. In conclusion, the Accounts Receivable Turnover ratio is a key metric in financial management that measures the efficiency of a company's collection process. It provides valuable insights into a company's liquidity and credit policies, allowing financial managers and investors to make informed decisions.

Accounts Receivable

Accounts Receivable refers to the amount of money owed by customers to a company for goods or services that have been delivered but not yet paid for. In financial management, it is a critical aspect of a company's working capital, representing the funds that are expected to be received in the near future. The Accounts Receivable balance on a company's balance sheet is a reflection of its credit sales and payment terms. When a customer purchases goods or services on credit, a receivable is created, and the customer becomes a debtor of the company. The company records this as an increase in its Accounts Receivable balance and recognizes the revenue associated with the sale at the same time. The sale is considered complete, even though the payment is pending. Managing Accounts Receivable is crucial for companies as it impacts their cash flow and overall financial health. Companies need to strike a balance between granting credit to customers and ensuring timely payment. By monitoring the accounts receivable turnover ratio, a company can assess the efficiency of its credit policies and collection efforts. Accounts Receivable management involves several processes, including invoicing, credit evaluation, collection efforts, and customer communication. Invoicing should be accurate and timely to avoid payment delays. Companies often set credit limits for customers based on their creditworthiness to mitigate the risk of bad debts. Collection efforts are vital to ensuring timely payments. Companies may send reminders, make follow-up calls, or offer incentives for early settlement. They may also impose penalties for late payments. Effective customer communication is crucial in maintaining positive relationships and resolving any billing disputes promptly. Accounts Receivable is an asset in a company's balance sheet, representing the amount expected to be received from customers. It indicates the company's ability to generate sales and its liquidity. However, excessive levels of Accounts Receivable can indicate potential cash flow issues, and overdue receivables may lead to bad debts, impacting the company's profitability. In summary, Accounts Receivable in financial management refers to the outstanding money owed to a company by its customers for goods or services delivered on credit. Its management plays a vital role in maintaining cash flow and ensuring timely payment, contributing to the financial stability and success of the company.

Accrual Accounting

Accrual accounting is a method of recording and reporting financial transactions in the period in which they occur, regardless of when payment is actually made or received. It is based on the accrual principle, which states that revenues and expenses should be recognized when they are earned or incurred, rather than when cash is exchanged. Under accrual accounting, transactions are recorded in two main categories: revenues and expenses. Revenues represent the inflow of

4

assets or settlement of liabilities resulting from the sale of goods or services, while expenses represent the outflow of assets or incurrence of liabilities in the process of generating revenues. These transactions are recorded in the accounting system as they occur, even if the associated cash flows happen at a later time. One of the key advantages of accrual accounting is that it provides a more accurate representation of the financial performance and position of a business. By recognizing revenues and expenses in the period in which they occur, accrual accounting allows for a better matching of revenues and expenses, giving a clearer picture of the profitability and efficiency of an organization. In addition, accrual accounting enables businesses to adhere to generally accepted accounting principles (GAAP) and international financial reporting standards (IFRS). These standards require the use of accrual accounting to ensure consistency and comparability in financial reporting across different organizations. Accrual accounting also provides better insight into cash flow management, as it allows businesses to identify and plan for future cash outflows and inflows. By recognizing revenues and expenses when they are earned or incurred, businesses can make more informed decisions regarding investments, financing, and operational activities. Furthermore, accrual accounting facilitates the creation of financial statements, such as the income statement, balance sheet, and statement of cash flows. These statements provide a summary of the financial performance and position of a business and are used by investors, lenders, and other stakeholders to assess the profitability, solvency, and liquidity of an organization. In conclusion, accrual accounting is a method of recording and reporting financial transactions in the period in which they occur, regardless of when cash is exchanged. It provides a more accurate representation of financial performance, enables adherence to accounting standards, improves cash flow management, and facilitates the creation of financial statements.

Accrual Basis Accounting

Accrual basis accounting is the method used in financial management to record revenues and expenses when they are incurred, rather than when cash is received or paid. Under this accounting method, financial transactions are recorded in the books at the time they take place, regardless of when the associated cash flows occur. This accounting method recognizes the income and expenses as they are earned or incurred, matching them to the appropriate accounting period. It provides a more accurate picture of a company's financial performance and position by capturing all revenue and expenses during the period, regardless of when the cash is exchanged. Accrual basis accounting follows the matching principle, which states that expenses should be recognized in the same period as the revenue they generate. This ensures that the financial statements reflect the true profitability of the business, as it considers all associated costs and benefits within the same accounting period. For example, if a company provides services to a customer in December but does not receive payment until January of the following year, under accrual basis accounting, the revenue is recorded in December when the service was provided. The cash inflow is recognized separately when it occurs in January. This approach allows for a more accurate reflection of the company's revenue and expenses in December. Accrual basis accounting is considered the most accurate method of financial reporting, as it provides a comprehensive view of a company's financial performance. It allows for better comparison of financial statements over time and enables decision-makers to make more informed judgments based on complete and timely information.

Accrual Method

The accrual method is a financial management method that recognizes and records revenue and expenses when they are earned or incurred, regardless of when the cash is actually received or paid. This method follows the Generally Accepted Accounting Principles (GAAP) and is widely used by businesses to provide a more accurate representation of their financial position. Under the accrual method, revenue is recognized when it is earned, meaning when the goods or services are delivered or rendered, regardless of when the payment is received. Similarly, expenses are recognized when they are incurred, regardless of when the payment is made. This method allows businesses to match their revenues and expenses in the same accounting period, providing a clearer picture of their profitability.

Accruals

Accruals refer to the recognition of revenues or expenses in a company's financial statements before the actual cash transaction occurs. It is an accounting method that aims to provide a more accurate representation of a company's financial position and performance by matching revenues with expenses in the period in which they are incurred, regardless of when the cash is received or paid. Accrual accounting is based on the accrual principle, which states that economic events should be recorded in the period in which they occur, rather than when cash is exchanged. This principle ensures that financial statements reflect the true financial performance and position of a company, as it recognizes revenues and expenses when they are earned or incurred, rather than when the cash is received or paid. Accruals consist of two main components: accrual of revenues and accrual of expenses. The accrual of revenues refers to the recognition of revenue in the accounting period in which it is earned, even if the cash is received at a later date. For example, if a company provides goods or services to a customer in one accounting period but receives the payment in the following period, the revenue should be recognized in the period in which the goods or services were provided. The accrual of expenses, on the other hand, refers to the recognition of expenses in the accounting period in which they are incurred, even if the payment is made at a later date. For example, if a company receives an invoice for utilities expenses in one accounting period but pays the invoice in the following period, the expenses should be recognized in the period in which the utilities were used. Accruals play a crucial role in financial management as they provide a more accurate and comprehensive view of a company's financial performance and position. By matching revenues with expenses in the appropriate accounting period, accrual accounting allows investors, creditors, and other stakeholders to make informed decisions based on the company's true financial status. It also helps in achieving comparability between different accounting periods, allowing for better trend analysis and financial forecasting. In conclusion, accruals are an essential concept in financial management that involves recognizing revenues and expenses in the accounting period in which they are incurred, regardless of when the cash is exchanged. This accrual accounting method provides a more accurate representation of a company's financial performance and position, aiding in decision-making and financial analysis.

Accrued Interest

Accrued interest refers to the interest that has been earned but not yet received or paid. It is a crucial concept in financial management, particularly in the context of investing and borrowing. When a financial instrument, such as a bond or a loan, generates interest that is not paid immediately, it accrues over time. This means that the interest amount continues to increase until it is eventually paid or received. Accrued interest is typically calculated based on the amount of the principal, the interest rate, and the time period for which it has been accrued.

Accumulated Depreciation

Accumulated Depreciation is a crucial concept in the field of Financial Management. It refers to the total depreciation expense that has been charged against an asset over its useful life up to a specific point in time. This amount represents the decrease in the value of an asset due to factors such as wear and tear, obsolescence, and technological advancements. Accumulated Depreciation is recorded on the balance sheet as a contra-asset account, which means it is subtracted from the asset's value to derive its net book value.

Accumulated Earnings And Profits (AE&P)

Accumulated Earnings and Profits (AE&P) refers to the amount of a corporation's net income that has not been distributed to shareholders as dividends. It is a key concept in financial management that helps determine the amount of retained earnings available for reinvestment or distribution to shareholders. AE&P is an essential metric for assessing a company's financial health and its ability to generate and retain profits over time. It represents the cumulative total of all past profits that have not been paid out to shareholders, including both taxable and non-taxable income. AE&P is calculated by subtracting dividends paid from the corporation's net income since its inception. One of the primary purposes of AE&P is to provide a measure of the corporation's ability to pay dividends to shareholders. When a company decides to distribute dividends, it is typically required to use its accumulated earnings and profits. If the company does not have sufficient AE&P to cover the dividends, it may need to resort to other sources of funds such as borrowing or issuing new shares. AE&P also plays a crucial role in determining the tax treatment of dividends. In the United States, for example, dividends paid out of current earnings and profits (CE&P) are generally taxable to shareholders as ordinary income. However, if the dividends exceed CE&P and are paid out of AE&P, they may be treated as a tax-free return of capital or a capital gain distribution. Financial managers use AE&P as a valuable tool for making strategic financial decisions. It helps them assess the financial capacity of the company, plan for dividend payments, evaluate the feasibility of new investments, and determine the optimal capital structure. By analyzing AE&P, financial managers can gain insights into the company's historical profitability, its dividend payment history, and its ability to generate sustainable earnings in the future.

Accumulated Other Comprehensive Income (AOCI)

Accumulated Other Comprehensive Income (AOCI) refers to the part of a company's equity that includes gains and losses that have not been recognized in the income statement yet. It is a key concept in financial management as it provides information on the overall financial performance and stability of a company. AOCI includes various items that can impact a company's financial position but are not included in the net income calculation. These items are typically related to unrealized gains and losses that result from changes in the fair value of certain assets and liabilities, such as investments in stocks or bonds, foreign currency transactions, and pension plan adjustments. By recognizing these gains and losses in AOCI, companies can provide a more accurate picture of their comprehensive income, which includes both realized and unrealized gains and losses. AOCI is presented as a separate component in the equity section of the balance sheet. It is important to note that AOCI does not represent actual cash flows but rather changes in the value of certain assets or liabilities that have not yet been realized. Companies are required to disclose the details of the components of AOCI in their financial statements to provide transparency and help investors and stakeholders understand the impact of these items on their financial position. One of the significant advantages of AOCI is its ability to smooth out the volatility in a company's financial results caused by changes in the fair value of certain assets and liabilities. By recognizing these gains and losses in AOCI, companies can avoid large swings in their net income statement, which may not accurately reflect the operating performance of the business. This can be particularly relevant for companies that hold a significant amount of investments or engage in activities exposed to fluctuating currencies. In summary, AOCI is the part of a company's equity that includes gains and losses resulting from changes in the fair value of certain assets and liabilities. It provides a more comprehensive view of a company's financial performance and stability by including unrealized gains and losses that have not been recognized in the income statement yet. AOCI is an essential tool in financial management as it helps investors and stakeholders understand the impact of these items on the company's financial position.

Acquisition Cost

Acquisition Cost refers to the total cost incurred by a company to acquire a new asset or business. It includes all the expenses directly associated with the acquisition process, such as the purchase price, legal fees, due diligence costs, and other related expenses. The acquisition of assets or businesses is a common strategy used by companies to expand their operations, gain access to new markets, or increase their market share. The acquisition cost is an important aspect of financial management as it helps determine the overall financial impact of the acquisition on the company's financial statements.

Acquisition

Acquisition refers to the process by which one company acquires ownership or control over another company, either through a direct purchase of its assets or through a merger or consolidation. In the context of financial management, acquisition plays a crucial role in shaping the growth and strategy of a company. It is a strategic move that allows a company to expand its market presence, diversify its product or service offerings, increase its customer base, enter new geographical locations, or gain access to new technologies or expertise.

Active Investing

Active investing refers to a strategy in financial management where investors actively make investment decisions and frequently trade securities in order to generate a higher return on their investments compared to passive investing. Unlike passive investing, which typically involves buying and holding a diverse portfolio of securities, active investing involves a more hands-on approach that aims to outperform the market through active decision-making. In active investing, investors actively analyze market conditions and various investment options to identify mispriced securities or undervalued opportunities. They utilize fundamental analysis, technical analysis, or a combination of both to evaluate the financial health, growth potential, and future prospects of companies, sectors, or asset classes. By actively researching and assessing market conditions, active investors aim to uncover investment opportunities that can potentially generate superior returns. To implement an active investing strategy, investors may frequently buy and sell securities based on their analysis and market insights. They may make shorter-term trades, seeking to take advantage of market fluctuations or specific events that can impact the value of their investments. This active trading approach requires investors to closely monitor their portfolios and stay updated on market news, economic indicators, and corporate developments that may impact their investment decisions. Active investing requires a high level of knowledge, skill, and experience, as it involves actively managing portfolios and making informed decisions regarding asset allocation, timing, and security selection. It also requires considerable time and effort to stay informed about market trends and to analyze and monitor investments. Active investors may also face higher transaction costs, such as brokerage fees and taxes, associated with their frequent trading activities. While active investing has the potential to generate higher returns, it is also associated with higher risks. The success of active investing depends on the investor's ability to consistently make accurate investment decisions, time the market effectively, and navigate market volatility. Failure to do so may result in underperformance, higher costs, and potential losses. In summary, active investing is a proactive investment strategy where investors make frequent investment decisions and actively manage their portfolios in an attempt to outperform the market. It involves analyzing market conditions, researching investment options, and making informed decisions through active trading and asset allocation. While it offers the potential for higher returns, it also carries higher risks and requires expertise, time, and effort to execute successfully.

Active Management

Active management in the context of financial management refers to the practice of actively selecting and managing investments in order to outperform a particular benchmark or index. This approach involves making strategic investment decisions based on careful analysis and research, with the aim of generating superior returns for investors. In active management, fund managers or investment professionals utilize various techniques and strategies to identify and capitalize on market inefficiencies, mispricings, and opportunities. They conduct in-depth analysis of individual securities, industries, and market trends to make informed investment decisions. Active managers typically have a more hands-on approach compared to passive managers who aim to match the performance of a specific market index. Active management involves actively buying and selling securities within a portfolio to take advantage of potential market fluctuations and changes in the economic landscape. There are several key characteristics and strategies associated with active management. These include stock picking, where managers select individual stocks based on their potential for growth or undervaluation. Another strategy is market timing, where managers try to predict the overall direction of the market or specific sectors and adjust their portfolio accordingly. Active management also involves risk management, where managers actively monitor and adjust the portfolio's risk exposure to mitigate potential downsides. They may use hedging techniques, derivatives, or other financial instruments to protect against adverse market movements. It is important to note that active management is not without its challenges and limitations. It requires skilled and knowledgeable professionals who can consistently make accurate predictions and identify profitable investment opportunities. Additionally, active management typically involves higher fees compared to passive management due to the increased research and trading costs. In summary, active management in financial management is the practice of actively selecting and managing investments with the goal of outperforming a benchmark or index. It involves careful analysis, strategic decision-making, and ongoing monitoring to generate superior returns for investors.

Active Portfolio Management

Active Portfolio Management refers to the practice of actively managing a portfolio of investments to maximize returns and outperform a specific benchmark or market index. It involves making strategic investment decisions based on market conditions, economic trends, and individual security analysis. The goal of active portfolio management is to generate superior performance by taking advantage of market inefficiencies and mispricings. Unlike passive portfolio management, which focuses on tracking an index and maintaining a diversified portfolio, active portfolio managers actively buy and sell securities based on their analysis and judgment.

Active Portfolio Strategy

An active portfolio strategy is an investment approach that involves frequent buying and selling of securities in order to outperform a specific benchmark or market index. This strategy is based on the belief that portfolio managers can consistently identify mispriced securities and take advantage of short-term market inefficiencies to earn higher returns. The goal of an active portfolio strategy is to generate alpha, which refers to the excess return earned by a portfolio above what would be expected based on its risk level. Portfolio managers who employ this strategy rely on various techniques, including fundamental analysis, technical analysis, and quantitative models, to identify securities that are undervalued or overvalued. They then make trades to take advantage of these perceived market inefficiencies. Active portfolio management requires a high level of expertise and research capabilities. Portfolio managers need to have a deep understanding of financial markets, economic trends, and individual companies to make informed investment decisions. They also need to constantly monitor the portfolio and make adjustments as market conditions change. One advantage of active portfolio management is the potential for higher returns compared to a passive strategy, which involves holding a diversified portfolio of securities that mirrors a benchmark index. Active managers believe they can generate excess returns by exploiting market inefficiencies and taking advantage of short-term trading opportunities. However, active portfolio management also involves higher costs and risks compared to a passive strategy. Frequent trading can result in higher transaction costs and taxes, which can eat into the overall returns. Additionally, active managers are exposed to the risk of poor investment decisions and underperformance compared to the benchmark index. In conclusion, active portfolio strategy is an investment approach that aims to outperform a specific benchmark or market index through frequent buying and selling of securities. While it has the potential for higher returns, it also comes with higher costs and risks. Successful active management requires a combination of expertise, research capabilities, and diligent monitoring of market conditions.

Adjusted Gross Income (AGI)

Adjusted Gross Income (AGI) is a crucial financial metric used in the field of financial management to assess an individual's or organization's overall taxable income after certain adjustments. AGI serves as a fundamental calculation in determining income tax liability, eligibility for certain tax deductions, and eligibility for various tax credits and benefits. To calculate AGI, an individual or organization starts with their total income from all sources, including wages, salaries, tips, interest, dividends, rental income, and business income. This total income is commonly known as gross income. However, AGI factors in several deductions and adjustments to arrive at a net figure that reflects a more accurate representation of an individual's or organization's financial standing. The deductions and adjustments subtracted from gross income to arrive at AGI can include contributions to retirement savings accounts, certain business expenses, student loan interest, alimony payments, and other eligible expenses. These deductions and adjustments are known as "above-the-line" deductions, as they are subtracted from gross income before arriving at AGI. AGI is a significant metric in financial management as it not only determines an individual's or organization's taxable income but also affects their eligibility for various tax benefits and credits. For example, AGI is utilized to calculate an individual's or organization's eligibility for deducting certain medical expenses, mortgage interest, and charitable contributions, among other deductions. Furthermore, AGI affects an individual's or organization's eligibility for certain tax credits and benefits, such as the earned income tax credit (EITC), the child tax credit, and the American opportunity credit for education expenses. In some cases, higher AGI can reduce or eliminate eligibility for these credits and benefits. In summary, AGI is a critical financial management metric that provides a comprehensive assessment of an individual's or organization's taxable income after specific deductions and adjustments. It helps determine income tax liability, eligibility for deductions, tax credits, and benefits, and overall financial standing.

Adverse Selection

Adverse selection in Financial Management refers to the tendency of individuals, who are more likely to face negative outcomes, to be the ones who seek out certain financial products or services. This phenomenon occurs because individuals have more information about their own risk level than the financial institution or insurer providing the product or service. As a result, adverse selection can lead to unbalanced risk exposure for the financial institution and its customers. One common example of adverse selection is in the insurance industry. When individuals apply for insurance, they are typically required to disclose information about their health, lifestyle, and other factors that may impact their risk profile. However, individuals with a higher likelihood of health problems or accidents may be more motivated to seek out insurance coverage, as they anticipate needing it more frequently. On the other hand, individuals with lower risk levels may be less inclined to purchase insurance. This creates a situation where the insurance provider has a higher proportion of customers who are more likely to file claims, leading to increased costs for the company.

Agency Costs

Agency Costs Agency costs refer to the expenses incurred by the principal (shareholders) in an organization to ensure that the actions of the agent (management) align with the best interests of the principal. These costs arise due to the separation of ownership and control in corporations, where the shareholders delegate decision-making authority to managers to run the business on their behalf. The concept of agency costs can be analyzed from two perspectives: agency costs of equity and agency costs of debt. Agency costs of equity arise because shareholders and managers may have conflicting interests. Shareholders want the company to maximize its value and increase the stock price, while managers may prioritize their own interests, such as job security or personal financial gains. These conflicts can result in actions that may not be in shareholders' best interest, such as excessive executive compensation, ineffective monitoring, or pursuing projects with low returns but personal benefits for managers. The costs incurred by shareholders to mitigate these conflicts, such as hiring external auditors or implementing corporate governance mechanisms, are considered agency costs of equity. On the other hand, agency costs of debt emerge due to conflicts between shareholders and debtholders. Shareholders may have an incentive to pursue risky projects that increase the value of their equity but put debtholders' repayment at risk. To protect their interests, debtholders require higher interest rates or place restrictive covenants on the company, which increase the company's borrowing costs. These additional expenses incurred by the company to address the conflicts between shareholders and debtholders represent agency costs of debt. In summary, agency costs in financial management are the expenses incurred by shareholders to ensure that management acts in the best interest of the company and its shareholders. They arise due to the conflicts of interest between different stakeholders within an organization and include costs related to monitoring, implementing control mechanisms, and managing conflicts between equity and debt holders.

Agency Theory

Agency Theory is a concept that refers to the relationship between two parties, known as the principal and the agent, in the context of financial management. It involves the delegation of decision-making authority and the consequent need for monitoring and control mechanisms to ensure that the agent acts in the best interests of the principal. The principal-agent relationship exists when one party, the principal, hires another party, the agent, to perform certain tasks on their behalf. This relationship is commonly seen in financial management when shareholders (principal) appoint managers (agents) to run the company's operations. The principal-agent problem arises due to the inherent conflict of interest between the principal and the agent. The principal seeks to maximize their own wealth and expects the agent to act in a manner that aligns with their interests. However, the agent may have different goals or priorities, such as maximizing their own compensation or job security. This creates a divergence of interests between the two parties, leading to potential agency conflicts.

Aggregate Demand

Aggregate Demand refers to the total demand for goods and services within an economy at a given price level during a specified period. It represents the sum of individual demands across all sectors, including consumption by households, investment by businesses, government spending, and net exports. In financial management, understanding aggregate demand is essential for analyzing and predicting economic trends and making informed business decisions. By evaluating the factors that influence aggregate demand, financial managers can assess the overall demand for their products or services and adjust their strategies accordingly.

Alien Corporation

An Alien Corporation, in the context of financial management, refers to a type of corporation that is incorporated in a country or jurisdiction different from the country in which it operates its primary business activities. It is also commonly known as a foreign corporation. Alien corporations are established by companies seeking to expand their operations beyond their home country's borders. These corporations may be subsidiaries of a parent company or independent entities. They are subject to the laws and regulations of the jurisdiction in which they are incorporated, as well as the laws and regulations of the countries in which they conduct their business activities.

Alpha Generation

Alpha Generation in the context of Financial Management refers to the ability of a portfolio manager or investment strategy to generate excess returns above a given benchmark or the market as a whole. Alpha is essentially a measure of the manager's skill in selecting and managing investments in order to outperform the market. It represents the portion of a portfolio's return that is not attributable to market movements. A positive alpha suggests that the manager has generated returns above what would be expected based on the risk taken, while a negative alpha indicates underperformance.

Alpha

Financial management is the process of planning, organizing, controlling, and monitoring the financial resources of an organization. It involves making strategic decisions regarding the allocation and utilization of funds to meet the organization's objectives and maximize value for its stakeholders. Financial management encompasses various areas, including financial planning, budgeting, investment management, and financial analysis. It aims to ensure that the organization has the necessary financial resources and uses them efficiently to achieve its goals.

Alternative Minimum Tax (AMT)

The Alternative Minimum Tax (AMT) is a tax regulation implemented by the Internal Revenue Service (IRS) of the United States that ensures taxpayers with high incomes pay a minimum amount of tax, regardless of deductions and credits they may be eligible for under the regular tax system. The AMT was introduced in 1969 in response to widespread tax avoidance by wealthy individuals and corporations who were able to exploit loopholes and deductions to significantly reduce their tax liabilities. The purpose of the AMT is to prevent high-income earners from using various tax planning strategies to completely avoid federal income taxes.

Amortization Expense

Amortization Expense refers to the gradual recognition and allocation of intangible assets' costs over their useful life. In financial management, this term represents the expense associated with intangible assets like patents, copyrights, and goodwill. When a company acquires an intangible asset, such as a patent, it is recognized as an asset on the balance sheet. However, since intangible assets have no physical presence and provide benefits over a specific period, their costs need to be expensed over time to reflect their consumption and generate an accurate representation of the company's financial position. This gradual recognition of the asset's cost is referred to as amortization. Amortization expense is calculated by dividing the initial cost of an intangible asset by its expected useful life. The resulting annual expense is then recorded in the income statement, reducing the company's net income. It is important to note that the process of amortization is different from depreciation, which is the expense allocation for tangible assets like buildings and equipment. The amortization expense allows the company to match the cost of an intangible asset with the revenue it generates over its useful life. By recognizing the expenses over time, the company avoids a substantial impact on its income statement in the year of acquisition. This method provides a more accurate reflection of the asset's value and its contribution to the company's operations. Moreover, amortization expense plays a significant role in financial analysis and decision-making. It helps investors and analysts assess a company's profitability and understand the ongoing costs associated with intangible assets. Additionally, it allows for better comparability between companies by adjusting for the differences in their asset recognition and expense allocation practices.

Amortization Schedule

An amortization schedule refers to a table that displays the breakdown of loan payments over time, showing the distribution of principal and interest amounts. It is commonly used in financial management to understand and plan loan repayments, primarily for mortgages and other long-term loans. The key components of an amortization schedule include the initial loan amount, the interest rate, the loan term, and the payment frequency. With this information, the schedule calculates the periodic payment amount, the loan balance, and the interest and principal portions of each payment. The schedule typically starts with the first payment and extends until the loan is fully repaid. It outlines the monthly or periodic payments, tracking the allocation of funds to interest payments and principal repayments. Initially, a large portion of the payment goes towards covering the interest, while the remaining amount is used to reduce the principal balance. Over time, as the principal balance decreases, the allocation towards interest decreases while the portion towards principal increases. The amortization schedule provides a comprehensive view of the loan repayment process, enabling borrowers to understand how their monthly payments are applied to reducing their debt. It allows them to analyze the impact of different payment frequencies or extra payments on the overall loan duration and interest savings. Financial managers use amortization schedules to plan cash flows, assess the affordability of loan repayments, and make informed financial decisions. For example, businesses can evaluate different loan options by comparing the schedules, enabling them to choose loans with the most favorable terms and repayment structures. In conclusion, an amortization schedule is a valuable tool in financial management that visually breaks down loan payments, showcasing the distribution of principal and interest amounts over time. It provides a clear understanding of the loan repayment process, allowing borrowers and financial managers to make informed decisions regarding loan terms, payment frequencies, and overall affordability.

Amortization

Amortization is a key concept in financial management that refers to the process of allocating the cost or value of an intangible asset over a specific timeframe. It is primarily used in relation to loans and other financial obligations, where it helps determine the periodic repayment amounts and the total interest cost over the life of the loan. When a loan is taken out, the principal amount borrowed needs to be repaid to the lender along with interest over a predetermined period. Amortization calculates the portion of each payment that goes towards reducing the loan balance, known as the principal, and the portion that goes towards paying the interest. The most common method of amortization is known as the straight-line method, where an equal amount is allocated to each payment. This means that the principal reduction and interest payment remain constant throughout the repayment period. However, other methods such as declining balance or annuity methods may also be used depending on the specific terms and conditions of the loan. Amortization schedules are used to keep track of the loan repayment process. These schedules outline each payment, its allocation towards principal and interest, and the remaining loan balance after each payment. By analyzing an amortization schedule, borrowers can gain insights into how much of their monthly payments are being used to reduce the principal and how much is being applied to interest costs. Amortization plays a crucial role in financial management as it helps borrowers understand their repayment obligations and make informed decisions. By analyzing different amortization scenarios, borrowers can compare repayment options, assess the impact of different interest rates, and determine the length of the loan term that suits their financial goals.

Analyst

An analyst in the context of Financial Management refers to an individual who is responsible for collecting, analyzing, and interpreting financial data to assist in making informed decisions regarding investments, financial planning, and overall financial health of an organization. The primary role of a financial analyst is to assess the financial performance of a company by reviewing financial statements, conducting financial forecasting, and analyzing market trends. They use various tools and techniques to evaluate the company's profitability, liquidity, solvency, and overall financial stability. This analysis helps in identifying areas of improvement and potential risks that may affect the organization's financial position. Financial analysts play a crucial role in guiding management decisions by providing insights and recommendations based on their analysis. They provide reports and presentations that summarize their findings and offer strategies for improving financial performance. Additionally, they may also be involved in conducting industry and competitor analysis to identify opportunities and threats in the market. Furthermore, financial analysts are responsible for monitoring and tracking financial performance against established goals and benchmarks. They analyze financial data regularly to identify any deviations or discrepancies that may indicate potential issues. This helps management in taking corrective actions and ensuring financial objectives are met. Financial analysts often specialize in specific areas such as investment analysis, risk management, or financial planning. They utilize advanced knowledge of financial principles, accounting practices, and economic factors to conduct thorough analysis and provide accurate recommendations. They may also collaborate with other departments such as accounting, treasury, and sales to gather relevant information and ensure data accuracy. In summary, a financial analyst plays a critical role in the field of financial management by analyzing and interpreting financial data to support decision-making processes. Their insights and recommendations help organizations achieve their financial objectives while ensuring long-term financial stability and success.

Annual Report

An annual report, in the context of financial management, is a comprehensive document that provides an overview of a company's financial performance and activities over the course of a year. It typically includes a detailed analysis of the company's financial statements, such as the income statement, balance sheet, and cash flow statement. These statements provide a snapshot of the company's revenue, expenses, assets, liabilities, and cash flows, which are crucial in assessing its financial health and profitability.

Annuity

An annuity refers to a financial product or investment vehicle that provides a stream of regular payments, either fixed or variable, to the annuitant over a specified period. It involves a contract between an individual (the annuitant) and a financial institution or insurance company that agrees to make these periodic payments. There are two main types of annuities: immediate and deferred. Immediate annuities start making payments to the annuitant shortly after the initial investment, while deferred annuities accumulate funds over a specific period before starting the payment stream. Annuities can be further classified into fixed, variable, or indexed based on the underlying investment and risk factors involved. The primary purpose of an annuity is to provide a steady, predictable income stream during retirement. It gives individuals the option to convert their savings or lump sum amount into regular payments, ensuring a stable financial future. For example, an individual can invest a portion of their retirement savings in an annuity to receive monthly payments after retiring. Annuities offer several advantages, such as tax deferral on investment gains, the potential for guaranteed income for life, and the ability to customize payment options to meet specific needs. However, they also come with certain limitations and complexities that individuals should consider. These include surrender charges for early withdrawals, fees associated with managing the annuity, and potential limitations on investment growth. Overall, annuities serve as an essential tool for retirement planning and provide individuals with a reliable source of income. They offer the peace of mind that comes from knowing there will be a regular stream of payments to cover living expenses during retirement. As with any financial instrument, it is crucial to understand the terms, conditions, and potential risks associated with annuities before making a decision.

Anti-Dilution Provision

An anti-dilution provision, also known as an anti-dilution clause or anti-dilution protection, is a financial management mechanism that protects existing shareholders from the potential negative effects of dilution during subsequent rounds of fundraising or the issuance of new shares. When a company decides to issue new shares or raise additional funds, it often does so by offering these new shares at a lower price than what existing shareholders paid for their shares. This can result in dilution, which reduces the ownership percentage and voting power of existing shareholders. The anti-dilution provision aims to protect the value of existing shareholders' investments by adjusting their ownership percentage and/or price per share in the event of future issuances of shares at a lower price. There are two commonly used types of anti-dilution provisions: 1. Full Ratchet: Under a full ratchet provision, if new shares are issued at a lower price than what existing shareholders paid, the conversion price of their shares is adjusted downward to match the new issuance price. This means that existing shareholders effectively receive additional shares for free, helping to maintain the value of their investment. 2. Weighted Average: The weighted average provision is more commonly used in practice and provides a more balanced approach. It calculates a new conversion price based on the average price paid for the new shares and the price paid by the existing shareholders. This ensures that the impact of dilution is less severe, as the adjustment is based on a weighted average of the old and new prices. Anti-dilution provisions are typically included in investment agreements, such as preferred stock agreements or convertible loan agreements. They are designed to protect investors, particularly those who participate in early-stage financing rounds, from the potential negative effects of future dilution. By providing these protections, anti-dilution provisions can help attract and retain investors, as they mitigate the risk of their ownership and investment value being significantly eroded.

Arbitrage Pricing Theory (APT)

The Arbitrage Pricing Theory (APT) is a financial management model that attempts to explain the relationship between expected returns on investments and their relevant risk factors. Developed by economist Stephen Ross in the 1970s as an alternative to the Capital Asset Pricing Model (CAPM), the APT is based on the concept of arbitrage, which involves exploiting price differences in different markets to make riskless profits. According to the APT, the expected return on an investment can be determined by analyzing the systematic risk factors that influence its price.

Arbitrage

Arbitrage refers to the practice of making profits by simultaneously buying and selling financial instruments or assets in different markets to take advantage of price disparities. It involves taking advantage of differences in the prices of the same asset or security on different exchanges, or exploiting pricing discrepancies between related assets or derivatives. The concept of arbitrage is based on the principle of the efficient market hypothesis (EMH), which assumes that prices of financial instruments reflect all available information and adjust instantaneously to any new information. However, in reality, market inefficiencies and delays in information dissemination can create temporary price discrepancies. Arbitrageurs are individuals or institutions who exploit these discrepancies by buying the undervalued asset in one market and simultaneously selling it at a higher price in another market, earning a risk-free profit from the price difference.

Arrears

Arrears refer to the outstanding balance or unpaid debts that are past their due date. In the context of financial management, it is crucial to monitor and address arrears effectively to maintain the financial stability of an individual, business, or organization. When a payment is not made by the agreed-upon deadline, it becomes an arrear. This can occur for various reasons, such as forgetting to pay, facing cash flow constraints, or intentionally delaying payment. Arrears can be associated with different financial obligations, including loans, mortgages, credit card bills, utility bills, rent, or any other payment agreement. For individuals, being in arrears can have significant consequences. It can lead to increased interest charges, late payment fees, and damage to their credit score. Moreover, repeated or prolonged arrears may result in legal action, such as debt collection or repossession of assets. Therefore, it is essential to prioritize and manage arrears to prevent further financial complications. In business or organizational settings, arrears can have severe implications for cash flow and overall financial health. Unpaid invoices or bills can disrupt the normal functioning of operations and strain relationships with suppliers or service providers. In addition, arrears can result in a negative reputation for the business, making it difficult to secure credit or attract potential clients. Effective arrears management involves several key steps. Firstly, regular monitoring and tracking of payment deadlines is crucial to identify arrears promptly. Once arrears are identified, it is important to communicate with the debtor to understand the reasons behind the non-payment and explore potential solutions. This can involve setting up alternative payment arrangements, negotiating revised terms, or implementing late payment penalties. Furthermore, maintaining accurate and up-to-date financial records is vital to streamline arrears management. Organizations should ensure that invoices, bills, and payment reminders are sent on time, and that proper follow-up procedures are in place to handle arrears cases. Investing in financial management software or hiring professionals can also support efficient arrears management, as they can provide tools for automating reminders, generating reports, and analyzing payment patterns. In conclusion, arrears refer to outstanding debts or unpaid balances that have surpassed their due date. Effective arrears management is crucial for individuals, businesses, and organizations to maintain financial stability and avoid potential consequences. Regular monitoring, proactive communication, and accurate financial record-keeping are essential components of successful arrears management.

Asset Allocation

Asset allocation refers to the process of dividing an investment portfolio among different asset classes such as stocks, bonds, cash, and real estate, based on the investor's financial goals, risk tolerance, and time horizon. It is a key strategy used in financial management to balance risk and reward, and to optimize returns for an investor's specific needs and circumstances. The primary objective of asset allocation is to maximize the potential return on investment while minimizing the associated risks. This is achieved by diversifying the portfolio across various asset classes, which have different levels of risk and return potential. By spreading investments across different asset classes, asset allocation aims to reduce the impact of any single investment's performance on the overall portfolio. Asset allocation is based on the principle that different asset classes have varying levels of correlation or interdependence with each other. While some asset classes may move in the same direction during certain market conditions, others may move in the opposite direction. By investing in a mix of asset classes that have a low or negative correlation, investors can potentially reduce overall portfolio volatility. Asset allocation strategies typically involve determining an investor's risk tolerance and investment objectives. Conservative investors, who prioritize the preservation of capital over growth, may opt for a more heavily weighted allocation towards lower-risk assets such as government bonds and cash. On the other hand, aggressive investors seeking higher returns may allocate a greater portion of their portfolio to higher-risk assets such as equities. It is important to note that asset allocation is not a one-time decision, but an ongoing process that requires periodic review and adjustments. As market conditions change, asset classes may perform differently, leading to a deviation from the desired allocation. In such cases, investors need to rebalance their portfolios by buying or selling assets to realign with their target asset allocation.

Asset Backed Securities (ABS)

Asset Backed Securities (ABS) are financial instruments that are created by pooling together various types of assets, such as mortgages, auto loans, credit card receivables, and student loans. These assets are then securitized and transformed into marketable securities, which are sold to investors. The process of creating ABS involves several steps. First, the originator of the assets, such as a bank or a financial institution, identifies a group of assets that have a similar risk profile and cash flow characteristics. These assets are then transferred to a special purpose vehicle (SPV), which is a separate legal entity created solely for the purpose of issuing the ABS. The SPV then issues the ABS in the form of bonds or notes. ABS are attractive to investors because they offer diversification and the potential for higher yields compared to traditional fixed income securities. The cash flows from the underlying assets, such as the mortgage payments or the loan repayments, serve as collateral for the ABS. This means that if the underlying borrowers default on their payments, the investors in the ABS have a claim on the underlying assets. ABS can be structured in different ways to meet the needs of different types of investors. For example, a senior/subordinated structure can be used, where the ABS are divided into different tranches, each with a different level of risk and return. The senior tranches have priority

15

claim on the cash flows from the underlying assets, while the subordinated tranches have a lower priority. The risks associated with ABS include credit risk, prepayment risk, and liquidity risk. Credit risk refers to the risk that the underlying borrowers will default on their payments. Prepayment risk refers to the risk that the borrowers will repay their loans earlier than expected, which can affect the cash flows to the ABS investors. Liquidity risk refers to the risk that the ABS may not be easily traded in the secondary market, which can make it difficult for investors to sell their holdings.

Asset Liability Management (ALM)

Asset Liability Management (ALM) is a financial management practice that aims to effectively manage the assets and liabilities of a financial institution in order to optimize its profitability and reduce the risk exposure. It involves the strategic management of a company's balance sheet to ensure that the institution's assets generate enough income to cover its liabilities and achieve its financial objectives. The primary goal of ALM is to manage the mismatch between assets and liabilities in terms of their maturities, interest rates, and cash flows. By closely monitoring and controlling these factors, financial institutions can mitigate liquidity risk, interest rate risk, and credit risk. In order to achieve effective ALM, financial institutions need to gather comprehensive and accurate data on their assets and liabilities, including their size, maturity, interest rate sensitivity, and cash flow characteristics. This data serves as the foundation for analyzing and interpreting the risks associated with the institution's balance sheet. Based on this analysis, ALM practitioners can develop strategies and make informed decisions to mitigate these risks and optimize the institution's balance sheet. This may involve adjusting the mix of assets and liabilities, pursuing asset-liability matching strategies, or using financial derivatives to hedge against interest rate and liquidity risks. Furthermore, ALM involves continuously monitoring and reviewing the institution's risk profile and making necessary adjustments as market conditions and regulatory requirements change. This proactive approach ensures that the institution can adapt to new challenges and seize opportunities as they arise. Overall, Asset Liability Management is an essential component of financial management for any institution that relies heavily on its balance sheet, such as banks, insurance companies, and investment firms. By effectively managing assets and liabilities, these institutions can enhance their profitability, maintain adequate liquidity, and safeguard against potential financial disruptions.

Asset Management Company

An asset management company, also known as an investment management company, is a financial institution that manages and invests funds on behalf of its clients. These clients can include individuals, corporations, pension funds, and governments. The primary goal of an asset management company is to maximize the return on investment for their clients while mitigating the associated risks. They achieve this by employing a team of experienced fund managers and analysts who carefully analyze and evaluate various investments options, such as stocks, bonds, real estate, and commodities. The asset management company develops and implements investment strategies that align with their clients' financial objectives and risk tolerance. This involves the selection of specific assets or securities to achieve the desired asset allocation and diversification. Additionally, they monitor and review the performance of the investments on an ongoing basis, making necessary adjustments as market conditions change. Another important aspect of an asset management company's role is providing personalized investment advice and financial planning services to their clients. They take into account their clients' financial goals, time horizon, and other specific requirements to develop tailored investment plans. Asset management companies also play a crucial role in providing liquidity to the financial markets. They buy and sell securities on behalf of their clients, contributing to the overall efficiency and stability of the market. In summary, an asset management company is a financial institution responsible for managing and investing funds on behalf of their clients. They strive to maximize returns while minimizing risks, through careful analysis, strategic asset allocation, and ongoing monitoring. Additionally, they provide personalized investment advice and contribute to the liquidity of the financial markets.

Asset Management Ratio

Asset management ratio is a financial management tool used to evaluate how efficiently a company is utilizing its assets to generate revenue. It involves analyzing a company's balance sheet to measure the relationship between different types of assets and their corresponding liabilities. By examining the ratio between these components, investors and analysts can assess the company's ability to generate profits and manage its resources effectively. There are various types of asset management ratios that provide insight into different aspects of a company's financial performance. Some of the most commonly used ratios include the current ratio, fixed asset turnover ratio, and total asset turnover ratio. The current ratio is a liquidity ratio that measures a company's ability to meet short-term obligations. It is calculated by dividing current assets by current liabilities. A higher current ratio indicates a greater ability to meet short-term liabilities, while a lower ratio may suggest potential liquidity problems. The fixed asset turnover ratio is an efficiency ratio that evaluates how effectively a company is utilizing its fixed assets to generate sales. It is calculated by dividing net sales by the average net fixed assets. A higher fixed asset turnover ratio indicates higher productivity and efficient use of fixed assets. The total asset turnover ratio measures a company's ability to generate revenue from its total assets. It is calculated by dividing net sales by average total assets. A higher total asset turnover ratio indicates better utilization of assets to generate sales. Asset management ratios are valuable tools for investors, as they provide insights into a company's financial health and efficiency. By analyzing these ratios, investors can identify potential investment opportunities, assess risk levels, and compare companies within the same industry. However, it is important to note that these ratios should be used in conjunction with other financial metrics and qualitative factors for a comprehensive evaluation of a company's financial performance.

Asset Management

Asset Management refers to the process of effectively managing a company's assets in order to optimize their performance, reduce costs, and minimize risks. It encompasses a range of activities, including the identification, acquisition, utilization, maintenance, and disposal of assets. In the context of financial management, asset management is crucial for organizations to ensure that their assets are properly utilized to generate maximum returns and add value to the business. This involves not only physical assets such as property, equipment, and vehicles but also intangible assets such as patents, trademarks, and intellectual property. The main objective of asset management is to maximize the value of assets while minimizing their associated costs and risks. This requires careful planning and decision-making, as well as ongoing monitoring and evaluation of asset performance. By effectively managing their assets, organizations can improve operational efficiency, increase profitability, and enhance shareholder value. Asset management involves various key activities. Firstly, it involves asset planning, which includes determining the objectives and strategies for managing assets based on the organization's goals and requirements. This involves assessing the current asset portfolio, identifying any gaps or deficiencies, and developing a comprehensive asset management plan. Secondly, asset management entails asset acquisition, which involves identifying the assets needed to support the business operations and acquiring them in the most cost-effective and efficient manner. This may involve purchasing or leasing assets, negotiating contracts, and assessing the financial implications of the acquisition. Thirdly, asset management encompasses asset utilization and maintenance, which involves effectively using and maintaining assets to maximize their operational performance and lifespan. This includes implementing maintenance schedules, conducting regular inspections, and ensuring that assets are utilized efficiently and effectively. Finally, asset management includes asset disposal, which involves the proper disposal or replacement of assets at the end of their useful life. This may involve selling assets, scrapping them, or repurposing them for alternative uses. In summary, asset management is a critical aspect of financial management that involves the effective and efficient management of an organization's assets. By optimizing asset performance, minimizing costs, and mitigating risks, asset management helps organizations achieve their strategic objectives and improve their financial performance.

Asset Turnover Ratio

The Asset Turnover Ratio is a financial management metric that measures the efficiency with which a company utilizes its assets to generate revenue. It indicates the company's ability to generate sales based on the amount of assets it possesses. The asset turnover ratio is calculated by dividing the net sales of a company by its average total assets. The net sales represents the revenue generated by the company after deducting sales returns, allowances, and discounts, while the average total assets is the average value of all the assets owned by the company during a specific period. A higher asset turnover ratio indicates that a company is generating more sales relative to its assets, which generally indicates better asset management and utilization. On the other hand, a lower ratio suggests that the company may be inefficient in using its assets to generate revenue, which can have negative implications for the company's profitability and overall financial performance. The asset turnover ratio is useful for comparing the performance of a company with its industry peers and for evaluating the company's historical performance over time. It can also be used to assess the impact of different strategies on asset utilization and to identify areas for improvement. However, it is important to note that the asset turnover ratio should be interpreted in the context of the industry in which the company operates. Different industries have different asset requirements and sales levels, which can affect the ratio. Additionally, the ratio should be used in conjunction with other financial ratios and metrics to get a more comprehensive understanding of the company's financial health and performance.

Asset Turnover

Asset Turnover is a financial metric used in the discipline of Financial Management to analyze the efficiency with which a company uses its assets to generate revenue. It is calculated by dividing the company's net sales by its average total assets. The net sales figure can be found on the company's income statement, and the average total assets figure can be found on the company's balance sheet. The average total assets figure is calculated by adding the company's total assets at the beginning and end of a period and dividing by 2.

Asset-Backed Commercial Paper (ABCP)

Asset-Backed Commercial Paper (ABCP) refers to a short-term debt instrument that is backed by a specific pool of underlying assets. It is a type of commercial paper that is often used by financial institutions to raise funds quickly and efficiently. ABCP is a vital aspect of financial management as it provides liquidity to banks and other financial institutions, allowing them to fund their operations and meet their lending obligations. ABCP is created through the process of securitization, where a financial institution bundles together a group of assets, such as mortgages, auto loans, or credit card receivables, and transfers them to a special purpose vehicle (SPV). The SPV issues the commercial paper to investors, who receive a fixed return in exchange for their investment. The underlying assets serve as collateral for the ABCP, providing a level of security to the investors. One of the key benefits of ABCP is its ability to diversify risk. By packaging different types of assets into a single security, the risk is spread across the pool of assets, reducing the likelihood of default. This makes ABCP an attractive investment option for institutional investors who are seeking short-term, low-risk investments. ABCP is typically structured as a variable rate instrument, meaning that the interest rate on the commercial paper may vary over time. The interest rate is usually tied to a benchmark, such as the London Interbank Offered Rate (LIBOR), and is adjusted periodically. This provides issuers with flexibility in managing their funding costs and allows investors to earn a competitive return based on prevailing market rates. In conclusion, Asset-Backed Commercial Paper (ABCP) is a short-term debt instrument that is backed by a specific pool of underlying assets. It provides financial institutions with a means to raise funds quickly, while also offering investors a low-risk investment option. Through securitization, ABCP allows for the diversification of risk and provides flexibility in managing funding costs. Overall, ABCP plays a crucial role in the financial management of institutions by enabling liquidity and supporting lending activities.

Asset-Backed Securities (ABS)

Asset-Backed Securities (ABS) are financial instruments that are created by pooling together a group of assets, such as loans, mortgages, or credit card receivables. These assets are then converted into tradable securities, which are backed by the cash flows generated from the underlying assets. ABS are typically issued by banks or other financial institutions to raise capital and transfer the risk associated with the underlying assets to investors. The underlying assets act as collateral, providing a level of security to the investors in case of default or non-payment. The process of creating ABS involves three key steps: 1. Pooling: The assets are grouped together based on their similar characteristics, such as credit quality, maturity, or type of loan. This pooling helps to diversify the risk associated with individual assets and enhance the overall credit quality of the securities. 2. Securitization: The pooled assets are then transferred to a special purpose vehicle (SPV), which is a separate legal entity created solely for the purpose

18

of issuing the ABS. The SPV issues the securities and uses the cash flows from the underlying assets to make interest and principal payments to the investors. 3. Tranching: ABS are often divided into different tranches, which represent different levels of risk and return. Each tranche has different priority in receiving cash flows from the underlying assets. The senior tranches have the highest priority and receive payment first, while the junior (or subordinated) tranches have a lower priority and bear the first loss in case of default. Investing in ABS offers several benefits to both issuers and investors. For issuers, ABS provide a way to quickly raise capital and reduce their exposure to risky assets, thereby improving their financial position. For investors, ABS offer the opportunity to invest in a diversified portfolio of assets and earn a steady stream of income from the cash flows generated by these assets. However, ABS also carry certain risks. The performance of ABS is highly dependent on the cash flows generated by the underlying assets. If these cash flows deteriorate or the default rate of the underlying assets increases, it can result in a decrease in the value of the ABS. Additionally, the complexity and lack of transparency in the underlying assets and the structure of ABS can make it difficult for investors to fully understand and assess the risks involved.

Asset-Backed Security (ABS)

An Asset-Backed Security (ABS) is a type of financial instrument that is created by pooling together various types of assets, such as mortgages, loans, or receivables, and then selling interests in the pooled assets to investors. These assets serve as collateral for the ABS, providing a degree of security for the investors. The process of creating an ABS involves transferring the ownership of the assets from the originator (the entity that originally owned the assets) to a special purpose vehicle (SPV) or a trust. The SPV or trust then issues the ABS to investors, who receive a share of the cash flows generated by the assets. The cash flows can come from the interest and principal payments on the underlying loans or mortgages, or from the payments on the receivables. The ABS market allows originators to remove assets from their balance sheets, thereby freeing up capital to finance new loans or investments. It also provides a way for investors to gain exposure to a diversified pool of assets, which helps to spread risk. In addition, ABS can be structured in different ways to suit the needs of both issuers and investors. One key feature of ABS is the process of securitization, which involves transforming illiquid assets into tradable securities. This process requires rigorous due diligence and analysis to assess the credit quality and cash flow characteristics of the underlying assets. The ABS is then assigned a credit rating by a rating agency, based on the likelihood of the cash flows being sufficient to meet the interest and principal payments to investors. ABS can be classified into different types, depending on the nature of the underlying assets. For example, mortgage-backed securities (MBS) are ABS backed by pools of residential or commercial mortgages, while collateralized debt obligations (CDO) are ABS backed by a combination of different types of debt instruments. Overall, ABS play an important role in the financial markets by providing a way for originators to raise funds and for investors to diversify their portfolios. However, they also carry risks, such as credit risk and liquidity risk, which need to be carefully managed and assessed by both issuers and investors.

At-The-Market (ATM) Offering

An At-the-Market (ATM) Offering is a type of securities offering in which a company sells its shares directly to the market through an underwriter on a "to-be-sold" basis. Unlike traditional offerings where shares are sold at a predetermined price, ATM offerings allow the company to sell its shares at prevailing market prices, providing flexibility and immediate access to capital. In an ATM offering, the company registers a certain number of shares with the Securities and Exchange Commission (SEC) and contracts with an underwriter to sell these shares as needed. The underwriter acts as an intermediary between the company and the market, executing the sales of shares on behalf of the company. ATM offerings are typically used by established companies that have a continuous need for capital, such as those in the biotech or pharmaceutical industry that require ongoing funding for research and development. These offerings are also suitable for companies facing uncertain market conditions or those that want to take advantage of favorable market prices without significantly diluting existing shareholders. The advantages of ATM offerings include the ability to access capital quickly, as shares can be sold as needed without time-consuming and costly traditional offering processes. Additionally, the flexibility of selling shares at prevailing market prices allows the company to maximize the amount of capital raised. ATM offerings also provide companies with greater control over the timing and size of share issuances, which can be adjusted based on market conditions and the company's capital requirements. However, there are also potential drawbacks to consider. Selling shares directly to the market may result in downward pressure on the company's stock price due to supply exceeding demand. Furthermore, ATM offerings may not be suitable for companies with limited trading volume or low market capitalization, as the increased supply of shares could lead to significant share price volatility. In conclusion, an ATM offering is a flexible and efficient method for companies to raise capital by selling shares directly to the market at prevailing market prices. It offers advantages such as quick access to capital and greater control over share issuances, but also carries potential risks of stock price dilution and volatility.

Audit Trail

An audit trail in the context of financial management refers to a systematic record of transactions, activities, and events that occur within an organization's financial system. It provides a chronological and detailed trail of evidence that documents the flow of financial information, ensuring transparency, accuracy, and accountability in financial management processes. The audit trail serves as a vital tool for monitoring and controlling financial activities, enabling organizations to maintain the integrity of their financial statements and comply with regulatory requirements. It plays a pivotal role in the identification and prevention of errors, fraud, and misstatements, as well as facilitating internal and external audits.

Audit

An audit is a systematic and independent examination of financial records, statements, transactions, and operations of an organization to ensure accuracy, compliance with regulations, and reliability of financial information. It is conducted by an independent professional, known as an auditor, who assesses the financial health and performance of the organization. The main purpose of an audit is to provide an objective evaluation of an organization's financial information, internal controls, and operational processes. During an audit, the auditor reviews financial statements, supporting documents, and other relevant records to verify their accuracy and integrity. This includes examining invoices, receipts, bank statements, ledgers, and other financial records. The auditor also interviews key personnel, such as management and staff, to gain a deeper understanding of the organization's operations and internal control systems. The audit process typically follows a well-defined set of procedures that adhere to generally accepted auditing standards. These standards provide guidelines and benchmarks for auditors to follow, ensuring consistency, professionalism, and quality in the audit process. The auditor assesses the adequacy and effectiveness of internal controls, identifies any weaknesses or deficiencies, and makes recommendations for improvement. The auditor expresses their opinion on the financial statements and issues an audit report, which communicates the findings, conclusions, and recommendations resulting from the audit. The report provides stakeholders with an independent and unbiased assessment of the organization's financial position, performance, and compliance with applicable laws and regulations. Audits have several benefits for organizations and stakeholders. They promote transparency, accountability, and trust by ensuring that financial information is accurate, reliable, and complete. Audits also help detect and deter fraud, misappropriation of assets, and other financial irregularities by identifying control weaknesses and implementing corrective measures. Furthermore, audits provide assurance to investors, creditors, regulators, and other stakeholders that the organization's financial statements present a true and fair view of its financial position and performance. In conclusion, an audit is a vital tool in financial management that provides an independent and objective assessment of an organization's financial information, internal controls, and operational processes. It helps ensure accuracy, compliance, and reliability of financial information, promotes transparency and accountability, and enhances stakeholders' confidence in the organization.

Average Annual Growth Rate (AAGR)

Average Annual Growth Rate (AAGR) refers to the average rate at which a company's key financial metric, such as revenue or earnings, has grown over a specified period of time, typically measured in years. AAGR is an important indicator for financial management as it helps assess the long-term performance and potential of a company. To calculate AAGR, the starting and ending values of the financial metric are needed, along with the number of years in the period. The formula for AAGR is as follows: AAGR = (Ending Value / Starting Value)^(1 /

20

Number of Years) - 1 For example, if a company's revenue was $1 million at the beginning of a 5-year period and grew to $1.5 million at the end of the period, the AAGR would be calculated as: AAGR = ($1.5 million / $1 million)^(1 / 5) - 1 = (1.5)^(0.2) - 1 ≈ 0.095 or 9.5% A positive AAGR indicates a growth trend, while a negative AAGR suggests a decline. AAGR can be used to compare the growth rates of different companies or sectors, helping investors and financial managers make informed decisions. However, it is important to note that AAGR does not provide details about the volatility or consistency of growth, and it should be considered alongside other financial metrics and qualitative factors.

Average Collection Period

Average Collection Period refers to the average number of days it takes for a company to collect payment from its customers for the goods or services provided. It is an important financial metric that helps in assessing the efficiency of a company's credit and collection policies. The calculation of average collection period involves dividing the total accounts receivable by the average daily credit sales. The formula is as follows: Average Collection Period = (Total Accounts Receivable) / (Average Daily Credit Sales) The total accounts receivable represents the amount of money owed to the company by its customers for credit sales. This includes invoices that have not been paid yet. The average daily credit sales is calculated by dividing the total credit sales by the number of days in the period under consideration. An average collection period is a measure of how quickly a company can convert its accounts receivable into cash. A shorter average collection period indicates that a company is able to collect payment from its customers in a timely manner and has effective credit and collection policies in place. On the other hand, a longer average collection period may suggest that the company's credit and collection policies are not efficient, resulting in delayed payments from customers. It is important for companies to closely monitor their average collection period as it directly affects their cash flow and liquidity. A longer average collection period means that the company has to wait longer to receive its cash, which may lead to cash flow issues and hinder its ability to meet its financial obligations. Additionally, a longer average collection period also increases the risk of bad debts, as there is a higher chance of customers defaulting on their payments. By analyzing the average collection period, companies can identify potential issues in their credit and collection processes and take corrective actions. They can implement strategies to reduce the average collection period, such as offering discounts for early payment, tightening credit policies, improving the collection process, or using collection agencies to recover overdue payments.

Average Rate Of Return

The average rate of return, in the context of financial management, is a metric used to determine the profitability of an investment or a portfolio over a specific period of time. It is a key performance measure that provides investors or managers with insights into the overall effectiveness of their investment decisions. Mathematically, the average rate of return is calculated by taking the average of the annual returns achieved over a given time period. This is done by summing up the annual returns and then dividing the sum by the number of years in the period. The result is expressed as a percentage. For example, let's say an investor has a portfolio that generates annual returns of 5%, 10%, 8%, and 12% over a period of four years. To calculate the average rate of return, the investor would sum up these returns (5 + 10 + 8 + 12 = 35) and then divide the sum by the number of years (4), resulting in an average rate of return of 8.75%. By analyzing the average rate of return, investors can gain insights into the performance of their investments relative to their expectations or benchmarks. A higher average rate of return indicates a more profitable investment, while a lower average rate of return suggests underperformance. Furthermore, the average rate of return can be used to compare the profitability of different investments or portfolios. By calculating and comparing the average rates of return, investors can determine which investment options are more attractive and potentially adjust their allocation accordingly.

Back-End Load

The back-end load, in the context of financial management, refers to a type of sales charge or fee that is incurred when an investor sells or redeems shares of a mutual fund within a specified time period after purchase. Also known as a contingent deferred sales charge (CDSC) or redemption fee, the back-end load is typically expressed as a percentage of the total value of shares being redeemed. This fee is intended to discourage investors from frequently buying and selling shares of a mutual fund, as it is designed to recoup the costs associated with the initial purchase of the shares and compensate the mutual fund for lost potential income.

Backtesting

Backtesting refers to the process of evaluating the performance of a financial strategy or model using historical data. It is a crucial aspect of financial management as it helps assess the effectiveness and reliability of investment or trading strategies before implementing them in real-time. In backtesting, historical market data is used to simulate and test the performance of a specific strategy or model. This data includes details such as price movements, volume, and other relevant factors. By applying the strategy to this historical data, the goal is to understand how it would have performed in the past, providing insights into its potential success or failure in the future.

Bad Debt Expense

Bad Debt Expense refers to the amount of money that a company determines is unlikely to be collected from its customers. It is a provision made by a company to account for the possibility of customers defaulting on their payments. When a customer fails to make a payment, the company must decide whether to pursue collection efforts or write off the debt as a loss. Bad Debt Expense is the financial recognition of the latter option, where the company acknowledges that it is no longer feasible to recover the outstanding balance.

Bad Debt Recovery

Bad debt recovery in the context of financial management refers to the process of collecting unpaid or delinquent debts that are considered to be irrecoverable by a business or organization. It is often necessary for companies to make provisions for bad debts, as some customers or clients may default on their payment obligations, resulting in a loss for the business. When a debt is classified as bad, it means that the likelihood of collecting the outstanding balance is extremely low. In such cases, the business may choose to write off the debt as a loss on their financial statements. However, bad debt recovery attempts to minimize this loss by implementing strategies and processes to recover as much of the unpaid debt as possible.

Balance Sheet

A balance sheet is a financial statement that provides a snapshot of a company's financial position at a specific point in time. It presents a summary of a company's assets, liabilities, and equity, allowing stakeholders to assess the company's financial health and its ability to meet its financial obligations. The balance sheet follows the fundamental accounting equation, which states that assets must equal liabilities plus equity. This equation serves as the foundation for double-entry bookkeeping, ensuring that every financial transaction is recorded and balanced. The balance sheet is divided into two main sections: assets on one side and liabilities and equity on the other side. The assets section lists all the resources owned or controlled by the company that have economic value. These can include cash, accounts receivable, inventory, investments, property, plant, and equipment. Assets are categorized into current assets - those that are expected to be converted into cash within one year - and long-term assets, which have a longer life span. The liabilities and equity section represents the company's sources of funds. Liabilities include obligations that the company owes to external parties, such as accounts payable, loans, and accrued expenses. Equity represents the owners' interest in the company and is calculated as the difference between total assets and total liabilities. It includes common stock, retained earnings, and additional paid-in capital. The balance sheet provides important information for investors, creditors, and management. Investors can use it to assess the company's financial stability and evaluate its potential for growth. Creditors use the balance sheet to determine the company's ability to repay its debts and assess its creditworthiness. Management relies on the balance sheet to make informed decisions about resource allocation, investment opportunities, and financing strategies. In summary, the balance sheet is a crucial financial statement that provides a snapshot of a company's financial position. It helps stakeholders evaluate the company's liquidity, solvency, and overall financial performance.

Balance Of Trade

The balance of trade is a measure that calculates the difference between a country's exports and imports of goods and services over a specific period. It is an essential indicator in financial management as it provides insight into the economic performance of a country in terms of international trade. The balance of trade is also known as the trade balance or the net export/import balance.

Balanced Fund

A balanced fund is a type of investment fund that aims to provide investors with a diverse portfolio by allocating assets across multiple asset classes, such as stocks, bonds, and cash equivalents. The purpose of a balanced fund is to balance the potential for growth offered by stocks with the stability provided by bonds and cash. This approach is intended to reduce investment risk and achieve a moderate level of return. In financial management, the main objective of a balanced fund is to achieve a balance between capital preservation and capital growth. By investing in a mix of stocks, bonds, and cash, the fund aims to protect the investor's initial capital investment while also seeking opportunities for capital appreciation. The allocation of assets within the fund is actively managed by professional fund managers who use various strategies to adjust the weights of each asset class based on market conditions and the fund's investment objectives.

Balanced Scorecard

The Balanced Scorecard is a strategic management tool that provides a comprehensive view of an organization's performance by evaluating key performance indicators across four different perspectives: financial, customer, internal business processes, and learning and growth. In the context of financial management, the Balanced Scorecard helps organizations track and measure their financial performance in a more holistic manner. Traditionally, financial metrics such as revenue, profits, and return on investment have been the primary focus for assessing financial health. While these indicators are important, the Balanced Scorecard recognizes the need to consider other factors that contribute to long-term financial success. By incorporating financial measures alongside non-financial measures, the Balanced Scorecard enables organizations to gain a more complete understanding of their financial performance and make informed decisions. The financial perspective in the Balanced Scorecard includes metrics such as revenue growth, profitability, return on investment, and cash flow. Furthermore, the Balanced Scorecard encourages organizations to identify and measure the drivers of financial performance, rather than solely focusing on lagging indicators. For example, instead of solely monitoring revenue growth, organizations may also track customer satisfaction (customer perspective) and process efficiency (internal business process perspective) as leading indicators that contribute to long-term financial success. By actively monitoring and managing performance across all four perspectives, organizations can identify areas for improvement and align their strategies with their financial goals. The Balanced Scorecard provides a framework for setting targets, measuring progress, and aligning initiatives across different functional areas and departments within the organization. In summary, the Balanced Scorecard is a strategic management tool that assesses an organization's financial performance in conjunction with other key performance indicators. It promotes a more holistic approach to financial management and enables organizations to make informed decisions by considering multiple perspectives.

Balloon Payment

A balloon payment is a large lump sum payment that is made at the end of a loan term, commonly used in financial management. It is typically seen in loans that have low monthly payments but a significant final payment. In financial management, a balloon payment can serve multiple purposes. It can provide favorable terms for borrowers, especially those who want to minimize their monthly cash flow or those who expect to have a significant influx of funds in the future. Additionally, it allows lenders to receive increased interest income over the course of the loan term.

Bank Reconciliation

A bank reconciliation is a process in financial management that compares the company's accounting records of cash transactions with the bank statement records. The purpose of a bank reconciliation is to ensure that the company's records accurately reflect the cash position by identifying any discrepancies or errors between the two sets of records. During a bank reconciliation, the company's cash receipts and cash disbursements are compared with the bank statement to identify any differences. These differences can occur due to various reasons, such as timing differences in recording transactions, bank fees, interest income or expense, and bank errors. The bank reconciliation process involves adjusting the company's records to reflect the correct cash balance by adding or deducting these differences.

Bankers' Acceptance

Bankers' Acceptance refers to a financial instrument that is issued by a bank on behalf of a customer and guarantees payment on a specified future date. It is commonly used in international trade transactions as a means of providing assurance to the seller that they will be paid for the goods or services they have provided. When a customer wishes to engage in a trade transaction with a seller, they may request a bankers' acceptance from their bank. The bank, after evaluating the creditworthiness of the customer, issues the acceptance, which is essentially a promise to pay the seller a certain amount of money on a specific future date. The bank's name and signature on the acceptance add credibility and provide assurance to the seller that they will receive payment as agreed.

Bankruptcy Risk

Bankruptcy risk refers to the probability or likelihood that a company will become insolvent and unable to meet its financial obligations. It is a measure of the financial health and stability of a company and is a critical factor in assessing its creditworthiness and potential investment risks. Bankruptcy risk is influenced by various internal and external factors, including the company's financial structure, profitability, liquidity, business model, industry dynamics, economic conditions, and regulatory environment. A high bankruptcy risk indicates that a company is more vulnerable to financial distress and may face difficulties in repaying its debts or meeting its operational expenses. A company with a high bankruptcy risk is typically characterized by declining revenues, negative cash flows, excessive debt burden, low profitability, and insufficient liquidity. It may struggle to generate sufficient cash flow to cover its debt payments and sustain its operations. In such cases, the company may resort to measures like borrowing more money, selling assets, or restructuring its debt to avoid bankruptcy. Financial managers play a critical role in managing and mitigating bankruptcy risk. They employ various strategies and techniques to improve the company's financial position, reduce debt levels, optimize capital structure, enhance profitability, and enhance overall liquidity. This may include implementing cost-cutting measures, improving operational efficiency, diversifying revenue streams, negotiating favorable terms with lenders, and conducting rigorous financial analysis and forecasting. A comprehensive assessment of bankruptcy risk involves analyzing various financial ratios and indicators, such as debt-to-equity ratio, interest coverage ratio, current ratio, quick ratio, and cash flow adequacy. These ratios provide insights into the company's ability to fulfill its financial obligations and withstand economic downturns and adverse events. Overall, bankruptcy risk is a crucial concept in financial management as it helps stakeholders evaluate the financial stability and creditworthiness of a company. By identifying and managing bankruptcy risk effectively, companies can safeguard their financial health, maintain investor confidence, and optimize their long-term growth and profitability prospects.

Bankruptcy

Bankruptcy refers to a legal process in which an individual or a business declares their inability to repay their debts to creditors. It is a financial state where the liabilities of the debtor exceed their assets, making it impossible to fulfill their financial obligations.This legal status is initiated by the filing of a bankruptcy petition by the debtor or a creditor. The main objective of bankruptcy is to provide relief from overwhelming debt to individuals or businesses that are incapable of paying their creditors.

Barter System

The barter system, in the context of financial management, refers to a method of exchange where goods and services are traded directly without the use of a common medium of exchange, such as money. It is a system that predates the use of currency and has been utilized by various societies throughout history. In a barter system, individuals or businesses trade goods or services they possess in exchange for other goods or services that they need. Unlike modern monetary transactions, barter involves a direct exchange between two parties, without the involvement of a third party or any form of currency. The value of each item being exchanged is determined through mutual agreement between the parties involved.

Base Currency

A base currency, in the context of financial management, refers to the currency in which an entity conducts its primary business operations and maintains its accounting records. It serves as the reference point for measuring and valuing all other currencies in a company's financial statements. The base currency is typically chosen based on the location of the company's headquarters or the country where it operates predominantly. The selection of a base currency is an important decision for companies engaged in international business or those with subsidiaries in multiple countries. It affects various aspects of financial management, including financial reporting, budgeting, forecasting, and risk management. One of the key reasons for choosing a base currency is to provide stability and consistency in financial reporting. By using a single currency as the base, companies can minimize the effects of currency fluctuations on their financial statements. This allows for better comparability and analysis of financial performance over time. Furthermore, having a base currency facilitates the consolidation of financial statements for multinational companies. When a company has subsidiaries operating in different countries using different currencies, consolidating the financials becomes challenging. By converting all subsidiary currencies to the base currency, companies can present a more accurate and comprehensive view of their overall financial position. Another advantage of having a base currency is that it simplifies the budgeting and forecasting processes. Companies can set their targets and make projections using a single currency, making it easier to monitor and evaluate performance against these goals. Risk management is also a crucial aspect influenced by the choice of base currency. It helps companies mitigate currency exchange rate risks, which can significantly impact profitability. By conducting transactions and maintaining financial records in the base currency, companies can reduce their exposure to currency fluctuations and manage their foreign exchange risks more effectively.

Basis Point (BP)

A basis point (BP) is a unit commonly used in financial management to describe a small percentage change in a financial instrument or a measure of interest rates. It represents one-hundredth of a percentage point, or 0.01%.This term is primarily used in the finance industry to measure changes in interest rates, yields, spreads, and other financial indicators. It provides a convenient way to express small changes that may have a significant impact on financial calculations and decisions.

Basis Point (BPS)

A basis point (BPS) is a unit of measurement used in the field of financial management. It is commonly used to express small changes in interest rates, bond yields, or other financial metrics. One basis point is equal to one-hundredth of a percentage point, or 0.01%. The use of basis points allows for precise and standardized measurement of changes in financial variables. It helps to eliminate confusion and provides a common language for discussing and comparing different rates and yields. For example, if the interest rate on a loan increases by 25 basis points, it means the rate has increased by 0.25%.

Bear Market

A bear market refers to a condition in the financial market wherein prices of securities, such as stocks, decline significantly over an extended period. It is characterized by widespread pessimism and a general decline in the overall value of the market. This bearish trend often results in a downward spiral as investors tend to sell their holdings, further pushing prices downward. Bear markets are typically associated with economic downturns or financial crises, and they are considered the opposite of bull markets, which signify a rising market trend. During a bear market, investor confidence is low, and there is a prevalent negative sentiment in the market.

Bearer Bond

A bearer bond refers to a type of debt instrument that is owned by the person who physically holds the bond certificate, known as the bearer. It is a form of bond that is unregistered and does not have the owner's name recorded in any database or on the bond certificate itself. The holder of a bearer bond is entitled to receive periodic interest payments and the principal amount at maturity. Bearer bonds are typically issued in large denominations and are often used by corporations or governments to raise capital. Unlike registered bonds, which have the owner's information recorded and require a transfer of ownership to be made, bearer bonds are negotiable instruments that can be easily transferred by simply handing over the physical certificate to someone else.

Behavioral Biases

Behavioral biases, in the context of financial management, refer to the systematic and predictable deviations from rational decision-making that individuals exhibit when it comes to managing their finances. These biases arise due to the inherent cognitive and emotional limitations of human beings, which often lead to irrational and suboptimal financial choices. One common behavioral bias in financial management is known as the confirmation bias. This bias occurs when individuals seek out information or only pay attention to evidence that supports their existing beliefs or opinions, while disregarding or ignoring contradictory information. For example, an investor may only focus on positive news about a particular stock or investment, dismissing any negative news that may suggest a decline in its value. This bias can prevent individuals from objective analysis and evaluation of investment options, leading to potential losses.

Behavioral Economics

Behavioral Economics is a branch of economics that seeks to understand and explain human behavior and decision-making in the context of financial management. It combines insights from psychology and economics to explore how individuals make financial decisions and how these decisions deviate from traditional economic theory. Traditional economic theory assumes that individuals make decisions based on rationality, self-interest, and complete information. However, behavioral economics challenges these assumptions by recognizing that humans often deviate from rationality and are influenced by cognitive biases and emotions when making financial decisions.

Behavioral Finance

Behavioral finance is a field of study that explores how psychological factors and biases influence the decision-making process of individuals and market participants in the realm of financial management. Traditional finance assumes that individuals and markets behave rationally, making decisions that maximize their own self-interests based on all available information. However, behavioral finance challenges this assumption by recognizing that human beings are not always rational and that their decisions can be influenced by a range of cognitive and emotional biases. One key aspect of behavioral finance is the concept of heuristics, which are mental shortcuts that individuals use to make quick and efficient decisions. These heuristics can sometimes lead to biases, such as the tendency to overestimate the probability of rare events or the inclination to rely on past experiences as a basis for decision-making. Another important area of study in behavioral finance is the field of prospect theory, which suggests that individuals do not evaluate potential gains and losses objectively. Instead, they tend to weigh potential losses more heavily than gains and are often risk-averse when faced with the possibility of incurring losses. Additionally, behavioral finance examines the influence of social and emotional factors on financial decision-making. Market sentiment, for example, can be influenced by herd mentality, where individuals tend to follow the actions of the group rather than making independent decisions. Emotional biases, such as overconfidence or fear, can also impact investment decisions. Understanding behavioral finance is crucial for financial managers, as it helps explain why markets can be inefficient and why investors may make suboptimal decisions. By recognizing the presence of biases and other psychological factors, financial managers can develop strategies to mitigate their impact and make more informed decisions. In conclusion, behavioral finance is a branch of finance that considers how psychological factors and biases can affect decision-making in financial management. By studying these influences, financial managers can gain a deeper understanding of market behavior and make more effective decisions to achieve their financial goals.

Benchmark Index

A benchmark index is a standardized measure that is used to evaluate the performance of a specific investment or portfolio in relation to the broader market or a specific market segment. It serves as a reference point to assess the relative success or failure of an investment strategy. In financial management, benchmark indexes play a crucial role in comparing the performance of a fund manager, investment strategy, or investment portfolio. The benchmark index represents a hypothetical portfolio of assets, typically chosen to reflect the characteristics of a specific market or industry. It serves as a benchmark against which the performance of a fund or investment can be measured.

Benchmark Rate

A benchmark rate is a standardized reference rate that is used to evaluate or compare the performance of financial instruments, portfolios, or investment strategies. It serves as a point of comparison for measuring the relative returns or risk-adjusted returns of different types of investments. In the context of financial management, benchmark rates are commonly used as a yardstick to assess the performance of investment funds, such as mutual funds or hedge funds. These rates provide a standardized performance measure for evaluating the investment managers' ability to generate returns above or below the benchmark rate.

Beta Coofficient

The beta coefficient, also known as beta, is a measure used in financial management to assess the systematic risk associated with an investment. It quantifies the sensitivity of an asset's returns to changes in the overall market returns. Beta is commonly used by investors and analysts to evaluate the risk-reward trade-off of a particular security or portfolio. The beta coefficient is calculated by regressing the historical returns of the asset against the returns of a designated benchmark index, typically the overall market index. The resulting beta value represents the asset's volatility relative to the benchmark. A beta greater than 1 indicates that the asset is more volatile than the market, while a beta less than 1 suggests lower volatility.

Beta Risk

Beta risk, in the context of financial management, refers to the measure of the sensitivity of a particular investment or stock's returns in relation to the overall market returns. It is a statistical measure that helps investors evaluate the level of systematic risk associated with an investment. More specifically, beta risk is calculated by comparing the historical price movements of a specific asset with that of a benchmark index, such as the S&P 500. The beta coefficient resulting from this calculation indicates the degree to which an investment is likely to move in relation to the broader market.

Bid-Ask Spread

The bid-ask spread refers to the difference between the highest price a buyer is willing to pay for a security (bid price) and the lowest price a seller is willing to accept for it (ask price). It is a key concept in financial management, particularly in trading and investment analysis. The bid price represents the maximum amount that a buyer is willing to pay for a security, while the ask price represents the minimum amount that a seller is willing to accept. The difference between these two prices is the bid-ask spread. The bid-ask spread serves as an indicator of market liquidity and transaction costs. It represents the cost of executing a trade, as the buyer must be willing to pay a higher price than what the seller is willing to accept. A narrow bid-ask spread suggests a liquid market with low transaction costs, while a wide spread indicates illiquidity and higher costs. Market makers, such as brokers and dealers, play a crucial role in determining bid-ask spreads. They serve as intermediaries between buyers and sellers, and profit from the difference between the bid and ask prices. Market conditions, such as supply and demand dynamics, also influence the spread. Increased competition among market makers tends to reduce spreads, while decreased competition or market uncertainty can lead to wider spreads. Traders and investors closely monitor bid-ask spreads to assess market conditions and determine the potential profitability of a trade. A narrower spread is generally preferable, as it allows for more efficient trading and reduces transaction costs. However, it is important to consider the size of the spread in relation to the security's price, as smaller spreads may be relatively larger for lower-priced securities. In summary, the bid-ask spread is the difference between the highest price a buyer is willing to pay and the lowest price a seller is willing to accept for a security. It serves as an indicator of liquidity and transaction costs in the market. Traders and investors use bid-ask spreads to assess market conditions and potential profitability of trades.

Black Swan Event

A black swan event refers to an unpredictable and rare occurrence that has a severe impact on the financial markets and the overall economy. It is characterized by its extreme rarity, high impact, and the difficulty in predicting or preparing for it. The concept of a black swan event was popularized by Nassim Nicholas Taleb in his book "The Black Swan: The Impact of the Highly Improbable." In the context of financial management, a black swan event poses significant challenges and risks for organizations and investors. These events are often external shocks that can lead to market disruptions, economic downturns, and financial crises. Examples of black swan events include the 2008 global financial crisis, the dot-com bubble burst in 2000, and the 9/11 terrorist attacks. One key characteristic of a black swan event is that it is typically unforeseen or considered highly unlikely before its occurrence. Traditional risk management models and techniques are often insufficient in predicting or mitigating the impacts of such events. This is because they are usually based on historical data and assumptions about market behavior, which may not hold true during a black swan event. These events can result in significant losses and financial instability, as they have the potential to disrupt financial markets, damage investor confidence, and lead to widespread economic contractions. Organizations may face challenges such as liquidity and solvency concerns, declining asset values, and increased uncertainties in decision-making. To manage the risks associated with black swan events, financial managers may employ various strategies, such as diversification, stress testing, and scenario analysis. These approaches aim to enhance the organization's resilience and ability to withstand sudden shocks to the financial system. Additionally, organizations may also focus on enhancing their risk detection and response capabilities, as well as establishing robust contingency plans. In conclusion, a black swan event is an unpredictable and highly impactful occurrence in the financial markets. It poses significant challenges for financial managers and requires the implementation of proactive risk management strategies to mitigate its potential adverse effects.

Black-Scholes Model

The Black-Scholes model is a mathematical formula used in financial management to determine the value of options, specifically European-style options. Developed by economists Fischer Black and Myron Scholes in 1973, the model provides a theoretical framework for pricing options based on various factors. The model takes into account five key variables to calculate the theoretical price of an option: the current price of the underlying asset, the strike price of the option, the time to expiration, the risk-free interest rate, and the volatility of the underlying asset's price. By inputting these variables into the Black-Scholes formula, financial managers can estimate the fair value of an option. The Black-Scholes model assumes that markets are efficient and that the price of the underlying asset follows a geometric Brownian motion with constant volatility. It also assumes that there are no transaction costs, no dividends are paid during the life of the option, and that the risk-free interest rate remains constant over the life of the option. Additionally, the Black-Scholes model provides two key insights into option pricing. Firstly, it demonstrates that the value of an option is influenced by the volatility of the underlying asset's price. As volatility increases, the value of the option also increases. Secondly, it introduces the concept of delta, which measures the sensitivity of an option's price to changes in the price of the underlying asset. Delta ranges from 0 to 1 for call options and from -1 to 0 for put options. While the Black-Scholes model is widely used in financial management, it does have certain limitations. It assumes that the underlying asset's price follows a continuous geometric Brownian motion, which may not always be accurate. It also assumes constant volatility and a constant risk-free interest rate, which may not hold true in real-world scenarios. Nevertheless, the Black-Scholes model remains a valuable tool for pricing options and assessing their fair value in financial management.

Blue Chip Stocks

Blue chip stocks are shares of well-established companies with a stable financial performance, a history of consistent dividend payments, and a strong market presence. These stocks are generally considered to be safe and reliable investments due to their ability to maintain stability and generate decent returns over a long period of time. Blue chip stocks are typically associated with large, reputable companies that have a strong track record of profitability, proven business models, and a solid position within their respective industries. These companies are often leaders in their sectors and enjoy a competitive advantage, which further contributes to their stability and potential for growth.

Blue Chip

A blue chip refers to a high-quality, well-established, and financially stable company that has a strong reputation in the market and has a track record of delivering consistent performance over time. Blue chip stocks are shares of these companies, typically large and well-known, which are considered to be less risky investments compared to other stocks. Blue chip companies are usually leaders in their respective industries and have a proven history of generating substantial revenue and profits. They often have a significant market presence, strong brand recognition, and a wide customer base. These companies are known for their ability to withstand economic downturns and recover quickly, making them a popular choice for investors seeking stability and long-term growth.

Blue Sky Laws

The Blue Sky Laws are state regulations that aim to protect investors from fraudulent securities practices. These laws require companies and individuals issuing securities to register their offerings and provide potential investors with comprehensive and accurate information about the securities. The term "Blue Sky Laws" was coined to reflect the idea that these regulations provide a "blue sky" of protection for investors, shielding them from unscrupulous individuals and companies who may attempt to defraud them through deceptive securities offerings.

Bollinger Bands

Bollinger Bands is a technical analysis tool used in financial management to measure volatility and identify potential overbought or oversold conditions in the price of a security. Developed by John Bollinger in the 1980s, it consists of three lines plotted on a price chart: a middle band, an upper band, and a lower band. The middle band is typically a simple moving average (SMA) of the security's price over a specified period, while the upper and lower bands are calculated by adding and subtracting a multiple of the standard deviation of the price from the middle band. The standard deviation is a measure of the dispersion of the price data, representing volatility.

Bond Fund

A bond fund is a type of mutual fund that invests primarily in bonds, which are debt securities issued by governments, municipalities, and corporations. Bond funds provide individual investors with access to a diversified portfolio of bonds, which can be more cost-effective compared to purchasing individual bonds. The fund manager of a bond fund selects a mix of bonds to align with the fund's investment objectives, such as income generation, capital preservation, or inflation protection. Bond funds can invest in various types of bonds, including government bonds, municipal bonds, corporate bonds, and mortgage-backed securities. Each type of bond has its own risk and return characteristics, and the allocation of these bonds within the fund can vary depending on the fund's investment strategy and risk tolerance. The fund manager may also consider factors such as interest rate risk, credit risk, and liquidity risk when constructing the bond portfolio. Investors in bond funds can benefit from regular income payments in the form of interest or dividends, which are typically paid out monthly or quarterly. The income generated from the bond portfolio is distributed to shareholders in proportion to their investment in the fund. Additionally, bond funds provide the potential for capital appreciation if the prices of the bonds held in the portfolio increase. However, it is important to note that bond prices can fluctuate based on changes in interest rates, credit ratings, and market conditions. Bond funds offer investors the advantages of professional management, diversification, and liquidity. The fund manager employs their expertise to actively manage the bond portfolio, making investment decisions based on market trends and economic conditions. The diversification provided by bond funds helps to spread out the risk among different types of bonds, reducing the impact of a default by a single issuer. Furthermore, investors can buy and sell shares of bond funds on any business day, allowing for easy liquidity compared to purchasing individual bonds.

Bond Indenture

A bond indenture is a legally binding agreement between the issuer of a bond and the bondholders that outlines the terms and conditions of the bond. It is a crucial document in financial management as it provides vital information about the rights and obligations of both parties involved in the bond issuance. The bond indenture typically includes details such as the principal amount of the bond, the interest rate, the maturity date, and any other provisions related to the bond. It also specifies how the interest will be paid, the frequency of interest payments, and any potential events of default or remedies available to bondholders in case of non-compliance by the issuer. The bond indenture serves as a contractual agreement that governs the relationship between the issuer and the bondholders. It outlines the rights of the bondholders, which may include the ability to take legal action in case of default or seek repayment of their investment. Similarly, it details the responsibilities and obligations of the issuer, including the timely payment of interest and repayment of the principal amount on maturity. Furthermore, the bond indenture may also include provisions regarding the use of collateral or other security to protect bondholders' interests. It may specify the steps to be taken in case of bankruptcy or liquidation of the issuer, ensuring that bondholders have a priority claim on the issuer's assets. In summary, a bond indenture is a legally binding agreement that outlines the terms and conditions of a bond issuance. It provides critical information about the rights and obligations of both the issuer and the bondholders. This document is essential in financial management as it ensures transparency and clarity in the bond issuance process, protecting the interests of both parties involved.

Bond Ladder

A bond ladder is a financial management strategy that involves diversifying the risk and maximizing returns in a bond portfolio. It is based on the concept of staggering the maturity dates of bonds in order to create a consistent stream of income and maintain liquidity. In a bond ladder, a portfolio is constructed by purchasing bonds with different maturity dates, typically with equal intervals between them. For example, if a bond ladder is created with five-year intervals, bonds with maturities of 1 year, 6 years, 11 years, and so on, would be purchased.

Bond

A bond is a fixed income instrument that represents a loan made by an investor to a borrower, which is typically a government or a corporation. It is a form of debt security, where the borrower agrees to pay a fixed amount of interest over a predetermined period of time and return the face value of the bond upon maturity. Bonds are widely used in financial management as they offer a reliable source of funding for both governments and corporations. They are commonly issued in the primary market, where the borrower sells the bonds directly to investors, and are subsequently traded in the secondary market.

Bondholder

A bondholder is an individual or entity that owns the debt instrument known as a bond. Bonds are used by corporations, municipalities, and governments to borrow money from investors. When an investor purchases a bond, they become a bondholder and are entitled to receive regular interest payments and the return of the principal amount at maturity.

Bonds Payable

Bonds Payable refers to a long-term debt instrument issued by a company or organization to raise funds. It represents the amount borrowed by the entity, which is typically repaid over a specified period with periodic interest payments. When a company decides to issue bonds, it essentially borrows money from investors or lenders. The bond represents a contractual obligation to repay the principal amount borrowed, known as the face value or par value of the bond, at a predetermined maturity date. This maturity date can range from a few years to several decades. Bonds Payable involve two primary components: the principal and the interest. The principal is the initial amount borrowed and is repaid at maturity. The interest, which is typically a fixed rate stated as a percentage of the principal, is paid periodically, usually semi-annually or annually, over the life of the bond. Companies use bonds as a method of financing their operations or expansion plans. By issuing bonds, they can tap into the debt market to raise capital from a wide range of investors. This allows companies to diversify their funding sources and access larger amounts of capital compared to bank loans or equity financing. Investors who purchase bonds become creditors of the issuing company. They receive periodic interest payments as compensation for lending their money and expect the repayment of the principal amount at maturity. The interest rate on bonds, also known as the coupon rate, is determined based on various factors such as prevailing market rates, creditworthiness of the issuer, and the term of the bond. Bonds Payable play a crucial role in the financial management of a company. It helps in maintaining a healthy capital structure by balancing the mix of debt and equity. Bonds are attractive to investors seeking fixed income investments and are often considered less risky than stocks. The interest paid on bonds is tax-deductible, resulting in potential tax savings for the issuing company. In summary, Bonds Payable represent a long-term debt obligation issued by a company to raise funds, involving a principal amount to be repaid at maturity and periodic interest payments. They are an important source of financing for businesses and provide investors with a fixed income investment option.

Book Runner

The term "book runner" is commonly used in the field of financial management and refers to a financial institution or an underwriting firm that is responsible for managing the issuance of securities, such as stocks or bonds, on behalf of a company or government entity. When a company or government entity decides to raise capital by issuing securities, they typically engage the services of a book runner. The book runner plays a crucial role in the issuance process, acting as the intermediary between the issuer and potential investors. The primary responsibility of the book runner is to coordinate the entire issuance process, from the initial planning and structuring of the offering to the final distribution of the securities. This involves working closely with the issuer to determine the appropriate timing, pricing, and terms of the offering, as well as conducting due diligence to ensure compliance with regulatory requirements. Once the offering is ready, the book runner takes on the task of marketing and distributing the securities to potential investors. This may involve conducting roadshows, arranging meetings with institutional investors, and promoting the offering through various channels. The book runner also handles the allocation of the securities to investors, ensuring a fair and efficient distribution process. In addition to managing the issuance process, book runners often play a key role in underwriting the securities. This means that they commit to purchasing a certain amount of the securities from the issuer, either directly or through a syndicate of underwriters. By underwriting the offering, the book runner takes on the risk of not being able to sell all of the securities to investors, but stands to profit from the difference between the purchase price and the sale price. Overall, the book runner serves as a crucial link between the issuer and the investing public, facilitating the smooth and efficient issuance of securities. Their expertise in financial markets, as well as their extensive network of investor contacts, allows them to provide valuable guidance to issuers and ensure the success of the offering.

Book Value Per Share

Book Value per Share is a financial metric used in the field of Financial Management to assess the intrinsic value of a company's shares. It is calculated by dividing the total shareholder's equity by the number of outstanding shares. The total shareholder's equity represents the net assets of the company after deducting liabilities. It is a measure of the company's net worth and represents the ownership interest of the shareholders. The number of outstanding shares represents the total number of shares issued by the company and held by investors. By dividing the total shareholder's equity by the number of outstanding shares, Book Value per Share

31

provides a measure of the value allocated to each individual share. It indicates the amount of money that shareholders would receive for each share if the company were to liquidate its assets and pay off its liabilities. Book Value per Share is an important metric for investors as it provides insight into the financial health and stability of a company. A higher Book Value per Share indicates that the company has a larger amount of equity relative to its outstanding shares, which can be seen as a positive sign. It suggests that the company has a solid financial foundation and is less reliant on debt financing. Investors often use Book Value per Share as a benchmark to compare the market price of a company's shares. If the market price is lower than the Book Value per Share, it may be considered undervalued, indicating that the stock may be a good investment opportunity. Conversely, if the market price is higher than the Book Value per Share, it may be considered overvalued, suggesting that the stock may be overpriced. However, it is important to note that Book Value per Share is just one of several factors to consider when evaluating the investment potential of a company. It does not take into account factors such as future earnings potential, market conditions, or industry trends. Therefore, it should be used in conjunction with other financial ratios and metrics to make informed investment decisions.

Book Value

Book value refers to the net worth of a company as shown on its balance sheet. It is the total value of a company's assets minus its liabilities, which provides an indication of the value of the company's equity. To determine the book value of a company, all of its assets are recorded at their historical cost, minus any accumulated depreciation and impairment. This includes tangible assets such as buildings, equipment, and inventory, as well as intangible assets such as patents and trademarks. Liabilities, on the other hand, include debts, loans, and other obligations that the company owes to external parties. The book value of a company is important for various reasons. It serves as a benchmark for investors to evaluate the financial health and stability of a company. A higher book value generally indicates a more valuable company, while a lower book value may suggest financial challenges or a less valuable company. The book value per share, which is derived by dividing the book value by the number of outstanding shares, is often used by investors as a basis for determining the intrinsic value of a company's stock. In addition, book value is a key factor in determining a company's net asset value (NAV) for investment funds. The NAV represents the per-share value of an investment fund's assets minus its liabilities. Investors use NAV as a basis for pricing and trading shares of the fund. It is worth noting that book value does not necessarily reflect the market value of a company. The market value takes into account factors such as market demand, investor sentiment, and future growth prospects. In some cases, the book value may be higher than the market value, indicating that the company's assets are overvalued. On the other hand, the market value may be higher than the book value, suggesting that the market is valuing the company's assets at a premium due to factors such as growth potential or brand value.

Borrowing Base

A borrowing base is a financial management tool used by lenders to determine the maximum amount of money they are willing to lend to a borrower based on the collateral provided. It serves as a way for lenders to assess the risk associated with extending credit and helps protect their interests in case of default. The borrowing base is calculated by taking a percentage of the value of eligible collateral and subtracting any outstanding liens or encumbrances. The eligible collateral typically includes assets such as accounts receivable, inventory, equipment, and real estate. The specific percentage used to calculate the borrowing base depends on the type and quality of the collateral, as well as the lender's risk appetite. For example, let's say a company is seeking a loan and has $500,000 in accounts receivable, $1,000,000 in inventory, and a piece of real estate valued at $2,000,000. The lender may calculate the borrowing base at 70% for accounts receivable, 50% for inventory, and 80% for real estate. They would then subtract any outstanding liens or encumbrances on each asset to arrive at the final borrowing base. Once the borrowing base has been determined, the lender will typically set a loan limit that is lower than the borrowing base to provide a margin of safety. This cushion helps protect the lender's interests in the event of a decline in the value of the collateral or other unforeseen circumstances. Regular monitoring and reporting of the borrowing base is essential for both the borrower and the lender. The borrower needs to ensure that the value of their collateral remains sufficient to support their borrowing needs, while the lender must verify that the collateral is adequately protected and that the borrower is not in violation of any loan covenants.

Break-Even Analysis

A break-even analysis is a financial management tool used to determine the point at which a company's total revenue equals its total expenses, resulting in neither profit nor loss. It helps businesses assess the minimum level of sales they need to generate in order to cover their costs and begin making a profit. Break-even analysis is based on the concept of fixed and variable costs. Fixed costs are expenses that do not change regardless of the level of production or sales, such as rent, salaries, and insurance. Variable costs, on the other hand, fluctuate with the level of production or sales, such as raw materials, direct labor, and commission. By distinguishing between fixed and variable costs, break-even analysis enables businesses to understand how changes in sales volume affect their profitability.

Break-Even Point (BEP)

The Break-Even Point (BEP) is a financial management concept that refers to the level of sales or revenue at which a company neither makes a profit nor incurs a loss. It is the point where total revenue equals total costs, resulting in zero net income. At the BEP, a company's sales revenue covers all of its variable and fixed costs. Variable costs include items directly related to the production or delivery of goods or services, such as raw materials, labor, and utilities. Fixed costs, on the other hand, are expenses that remain constant regardless of the volume of sales, such as rent, salaries, and depreciation. The BEP can be calculated using a simple formula. It is determined by dividing the total fixed costs by the contribution margin per unit, which is the difference between the selling price per unit and the variable cost per unit. The resulting BEP can be expressed as a number of units sold or as a sales revenue amount. Knowing the BEP is important for several reasons. Firstly, it helps businesses understand the minimum level of sales they need to achieve in order to cover their costs and avoid losses. This information can be useful for setting sales targets and pricing strategies. Additionally, the BEP can serve as a benchmark for evaluating the financial health and profitability of a company. If a company's actual sales exceed the BEP, it indicates a profit; if sales are below the BEP, it implies a loss. The concept of the BEP is particularly relevant in decision-making processes such as introducing a new product, determining the impact of changes in costs or prices, setting sales volume targets, and evaluating the profitability of different business segments. By analyzing the BEP, businesses can assess the financial implications of these decisions and make informed choices that align with their strategic goals.

Break-Even Point

The break-even point in financial management is the point at which total revenue equals total costs, resulting in neither profit nor loss. It is the level of sales at which a business covers all of its fixed and variable costs, and begins to make a profit. At the break-even point, the business is said to be "breaking even," because there is no net income or loss. This point is essential for financial managers to determine the viability and profitability of a business or a specific product or service.

Bretton Woods Agreement

The Bretton Woods Agreement was a landmark international agreement in the field of financial management. It was established in 1944 at the United Nations Monetary and Financial Conference held in Bretton Woods, New Hampshire, United States. The main objective of the Bretton Woods Agreement was to create a stable international monetary system in the aftermath of World War II. It aimed to promote economic growth, facilitate international trade, and prevent future financial crises. Under the agreement, participating countries agreed to fix their exchange rates to the U.S. dollar, which was pegged to gold. This meant that the value of each currency was directly linked to the value of gold and the U.S. dollar. The U.S. dollar, in turn, was convertible to gold at a fixed rate of $35 per ounce. In addition to the fixed exchange rate system, the Bretton Woods Agreement also established two important international institutions: the International Monetary Fund (IMF) and the International Bank for Reconstruction and Development (IBRD), now known as the World Bank. The IMF was created to provide financial assistance to countries facing balance of payments problems. It aimed to stabilize exchange rates and promote international monetary cooperation. Member countries contributed funds to the IMF, and those in need could borrow from the organization to address their economic challenges. The IBRD, on the other hand, was established to provide loans and financial support to countries for infrastructure projects and economic development. It aimed to reduce poverty and promote sustainable economic growth. The IBRD raised funds through issuing bonds and loans, which it then lent to member countries for their development projects. The Bretton Woods Agreement played a crucial role in shaping the global financial system in the post-war era. It facilitated international trade, provided a stable framework for exchange rates, and helped countries recover from the devastation of World War II. However, the agreement eventually collapsed in the early 1970s as countries faced economic challenges and the fixed exchange rate system became unsustainable. Despite its eventual demise, the Bretton Woods Agreement left a lasting legacy in the field of financial management. It set the stage for the creation of other international financial institutions, such as the World Trade Organization (WTO), and influenced subsequent negotiations on global economic issues.

Brokerage Account

A brokerage account is a financial account that allows an individual or entity to buy and sell various types of securities, such as stocks, bonds, mutual funds, and exchange-traded funds (ETFs), through a licensed brokerage firm. It serves as an intermediary platform between investors and the financial markets. When opening a brokerage account, the account holder must provide personal information and complete a registration process with their chosen brokerage firm. Once the account is established, the investor can deposit funds into the account and use those funds to purchase securities. Brokerage accounts offer investors a wide range of investment options, allowing them to diversify their portfolios and potentially earn returns on their investments. They provide access to a variety of financial products, including stocks, which represent ownership in a company; bonds, which are debt securities issued by governments or corporations; mutual funds, which pool money from multiple investors to invest in a diversified portfolio of securities; and ETFs, which are similar to mutual funds but trade on stock exchanges like individual stocks. Investors can place buy or sell orders for securities through their brokerage accounts. These orders are executed by the brokerage firm, which acts as an intermediary between the investor and the relevant financial markets. The brokerage firm may charge a commission or fee for executing trades on behalf of the account holder. Brokerage accounts also provide investors with access to important financial information and tools that can help them make informed investment decisions. This may include research reports, market analysis, news updates, and other resources that can assist in evaluating potential investment opportunities. Additionally, brokerage accounts allow investors to monitor the performance of their investments, view account statements, and track their portfolio's overall value. They often provide a user-friendly online platform or mobile application that makes it easy for investors to manage their accounts and stay informed about their investments. In summary, a brokerage account is a financial management tool that enables individuals and entities to buy and sell securities, diversify their investment portfolios, access important financial information, and monitor the performance of their investments. It serves as a connection between investors and the financial markets, providing a platform for executing trades and managing investment activities.

Budgeting

Budgeting is a financial management practice that involves planning and controlling the allocation of resources to achieve specific goals within a given time period. It is an essential tool for businesses and individuals to effectively manage their income, expenses, and investments. Through budgeting, organizations and individuals can create a comprehensive overview of their financial situation, set realistic financial goals, and make informed decisions based on their financial capabilities.

Bull Market

A bull market refers to a financial market characterized by rising prices, investor optimism, and increased buying activity. In this market, the overall direction of the market is upwards, and there is a strong belief among investors that prices will continue to rise. The term "bull market" is commonly used in the context of stock markets, but it can also apply to other types of financial markets, such as the bond market or the commodity market. When the majority of stocks, bonds, or commodities are experiencing significant price increases, it is an indication of a bull market.

Bullet Bond

A bullet bond is a type of bond that has a specific maturity date, typically ranging from one to ten years. It is called a "bullet" bond because it is designed to pay back the principal amount in a single lump sum payment on the maturity date, similar to a bullet being shot. Unlike other types of bonds that may have regular interest payments throughout their term, a bullet bond does not typically pay any interest until the maturity date. Instead, investors purchase the bond at a discount to its face value and earn a return through the price appreciation of the bond over time. The return earned on a bullet bond is called the yield to maturity.

Bullet Loan

A bullet loan is a type of loan that is structured with a large final payment, known as the balloon payment, that is due at the end of the loan term. This final payment is typically larger than the regular periodic payments made throughout the loan term, and it represents the remaining principal balance of the loan. This type of loan is commonly used in financial management for various purposes. It can be beneficial for borrowers who prefer to have lower monthly payments during the loan term and are confident in their ability to make the large balloon payment at the end. By deferring a significant portion of the loan repayment to the end, the borrower can use the funds for other investments or expenses during the loan term.

Business Risk

Business Risk is defined as the potential for loss or negative impact on a company's financial position, operations, or reputation due to external factors or internal weaknesses. In the context of financial management, it refers to the uncertainty and potential adverse consequences associated with financial decisions and activities. There are various types of business risks that organizations may face, including market risk, credit risk, operational risk, liquidity risk, legal and regulatory risk, reputational risk, and strategic risk. Each of these risks poses unique challenges and requires proactive management to mitigate their impact on the company's financial health and sustainability. Market risk arises from fluctuations in the market environment, including changes in interest rates, exchange rates, commodity prices, and market demand and supply. It can affect a company's profitability, value of assets and liabilities, and ability to generate cash flows. Effective risk management strategies may involve hedging, diversification of market exposure, and monitoring market trends and developments. Credit risk refers to the potential loss arising from the failure of customers or counterparties to fulfill their financial obligations, such as defaulting on loan repayments or failing to pay for goods or services. To manage credit risk, companies may establish credit assessment and monitoring procedures, set credit limits, and implement sound credit control and recovery mechanisms. Operational risk encompasses the potential losses arising from inadequate or failed internal processes, systems, or human actions. It includes risks related to fraud, errors, disruptions in supply chains, technology failures, health and safety issues, and legal and regulatory compliance. Implementing robust internal controls, conducting risk assessments, and providing regular training and monitoring can help mitigate operational risks. Liquidity risk arises from the inability to meet short-term obligations due to a shortage of cash or liquid assets. It can be caused by unexpected events or poor financial planning and management. Companies can manage liquidity risk by maintaining adequate cash reserves, establishing appropriate credit lines, and closely monitoring cash flows and working capital. Legal and regulatory risk pertains to the potential adverse impact of non-compliance with laws, regulations, and industry standards. Failure to comply with legal and regulatory requirements can result in fines, penalties, litigation, damage to reputation, and even business closure. It is crucial for companies to stay informed about relevant laws and regulations, establish internal controls and policies, and conduct regular audits and assessments. Reputational risk refers to the potential harm to a company's reputation or brand image due to negative publicity, customer dissatisfaction, unethical behavior, or poor quality products or services. It can have a significant impact on customer loyalty, investor confidence, and business relationships. Companies can mitigate reputational risk by delivering high-quality products and services, maintaining strong customer relationships, addressing complaints and issues promptly, and practicing transparent and ethical business conduct. Strategic risk relates to the uncertainty and potential adverse effects associated with a company's strategic decisions and actions. It includes risks arising from competition, changes in the business environment, technological advancements, and shifts in consumer preferences. Companies should regularly review and adjust their strategies, conduct market research, and monitor industry trends to navigate strategic risks effectively.

CDO (Collateralized Debt Obligation)

A Collateralized Debt Obligation (CDO) is a complex financial instrument that is created by pooling together various types of debt, such as loans, mortgages, and bonds, and repackaging them into a new security to be sold to investors. It is a form of securitization, where the cash flow generated from the debt assets is used to pay interest and principal to the investors in the CDO. The underlying assets in a CDO are typically grouped into different tranches based on their risk and return characteristics. These tranches have varying levels of credit quality and are structured in a way that senior tranches receive the first priority of payment, while junior tranches bear the first losses in case of defaults or delinquencies on the underlying assets. This hierarchical structure allows for the creation of different risk profiles and return potential, catering to the preferences of different types of investors. CDOs played a significant role in the financial crisis of 2008, as they were heavily exposed to subprime mortgage-backed securities. The lack of transparency, complexity, and inadequate risk assessment of CDOs led to significant losses for investors and contributed to the overall instability in the financial system. Despite the negative connotation associated with CDOs, they continue to exist as a financial tool for risk management and portfolio diversification. They allow banks and financial institutions to transfer risk off their balance sheets and free up capital to pursue other investment opportunities. Additionally, CDOs can provide investors with access to a diversified portfolio of debt assets, potentially offering higher yields compared to traditional fixed-income securities.

CFA Institute

The CFA Institute is a global association of investment professionals that sets the standard for professional excellence in the field of financial management. It is dedicated to promoting the highest ethical and professional standards among its members, as well as fostering global financial market integrity and investor protection. The CFA Institute offers the Chartered Financial Analyst (CFA) designation, which is widely recognized as the definitive standard for measuring competence and integrity in the fields of investment management and research. To earn the CFA designation, candidates must complete a rigorous program of study, pass three levels of examinations, accumulate relevant work experience, and adhere to a strict Code of Ethics and Standards of Professional Conduct set by the CFA Institute.

Call Option

A call option is a financial contract that gives the holder the right, but not the obligation, to buy a specified quantity of an underlying asset at a specified price, within a specified period of time. It is a type of derivative instrument commonly used in financial markets for hedging, speculation, or investment purposes. When an investor buys a call option, they are paying a premium to the option writer (seller) for the opportunity to purchase the underlying asset at a predetermined price, known as the strike price, on or before the expiration date of the option contract. The call option holder benefits from an increase in the price of the underlying asset, as it allows them to buy the asset at a lower cost than the market price. However, if the price of the underlying asset decreases or remains below the strike price, the call option may become worthless and the investor stands to lose their premium. Call options are commonly used by investors to speculate on the price movement of assets, hedge against potential losses, or to generate income through writing (selling) options. They offer the potential for significant leverage, as the capital required to purchase an option is typically much lower than the actual cost of owning the underlying asset. Option contracts are standardized and traded on organized exchanges, such as the Chicago Board Options Exchange (CBOE), providing liquidity and transparency to market participants. In addition to the strike price and expiration date, call options have other important characteristics. The premium, or price, of the option is determined by various factors including the volatility of the underlying asset, time to expiration, interest rates, and market supply and demand. The option contract also specifies the number of shares or units of the underlying asset that can be bought, known as the contract size. Overall, call options provide investors with flexibility and the potential to profit from price increases in the underlying asset, while limiting their downside risk. However, it is important to understand the risks and complexities associated with options trading, and to carefully consider one's investment objectives and risk tolerance before engaging in option transactions.

Callable Bond

A callable bond is a type of bond that gives the issuer the right to redeem or "call" the bond before its maturity date. This means that the issuer has the option to repay the bond's principal and terminate the bond before the scheduled maturity date. The main advantage of a callable bond for the issuer is that it provides flexibility in managing its debt obligations. By having the right to call the bond, the issuer can take advantage of favorable market conditions, such as declining interest rates, to refinance the debt at a lower cost. This can lead to cost savings for the issuer and improve its financial position. On the other hand, callable bonds carry certain risks for the bondholders. When a bond is called, bondholders receive the principal amount of the bond, but they may lose the opportunity to earn interest for the remaining period until the bond's original maturity date. This is because when the bond is called, the issuer typically repays the bond at a predetermined call price, which is usually higher than the bond's face value. The call price often includes a premium to compensate bondholders for the lost interest income. Investors who hold callable bonds face reinvestment risk. If their bond is called, they need to find other investment opportunities to generate the same level of income. This can be challenging, especially in a low-interest-rate environment. Moreover, callable bonds tend to have higher yields compared to non-callable bonds to compensate bondholders for the call risk they bear. Callable bonds often have specific call provisions that dictate when and under what conditions the issuer can call the bond. These provisions may include call dates, call prices, and call protection periods. The call dates specify when the bond can be called, while the call prices determine the amount the issuer must pay to call the bond. Call protection periods safeguard bondholders from early calls by setting a time period during which the bond cannot be called.

Callable Preferred Stock

Callable preferred stock refers to a type of preferred stock that is issued by a company and gives the company the right to call back or redeem the stock from the shareholders at a predetermined price and within a specified time period. The ability to call back the stock is a feature that is advantageous to the issuing company as it provides flexibility in managing its capital structure. Callable preferred stock typically offers higher dividend payments compared to common stock and may have other preferential rights, such as priority in the distribution of assets in the event of the company's liquidation. However, the call feature allows the company to repurchase the stock at a predetermined call price, which is usually higher than the stock's initial purchase price. This provides a potential disadvantage to investors as they may be forced to sell their shares at a price that is not favorable to them.

Capital Adequacy Ratio (CAR)

Capital Adequacy Ratio (CAR) is a key measure of a financial institution's ability to absorb potential losses and meet its financial obligations. It is an important indicator of the financial strength and stability of a bank or other financial institution. The CAR is calculated by dividing the bank's capital by its risk-weighted assets. The capital represents the lender's net worth and ability to cover losses, while the risk-weighted assets are the assets adjusted to reflect their credit risk. The CAR is expressed as a percentage, with higher percentages indicating a higher level of capital adequacy.

Capital Adequacy

Capital adequacy is a measure used in financial management to assess the financial strength and stability of a company or financial institution. It refers to the ability of an organization to meet its financial obligations and absorb any unexpected losses without jeopardizing its operations or the interests of its stakeholders. In other words, it is a measure of the extent to which a company has enough capital to support its activities and withstand financial shocks. The concept of capital adequacy is particularly important in the banking industry, where financial institutions must hold a sufficient amount of capital to mitigate potential risks and ensure the stability of the financial system. The capital adequacy framework for banks is typically regulated by authorities such as the Basel Committee on Banking Supervision (BCBS), which sets minimum capital requirements and establishes guidelines for the calculation and management of capital adequacy ratios. There are several capital adequacy ratios that are commonly used to assess a company's financial health. The most widely recognized ratio is the capital adequacy ratio (CAR), which compares a bank's capital to its risk-weighted assets. A higher CAR indicates a higher level of financial strength and stability, as it means that the bank has a larger capital buffer to absorb potential losses. Capital adequacy is crucial for financial institutions as it helps protect depositors, creditors, and shareholders from the risk of insolvency. By maintaining an adequate level of capital, banks can minimize the probability of default and reduce the potential impact of financial crises or economic downturns. Additionally, a strong capital base allows banks to support lending activities and contribute to economic growth by providing funds to individuals and businesses. In conclusion, capital adequacy is a fundamental aspect of financial management, especially within the banking industry. It ensures the stability and solvency of financial institutions, protects stakeholders, and contributes to the overall health of the financial system.

Capital Allocation Line (CAL)

The Capital Allocation Line (CAL) is a concept used in financial management to represent the trade-off between risk and return for a portfolio of investments. It helps investors assess the ideal combination of risky assets and risk-free assets to achieve their desired level of return while considering their risk tolerance. The CAL is constructed by plotting various combinations of risky assets and risk-free assets on a graph. The vertical axis represents the expected return of the portfolio, while the horizontal axis represents the standard deviation or level of risk. The CAL is a straight line that starts at the risk-free rate and extends upwards, reflecting the additional return an investor can achieve by taking on more risk.

Capital Asset Pricing Model (CAPM)

The Capital Asset Pricing Model (CAPM) is a financial tool used to determine the expected return on an investment based on its level of risk. It is a formula that calculates the required rate of return for an investment by taking into account the risk-free rate of return, the expected return of the market, and the beta coefficient of the investment. The CAPM formula is as follows: $Ra = Rf + (Rm - Rf) * \beta a$ Where: Ra = Expected return on investment a Rf = Risk-free rate of return Rm = Expected return of the market βa = Beta coefficient of investment a The risk-free rate of return is the return an investor would expect to receive from a risk-free investment, such as a government bond. The expected return of the market represents the average return of all investments in the market. The beta coefficient measures the sensitivity of an investment's price movement in relation to the overall market. It indicates how much an investment's returns will move in response to changes in the market returns. By using the CAPM, investors can estimate the return they should expect to earn on an investment considering its risk level. The CAPM assumes that investors are rational and risk-averse, meaning that they require additional compensation for taking on additional risk. It also assumes that the market is efficient, meaning that prices fully reflect all available information. However, it is important to note that the CAPM has its limitations. The model relies on several assumptions that may not always hold true in the real world. For example, it assumes a linear relationship between an investment's beta and its expected return. In reality, this relationship may not be so straightforward. Additionally, the CAPM does not account for specific risks that may affect an investment's return, such as industry or company-specific risks.

Capital Budgeting

Capital budgeting is a financial management process that involves evaluating potential long-term investment projects and determining whether they are worthwhile for a company. It aims to analyze the cash inflows and outflows associated with these investment opportunities to determine their feasibility and potential profitability for the organization. During the capital budgeting process, companies assess various investment projects and select the ones that align with their strategic goals and financial objectives. This involves estimating the future cash flows generated by each project and discounting them to determine their present values. By comparing the present value of cash inflows with the initial investment cost, companies can evaluate the profitability of potential projects. Capital budgeting decisions are critical for companies as they involve allocating scarce resources to different investment opportunities.

These decisions can impact the company's financial performance and long-term competitiveness. Therefore, it is essential to carefully evaluate and select investment projects that can generate positive returns and create value for shareholders. There are several techniques commonly used in capital budgeting, including the payback period, net present value (NPV), internal rate of return (IRR), and profitability index. Each technique has its strengths and weaknesses and provides different insights into the potential profitability of investment projects. The payback period measures the time required to recover the initial investment through cash inflows. It is a relatively simple method but does not consider the time value of money. The NPV calculates the present value of expected cash flows, taking into account the required rate of return. A positive NPV indicates a potentially profitable investment. The IRR, on the other hand, represents the discount rate at which the NPV becomes zero, indicating the project's internal rate of return. The profitability index compares the present value of cash inflows to the initial investment and provides a ratio that helps determine the project's profitability. In conclusion, capital budgeting is a financial management process that evaluates potential investment projects to determine their feasibility and potential profitability. By analyzing cash flows, discounting future cash inflows, and considering various investment appraisal techniques, companies can make informed investment decisions that enhance their financial performance and long-term value creation.

Capital Expenditure (CapEx)

Capital Expenditure (CapEx) in the context of Financial Management refers to the funds utilized by a company to acquire, upgrade, or maintain physical assets that are essential for its operations. These assets typically have a long useful life and provide future benefits to the organization. CapEx is an important aspect of financial planning and investment decision-making for businesses. It involves the determination of how much to invest in capital assets and the timing of such investments. Capital expenditures can take various forms, including the purchase of property, buildings, equipment, vehicles, and technology infrastructure. It can also include costs associated with constructing new facilities or renovating existing ones. These investments are crucial for organizations to expand their operations, improve efficiency, stay competitive, and generate future revenue streams. When deciding on capital expenditures, companies consider several factors. They assess the potential return on investment (ROI) by evaluating the future cash flows expected from the asset. Additionally, they carry out cost-benefit analyses to understand the economic feasibility and profitability of the investment. Companies may finance capital expenditures using internal funds, such as retained earnings, or by raising external capital through debt or equity financing. The financing decision depends on the company's financial position, cash flow situation, and the cost of capital. It is essential for businesses to carefully manage and control their capital expenditures to ensure optimal utilization of resources. This involves developing capital expenditure budgets, monitoring actual spending against planned budgets, and regularly reviewing and evaluating the performance of capital assets. Capital expenditures are typically distinguished from operating expenses, which refer to day-to-day costs incurred to sustain ongoing business activities. While operating expenses are recorded in the income statement and deducted from revenue, capital expenditures are capitalized and recorded in the balance sheet as assets. In conclusion, capital expenditure refers to the funds invested by a company to acquire long-term assets necessary for its operations. It is a critical component of financial management, requiring careful evaluation, budgeting, and monitoring to ensure effective utilization of resources.

Capital Expenditure

Capital expenditure refers to the funds allocated and spent by a company or organization for the acquisition, improvement, or maintenance of long-term assets. These assets typically have a useful life of more than one accounting period and are expected to generate future economic benefits for the entity. In financial management, capital expenditure is an essential component of the overall investment strategy of a business. It involves the commitment of significant financial resources to acquire or upgrade physical assets such as property, plant, equipment, and vehicles. Capital expenditure decisions are typically made with a long-term perspective, focusing on the potential return on investment and the expected cash flows generated by the assets over their useful lives. Capital expenditure plays a crucial role in the growth and development of a company. By investing in capital assets, organizations can enhance their productive capacity, increase operational efficiency, and improve the quality of their products or services. These investments are essential for companies to remain competitive in the market, expand their market share, and sustain their long-term profitability. Capital expenditure decisions are often subject to rigorous evaluation and analysis. Financial managers utilize various financial appraisal techniques, such as net present value (NPV), internal rate of return (IRR), and payback period, to assess the potential profitability and risk associated with different investment options. These evaluations help in determining the feasibility and prioritization of capital projects. In addition to the financial considerations, capital expenditure decisions also require careful planning and coordination with other functional areas within an organization. The procurement, installation, and maintenance of capital assets involve collaboration between finance, operations, engineering, and other departments to ensure successful implementation and optimal utilization of the assets.

Capital Gains Distribution

A capital gains distribution refers to the distribution of profits from the sale of assets or investments in a mutual fund or a real estate investment trust (REIT). It is a way for these entities to pass on the gains from the sale of assets to their shareholders or unit holders. When a mutual fund or REIT sells its assets at a profit, it is required by law to distribute a certain percentage of those gains to its investors. These distributions are typically made annually or semi-annually and are subject to certain requirements and regulations.

Capital Gains Tax

Capital gains tax is a type of tax levied on the profits generated from the sale or disposal of certain assets known as capital assets. These assets can include stocks, bonds, real estate, and other investments. The tax is imposed on the difference between the sale price of the asset and its original purchase price, resulting in a taxable gain. Capital gains tax is typically applied to long-term and short-term assets. Long-term assets are those that have been held for more than one year, while short-term assets are held for less than one year. The tax rates for long-term capital gains are usually lower than those for short-term capital gains, as the aim is to encourage long-term investments.

Capital Market

A capital market is a financial market where businesses and governments can raise long-term funds by issuing and trading securities. It is a market where individuals and institutions buy and sell financial instruments such as stocks, bonds, and derivatives. In the capital market, businesses and governments raise capital to finance their long-term investments and operations. They do this by issuing securities, which are financial instruments representing ownership or debt. These securities are traded between buyers and sellers in the capital market, allowing individuals and institutions to invest their money and earn returns. The main participants in the capital market are businesses, governments, investors, and financial institutions such as banks, investment banks, and stock exchanges. Businesses and governments issue securities such as stocks and bonds to raise funds for various purposes, including expanding their operations, investing in new projects, or paying off existing debts. Investors, on the other hand, buy these securities in the hope of earning a return on their investment. They can earn returns through capital appreciation, when the value of the securities they own increases over time, or through regular interest or dividend payments. Investors in the capital market may include individuals, pension funds, mutual funds, hedge funds, and other institutional investors. Financial institutions play a crucial role in the capital market as intermediaries. They facilitate the issuance and trading of securities by providing various services such as underwriting, market-making, and brokerage. They also provide advice and assistance to businesses and governments in raising capital and managing their finances. The capital market is an important component of the overall financial system as it supports economic growth and development. By enabling businesses and governments to raise capital, it provides the necessary funds for investments and expansion, which in turn create jobs, stimulate economic activity, and foster innovation. In summary, a capital market is a financial market where businesses and governments raise long-term funds through the issuance and trading of securities. It involves various participants such as businesses, governments, investors, and financial institutions, and plays a crucial role in supporting economic growth and development.

Capital Markets

Capital Markets refers to a segment of the financial market where individuals, companies, and governments can raise funds by issuing and trading various financial instruments. These instruments include stocks, bonds, derivatives, and other securities. Capital markets play a crucial role in facilitating the flow of capital from investors to those in need of funds. They serve as a platform for borrowers to access long-term financing through the issuance of debt securities such as bonds. At the same time, they provide opportunities for investors to earn returns on their investments by buying and selling these securities in the market. One of the primary functions of capital markets is the allocation of financial resources. It allows savers to invest their excess funds in productive activities, such as business expansions or infrastructure development. By investing in companies or governments, savers become shareholders or bondholders, enabling them to participate in the success and growth of these entities. Capital markets also enable price discovery by providing a platform for buyers and sellers to determine the fair value of securities. Through the forces of supply and demand, the prices of securities are determined, reflecting the market's perception of the issuer's financial health and future prospects. This price discovery mechanism ensures that securities are fairly valued and helps investors make informed decisions. Furthermore, capital markets enable risk management through the trading of derivatives. Derivatives, such as options and futures, allow investors to hedge against potential losses or speculate on future price movements. By providing this avenue for risk transfer, capital markets contribute to the stability and efficiency of the overall financial system. Overall, capital markets serve as the backbone of the global financial system, enabling the efficient flow of funds and providing investors with opportunities for investment and risk management. They play a vital role in supporting economic growth, fostering innovation, and facilitating the efficient allocation of capital.

Capital Structure

Capital structure refers to the mix of long-term sources of financing used by a company to finance its operations and investments. It represents the proportion of debt and equity used to fund a company's assets and activities. Debt capital, also known as borrowed funds, includes loans, bonds, and other forms of debt securities. It represents the money that the company has borrowed from external parties with an obligation to pay it back with interest over a specified period. Equity capital, on the other hand, represents the owner's funds or shareholders' investment in the company. It includes common stock, preferred stock, and retained earnings, which are the accumulated profits reinvested in the business. By deciding on the optimal capital structure, a company aims to find the right balance between debt and equity financing in order to maximize its value and minimize its cost of capital. This decision is crucial for the financial management of a company as it directly affects the risk and return profile. The capital structure decision involves several factors, such as the cost and availability of debt and equity, the company's financial risk tolerance, the stage of its life cycle, and the nature of its industry. A company with a higher risk tolerance or in a mature industry may have a higher proportion of debt in its capital structure as it can benefit from the tax advantages of interest expense deduction. On the other hand, a company with a lower risk tolerance or in a rapidly growing industry may prefer to rely more on equity financing to avoid excessive financial leverage and preserve flexibility in case of unexpected challenges. Overall, the capital structure decision is a strategic choice that requires careful evaluation and consideration of various factors. It should align with the company's financial goals, risk appetite, and the prevailing market conditions. By maintaining an optimal capital structure, a company can enhance its ability to generate profits, support growth, and withstand economic uncertainties.

Capitalization Rate

A capitalization rate, also known as a cap rate, is a financial metric used in the field of real estate and investment management. It is used to estimate the potential return on an investment property based on its net operating income (NOI). The capitalization rate is expressed as a percentage and is calculated by dividing the property's NOI by its market value. The capitalization rate represents the rate of return an investor can expect to earn from an investment property. It is used as a benchmark to compare different investment opportunities and determine the value of a property. A higher capitalization rate indicates a higher potential return, while a lower rate indicates a lower return. The formula to calculate the capitalization rate is as follows: Capitalization Rate = Net Operating Income / Market Value The net operating income is calculated by subtracting the operating expenses of the property from its total income. Operating expenses include property taxes, insurance, maintenance costs, and other expenses associated with managing the property. The market value of the property is typically determined through an appraisal or by comparing it to similar properties in the market. The capitalization rate is often used by real estate investors and appraisers to estimate the value of an income-producing property. By comparing the cap rates of similar properties, investors can determine if a property is overvalued or undervalued. Additionally, the cap rate can help investors assess the risk associated with an investment by considering factors such as location, property condition, and market trends. In conclusion, the capitalization rate is a key financial metric used in real estate and investment management to estimate the potential return on an investment property. It is calculated by dividing the property's net operating income by its market value and is expressed as a percentage. The cap rate helps investors compare different investment opportunities and assess the value and risk of a property.

Carried Interest

Carried interest is a term used in financial management to refer to a share of profits that is paid to investment managers or general partners of private equity funds, hedge funds, and other similar investment vehicles. This type of compensation is typically earned as a percentage of the profits generated by the fund's investments or investment activities. The concept of carried interest is often associated with the performance-based compensation structure commonly used in the alternative investment industry. Under this structure, investment managers or general partners receive a fixed management fee for their services, but the majority of their compensation is tied to the fund's performance. Carried interest serves as a performance incentive, aligning the interests of the managers with those of the investors. Carried interest is typically calculated as a percentage of the profits realized by the fund after a certain hurdle rate or preferred return is achieved. For example, if the hurdle rate is set at 8% and the fund generates a return of 15%, the carried interest may be calculated as a percentage of the 7% excess return above the hurdle rate. Carried interest is usually subject to a clawback provision, which means that if the fund underperforms in subsequent years and the managers have received a higher share of profits than they are entitled to, they may be required to return a portion of their carried interest to the fund's investors. This provision helps to ensure that the managers do not receive excessive compensation for poor performance.

Carry Trade

A carry trade refers to a strategy in financial management where an investor borrows money or sells securities in a country with low interest rates and uses the funds to invest in a country with higher interest rates. The goal of a carry trade is to take advantage of the interest rate differential between the two countries, known as the "carry," and earn a profit through the spread. The process of executing a carry trade involves several steps. First, the investor identifies two currencies, usually from different countries, where the interest rate differential is favorable. The investor then borrows or sells securities denominated in the currency with the lower interest rate and converts the funds to the currency with the higher interest rate. Once the investor has acquired the funds in the higher interest rate currency, they can invest in various assets such as bonds, stocks, or other financial instruments that offer higher returns. The investor aims to earn a profit not only from the interest rate differential but also from the appreciation of the higher interest rate currency against the lower interest rate currency. If the higher interest rate currency appreciates, the investor can sell it at a higher exchange rate and convert the proceeds back into the lower interest rate currency, thereby realizing a gain. However, carry trades come with risks that investors must consider. One of the main risks is exchange rate fluctuations, which can significantly impact the profitability of the trade. If the higher interest rate currency depreciates against the lower interest rate currency, the investor may face losses when converting the funds back. Additionally, changes in interest rates can influence the profitability of the carry trade. If the interest rate differential narrows or reverses, the potential returns may diminish or even become negative. Overall, a carry trade can be a profitable strategy when executed properly, taking into account the risks involved. Investors must carefully analyze the interest rate differentials, exchange rate trends, and market conditions to determine the viability of a carry trade and manage their positions effectively.

Cash Conversion Cycle (CCC)

The Cash Conversion Cycle (CCC) is a financial metric that measures the time it takes for a company to convert its investments in inventory and other resources into cash flows from sales and finally back into cash. It is an important tool in financial management as it helps assess the efficiency of a company's use of its working capital. The CCC is calculated by adding the number of days it takes for a company to sell its inventory (days sales of inventory, DSI), the number of days it takes to collect cash from its customers (days sales outstanding, DSO), and subtracting the number of days it takes to pay its suppliers (days payable outstanding, DPO). The DSI represents the average number of days it takes for a company to sell its inventory. A lower DSI indicates that a company is able to sell its inventory quickly, generating cash flow. On the other hand, a higher DSI suggests that a company's inventory is not moving as quickly, tying up capital and potentially increasing the risk of obsolescence. The DSO measures the average number of days it takes for a company to collect cash from its customers after a sale. A lower DSO indicates that a company is able to collect its accounts receivable quickly, converting sales into cash. Conversely, a higher DSO suggests that a company is taking longer to collect cash, which may indicate issues with credit policies or customer payment delays. The DPO represents the average number of days it takes for a company to pay its suppliers. A higher DPO means that a company takes longer to pay its suppliers, allowing it to hold onto its cash for a longer period of time. However, a high DPO can also strain supplier relationships if the company consistently delays payments beyond agreed-upon terms. By analyzing and managing these three components, a company can optimize its CCC to enhance its liquidity and financial performance. A shorter CCC indicates that a company can generate cash flows more quickly, improving its working capital management and potentially reducing its need for external financing. Conversely, a longer CCC can put strain on a company's cash flow, making it more vulnerable to liquidity issues and increasing its reliance on external funding sources.

Cash Conversion Cycle

The cash conversion cycle is a financial management metric that measures the time it takes for a company to convert its investments in inventory and other resources into cash flow from sales. It assesses the efficiency of a company's working capital management by considering the processes involved in purchasing inventory, converting it into finished goods, selling those goods, and collecting the resulting cash. The three components of the cash conversion cycle are the inventory conversion period, the accounts receivable collection period, and the accounts payable deferral period. The inventory conversion period reflects the average number of days it takes for a company to convert its inventory into finished goods. The accounts receivable collection period represents the average number of days it takes for a company to collect payments from its customers after a sale. The accounts payable deferral period indicates the average number of days it takes for a company to pay its suppliers. By subtracting the accounts payable deferral period from the sum of the inventory conversion period and the accounts receivable collection period, the cash conversion cycle provides insight into the company's liquidity and working capital management. A shorter cash conversion cycle indicates that a company is able to quickly convert its investments into cash, suggesting efficient management of working capital. Conversely, a longer cash conversion cycle suggests potential liquidity issues and inefficiencies in working capital management. The goal of managing the cash conversion cycle is to minimize the time it takes for a company to convert its investments into cash while maintaining an optimal level of working capital. By carefully managing inventory levels, streamlining the accounts receivable collection process, and negotiating favorable payment terms with suppliers, a company can reduce the cash conversion cycle and improve its overall financial health.

Cash Dividend

A cash dividend is a payment made by a company to its shareholders, typically in the form of cash, as a return on their investment in the company. It is one of the ways in which a company can distribute profits to its owners. Companies generate profits through their operations, such as sales of products or services. These profits belong to the shareholders, who are the owners of the company. However, instead of distributing all of the profits, companies may choose to reinvest a portion of them back into the business for future growth and expansion. The remaining portion of profits can be distributed to shareholders as dividends. Dividends are usually paid out on a regular basis, such as quarterly or annually, and the amount of the dividend is expressed as a fixed amount per share. For example, if a company declares a cash dividend of $1 per share and an investor owns 100 shares, they would receive a cash payment of $100. The decision to pay cash dividends is made by the company's board of directors, who consider several factors, including the company's financial performance, cash flow position, and future investment opportunities. Paying dividends can be seen as a signal of a company's financial health and stability, as it reflects the ability to generate consistent profits and have excess cash available for distribution. Investors often view cash dividends as a positive sign, as it provides them with a direct return on their investment in the company. It can also be a way for shareholders to realize some of the value of their investment without having to sell their shares. Additionally, cash dividends can be attractive to income-focused investors, such as retirees, who rely on regular income from their investments. However, not all companies pay cash dividends. Some companies, especially those in high-growth industries or early stages of development, may choose to reinvest all of their profits back into the business to fund expansion and innovation. In such cases, investors may instead benefit from potential capital appreciation of their shares.

Cash Equivalents

A cash equivalent refers to highly liquid investments that are easily convertible into cash with negligible risk of change in value. These investments typically have a short-term maturity period of three months or less from the date of acquisition. Cash equivalents play a crucial role in financial management as they provide companies with a safe and readily available source of funds. They are important for maintaining liquidity and meeting short-term cash obligations. Companies typically hold cash equivalents to ensure they have enough cash on hand to cover unexpected expenses, take advantage of investment opportunities, or meet any anticipated short-term cash needs.

Cash Flow Analysis

Cash flow analysis is a crucial aspect of financial management that involves the evaluation and interpretation of the movement of cash within an organization. It provides valuable insights into the inflows and outflows of cash, enabling businesses to make informed decisions and maintain financial stability. In essence, cash flow analysis involves examining the cash received and disbursed by a company over a specific period. It focuses on three main activities: operating activities, investing activities, and financing activities. Operating activities include the core business operations of a company, such as revenue generated from the sale of goods or services and the payment of expenses. Cash flow from operating activities helps assess the profitability and efficiency of a business, indicating whether it generates sufficient cash to cover day-to-day expenses. Investing activities involve the purchase or sale of long-term assets, such as equipment, property, or investments. Cash flow from investing activities provides insights into the company's investment decisions and potential for future growth. Financing activities involve the acquisition or repayment of funds to support business activities. These activities may include obtaining loans, issuing or repurchasing shares, or paying dividends. Cash flow from financing activities helps determine the company's ability to meet its financial obligations and indicates its capital structure. By analyzing cash flow, financial managers can assess the overall liquidity and solvency of a company. Positive cash flow indicates that the company is generating more cash inflows than outflows, which enhances its ability to cover expenses and invest in growth opportunities. Conversely, a negative cash flow suggests that the company is spending more cash than it is generating, which may lead to financial instability and an increased reliance on external financing sources. Cash flow analysis also enables financial managers to identify potential cash flow gaps or shortfalls, allowing them to take preemptive measures to address these issues. It aids in budgeting and forecasting, facilitating efficient cash management and ensuring that the company can meet its financial obligations in a timely manner.

Cash Flow Coverage Ratio

The cash flow coverage ratio is a financial metric used in financial management to assess a company's ability to cover its fixed expenses and debt obligations using its operating cash flow. It measures the company's capacity to generate enough cash flow from its normal operations to meet its financial obligations. The formula to calculate the cash flow coverage ratio is: Cash

Flow Coverage Ratio = Operating Cash Flow / Total Debt Service Where: - Operating Cash Flow refers to the cash generated by a company's core business operations, which includes revenue from sales, minus operating expenses. - Total Debt Service represents the total amount of principal and interest payments due on a company's outstanding debt over a given period. The cash flow coverage ratio is an important metric for both lenders and investors. It provides insights into a company's ability to generate sufficient cash flow to cover its financial obligations, which is crucial for assessing its solvency and financial health. A higher ratio indicates a stronger ability to meet debt obligations and suggests a lower risk of default or financial distress. However, it is important to note that the cash flow coverage ratio should be evaluated in conjunction with other financial metrics and considerations. It does not provide a comprehensive assessment of a company's overall financial condition, as it only focuses on the ability to cover fixed expenses and debt obligations from operating cash flow. Other factors such as liquidity, profitability, and market conditions should also be taken into account when evaluating a company's financial stability.

Cash Flow Forecast

A cash flow forecast is a financial management tool that predicts the inflows and outflows of cash in a business over a specific period of time. It provides a detailed projection of the company's cash position, allowing management to make informed decisions about the allocation and management of cash resources. The main purpose of a cash flow forecast is to help businesses plan and manage their finances effectively. By providing a detailed breakdown of expected cash inflows and outflows, it allows management to identify potential cash shortages or surpluses in advance and take appropriate actions to address them.

Cash Flow Forecasting

Cash flow forecasting is a financial management tool used to predict the inflows and outflows of cash within a business over a specific period. It involves estimating the timing and amount of future cash receipts and payments, allowing businesses to plan and make informed decisions about their cash position. A cash flow forecast is typically prepared on a monthly or quarterly basis and provides a detailed analysis of the expected cash flows. It takes into account various sources of cash inflows, such as sales revenue, loans, investments, and accounts receivable collections, as well as cash outflows, including operating expenses, loan repayments, inventory purchases, and accounts payable payments. The primary goal of cash flow forecasting is to ensure that a business maintains sufficient cash to cover its expenses and obligations, thereby avoiding cash shortages or liquidity issues. By projecting future cash flows, businesses can identify potential cash gaps or surpluses and take necessary actions to manage their cash effectively. Furthermore, cash flow forecasting helps businesses in budgeting and financial planning. It enables them to anticipate upcoming expenditures, such as equipment purchases or expansion projects, and plan their financing needs accordingly. It also allows businesses to evaluate the impact of different scenarios and determine the feasibility of undertaking certain initiatives. Additionally, cash flow forecasting is a crucial tool for financial decision-making. It helps businesses evaluate the timing and appropriateness of investments, assess the viability of borrowing or financing options, and determine the optimal allocation of cash resources. It also enables businesses to assess their overall financial health and identify trends or patterns that may require attention or corrective actions. In summary, cash flow forecasting is an essential process for businesses to manage their cash effectively, plan for the future, and make informed financial decisions. By accurately predicting cash inflows and outflows, businesses can maintain financial stability, optimize cash resources, and ensure a positive cash balance for continued operations and growth.

Cash Flow Hedge

A cash flow hedge is a financial risk management strategy that aims to mitigate the potential impact of fluctuations in cash flows on a company's financial performance. It involves the use of derivative instruments to offset the risk associated with changes in cash flows that may arise from fluctuations in interest rates, exchange rates, or commodity prices. Companies often enter into cash flow hedges to protect themselves from adverse changes in cash flows resulting from these market risks. By using derivative contracts such as interest rate swaps, currency forwards, or commodity futures, companies can minimize the potential negative impact of fluctuating cash flows on their financial statements.

Cash Flow Per Share (CFPS)

Cash Flow Per Share (CFPS) is a financial metric used in the field of financial management to assess the amount of cash generated per share by a company during a given period. It provides investors and analysts with a measure of a company's ability to generate cash and distribute it to its shareholders. CFPS is calculated by dividing the cash flow from operations (CFO) by the weighted average number of shares outstanding. The CFO represents the cash generated by a company's core operations, which includes the cash receipts from the sale of goods or services and the cash payments for operating expenses.

Cash Flow Statement Analysis

A cash flow statement analysis is a financial management tool that evaluates the cash inflows and outflows of a company during a specific period. It provides insights into the actual cash generated and used by the business, allowing management to assess its liquidity, solvency, and overall financial health. With this information, decision-makers can make more informed financial decisions and effectively plan for the future. The cash flow statement is divided into three main sections: operating activities, investing activities, and financing activities. Each section provides a breakdown of the cash inflows and outflows related to different aspects of the business. By analyzing these sections, financial managers can identify trends, assess financial risks, and evaluate the company's ability to generate cash. The operating activities section of the cash flow statement analyzes the cash flows directly related to the core operations of the business, such as sales, purchases, and expenses. It reflects the cash generated or used from day-to-day operations and gives an indication of the company's profitability. A positive cash flow from operating activities suggests that the company is generating enough cash to sustain its operations. The investing activities section focuses on the cash flows associated with the acquisition or disposal of long-term assets, such as property, plant, and equipment. It provides insights into the company's capital expenditures, investments, and divestments. By analyzing this section, financial managers can assess the company's investment decisions and its ability to generate future cash flows. The financing activities section examines the cash flows related to the company's capital structure, including debt, equity, and dividends. It reflects the cash generated or used from financing activities, such as issuing or repaying loans, issuing or buying back shares, and paying dividends. This section helps financial managers evaluate the company's financing strategy, its ability to meet debt obligations, and the impact of financing decisions on the overall cash flow of the business. In conclusion, a cash flow statement analysis is an essential tool in financial management. It provides a comprehensive view of a company's cash flow activities, allowing management to evaluate its financial performance and make informed decisions. By analyzing the cash inflows and outflows from operating, investing, and financing activities, financial managers can identify strengths, weaknesses, and potential risks, contributing to the overall financial success of the organization.

Cash Flow Statement (CFS)

A Cash Flow Statement (CFS) is a financial statement that provides information about the cash inflows and outflows of a company during a specific period of time. It is an essential tool in financial management as it helps to assess the liquidity and solvency of a business by tracking the movement of cash. The CFS consists of three sections: operating activities, investing activities, and financing activities. The operating activities section includes cash flows from day-to-day business operations, such as sales, purchasing inventory, and payment of expenses. It helps to determine the profitability of the company's core operations and its ability to generate cash from its normal business activities. The investing activities section reflects cash flows related to the acquisition or disposal of long-term assets, such as property, plant, and equipment, as well as investments in securities and other financial instruments. This section provides insights into how the company is allocating its funds for future growth and expansion. The financing activities section represents cash flows resulting from the issuance or repayment of debt, such as loans and bonds, as well as the issuance or repurchase of equity shares. It indicates how the company is financing its operations and whether it is relying more on debt or equity instruments. By analyzing the cash flow statement, financial managers can assess the company's ability to meet its short-term obligations, finance its long-term investments, and

46

generate sustainable cash flows. It also helps in evaluating the timing and magnitude of cash inflows and outflows, identifying any potential cash flow problems, and making informed decisions regarding financing, investment, and dividend policies. Moreover, the CFS is crucial for investors, creditors, and other stakeholders to evaluate the financial health and stability of a company. It provides a more accurate picture of a company's financial position compared to the income statement and balance sheet, which are based on accrual accounting. The CFS focuses solely on cash transactions, providing a clearer understanding of how cash is being utilized within the organization.

Cash Flow Statement

A cash flow statement is a financial statement that provides an overview of the inflows and outflows of cash within an organization over a specific period of time. It presents the cash generated from operating activities, investing activities, and financing activities. The cash flow statement is a crucial tool for financial management as it helps in assessing the liquidity and solvency of a company. It provides valuable information about the cash position of the organization, helping stakeholders make informed decisions.

Cash Flow

Cash flow is a key indicator of a company's financial health and refers to the movement of cash into and out of a business over a specific period of time. It is an essential aspect of financial management as it helps in analyzing the liquidity and profitability of a company. A positive cash flow indicates that a company is generating more cash than it is spending. This can result from various sources, such as sales revenue, investments, loans, and other external funding. Positive cash flow provides a company with the ability to meet its financial obligations, invest in growth opportunities, and distribute profits to shareholders. On the other hand, a negative cash flow means that a company is spending more cash than it is receiving. This can be due to various factors, such as excessive expenses, loan repayments, and low sales revenue. Negative cash flow can be a warning sign of financial distress, indicating that a company may not be able to meet its obligations and may require additional funding to sustain its operations. To effectively manage cash flow, companies employ various strategies, such as optimizing accounts receivable and accounts payable, managing inventory levels, and controlling expenses. Monitoring cash flow on a regular basis allows businesses to identify potential cash shortages or surpluses and take appropriate actions to mitigate risks or capitalize on opportunities. Cash flow forecasting is another crucial aspect of financial management. It involves predicting future cash inflows and outflows based on historical data, market conditions, and other relevant factors. By forecasting cash flow, companies can make informed decisions regarding budgeting, financing, and investment, and ensure that they have sufficient liquidity to support their operations. In summary, cash flow is the movement of cash into and out of a company over a specific period of time. It is a vital metric for financial management as it provides insights into a company's liquidity, profitability, and ability to meet its financial obligations. Effective cash flow management is essential for the long-term success of a business.

Cash And Cash Equivalents (CCE)

Cash and Cash Equivalents (CCE) refer to the most liquid assets held by a company, which can be readily converted into cash within a short period. These assets are crucial indicators of a company's short-term liquidity and are closely monitored by financial management to ensure the company's ability to meet its immediate obligations. Under the Generally Accepted Accounting Principles (GAAP), cash includes physical currency, such as banknotes and coins, as well as funds held in demand deposit accounts, such as checking or current accounts. Cash equivalents, on the other hand, are short-term investments that can be easily sold or converted into cash. These investments typically have a maturity period of three months or less from the date of purchase.

Central Bank

A central bank is a regulatory authority responsible for overseeing and controlling a country's money supply, interest rates, and banking system. It acts as a custodian of a nation's financial stability and performs various functions to ensure the smooth functioning of the economy. One of the primary roles of a central bank is to maintain price stability and control inflation. It achieves this by formulating and implementing monetary policy. Through tools like open market operations, reserve requirements, and interest rate adjustments, the central bank influences the amount of money circulating in the economy. By managing the money supply, it aims to keep inflation within a target range set by the government. Another crucial function of the central bank is to supervise and regulate the banking system. It establishes prudential regulations, sets capital requirements, and monitors the activities of commercial banks. This helps ensure the stability and integrity of the financial system, safeguarding public confidence in the banking sector. The central bank also acts as a lender of last resort, providing emergency liquidity to banks and financial institutions during times of crisis. By acting as a safety net, it prevents the collapse of individual banks that could have a widespread impact on the economy. This function promotes stability and mitigates financial contagion risks. Besides its regulatory role, a central bank often acts as the government's banker. It holds the government's accounts, manages public debt, and executes various transactions on behalf of the government. This relationship allows the central bank to influence fiscal policies and coordinate monetary measures with the government to achieve overall economic objectives. Additionally, a central bank plays a crucial role in managing foreign exchange reserves and maintaining currency stability. It intervenes in the foreign exchange market to stabilize the exchange rate and prevent extreme fluctuations. By managing the country's foreign reserves, the central bank helps ensure confidence in domestic and international trade. In summary, a central bank is a vital institution in the field of financial management. It serves as both a regulator and operator, using various tools and functions to maintain price stability, ensure a stable banking system, provide liquidity in times of crisis, manage public debt, influence fiscal policies, stabilize the currency, and promote economic growth.

Certificate Of Deposit (CD)

A Certificate of Deposit (CD) is a fixed-income financial instrument offered by banks and financial institutions. It is a type of time deposit where the investor deposits a specific amount of money for a fixed period of time, known as the term of the CD. In return, the investor receives a certificate as evidence of the deposit, which includes the principal amount, the interest rate, and the term. CDs are considered to be low-risk investments because they are insured by the Federal Deposit Insurance Corporation (FDIC) in the United States. This guarantee protects the investor's principal and interest up to a certain amount per account holder, per institution. This insurance provides peace of mind and makes CDs an attractive option for conservative investors who prioritize capital preservation and a fixed rate of return.

Certified Financial Planner (CFP)

A Certified Financial Planner (CFP) is a professional who specializes in providing comprehensive financial management services to individuals and businesses. They have undergone extensive training and education to achieve the CFP certification, which is recognized as a global standard for competence and ethics in the field of financial planning. CFPs assess their clients' financial situations by gathering information about their income, expenses, assets, and liabilities. They use this information to create personalized financial plans that help clients reach their financial goals and objectives. These plans typically involve strategies for saving, investing, retirement planning, tax planning, and estate planning.

Chartered Financial Analyst (CFA)

A Chartered Financial Analyst (CFA) is a professional designation given to individuals who have successfully completed the CFA Program, a globally recognized certification for professionals working in the field of financial management. The CFA Program is administered by the CFA Institute, a global association of investment professionals. The designation of CFA is widely considered as the gold standard in the investment management industry. It represents a high level of competence, integrity, and ethical conduct in the field of financial analysis and decision-making. CFAs possess a deep understanding of various aspects of financial management, including investment analysis, portfolio management, and asset valuation.

Clearing House

A clearing house is a financial institution that facilitates the settlement and clearing of financial transactions or contracts between multiple parties involved in the financial industry. It acts as an intermediary between buyers and sellers to ensure smooth and efficient transactions. The primary role of a clearing house is to mitigate counterparty risk by guaranteeing the completion of transactions even if one of the parties involved fails to meet their obligations. This is achieved through a process called novation, where the clearing house becomes the buyer to every seller and the seller to every buyer, effectively eliminating the risk of default. Clearing houses have become an integral part of the financial system, particularly in the trading of derivatives, such as futures and options contracts. When a trade is executed, the details of the transaction are transmitted to the clearing house, which then verifies the trade, calculates the obligations of each counterparty, and ensures proper settlement. In addition to mitigating counterparty risk, clearing houses also provide other important functions. They establish and enforce rules and regulations governing the trading and settlement process, ensuring fairness and transparency. They also act as a central repository for trade data, allowing for efficient record-keeping and regulatory oversight. Furthermore, clearing houses often act as central counterparties (CCPs), which means they become the buyer to every seller and the seller to every buyer, effectively standing between the two parties and assuming the credit risk. This enables standardization and centralization of transactions, leading to increased liquidity and lower trading costs. In conclusion, a clearing house is a critical institution in the financial industry that facilitates the settlement and clearing of financial transactions. By mitigating counterparty risk and providing other important functions, clearing houses play a crucial role in maintaining the stability and efficiency of the financial system.

Closed-End Fund

A closed-end fund is a type of investment fund that operates as a publicly traded entity on a stock exchange. It is a pooled investment vehicle that raises capital from investors through an initial public offering (IPO) and then issues a fixed number of shares which are traded on the stock exchange. Unlike open-end funds or mutual funds, closed-end funds have a fixed number of shares and do not continuously issue or redeem shares at the net asset value (NAV). This means that once the initial public offering has taken place, investors can only buy or sell shares on the secondary market through a broker or an exchange.

Coefficient Of Variation (CV)

The coefficient of variation (CV) is a statistical measure used in financial management to assess the relative variability of an investment's returns compared to its mean return. It is calculated as the ratio of the standard deviation of the investment's returns to the mean return, expressed as a percentage. The coefficient of variation provides investors and financial managers with a useful tool to evaluate and compare the risk and return characteristics of different securities or investment portfolios. By considering the CV, investors can gain insights into the consistency and stability of an investment's returns, making it easier to make informed decisions based on risk and return preferences.

Collateral Trust Bond

A collateral trust bond is a type of bond that is secured by collateral assets. These assets can include property, investments, or other types of valuable resources that the bond issuer pledges as a security for the repayment of the bond. The collateral trust bond is a form of debt instrument that is used by corporations or government entities to raise capital. When issuing a collateral trust bond, the issuer pledges specific assets as collateral to provide assurance to bondholders that they will be repaid in the event of default. The collateral serves as a guarantee that the bondholders will receive the principal amount and interest payments as agreed upon. Typically, the assets pledged as collateral are held in a separate trust account, which is managed by a trustee. The trustee is responsible for protecting the interests of the bondholders and ensuring that the collateral assets are maintained and used appropriately. In case of default, the trustee may liquidate the collateral assets to repay the bondholders. The use of collateral in a trust bond provides a level of security to investors, as it reduces the risk associated with default. Bondholders have a claim on the pledged assets in case the issuer fails to make the required payments. This reduces the credit risk of the bond and can result in lower borrowing costs for the issuer. Collateral trust bonds are often used by companies that may have lower credit ratings

49

or higher risk profiles. By offering collateral, these companies can attract investors who are seeking a higher level of security. Additionally, collateral trust bonds may be used to finance specific projects or acquisitions, where the assets being financed can serve as collateral.

Collateral

Collateral refers to an asset or property that is pledged by a borrower to a lender as a form of security for a loan or credit agreement. It is a risk management method used in financial management. When individuals or businesses need to borrow money, lenders typically require collateral to mitigate the risk of default. By pledging valuable assets, such as real estate, vehicles, stocks, or other investments, borrowers provide assurance that they will repay the loan.

Collateralized Debt Obligation (CDO)

A Collateralized Debt Obligation (CDO) is a financial instrument that pools together various types of debt obligations, such as mortgages, auto loans, and credit card debt, and then structures them into different levels of risk and return. These debt obligations are usually divided into tranches, which are then sold to investors. The purpose of a CDO is to redistribute the risk of default among a broader group of investors. By separating the underlying debt obligations into different tranches, each with its own level of risk and return, investors can choose the level of risk that matches their investment objectives. The tranches are typically rated by credit rating agencies, with higher-rated tranches being less risky and offering lower returns, while lower-rated tranches are riskier but potentially offer higher returns.

Collateralized Mortgage Obligation (CMO)

A Collateralized Mortgage Obligation (CMO) is a type of mortgage-backed security that is created by pooling together a group of mortgage loans and then repackaging them into individual securities with different risk and return characteristics. These securities are then sold to investors in the secondary market. CMOs are structured using the process of securitization, which involves transferring the cash flows from the underlying mortgage loans to the investors. The cash flows generated by the mortgage loans are separated into different tranches or classes, each with its own unique set of repayment priority and risk profile. There are several types of CMO tranches, including sequential-pay tranches, planned amortization class (PAC) tranches, floating-rate tranches, and support tranches. Each tranche is designed to cater to different investor preferences and risk appetites. Sequential-pay tranches provide a sequential order of principal and interest payments, while PAC tranches provide a stable and predictable cash flow schedule. Floating-rate tranches have interest rates that are periodically adjusted based on a reference rate, and support tranches provide credit enhancement to the other tranches. CMOs offer investors the opportunity to invest in a diversified portfolio of mortgage loans, which helps to spread the risk associated with individual loans. By pooling together a large number of loans, CMOs can achieve a higher level of diversification compared to holding individual loans. This diversification reduces the risk of default and helps to enhance the credit quality of the CMO securities. Investors in CMOs are primarily interested in the cash flows generated by the underlying mortgage loans. The timing and amount of these cash flows depend on factors such as the interest rates, prepayment rates, and default rates of the mortgage loans. Therefore, CMO investors must carefully analyze these factors to assess the potential return and risk associated with investing in CMOs.

Commercial Mortgage-Backed Security (CMBS)

A Commercial Mortgage-Backed Security (CMBS) refers to a type of financial instrument that is created by pooling together commercial mortgage loans and transforming them into investable securities. These securities are then sold to investors in the form of bonds or notes, providing them with an opportunity to invest in a diversified pool of commercial real estate loans. CMBS is typically issued by special purpose vehicles (SPVs), which are entities specifically created for this purpose. The SPVs purchase a portfolio of commercial mortgage loans from lenders, such as banks or other financial institutions. These loans are secured by commercial properties, such as office buildings, retail centers, or industrial facilities. The SPVs then organize the loans into different tranches, which represent different levels of risk and return. The tranches are structured in a way that prioritizes the payment of interest and principal to investors. Generally, the senior tranches have a higher credit quality and are considered less risky, while the junior tranches have a higher risk but offer higher potential returns. Investors in CMBS receive periodic interest payments based on the cash flows generated by the underlying mortgage loans. The cash flows consist of the principal and interest payments made by the borrowers on the commercial mortgages. In case of default on a loan within the pool, the recoveries from the collateral property are used to repay the investors. CMBS provide several benefits to investors. First, they offer an opportunity to invest in a diversified portfolio of commercial real estate loans, which helps to spread the risk. Additionally, CMBS have a relatively high yield compared to other fixed-income securities, making them attractive to investors seeking higher returns. Lastly, CMBS are highly liquid, as they can be bought and sold on secondary markets, providing investors with the flexibility to manage their portfolios.

Commercial Paper

Commercial paper refers to a type of short-term debt instrument that is commonly issued by large, creditworthy businesses and financial institutions to meet their immediate funding needs. It serves as an unsecured promissory note, essentially representing an IOU from the issuer to the holder of the paper. Typically, commercial paper has a maturity period of up to 270 days, but it is commonly issued for durations of less than 30 to 60 days. The maturity of the paper is determined by the issuer based on their cash flow requirements and the potential availability of alternative funding sources. The paper is typically issued at a discount to its face value, and the difference between the face value and the discounted price represents the interest payable to the investor.

Common Stock Equivalent (CSE)

Common Stock Equivalent (CSE) refers to any type of security or financial instrument that has the potential to be converted into common stock of a company. It is a term commonly used in financial management to denote the convertible securities or options that can be transformed into common shares, thereby giving the holder of the CSE the right to become a shareholder of the company. CSEs are typically issued by companies to raise capital by offering investors the opportunity to purchase these convertible securities or options. The main purpose is to attract investors who are looking for potential future upside in the company's common stock. By providing the option to convert the CSE into common stock, companies can offer investors a more flexible investment opportunity.

Common Stock

Common stock is a type of security that represents ownership in a company. When an individual or entity purchases common stock, they become a shareholder and have a claim on the company's assets and earnings. Common stockholders have the right to vote on company matters, including the election of the board of directors and other important decisions. In terms of financial management, common stock plays a crucial role. It is one of the main sources of equity financing for a company. When a company issues common stock, it raises capital by selling shares to investors. This capital infusion is essential for companies to fund their operations, invest in growth opportunities, and meet financial obligations. From a financial perspective, common stock represents a residual claim on a company's earnings and assets. This means that common stockholders have the lowest priority when it comes to receiving dividends or distributing assets in the event of liquidation. Preferred shareholders and debt holders have a higher claim on these earnings and assets. Common stockholders also have the potential for capital appreciation. If the company performs well and its stock price increases, shareholders can benefit from capital gains by selling their shares at a higher price than the purchase price. However, stock prices can also decrease, resulting in capital losses for shareholders. Furthermore, common stockholders have the right to vote at the company's annual general meetings. This allows them to participate in important decision-making processes and exercise their influence on the company's strategic direction. The number of votes typically corresponds to the number of shares owned by each stockholder. In summary, common stock represents ownership in a company, entitling shareholders to voting rights and potential capital appreciation. It is an important source of equity financing for companies and plays a significant role in financial management. However, common stockholders bear the

51

highest level of risk compared to other stakeholders as they have the lowest priority for receiving dividends and assets in the event of liquidation.

Comparative Advantage

Comparative advantage in the context of financial management refers to a situation where a business or individual has a lower opportunity cost of producing a particular good or service compared to others. It is based on the principle of specialization, where each party focuses on producing the goods or providing the services they can produce most efficiently. For example, consider two countries, Country A and Country B, producing two goods, Good X and Good Y. If Country A can produce more units of Good X per unit of resources compared to Country B, while Country B can produce more units of Good Y per unit of resources compared to Country A, then both countries can benefit from specializing in the production of the goods where they have a comparative advantage.

Compound Annual Growth Rate (CAGR)

Compound Annual Growth Rate (CAGR) is a metric utilized in financial management to measure the average annual rate of return over a specific period of time, assuming that the investment has been compounding during that period. CAGR allows investors to assess the growth of an investment over multiple periods, taking into account the compounding effect. This metric provides a standardized measure of growth, enabling comparison between investments with different holding periods and investment amounts.

Compound Interest Rate

Compound interest rate is a financial concept used in the field of financial management to calculate the interest earned or charged on an investment or a loan over a specific period of time. It refers to the interest that not only accumulates on the initial principal amount, but also on any previously accumulated interest. In other words, it is the interest that is earned on both the original investment or loan amount and the interest that has already been earned or charged. The compound interest rate is commonly expressed as an annual percentage rate (APR) and is a crucial factor in determining the growth of an investment or the cost of a loan. It is a fundamental concept in finance as it allows individuals and businesses to predict the future value of an investment or the total cost of borrowing. To calculate compound interest, the initial principal amount, the interest rate, and the time period are taken into consideration. The interest is compounded at regular intervals, typically annually, semi-annually, quarterly, or monthly. The resulting amount includes both the initial principal and the accumulated interest, which becomes the new principal for the next calculation period. As a result, the interest earned or charged increases over time due to the compounding effect. Compound interest is particularly advantageous for investors, as it allows for exponential growth over time. By reinvesting the accumulated interest, investors can compound their returns and potentially accumulate substantial wealth. This compounding effect is often referred to as the "miracle of compounding." On the other hand, compound interest can work against borrowers. With each compounding period, the interest owed on a loan increases, leading to a higher overall repayment amount. This is why it is crucial for borrowers to carefully consider the interest rate and compounding frequency when taking on debt. In conclusion, compound interest rate is a significant concept in financial management that determines the growth of investments and the cost of loans. It takes into account the compounding effect, wherein the interest earned or charged accumulates on both the initial principal amount and the previously accumulated interest. This concept is essential for individuals and businesses to make informed financial decisions and anticipate the future value of their investments or the total cost of borrowing.

Compound Interest

Compound interest is a concept in financial management that refers to the interest earned on the initial amount of money, also known as the principal, as well as on any accumulated interest from previous periods. It is the process of earning interest on both the principal and the interest that has already been earned. When calculating compound interest, the interest is added to the principal at regular intervals, such as annually, semi-annually, quarterly, or monthly. The interest is then calculated based on the new total, including both the principal and the previously earned interest. This results in a compounding effect, where the interest earned in each period is reinvested to generate additional interest in the following periods.

Concentration Risk

Concentration risk, in the context of financial management, refers to the possibility of suffering significant losses or negative impacts due to the over-reliance on a single asset, investment, market, or counterparty. It arises when a significant portion of an individual or organization's portfolio is concentrated in a single area or with a single entity, leading to a lack of diversification and increased vulnerability to specific risks. Concentration risk can manifest in various forms within the financial industry. One common example is sector concentration risk, which occurs when a portfolio has a large allocation to a specific industry or sector. This puts the portfolio at higher risk of financial downturns or disruptions that may directly impact that particular sector. For example, a portfolio heavily weighted in the technology sector would be susceptible to losses if there was a significant industry-wide decline or if regulatory changes adversely affected the sector. Another type of concentration risk is geographical concentration risk. This occurs when a portfolio or investment is heavily concentrated in one geographic region or country. Geopolitical events, economic downturns, natural disasters, or currency fluctuations specific to that region can significantly impact the portfolio's value. For instance, a portfolio heavily invested in emerging markets may face heightened concentration risk due to the potential for political instability or regulatory changes in those countries. Counterparty concentration risk is yet another form of concentration risk. It arises from a significant exposure to a single counterparty or a small group of counterparties. In this scenario, if the counterparty defaults or faces financial difficulties, the entity with the concentrated exposure may suffer significant losses. This is commonly seen in situations where an organization relies heavily on one key customer or supplier. Overall, concentration risk poses significant challenges to financial management as it reduces the benefits of diversification and increases vulnerability to specific risks. To mitigate concentration risk, it is essential for individuals and organizations to employ effective risk management strategies such as diversifying their portfolios across different assets, sectors, and geographies, monitoring exposure to individual counterparties, and regularly reassessing and adjusting their investment allocations.

Conduit Financing

Conduit financing refers to a financial structure in which a special purpose vehicle (SPV) is established to raise funds by issuing debt securities. The SPV acts as a conduit, or intermediary, between the issuer of the securities and the investors, allowing for the transfer of funds from the investors to the issuer. The main purpose of conduit financing is to provide funding for specific projects or assets without the issuer assuming direct liability for the debt. Instead, the SPV is created to issue the securities and holds the assets or cash flows that serve as collateral for the debt. This structure allows the issuer to obtain capital at a lower cost and with less risk, as the SPV separates the debt from the issuer's balance sheet. Conduit financing is commonly used in various industries, such as real estate, infrastructure, and energy. For example, a real estate developer may utilize conduit financing to fund the construction of a new project. The developer creates an SPV, which issues bonds to investors, with the proceeds used to finance the construction. The income generated from the completed project, such as rental income or sales proceeds, is then used by the SPV to repay the bondholders. One key advantage of conduit financing is the ability to access capital markets and attract a wide range of investors. By issuing debt securities, the SPV can tap into the bond market to raise funds, which may not be possible for the issuer directly. This allows for greater flexibility in terms of the size and tenure of the debt, as well as the ability to structure the securities to meet investor preferences. Furthermore, conduit financing can help mitigate risks for the issuer. As the debt is held by the SPV and not the issuer, any potential default or bankruptcy of the issuer would not directly impact the bondholders. This is particularly beneficial for entities with a higher risk profile or limited financial capacity, as conduit financing provides a means to access funding while minimizing their exposure.

Consumer Confidence Index (CCI)

The Consumer Confidence Index (CCI) is a statistical measure used in the field of financial management to assess the level of confidence that consumers have in the overall state of the economy. It is a reflection of consumers' expectations regarding their financial situation, job prospects, and the general economic conditions. The CCI is widely recognized as an important indicator of the overall health and stability of the economy and is closely monitored by economists, investors, policymakers, and financial analysts. The CCI is calculated through surveys and interviews conducted with a representative sample of consumers from various demographic groups. Participants are asked questions about their current financial situation, their expectations for the future, and their willingness to make major purchases. The responses to these questions are then aggregated and analyzed to determine the level of consumer confidence. The index is typically measured on a scale of 0 to 100, with a higher score indicating a higher level of consumer confidence. A score above 50 is generally considered to be positive and indicative of an optimistic outlook, while a score below 50 suggests a more pessimistic sentiment. Changes in the CCI over time can provide insights into consumer spending patterns and economic trends. The CCI is useful for financial management as it provides valuable information for businesses, investors, and policymakers. For businesses, a higher CCI suggests that consumers are more likely to spend money, which can help inform marketing strategies and sales forecasts. Investors can use the CCI to assess the potential profitability of certain industries or sectors, as consumer spending is a key driver of economic growth. Policymakers can also use the index as a guide for implementing economic policies and making decisions that can promote consumer confidence and stimulate economic activity. In conclusion, the Consumer Confidence Index is a significant measurement used in financial management to gauge consumer sentiment and expectations regarding the economy. It plays a crucial role in providing insights into consumer spending patterns and economic trends, and it is an important tool for businesses, investors, and policymakers in making informed decisions.

Consumer Price Index (CPI)

The Consumer Price Index (CPI) is an economic indicator used in financial management to measure changes in the average price level of a basket of goods and services consumed by households. It provides a way to monitor inflation and evaluate the impact of price changes on the cost of living for consumers. The CPI is calculated by collecting data on the prices of a specific set of goods and services, known as the market basket, which represents the typical spending patterns of urban consumers. These items include food, housing, transportation, healthcare, and various other goods and services. The prices of these items are then compared to a base period, which serves as a reference point for measuring price changes over time. The CPI is constructed using a weighted average method, where the prices of each item in the market basket are assigned a weight based on their relative importance in total consumer spending. This weighting reflects the purchasing patterns of households and ensures that the index accurately reflects changes in the cost of living for the average consumer. Financial managers and analysts use the CPI as a tool to analyze and forecast inflation, which is a critical factor in making financial decisions. By monitoring changes in the CPI, they can assess the impact of rising prices on consumer purchasing power and adjust their strategies accordingly. For example, if the CPI indicates increasing inflation, financial managers may consider adjusting pricing strategies, investment decisions, and budgeting to mitigate the effects of rising costs. In addition, the CPI is also used to adjust financial data for inflation, such as measuring real wage growth or calculating the true return on investments. This allows financial managers to make more accurate comparisons over time, accounting for the impact of inflation on financial performance.

Contingent Convertible (CoCo) Bond

A Contingent Convertible (CoCo) Bond is a type of hybrid financial instrument that combines the characteristics of both debt and equity. It is issued by a financial institution, usually a bank, to raise capital. CoCo Bonds have specific features that make them different from traditional bonds. One of the key features is the contingency aspect, which means that the bond can be converted into equity if a specific trigger event occurs. These trigger events are predetermined and are usually linked to the financial condition of the issuing institution. For example, if the bank's capital falls below a certain threshold, the bond may automatically convert into shares of the bank's stock. CoCo Bonds provide several benefits for both issuers and investors. For issuers, these bonds can enhance their regulatory capital buffers and improve their ability to absorb losses during periods of financial stress. This is because the bondholders bear the risk of conversion into equity, which provides a cushion for the bank's capital position. For investors,

CoCo Bonds offer the potential for higher returns compared to traditional bonds. This is because the conversion into equity can result in capital gains if the bank's stock price increases. However, investing in CoCo Bonds also involves additional risks. In addition to the credit risk associated with the issuing institution, there is also the risk of conversion into equity, which can lead to a loss of principal if the stock price declines. CoCo Bonds have gained popularity in recent years as regulators have encouraged banks to strengthen their capital positions and improve their ability to absorb losses. These bonds have become an important tool for banks to raise capital in a cost-effective manner. However, they are complex instruments and require careful analysis and understanding of their features before investing.

Contingent Liability

A contingent liability refers to a potential obligation or liability that may arise in the future, depending on the outcome of a specific event. It is an uncertain obligation, the existence of which depends on the occurrence or non-occurrence of a particular event. In financial management, contingent liabilities are important to consider as they have the potential to impact a company's financial position and performance. Contingent liabilities are typically disclosed in the footnotes to a company's financial statements, as they are not yet actual liabilities but have the possibility of becoming so. These footnotes provide additional information about the nature of the contingent liability, the likelihood of it occurring, and an estimate of the potential financial impact. Examples of contingent liabilities include pending lawsuits, warranty claims, tax disputes, and guarantees or indemnifications provided by the company.

Contingent Value Rights (CVRs)

Contingent Value Rights (CVRs) are financial instruments that are issued by a company to investors as an additional incentive or compensation. These rights are contingent upon the occurrence of specific events or milestones, typically related to the company's performance or certain corporate actions. CVRs are often used in merger and acquisition (M&A) transactions, particularly in cases where the acquiring company offers a combination of cash and stock as consideration. The purpose of issuing CVRs is to provide the shareholders of the acquired company with an opportunity to participate in the future success or value creation of the merged entity.

Continuous Compounding

Continuous compounding refers to a method of calculating interest on a loan or investment where the interest is added to the principal continuously, resulting in exponential growth. This approach is commonly used in the field of financial management to determine the value of investments, loans, and other financial products. In continuous compounding, the interest is calculated based on a constant interest rate and is added to the principal at infinitesimally small time intervals. As a result, the compounding of interest occurs instantaneously, leading to the exponential growth of the investment or loan balance.

Contract For Difference (CFD)

A Contract for Difference (CFD) is a financial derivative instrument that allows traders to speculate on the price movement of various assets, such as stocks, commodities, indices, and currencies, without actually owning the underlying asset. It is a popular trading product in the financial markets, offering potential opportunities for profit through both long and short positions. CFDs are essentially agreements between a trader and a broker to exchange the difference in the value of an asset at the start and end of the contract. The trader does not take physical ownership of the asset but rather enters into a contract with the broker to settle the difference in cash. This allows traders to profit from the price movements of the underlying asset without the need to invest a large amount of capital. CFD trading requires the trader to deposit an initial margin, which is a percentage of the total contract value. The margin acts as a form of collateral, allowing traders to gain exposure to larger positions than their initial investment would allow. However, it is important to note that trading on margin also carries the risk of magnifying both potential profits and losses. One of the key features of CFDs is the ability to go long or short on an asset. Going long involves buying a CFD in anticipation of the price rising, while going short involves selling a CFD in anticipation of the price falling. This flexibility allows traders to profit in both rising and falling markets. CFDs offer traders a wide range of underlying assets to trade, including equities, commodities, indices, and currencies. They provide access to global markets, allowing traders to diversify their portfolios and take advantage of different market conditions. CFDs also offer leverage, which can amplify potential returns, but it is important to use leverage responsibly and understand the associated risks.

Contribution Margin

The contribution margin is a financial metric used in financial management to assess the profitability of a company's products or services. It represents the amount of revenue that remains after deducting variable costs associated with producing or delivering the goods or services. Essentially, the contribution margin measures how much revenue is available to cover fixed costs and contribute to the company's operating income or profit. It is a crucial factor in evaluating the financial viability of a company's products or services, as it helps determine the level of profitability at different levels of sales volume. To calculate the contribution margin, the variable costs associated with producing or delivering the products or services are subtracted from the revenue generated. Variable costs are expenses that vary in direct proportion to the volume of goods or services sold, such as raw materials, direct labor, and sales commissions. The contribution margin can be expressed as a percentage or a dollar amount. The contribution margin ratio is calculated by dividing the contribution margin by the total revenue. This ratio indicates the proportion of revenue that contributes to covering fixed costs and generating profit. By analyzing the contribution margin, financial managers can make informed decisions about pricing strategies, product mix, and cost management. A higher contribution margin indicates that a larger portion of revenue is available to cover fixed costs and contribute to profit. This may imply that the company has a competitive advantage, as it can generate more profit from each unit sold. On the other hand, a low contribution margin may indicate that the company's products or services are not generating sufficient profit to cover fixed costs. In such cases, financial managers may need to evaluate cost reduction strategies, increase product prices, or consider discontinuing products or services with low contribution margins. In summary, the contribution margin is a vital financial metric in evaluating the profitability of a company's products or services. It provides insights into the amount of revenue available to cover fixed costs and generate profit. By monitoring and managing the contribution margin, financial managers can make informed decisions to improve the financial performance of the company.

Control Premium

Control premium refers to the amount paid by one party in a transaction to gain control or majority ownership of another party. It is the additional amount paid above the fair market value of the target company's shares, reflecting the potential benefits and synergies that can be achieved through controlling the company. In financial management, control premium plays a significant role in determining the valuation of a company. When acquiring a company, the acquiring party usually pays a control premium to gain control over the target company's assets, operations, and decision-making processes. This premium compensates the target company's shareholders for the loss of control and the potential future benefits they might have gained by holding onto their shares. The control premium is influenced by various factors, including the level of control acquired, the strategic value of the target company, the potential synergies, and the estimated future cash flows generated by the combined entity. The acquiring party performs a thorough analysis to determine the value of the control premium and assess the potential returns from the investment. Control premiums are commonly observed in mergers and acquisitions (M&A) transactions, where one company acquires another to enhance its market position, expand its product portfolio, or gain access to new markets. The acquirer may pay a control premium to convince the target company's shareholders to sell their shares and transfer control. This incentive can be critical, especially when a hostile takeover is attempted, as it encourages shareholders to support the acquisition. Investors and financial analysts use control premiums as indicators to assess the likelihood and potential success of M&A deals. A higher control premium usually suggests that the acquiring party is highly motivated to gain control and expects substantial benefits from the transaction. Conversely, a lower control premium may signal a less compelling offer or a lack of strategic alignment between the parties. While control premiums can create value for the acquiring party, it is essential to evaluate the potential risks and challenges associated with integration, management control, and achieving synergies. A thorough due diligence process is critical to understanding the target company's operations, financial performance, and potential synergies before determining an appropriate control premium. This analysis helps the acquiring party assess the overall feasibility and potential returns of the transaction.

Controlling Interest

Controlling Interest refers to the ownership or majority stake in a company that enables an individual or entity to govern the decision-making process and exert significant influence over the organization's operations and strategic direction. It signifies the power to control key activities, including financial management, policy-making, and the appointment of senior executives. In Financial Management, controlling interest plays a crucial role as it allows the controlling party to define the company's objectives, influence major business decisions, and determine how resources are allocated. The controlling interest holder typically possesses more than 50% ownership of the company's voting shares, giving them the authority to control the board of directors and shape corporate policies. The primary advantage of controlling interest lies in its ability to facilitate long-term planning and optimize the company's performance. It enables the controlling party to align corporate strategies with their own objectives and drive the company towards desired outcomes. This involvement can lead to improved operational efficiency, increased profitability, and enhanced shareholder value. Controlling interest holders have the power to make critical decisions related to capital investments, mergers and acquisitions, financing options, and dividend distributions. They can also influence corporate governance practices and either support or oppose management decisions. As a result, they may implement changes such as cost-cutting measures, restructuring initiatives, or expansion plans to improve the company's financial health. Nevertheless, controlling interest also entails responsibilities and potential risks. The controlling party has a fiduciary duty towards minority shareholders, ensuring their interests are protected and not overshadowed by personal agendas. They must act in the best interest of the company and adhere to legal and ethical standards. In summary, controlling interest in the context of financial management refers to the ownership or majority stake in a company that grants an individual or entity significant control over the organization's strategic decisions and operational activities. It empowers the controlling party to shape the company's overall direction and maximize its financial performance, while also carrying the responsibility of safeguarding minority shareholders' interests.

Conversion Price

Conversion price is a crucial concept in financial management that represents the price at which a security, typically a bond or preferred stock, can be converted into a predetermined number of common shares. This conversion process is primarily used to provide investors with the opportunity to convert their holdings into shares of common stock, which generally offers greater potential for capital appreciation. The conversion price is determined at the time of issuance of the security and is specified in the terms of the offering. It is typically set at a premium to the market price of the common stock at the time of issuance to compensate investors for the additional risk they take on by investing in a security that could potentially be converted into common shares. The premium is usually expressed as a percentage above the market price. The conversion price is a critical factor in determining the value of the security because it dictates the number of common shares that investors will receive upon conversion. The higher the conversion price, the fewer shares investors will receive, and vice versa. In this sense, the conversion price plays a significant role in the potential return on investment for investors who hold the convertible security. In addition to determining the number of shares received upon conversion, the conversion price also affects the conversion ratio, which is the number of common shares investors receive for each unit of the convertible security. The conversion ratio is calculated by dividing the par value or face value of the convertible security by the conversion price. A higher conversion price results in a lower conversion ratio, and vice versa. The conversion price is subject to adjustment in certain circumstances, such as stock splits, stock dividends, or other corporate events that could impact the value of the common stock. These adjustments aim to maintain the economic value of the convertible security and ensure that investors are not disadvantaged by changes in the underlying stock. Overall, the conversion price is a crucial element in convertible securities, as it determines the potential return on investment for investors and establishes the conversion ratio for the securities. Understanding the conversion price is essential for financial managers, investors, and other market participants involved in analyzing, valuing, and trading convertible securities.

Convertible Bond

A convertible bond is a type of bond that gives the bondholder the option to convert the bond into a specified number of shares of the issuing company's common stock, usually at a predetermined conversion price. It is essentially a combination of a bond and a stock option, offering both fixed income and potential equity ownership. Convertible bonds are typically issued by companies that want to raise capital without diluting existing shareholders' ownership. By offering the bondholders the option to convert their bonds into shares, the company can attract investors who are seeking potential upside from the stock price appreciation. At the same time, the company benefits from the lower interest rate associated with issuing a bond compared to issuing shares directly.

Convertible Preferred Stock

Convertible Preferred Stock is a type of investment instrument issued by a company that combines features of both common stock and debt. It offers investors certain benefits and features not found in regular preferred or common stock. Convertible Preferred Stock can be converted into a predetermined number of common shares of the issuing company at the option of the holder. This conversion feature provides flexibility to investors, allowing them to participate in any potential appreciation of the company's stock price. The conversion ratio is typically set at a pre-determined level, which represents the number of common shares the convertible preferred stock will convert into. One key advantage of Convertible Preferred Stock is that it offers investors a fixed dividend payment, similar to regular preferred stock. This fixed dividend is paid out to the investor on a regular basis and takes precedence over the common stock dividend. The fixed dividend provides investors with a steady income stream and adds a layer of stability to their investment. In the event of liquidation or bankruptcy, holders of Convertible Preferred Stock have a higher claim on the company's assets compared to common stockholders. They are prioritized in the distribution of remaining assets ahead of the common stockholders, which offers additional downside protection to investors. Convertible Preferred Stock often appeals to investors who desire a balance between fixed income and potential capital appreciation. It allows them to participate in the growth of the company's stock price while providing the stability of a fixed dividend payment. Companies issue Convertible Preferred Stock as a means of raising capital without diluting the ownership stake of existing common stockholders. It can also be an attractive option for investors seeking a lower risk investment compared to common stock, but with the opportunity for greater returns if the company's stock price increases. In summary, Convertible Preferred Stock is a hybrid investment instrument that offers investors the potential for capital appreciation through conversion into common stock, along with the benefit of a fixed dividend payment. Its conversion feature, higher claim on assets, and stability make it an attractive option for both companies and investors.

Convertible Securities

Convertible securities are a type of financial instrument that combines features of both debt and equity. These securities grant the holder the right to convert them into a predetermined number of common shares of the issuing company, usually at a specified conversion price and within a certain time frame. Convertible securities are typically issued by companies as a way to raise capital. They offer the issuer the advantage of obtaining funding through the issuance of debt without the obligation to make periodic interest payments or to repay the principal amount at maturity. This can be particularly attractive for companies that may have difficulty securing financing through traditional debt instruments or that want to avoid the dilution of ownership associated with issuing additional shares of common stock. For investors, convertible securities offer the potential for both income through periodic interest payments and the opportunity to participate in any appreciation of the underlying company's common stock. If the company's stock price increases significantly, the holder can choose to convert the securities into common shares and benefit from the price appreciation. On the other hand, if the stock price remains relatively stable or declines, the investor can retain the securities as debt and continue to receive interest payments until maturity. The conversion feature of these securities gives them a unique risk-return profile. The value of convertible securities is influenced by multiple factors, including the price and volatility of the underlying common stock, interest rates, and the time remaining until conversion. As a result, convertible securities generally exhibit a mix of debt-like features, such as income generation and a principal value that can be repaid at maturity, and equity-like features, such as the potential for capital appreciation and the ability to participate in dividends and other shareholder rights. The valuation of convertible securities can be complex and often involves sophisticated mathematical models that take into account various factors and assumptions. It requires considering the interplay between the fixed income component and the equity component of these securities, as well as the potential dilution effect on existing shareholders if conversion occurs. In summary, convertible securities are hybrid financial instruments that provide both debt and equity characteristics. They offer companies a flexible source of funding and investors the potential for income and participation in stock price appreciation. Their unique risk-return profile and valuation complexities make them an important tool in financial management.

Convertible Security

Convertible Security refers to a financial instrument that can be converted into a predetermined number of common stock shares at the discretion of the holder. This type of security combines the features of both debt and equity instruments, offering investors the possibility to benefit from the upside potential of the issuer's common stock while providing a fixed interest rate or dividend until conversion occurs. A convertible security can take various forms, such as convertible bonds, convertible preferred stocks, or convertible debentures. These securities are issued by companies looking to raise capital while offering investors the option to convert their holdings into equity. This flexibility attracts investors who seek potential capital appreciation and the opportunity to participate in the future success of the issuing company. One key characteristic of convertible securities is the conversion ratio, which determines the number of common stock shares that can be obtained by converting one unit of the security. For example, if the conversion ratio is set at 50, a holder could convert $1,000 of the security into 50 common stock shares. The conversion ratio is usually adjusted for events like stock splits or stock dividends to ensure the conversion terms remain equitable. In addition to the conversion feature, convertible securities typically offer a fixed interest rate or dividend payment until conversion occurs. This fixed income component provides investors with regular cash flows and acts as a buffer against potential downside risks associated with the issuer's common stock price. The interest rate or dividend yield is predetermined at the time of issuance and tends to be lower compared to similar non-convertible securities to compensate investors for the added conversion feature. The conversion option is valuable to investors when the price of the underlying common stock increases over time, making the conversion ratio more favorable. If the stock price surpasses a predetermined conversion price or strike price, holders usually exercise their right to convert the security into common stock shares, allowing them to participate in any future price appreciation. Convertible securities provide issuers with a flexible financing option, allowing them to raise capital at a potentially lower cost compared to traditional debt offerings. This is because the conversion feature may appeal to investors who are willing to accept a lower interest rate or dividend in exchange for the possibility of capital gains. However, issuers run the risk of diluting existing shareholders if a large number of convertible securities are converted into common stock. In summary, a convertible security is a hybrid financial instrument that combines features of debt and equity. It provides investors with the option to convert their holdings into common stock while receiving fixed income until conversion occurs. This type of security allows companies to raise capital while offering investors the potential for capital appreciation.

Core Competencies

Core competencies refer to the unique set of skills, knowledge, and abilities that an organization possesses and leverages to gain a competitive advantage in the market. In the context of financial management, core competencies are the fundamental capabilities that enable an organization to effectively manage and optimize its financial resources. One core competency in financial management is financial analysis. This involves the ability to analyze financial data, such as income statements and balance sheets, to assess the financial health and performance of the organization. Financial analysis also encompasses the evaluation of investment opportunities and risk management strategies, aiding in the decision-making process regarding resource allocation. Another core competency is financial planning and budgeting. This entails developing comprehensive financial plans and budgets that align with the organization's strategic objectives. Effective financial planning involves forecasting future revenues and expenses, determining funding requirements, and establishing financial targets and performance metrics to monitor and control financial performance. Risk management is also a critical core competency in financial management. This involves identifying, assessing, and mitigating financial risks that may impact the organization's ability to achieve its financial goals. Examples of financial risks include market volatility, credit risks, and liquidity risks. A well-developed risk management capability allows the organization to safeguard its financial resources and optimize risk-return trade-offs. Another core competency is financial reporting and compliance. This involves ensuring accurate and timely financial reporting, in accordance with regulatory requirements and accounting standards. It includes preparing financial statements, such as the income statement and balance sheet, and communicating financial information to stakeholders, such as investors and regulatory agencies. Compliance with financial reporting standards fosters transparency, accountability, and reliability in financial reporting. Lastly, strategic financial management is a core competency that encompasses the organization's ability to align financial decisions with its overall strategic objectives. This involves evaluating investment opportunities, assessing capital structure and financing options, and optimizing the organization's cost of capital. Strategic financial management ensures that financial resources are allocated in a manner that maximizes shareholder value and supports long-term growth and sustainability. In summary, core competencies in financial management revolve around financial analysis, planning and budgeting, risk management, financial reporting and compliance, and strategic financial management. Developing and leveraging these core competencies enable organizations to effectively manage their financial resources, ensure financial stability, and create value for their stakeholders.

Core Inflation

Core inflation is a term used in financial management to describe the measure of inflation that excludes certain volatile components. It refers to the underlying trend in price changes of goods and services in an economy by eliminating the effects of temporary or unusual factors that can distort the overall inflation rate. In calculating core inflation, economists exclude volatile elements such as energy, food, and other items that are subject to temporary supply or demand shocks. These elements can have a significant impact on the overall inflation rate but may not accurately reflect the underlying inflationary pressure in the economy.

Corporate Bonds

Corporate bonds are debt securities issued by corporations to raise capital for various purposes, such as funding new projects, acquiring assets, or refinancing existing debt. These bonds are commonly used in financial management as a means of borrowing money from investors, who receive regular interest payments in return for lending their funds. Unlike stocks, which represent ownership in a company, corporate bonds represent a contractual agreement between the issuer, typically a corporation, and the bondholder. The terms of the bond, including the interest rate, maturity date, and other provisions, are specified in a legal document known as a bond indenture.

Corporate Finance

Corporate Finance refers to the set of activities and decisions related to the financial management of a corporation. It involves analyzing and evaluating financial data, making strategic decisions, and implementing various financial strategies to maximize the value of the company for its shareholders.In essence, corporate finance is concerned with how corporations raise funds, allocate resources, and make investment decisions to achieve their financial goals. It encompasses a broad range of financial activities, including financial planning, budgeting, capital budgeting, capital structure decisions, dividend policy, and working capital management.

Corporate Governance

Corporate governance refers to the system of rules, practices, and processes through which a company is directed and controlled. It encompasses the relationships between various stakeholders such as shareholders, management, and the board of directors, as well as the framework for making decisions and ensuring accountability. In the context of financial management, corporate governance plays a critical role in ensuring the transparency, integrity, and accountability of a company's financial operations. It involves establishing and maintaining effective financial management policies and practices that safeguard the interests of shareholders and other stakeholders.

Cost Of Capital

The cost of capital is a financial metric used by companies to determine the minimum return rate required on investments to maintain or increase the value of the business. It represents the cost of obtaining funds to finance investment opportunities and is a critical factor in the decision-making process for capital budgeting. There are two main components of the cost of capital: the cost of debt and the cost of equity. The cost of debt is the interest rate a company pays on its debt obligations, such as loans and bonds. It is determined by factors such as the company's credit rating and prevailing market interest rates. The cost of equity, on the other hand, is the return expected by investors in exchange for their ownership stake in the company's stock. It is influenced by factors such as the company's growth prospects, risk profile, and market conditions.

Cost Of Carry

Cost of Carry refers to the expenses associated with holding an investment or asset over a certain period. It is an important concept in financial management as it helps calculate the total cost of owning an asset and assess the profitability of investments. The cost of carry includes various elements such as financing costs, storage costs, insurance costs, and other expenses related to holding an asset. These costs vary depending on the type of asset and the duration of holding.

Cost Of Debt

Cost of Debt is a financial ratio that measures the cost of borrowing for a company or organization. It is calculated by comparing the interest expense on a company's debt to the total amount of debt. This ratio provides insight into the financial health and risk of a company's capital structure. The cost of debt is an important metric for financial management as it helps determine the overall cost of capital for a company. It is essential for companies to understand their cost of debt as it directly affects their profitability and ability to generate returns for shareholders.

Cost Of Equity

Cost of Equity refers to the rate of return that a company requires to compensate its equity investors for the risk they undertake by investing in the company's stock. It is a key component of calculating the company's weighted average cost of capital (WACC), which is used to determine the minimum rate of return the company needs to earn in order to meet its financial obligations. The cost of equity is calculated by using the dividend discount model (DDM) or the capital asset pricing model (CAPM). The DDM estimates the fair value of a stock by forecasting its future dividends and discounting them back to their present value. The cost of equity is then derived from this fair value by calculating the rate of return that investors would expect from holding the stock.

Cost Of Goods Available For Sale (COGS)

Cost of Goods Available for Sale (COGS) is a financial metric that represents the total cost incurred by a company to acquire or produce the goods that are available for sale during a specific period. It is a crucial measure for businesses in evaluating their inventory management and determining the cost associated with the goods sold. The COGS calculation is derived by summing up the cost of the beginning inventory and the cost of additional purchases or production during the period. This provides a comprehensive view of the total cost that a company has invested in the goods that are available for sale. The formula for calculating COGS is as follows: COGS = Beginning Inventory + Additional Purchases or Production Beginning Inventory refers to the cost of goods that were held in inventory at the beginning of the period. This includes any unfinished goods that are in the process of being produced or assembled. Additional Purchases or Production refers to the cost of acquiring or producing additional goods during the period. It includes the cost of raw materials, labor, and any other expenses directly associated with the production or acquisition of the goods. The COGS figure is an essential component in the calculation of gross profit and determining the overall profitability of a company. It is subtracted from the total revenue generated from the sale of goods to arrive at the gross profit figure. This provides insights into the efficiency of the company's inventory management and the profitability of its core operations. Moreover, COGS is also used in various financial ratios like gross profit margin and inventory turnover ratio. The gross profit margin represents the percentage of revenue that is left after deducting the COGS, indicating the company's ability to generate profit from its core operations. The inventory turnover ratio measures the number of times a company's inventory is sold and replaced within a specific period, reflecting how efficiently the company manages its inventory and the liquidity of its products. In conclusion, Cost of Goods Available for Sale (COGS) is a fundamental financial metric that calculates the total cost associated with the goods available for sale during a specific period. It is a crucial measure for evaluating inventory management efficiency and determining gross profit. By analyzing COGS, businesses can gain valuable insights into their profitability and make informed decisions regarding pricing, production, and inventory management.

Cost Of Goods Sold (COGS)

Cost of Goods Sold (COGS) is a critical financial metric used in financial management to calculate the direct expenses incurred in producing or manufacturing goods or services sold by a company during a specific period. COGS reflects the direct costs of production, including the cost of raw materials, direct labor, and other related production costs such as factory overheads and utilities. It excludes costs that are not directly tied to producing goods or services, such as sales and marketing expenses, administrative costs, and research and development expenses. COGS is an essential component in determining a company's gross profit and evaluating its operational efficiency. By subtracting COGS from the company's net sales or revenue, one arrives at the gross profit margin, which indicates the profitability of a company's core business operations. Calculating COGS requires a detailed analysis of the direct costs involved in the production process. This typically involves identifying and tracking the cost of raw materials used to produce the goods, including any shipping or handling costs associated with acquiring those materials. Additionally, direct labor costs, including wages, salaries, and benefits of the workers directly involved in the production process, need to be considered. Lastly, any other direct costs such as factory rent, utilities, or equipment depreciation that are specifically incurred as part of the production process should be included. COGS is important for financial management as it helps in understanding the profitability of a company's core operations and in making informed decisions related to pricing, cost control, and inventory management. Comparing COGS with net sales or revenue allows for the calculation of the gross profit margin, which is a crucial performance indicator for assessing a company's competitiveness and financial health. Overall, COGS provides insights into the direct costs involved in producing goods or services and is a key measure used by financial managers to analyze a company's operational efficiency and profitability.

Coupon Payment

A Coupon Payment, in the context of Financial Management, refers to the periodic interest payment made to the holders of a bond or other fixed-income security. When a company or government entity issues a bond, they are essentially borrowing money from investors. The bond has a stated interest rate, often referred to as the coupon rate, which is used to calculate the coupon payment. The coupon rate is typically fixed for the life of the bond.

Coupon Rate

A coupon rate refers to the annual interest rate that a bond issuer promises to pay to bondholders. It is the fixed percentage of the bond's face value that the bondholder will receive as interest income. When a company or government entity issues a bond to raise money, it agrees to make regular interest payments to bondholders as compensation for investing in the bond. The coupon rate determines the amount of interest that will be paid out each year. For example, a bond with a face value of $1,000 and a coupon rate of 5% will pay out $50 in interest annually.

Coupon Yield

Coupon yield is a financial measure used in the field of financial management to determine the return on investment (ROI) of a fixed-income security, such as a bond or a debenture. It represents the annual interest rate paid by the issuer to the holder of the security, expressed as a percentage of the face value or par value of the security. The coupon yield is calculated by dividing the annual coupon payment by the face value of the bond and multiplying the result by 100 to convert it into a percentage. The coupon payment is the fixed amount of interest paid by the issuer to the bondholder at fixed intervals, typically semi-annually or annually. The face value or par value is the amount that the issuer promises to repay to the bondholder at maturity, which is usually the original price at which the bond was issued. Coupon yield is an important measure for investors as it helps them assess the potential return on their investment in fixed-income securities. It provides an estimate of the interest income that the investor can expect to earn annually from the bond, relative to its current market price. This information can be useful in comparing different fixed-income securities and making investment decisions based on their respective coupon yields. Moreover, the coupon yield also influences the market price of fixed-income securities. When market interest rates rise above the coupon yield, the bond's market price tends to decrease, as investors can find more attractive investment opportunities elsewhere. Conversely, when market interest rates fall below the coupon yield, the bond's market price tends to increase, as investors are willing to pay a premium for higher fixed interest payments. In summary, coupon yield is a financial measure that represents the annual interest rate paid by a fixed-income security, such as a bond or debenture. It helps investors assess the potential return on their investment and affects the market price of the security. By understanding coupon yield, investors can make informed investment decisions and manage their financial portfolios effectively.

Covenant

A covenant refers to a legally binding agreement between two parties that outlines specific terms and conditions related to financial management. These agreements are commonly used in the context of loans, bonds, and other financial transactions. Covenants are put in place to protect the interests of both parties and to ensure certain obligations are met. In financial management, covenants often impose restrictions or requirements on the borrower or issuer of a financial instrument. These restrictions can include limitations on the borrower's ability to take certain actions, such as incurring additional debt, paying dividends, or making significant investments. Additionally, covenants may require specific financial ratios or benchmarks to be maintained, such as debt-to-equity ratios or minimum levels of working capital.

Cram-Down

A cram-down is a term used in financial management to refer to a legal process that allows a bankruptcy court to approve a reorganization plan even if it is not approved by all creditors. This process is used when the debtor (typically a company) is unable to reach a voluntary agreement with its creditors to restructure its debts. In a cram-down, the court has the authority to impose the reorganization plan on all creditors, even those who have not consented to it. The purpose of a cram-down is to ensure that the debtor's reorganization plan is fair and equitable, and that it provides the best possible outcome for all parties involved.

Credit Analysis

Credit analysis is a process of evaluating the creditworthiness of a borrower, whether it be an individual or a company, to determine their ability to repay a loan or fulfill their financial obligations. It involves a thorough assessment of the borrower's financial history, business operations, and market conditions to form an informed opinion on their credit risk. During the credit analysis process, financial analysts collect and analyze various types of financial information, such as income statements, balance sheets, cash flow statements, tax returns, and credit ratings. They also review the borrower's industry, competitive landscape, and macroeconomic factors that could impact their ability to generate revenue and repay debt. By scrutinizing these financial and non-financial indicators, credit analysts aim to assess the likelihood of default or delay in repayment. The main objectives of credit analysis are to determine the borrower's ability to generate sufficient cash flows to meet their financial obligations, gauge the borrower's capital structure and leverage levels, measure the borrower's liquidity position, and assess the borrower's overall business and financial risk. Through this comprehensive evaluation, credit analysts provide credit rating recommendations or credit limits to creditors or lenders, helping them make informed decisions regarding loan approval, interest rates, loan terms, or credit extensions. Credit analysis involves several key components, such as analyzing the borrower's financial statements to evaluate their profitability, debt levels, and cash flow generation capabilities. It also requires assessing the borrower's management team, competitive advantages, and market positioning to understand their ability to adapt to changing market conditions and successfully operate their business. Additionally, credit analysts consider external factors, such as market trends, regulatory environment, and geopolitical risks, which could impact the borrower's ability to meet their financial obligations. Overall, credit analysis plays a crucial role in financial management by providing lenders and creditors with an objective assessment of a borrower's creditworthiness. By carefully evaluating various financial and non-financial factors, credit analysts help mitigate credit risk, optimize lending decisions, and ultimately contribute to financial stability in both individual and business lending scenarios.

Credit Default Risk

Credit default risk refers to the potential for a borrower to default on their debt obligations, such as failing to make timely interest or principal payments. This risk is an integral part of financial management and is a crucial factor for lenders and investors to consider when assessing the creditworthiness of a borrower. In financial management, credit default risk is assessed through various indicators and models, such as credit ratings, credit spreads, and credit default swaps. These tools help financial institutions and investors gauge the likelihood of a borrower defaulting on their debt payments. The higher the risk of default, the lower the credit rating and the wider the credit spread will be. Credit default risk can be influenced by various factors, including the financial health of the borrower, prevailing economic conditions, industry-specific risks, and market sentiment. For example, during economic downturns or recessions, credit default risk tends to increase as businesses and individuals face financial hardships, reducing their ability to meet their debt obligations. Financial management involves managing credit default risk through a range of strategies. Lenders and investors may diversify their portfolios to minimize exposure to any single borrower. They may also implement risk management techniques, such as setting credit limits, monitoring creditworthiness, and conducting regular reviews of their loan portfolios. Furthermore, financial management also involves assessing the price of credit default risk. Lenders and investors demand compensation for bearing the risk of default in the form of higher interest rates, fees, or spreads. This additional cost helps to offset potential losses in the event of default and incentivizes lenders to extend credit to borrowers with higher credit default risk.

Credit Default Swap (CDS) Index

A Credit Default Swap (CDS) Index is a financial derivative instrument that allows investors to manage and transfer credit risk in the form of default on a particular bond or a basket of bonds. It is considered an important tool in the field of financial management. The CDS Index acts as a benchmark for credit risk in the market. It provides a way to trade or hedge credit risk based on an index that represents a specific group of bonds or entities. The index is typically composed of credit default swaps on a variety of debt securities or reference entities.

Credit Default Swap (CDS)

A Credit Default Swap (CDS) is a financial derivative instrument that allows investors to transfer or mitigate credit risk. It is essentially a contract between two parties, commonly referred to as the protection buyer and the protection seller. The protection buyer pays regular premium payments to the protection seller in exchange for protection against the default of a specific reference entity, such as a corporate bond or loan. In the event of a default, the protection seller is obligated to compensate the protection buyer for the loss incurred on the reference entity. The CDS market emerged in the early 2000s and quickly gained popularity as a means for investors to hedge their credit exposures or speculate on the creditworthiness of a particular entity. It is considered an over-the-counter (OTC) instrument, meaning that transactions take place directly between counterparties rather than on a centralized exchange. One of the key features of a CDS is its flexibility. The protection buyer can choose the reference entity and the notional amount, which represents the face value of the reference entity's debt. This allows investors to tailor their risk exposure to specific credits or sectors. The notional amount does not represent an actual cash flow but serves as the basis for determining the payout in the event of a default. When a default occurs, the protection buyer may choose to deliver the defaulted debt to the protection seller in exchange for the face value of the debt. Alternatively, they can settle in cash based on the difference between the face value and the market value of the defaulted debt. The protection buyer may also opt to sell the CDS contract to a third party before expiration. Credit Default Swaps played a significant role in the global financial crisis in 2008, as their widespread use amplified the impact of the subprime mortgage crisis. The complex web of interconnected CDS contracts contributed to the contagion effect, leading to the collapse of major financial institutions. While CDS can provide valuable risk management tools, they also pose systemic risks and require careful regulatory oversight. The inherent complexity and potential for misuse make them subject to scrutiny and regulation by financial authorities worldwide.

Credit Limit

A credit limit is the maximum amount of money that a borrower is allowed to borrow from a lender or a financial institution, based on their creditworthiness and financial stability. It is determined by the lender and serves as a boundary or a cap on how much credit can be extended to the borrower. The credit limit is typically established when an individual or a business applies for a line of credit, such as a credit card or a loan. The credit limit is calculated by taking into consideration several factors, such as the borrower's credit history, income, existing debt obligations, and overall financial health. Lenders use this information to assess the borrower's ability to repay the borrowed funds and manage their credit responsibly. A higher credit limit indicates that the borrower is considered to be more creditworthy and capable of handling larger amounts of debt. Once the credit limit is established, the borrower is free to use the credit up to the assigned limit. For example, if a credit card has a credit limit of $5,000, the cardholder can make purchases or withdraw cash up to that amount. However, exceeding the credit limit may result in penalties, such as over-limit fees or increased interest rates. It is important for borrowers to manage their credit usage within their credit limit to avoid incurring additional costs and negatively impacting their credit score. The credit limit is not a fixed amount and can be adjusted over time based on the borrower's creditworthiness, financial situation, and relationship with the lender. Lenders may periodically review the credit limit and make changes accordingly. Borrowers can also request a credit limit increase if they believe they can handle additional credit responsibly. However, lenders may require further evaluation before approving such requests.

Credit Rating

Credit Rating is a financial assessment or evaluation conducted by agencies to determine the creditworthiness or the risk associated with lending money to individuals, companies, or governments. It is an important tool used by investors, lenders, and other financial institutions to assess the potential risk of default or non-payment by the borrower. These credit rating agencies analyze various factors, such as the borrower's financial history, income, assets, debt levels, and past payment behavior, among other factors. Based on this analysis, the agencies assign a credit rating to the borrower, which serves as an indicator of the borrower's ability to repay the debt and the likelihood of default.

Credit Risk Assessment

Credit risk assessment refers to the evaluation and analysis of the potential risk of default on a loan or debt by a borrower or issuer. It is an essential process within financial management that allows lenders, investors, and financial institutions to assess the creditworthiness of individuals, businesses, or other entities before extending credit or entering into a financial transaction. The aim of credit risk assessment is to determine the likelihood of default and quantify the potential loss that might occur if default does happen. By evaluating the credit risk, lenders can make informed decisions regarding the interest rate to charge, the amount of credit to extend, or whether to approve or deny a loan or credit application. This assessment is crucial in protecting the lender's investment and ensuring the overall stability of the financial system. There are several factors that are typically considered during the credit risk assessment process. These include the borrower's credit history, financial stability, income, assets, debt-to-income ratio, and collateral if applicable. The assessment may also involve evaluating the borrower's industry, market conditions, and economic factors that could influence their ability to repay the loan. Once the necessary information is gathered, a credit risk assessment is typically performed using various quantitative and qualitative analysis techniques. This may involve assigning a credit score or rating to the borrower, which indicates their creditworthiness. These scores or ratings are often based on statistical models, past credit performance, and industry benchmarks. In addition to assessing individual credit risk, credit risk assessment is also conducted at an institutional or portfolio level. In this case, the focus is on assessing the overall credit quality and potential risk exposure of a collection of loans or investments. This allows institutions to assess the diversification and concentration of their credit portfolios and manage risk on a broader level. Overall, credit risk assessment plays a vital role in the decision-making process for lenders and investors. It allows them to evaluate the potential risk of default and make informed decisions regarding extending credit or entering into financial transactions. By effectively managing credit risk, financial institutions can maintain the stability and profitability of their operations.

Credit Risk

Credit risk refers to the potential for a borrower or debtor to fail to meet their financial obligations, resulting in a loss for the lender or creditor. It is a critical aspect of financial management as it directly affects the financial health and stability of an organization. When an individual, company, or government entity borrows money, they enter into a contractual agreement with the lender, which typically includes specific terms and conditions for repayment. However, there is always a risk that the borrower may default on their loan or be unable to fulfill their contractual obligations due to various factors such as economic downturns, financial mismanagement, or unforeseen circumstances. Managing credit risk is crucial for financial institutions and organizations that engage in lending activities, as it helps them evaluate and quantify the potential risks associated with different borrowers. By assessing credit risk, lenders can make informed decisions about whether to extend credit to a particular borrower, as well as determine the terms, conditions, and interest rates that are appropriate for a given lending arrangement. There are several methods utilized by financial managers to analyze and mitigate credit risk. One common approach is to assess the creditworthiness of borrowers by conducting thorough credit checks, analyzing their financial statements and credit history, and evaluating their ability to generate sufficient cash flows to service their debts. Financial institutions also utilize credit risk models and statistical tools to predict the likelihood of default and estimate potential losses in the event of borrower non-payment. These models consider various factors such as the borrower's credit score, industry risk factors, macroeconomic indicators, and the overall economic environment to assess and quantify credit risk. In order to mitigate credit risk, lenders often employ risk mitigation techniques such as setting appropriate loan-to-value ratios, requiring collateral or guarantees, structuring diversified loan portfolios, and implementing effective credit risk management systems and policies. Overall, credit risk is a fundamental consideration in financial management, as it assists organizations in making prudent lending decisions, managing their loan portfolios effectively, and minimizing potential losses arising from borrower defaults.

Creditor

A creditor, in the context of financial management, refers to an entity or individual to whom money or other valuable assets are owed. In simple terms, a creditor is a party that has provided goods, services, or funds to another party under the expectation of being repaid in the future. There are various types of creditors, including financial institutions, such as banks and credit unions, as well as suppliers, vendors, and individuals. Creditors play a vital role in the financial ecosystem as they provide the necessary capital for businesses and individuals to meet their financial needs and obligations.

Cross Margining

Cross margining is a financial management strategy that allows investors to offset the risks and costs associated with multiple positions or transactions by consolidating them into a single margin account. This approach enhances efficiency and reduces the amount of margin required to maintain these positions. Under cross margining, investors can consolidate their margin requirements across different types of financial instruments or assets that are held within the same clearinghouse or exchange. This can include derivatives, such as futures and options, as well as securities, such as stocks and bonds. By combining these positions, investors are able to reduce the overall margin required, freeing up capital that can be used for other investments or business purposes.

Cross-Border Financing

Cross-border financing refers to the provision of funds from one country to another for the purpose of financing economic activities. It typically involves companies or individuals seeking capital from foreign investors or financial institutions to support their business operations, investments, or projects. One of the primary reasons why companies engage in cross-border financing is to access funding sources that may not be available domestically. By tapping into international markets, businesses can take advantage of different interest rates, currencies, and financing terms, potentially allowing for more favorable borrowing conditions. Additionally, cross-border financing can help companies diversify their funding sources, reducing dependence on local markets and increasing financial resilience. There are several types of cross-border financing, including foreign direct investment (FDI), international bank loans, bonds, and trade finance. FDI involves the establishment of physical operations in a foreign country, which often requires significant investment in infrastructure, equipment, or facilities. International bank loans are provided by foreign banks to borrowers in need of capital, while bonds are debt securities issued by companies or governments seeking to raise funds from international investors. Trade finance, on the other hand, refers to the provision of short-term financing to facilitate international trade transactions. This can include pre-export financing, which provides working capital for companies before they ship goods abroad, or import financing, which enables businesses to pay for imported goods or services before receiving them. Trade finance instruments commonly used in cross-border financing include letters of credit, export credit insurance, and factoring. However, cross-border financing is not without risks. Exchange rate fluctuations, political instability, regulatory differences, and legal complexities are among the factors that can impact the availability and cost of financing. Companies engaging in cross-border financing must carefully evaluate these risks and develop appropriate strategies to mitigate them. In conclusion, cross-border financing is the process of obtaining funds from foreign sources to support economic activities. It offers companies access to diverse funding options and can help them reduce dependency on domestic markets. However, it also comes with risks that need to be carefully managed.

Cross-Currency Swap

A cross-currency swap is a financial management tool used by multinational corporations to manage their foreign exchange exposure. In simple terms, it is an agreement between two parties to exchange the principal and interest payments of two different currencies over a specified period. Typically, the two parties involved in a cross-currency swap are looking to convert their cash flows from one currency to another without incurring any foreign exchange market risk. This is achieved by exchanging cash flows at a predetermined exchange rate, known as the swap rate. The swap rate is often quoted as the difference between the spot exchange rates of the two currencies involved. The key components of a cross-currency swap include the notional amount, the duration of the swap, and the swap rate. The notional amount represents the principal on which the swap is based. It is often a large amount, but no actual principal is exchanged between the parties. Instead, the notional amount is used to calculate the interest payments that are exchanged throughout the life of the swap. The duration of a cross-currency swap is typically fixed, ranging from a few months to several years, depending on the needs of the parties involved. During the life of the swap, the parties make periodic interest payments to each other based on the notional amount and the swap rate. These interest payments are typically based on a fixed interest rate for one currency and a floating interest rate, such as LIBOR, for the other currency. At the end of the swap agreement, the parties exchange the notional amount back at the original exchange rate, effectively unwinding the swap. This allows the parties to convert their cash flows back into their original currencies without incurring any foreign exchange market risk. Overall, a cross-currency swap provides multinational corporations with a flexible and cost-effective way to manage their foreign exchange exposure. By exchanging cash flows at a predetermined exchange rate, the parties can mitigate the impact of exchange rate fluctuations on their business operations and financial performance.

Cumulative Preferred Stock

Cumulative Preferred Stock is a type of stock that offers priority in receiving dividend payments over common stock and has a feature that allows accumulated unpaid dividends to be paid in the future. This means that if a company is unable to pay dividends to its preferred stockholders in a particular period, the dividends will accumulate and must be paid before any dividends are distributed to common stockholders in the future. Unlike common stockholders, who have voting rights and may benefit from potential increases in the company's value, preferred stockholders do not typically have voting rights and their shares are less risky. In the event of liquidation, preferred stockholders are entitled to be paid their original investment amount and any unpaid accumulated dividends before common stockholders receive anything.

Currency Exchange Risk

Currency exchange risk, also known as foreign exchange risk or FX risk, refers to the potential financial loss that an organization or individual may incur due to fluctuations in exchange rates between different currencies. In the context of financial management, currency exchange risk is a significant aspect that businesses and investors need to consider when engaging in international transactions or investments. It arises when there is a difference in the value of currencies involved in a transaction at the time of initiation and settlement. Exchange rates are influenced by various factors such as interest rates, inflation, political stability, economic performance, and market sentiment. Therefore, they are subject to constant fluctuations and can change rapidly. These changes can have a profound impact on the value of international transactions, investments, cash flows, and overall profitability. The currency exchange risk can be of two types: transaction risk and translation risk. Transaction risk occurs when the exchange rate changes between the time when a transaction is executed and when it is settled. This can result in a gain or loss, depending on whether the domestic currency strengthens or weakens against the foreign currency. Translation risk, on the other hand, is associated with the conversion of financial statements from one currency to another for consolidation purposes. It primarily affects multinational corporations that operate in multiple countries and have assets, liabilities, revenues, and expenses denominated in different currencies. To mitigate currency exchange risk, organizations can employ various risk management techniques such as hedging, forward contracts, options, and currency swaps. These strategies help to minimize the potential impact of exchange rate fluctuations and provide a certain degree of certainty in managing cash flows and financial performance. In conclusion, currency exchange risk is a crucial consideration in financial management. It has the potential to significantly impact the financial performance and stability of organizations operating in the international arena. Consequently, it is essential for businesses and investors to carefully analyze and manage this risk to protect their financial interests.

Currency Risk

Currency risk, also known as exchange rate risk or foreign exchange risk, refers to the potential for financial loss or gain faced by individuals or businesses due to fluctuations in currency exchange rates. It is a significant concern for multinational corporations, investors, and individuals engaged in international trade and investment. When conducting transactions in different currencies, changes in exchange rates can have a substantial impact on the value of assets, liabilities, revenues, and expenses. Currency risk arises because exchange rates are volatile and can fluctuate due to various factors such as economic conditions, political events, inflation rates, and market speculation. For multinational corporations, currency risk can affect their financial performance and profitability. Companies that operate in multiple countries are exposed to foreign exchange risk when they have assets, liabilities, revenues, or expenses denominated in foreign currencies. Fluctuations in exchange rates can result in translation, transaction, and economic exposures. Translation exposure refers to the potential impact of exchange rate changes on the value of a company's assets and liabilities denominated in foreign currencies when they are translated into the reporting currency. It affects the consolidated financial statements and can result in gains or losses on translation. Transaction exposure arises from future transactions that are denominated in foreign currencies. It occurs when a company has committed to buying or selling goods or services at a future date at pre-agreed prices in a foreign currency. Fluctuations in exchange rates can affect the profitability and competitiveness of these transactions. Economic exposure, also known as operating exposure, refers to the impact of exchange rate fluctuations on a company's future cash flows and competitive position. It is caused by changes in demand, competition, and market conditions resulting from currency movements. Economic exposure is more difficult to measure and manage compared to translation and transaction exposures. Investors and individuals engaged in international trade also face currency risk. They may hold investments or conduct business in foreign currencies, and fluctuations in exchange rates can affect the value of their holdings or the cost of their transactions.

Current Assets

Current Assets are a category of assets on a company's balance sheet that are expected to be converted into cash or used within one year or the operating cycle, whichever is longer. These assets are short-term resources that can readily be liquidated into cash or are used to support the daily operations of a business. Current assets play a crucial role in financial management as they provide information about a company's liquidity and its ability to meet its short-term obligations. Examples of current assets include cash and cash equivalents, accounts receivable, inventory, short-term investments, and prepaid expenses. Cash and cash equivalents refer to currency, checks, or any other form of cash held by a business. Accounts receivable represent the amount of money owed to the company by its customers for goods or services sold on credit. Inventory consists of goods held by a company for sale or raw materials used in production. Short-term investments are financial instruments that can be easily converted into cash, such as marketable securities. Prepaid expenses are payments made in advance for goods or services that will be received in the future.

Current Ratio

The Current Ratio is a financial metric used in financial management to assess a company's short-term liquidity. It measures the ability of a company to cover its short-term liabilities with its short-term assets. The formula for calculating the current ratio is as follows: Current Ratio = Current Assets / Current Liabilities Current assets are the assets that a company expects to convert into cash or consume within one year, including cash, accounts receivable, inventory, and prepaid expenses. Current liabilities, on the other hand, are the obligations that a company expects to settle within one year, including accounts payable, accrued expenses, and short-term debt. By comparing current assets to current liabilities, the current ratio provides an indication of a company's ability to meet its short-term obligations. A ratio of greater than 1 suggests that a company has more assets than liabilities, indicating a healthier financial position. A ratio below 1 implies that a company may struggle to meet its short-term obligations. However, it is essential to interpret the current ratio in the context of the industry in which the company operates. Some industries, such as retail, have higher inventory levels, resulting in a higher current ratio. In contrast, industries that rely more on services may have lower inventory levels and a lower current ratio. Additionally, a very high current ratio may indicate that a company is not efficiently utilizing its current assets or has excessive working capital. Conversely, a very low current ratio may suggest potential liquidity issues or an inability to pay short-term obligations. The current ratio should be used in conjunction with other financial ratios and analysis tools to gain a comprehensive understanding of a company's financial health. It is important to consider trends over time, industry benchmarks, and the company's specific circumstances. In conclusion, the current ratio is a vital tool in financial management that helps assess a company's ability to meet its short-term liabilities. It provides insight into a company's liquidity and should be used alongside other financial ratios for a more robust evaluation.

Current Yield

Current Yield refers to a financial metric used in the field of financial management that calculates the annual return on an investment in relation to its current market price. It is primarily utilized to evaluate and compare the relative attractiveness of different investment options, particularly fixed-income securities, such as bonds or preferred shares. The formula for calculating the current yield is straightforward and can be expressed as follows: Current Yield = Annual Interest Payment / Current Market Price of the Investment The annual interest payment refers to the income generated by the investment on an annual basis, while the current market price represents the price at which the investment is currently being traded in the market. By dividing the annual interest payment by the current market price, the current yield provides a percentage that indicates the anticipated rate of return for an investor based on the investment's current market value. Investors commonly use current yield as a preliminary tool to assess the attractiveness of fixed-income securities, especially when comparing multiple options. However, it is important to note that current yield does not take into account the potential capital gains or losses that an investor may experience over the holding period of the investment. Additionally, it assumes that the investment will be held until maturity, which may not always be the case. Moreover, current yield is most commonly applied to fixed-income securities where interest payments are made periodically and reliably. It is less applicable to other types of investments, such as equities or real estate, where anticipated returns are often driven by factors other than periodic interest or dividend payments.

Custodian Bank

A custodian bank, in the context of financial management, refers to a financial institution or entity that holds and safeguards assets on behalf of its clients. The primary role of a custodian bank is to ensure the safekeeping and administration of various types of investments, such as securities, cash, and other financial assets. Custodian banks play a crucial role in the financial industry by providing custody services to institutional investors, including pension funds, mutual funds, insurance companies, and other asset management firms. These institutions typically have a large portfolio of investments, which require professional custody services to ensure their safekeeping and proper management. One of the key responsibilities of a custodian bank is to maintain accurate records of all the assets it holds on behalf of its clients. This includes tracking the ownership of securities, processing corporate actions, such as dividend payments and stock splits, and providing regular reporting to clients regarding their investment holdings. Through these services, custodian banks help investors have a clear understanding of their portfolio's composition and performance. In addition to safekeeping and record-keeping, custodian banks also provide a range of ancillary services to their clients. These services may include settlement of transactions, which involves the transfer of securities and cash between buyers and sellers, as well as handling corporate events, such as proxy voting and shareholder meetings. Custodian banks may also facilitate the collection of income on behalf of clients, such as interest payments and dividends. Custodian banks are usually regulated entities, subject to specific rules and regulations, to ensure the safety and integrity of the assets they hold. They are often required to maintain strict operational and financial controls to prevent fraud and misconduct. Furthermore, custodian banks are typically required to segregate clients' assets from their own, providing an extra layer of protection to investors in the event of insolvency. In summary, a custodian bank plays a critical role in the safekeeping and administration of financial assets on behalf of institutional investors. By providing custody services, record-keeping, settlement, and other ancillary services, custodian banks help ensure the integrity of the financial system and provide investors with confidence in the security and management of their investments.

Custody Account

A custody account, in the context of financial management, refers to a type of account that is held by a financial institution on behalf of an individual or entity to hold and manage their investment assets. It is commonly used in the field of securities trading and investment management. When an investor wants to hold their assets in a custody account, they transfer the ownership of the assets to the custodian, typically a bank or a brokerage firm. The custodian then takes responsibility for the safekeeping and administration of the assets, ensuring that they are held securely and accurately reported.

Cyclical Industry

A cyclical industry is a type of industry that is highly sensitive to changes in the overall economic condition and tends to experience periodic fluctuations in its revenue, earnings, and operations. This type of industry is often associated with business sectors that produce goods and services that are considered non-essential or discretionary, as opposed to industries like healthcare or utilities that are more essential and less impacted by economic cycles. In a cyclical industry, the demand for goods and services is closely tied to the overall health of the economy. During periods of economic expansion or prosperity, consumer spending tends to increase, leading to higher demand for non-essential goods and services. This results in higher revenues, earnings, and overall profitability for companies operating in cyclical industries. Conversely, during periods of economic contraction or recession, consumer spending tends to decline, leading to lower demand for non-essential goods and services. This can have a significant negative impact on companies in cyclical industries, as they may experience lower revenues, earnings, and profitability. Additionally, companies in cyclical industries may also face challenges such as increased competition, pricing pressure, and reduced access to credit during economic downturns. Examples of cyclical industries include automotive, construction, airlines, hotels, retail, and leisure. These industries are particularly sensitive to changes in consumer confidence, interest rates, and employment levels, among other economic factors. Companies operating in cyclical industries often employ strategies such as cost-cutting, capacity adjustments, and diversification to mitigate the impact of economic cycles and maintain profitability. In conclusion, a cyclical industry is a type of industry that experiences periodic fluctuations in its financial performance due to changes in economic conditions. Companies operating in cyclical industries need to closely monitor and adapt to these economic cycles to ensure their long-term viability and success.

Cyclical Stock

A cyclical stock is a type of stock that tends to follow the ups and downs of the overall market or a specific sector or industry. These stocks often experience significant fluctuations in price and performance in response to changes in the economy and business cycles. Unlike defensive stocks, which are relatively stable and less affected by economic changes, cyclical stocks are highly sensitive to economic conditions. They perform well when the economy is growing and in expansionary phases of the business cycle. However, they can also underperform during downturns and recessionary periods.

Cyclical Stocks

Cyclical stocks are a category of stocks that are highly sensitive to the overall state of the economy. These stocks tend to move in sync with the business cycle, experiencing periods of growth during economic expansions and declines during economic contractions. Companies that fall into the cyclical stock category typically operate in industries that are directly influenced by consumer spending and business investment, such as automotive, housing, retail, and manufacturing. When the economy is strong and consumer confidence is high, these industries thrive, leading to increased sales and profitability for the companies within them. Conversely, during economic downturns or periods of uncertainty, consumer spending tends to slow down, negatively impacting the performance of cyclical stocks.

Debenture Bond

A debenture bond is a type of long-term debt instrument that is issued by a corporation or government entity to raise capital. It is essentially a loan agreement between the issuer, who acts as the borrower, and the debenture bondholders, who act as the lenders. Debenture bonds are typically unsecured, meaning that they are not backed by any specific collateral. Instead, the bondholders rely on the general creditworthiness and financial strength of the issuer to receive interest payments and repayment of the principal amount at maturity. This makes debenture bonds riskier than secured bonds but potentially offers higher yields to investors.

Debenture

A debenture is a type of long-term debt instrument that is issued by a company or a government entity to raise funds for various purposes, such as financing operations, capital expenditure, or restructuring existing debt. It is a formal agreement between the issuer (the borrower) and the holder (the lender) that outlines the terms and conditions of the loan, including the repayment schedule, interest rate, and any additional provisions. Unlike other forms of debt, such as bank loans, debentures are typically unsecured, meaning that they are not backed by any specific collateral. This means that the only assurance for the debenture holder is the promise of the issuer to repay the principal amount and interest on the specified due dates. To compensate for the higher risk associated with unsecured debt, debentures generally carry a higher interest rate compared to secured debt instruments. Debentures can be classified into various types based on their features and characteristics. Some common types include convertible debentures, redeemable debentures, and perpetual debentures. Convertible debentures give the holder the option to convert the debenture into equity shares of the issuing company at a predetermined conversion rate. This provides the holder with the opportunity to participate in any future appreciation in the value of the company's shares. Redeemable debentures have a fixed maturity date, at which point they are redeemed by the issuer. The issuer may repay the principal amount in full or in installments over the life of the debenture. This provides the issuer with flexibility in managing its debt obligations. Perpetual debentures, on the other hand, do not have a fixed maturity date and can be considered as a form of perpetual debt. The issuer pays interest on the debenture indefinitely, without any obligation to repay the principal amount. This type of debenture is relatively rare and is typically issued by governments or public entities. In conclusion, a debenture is a long-term debt instrument that is issued by a company or government entity to raise funds. It is a formal agreement between the issuer and the holder that outlines the terms and conditions of the loan. Debentures can be categorized based on their features, such as convertibility, redeemability, and perpetuity.

Debt Capital Markets (DCM)

Debt Capital Markets (DCM) are a sector of the financial markets that involve the issuance and trading of debt securities. These securities are issued by governments, corporations, and other organizations to raise funds from investors. DCM plays a crucial role in facilitating the borrowing needs of these entities. DCM primarily deals with the issuance and trading of bonds, which are debt instruments with fixed interest payments and maturity dates. Bonds can be classified based on various factors including the issuer, currency, interest rate, and credit rating. DCM market participants include investment banks, institutional investors, and individual investors.

Debt Consolidation

Debt consolidation is a financial management strategy that involves combining multiple debts into a single loan or payment plan. This approach is typically used when an individual or organization is struggling to manage multiple debts with varying interest rates, payment schedules, and lenders. The primary goal of debt consolidation is to simplify the debt repayment process and potentially reduce the overall cost of the debt. By consolidating multiple debts into one, the borrower can streamline their financial obligations and make a single payment each month, rather than dealing with multiple payments to different creditors. There are several methods of consolidating debt, including taking out a consolidation loan, transferring balances to a new credit card with a lower interest rate, or using a debt management program. The choice of method often depends on the borrower's financial situation, credit score, and available options. One common method of debt consolidation involves obtaining a consolidation loan from a bank, credit union, or online lender. This loan is typically used to pay off the existing debts, leaving the borrower with a single loan to repay. The consolidation loan often offers a lower interest rate than the original debts, which can help reduce the overall cost of the debt over time. Another option is to transfer balances from high-interest credit cards to a new card with a lower interest rate or a promotional period with no interest. This can provide temporary relief from high interest charges and simplify monthly payments. However, it is important to carefully read the terms and conditions, as there may be fees associated with balance transfers or interest rates that increase after the promotional period ends. For individuals or organizations with overwhelming debt and limited options, a debt management program may be a viable solution. This involves working with a nonprofit credit counseling agency that negotiates with creditors on behalf of the borrower. The agency may be able to lower interest rates, eliminate fees, and consolidate the debts into a more manageable payment plan. Overall, debt consolidation is a financial management strategy that allows individuals and organizations to combine multiple debts into a single loan or payment plan. It can simplify the repayment process, potentially reduce the overall cost of debt, and provide a path towards financial stability and freedom.

Debt Covenant

A debt covenant refers to a legal agreement or a set of financial requirements that a borrower must adhere to while taking on debt. These covenants are put in place by lenders or bondholders to protect their investment and minimize the risk associated with lending funds. Debt covenants typically outline certain financial ratios, performance metrics, or restrictions that the borrower must meet or abide by. They serve as a mechanism to ensure the borrower's creditworthiness and reduce the likelihood of default. These agreements are often included in loan contracts, bond indentures, or other debt documents.

Debt Covenants

Debt covenants, in the context of financial management, refer to the conditions and restrictions set by lenders in loan agreements to protect their interests and ensure the borrower's ability to meet the repayment obligations. These covenants act as a safety net for lenders, allowing them to monitor and control the borrower's financial activities, thereby minimizing the risk associated with lending. The primary objective of debt covenants is to safeguard the lender's investment by imposing certain limitations and requirements on the borrower. These restrictions are designed to maintain the borrower's financial health and prevent any actions that could potentially impair the borrower's ability to repay the debt. There are two main types of debt covenants: affirmative covenants and negative covenants. Affirmative covenants outline the actions that the borrower must take or comply with, such as providing regular financial statements, maintaining adequate insurance coverage, or paying taxes on time. These covenants ensure that the borrower fulfills certain obligations, which are essential for the smooth operation of the business. On the other hand, negative covenants refer to the actions that the borrower is restricted from taking without the lender's consent. These limitations aim to protect the lender's position and prevent any actions that could jeopardize the borrower's ability to repay the debt. Negative covenants commonly include restrictions on additional borrowing, dividend payments, asset sales, or entering into new contracts without the lender's approval. Debt covenants play a crucial role in managing the lender-borrower relationship and reducing the lender's risk exposure. By imposing restrictions and requirements, lenders can ensure that the borrower maintains financial discipline and protects their ability to recover their investment. Violating debt covenants can have severe consequences for the borrower, including higher interest rates, penalties, or even default. Therefore, it is essential for borrowers to carefully analyze and comply with the covenants specified in their loan agreements. Overall, debt covenants are an integral part of financial management, providing lenders with a mechanism to protect their interests and assess the borrower's creditworthiness continuously. By establishing clear conditions and limitations, debt covenants help maintain a mutually beneficial relationship between lenders and borrowers and contribute to the overall stability of the financial system.

Debt Equity Ratio

The debt equity ratio is a financial ratio that compares the total debt of a company to its total equity. It is a measure of the proportion of a company's financing that comes from debt compared to equity. In financial management, the debt equity ratio is an important metric as it provides insight into a company's capital structure and financial risk. It reflects the extent to which a company relies on borrowed funds versus funds contributed by its shareholders. By analyzing the debt equity ratio, investors and financial managers can assess a company's ability to meet its financial obligations and its overall financial stability. A higher debt equity ratio indicates that a company has a larger proportion of debt in its capital structure, which may increase its financial risk. Conversely, a lower debt equity ratio suggests a more conservative capital structure and less financial risk. In general, a debt equity ratio of less than 1 is considered favorable, as it indicates that a company has more equity than debt. This implies that the company is relying more on its own funds rather than external borrowing, which can enhance financial stability and flexibility. However, it is important to note that the optimal debt equity ratio varies across industries and depends on factors such as the company's risk tolerance, profitability, and cash flow generation. Industries that are more capital-intensive, such as manufacturing or infrastructure, may have higher debt equity ratios compared to service-based industries.

Debt Financing

Debt financing refers to a financial strategy in which a company raises funds by borrowing money from lenders or issuing bonds to investors, with an obligation to repay the borrowed amount along with interest within a specific time period. This method of financing involves taking on debt to meet the company's financial requirements or to fund business operations, investments, or capital expenditures. Debt financing can be categorized into two main types: short-term and long-term debt. Short-term debt typically includes loans or credit lines with a maturity period of less than a year, whereas long-term debt usually consists of loans, bonds, or debentures with a maturity period of more than a year. One of the primary advantages of debt financing is that it allows a company to acquire necessary funds without diluting ownership or control. By borrowing money, the company can maintain full ownership and control over its operations while using the borrowed funds to achieve its strategic objectives, such as expanding the business or investing in new projects. Furthermore, debt financing often provides tax benefits to companies, as the interest paid on the borrowed funds is tax-deductible. This can help reduce the overall tax liability of the company, increasing its profitability and cash flow. However, debt financing also involves certain risks and considerations. The company must carefully manage its debt levels to avoid an excessive burden of interest payments, which can negatively impact its financial health and solvency. High levels of debt can increase the company's financial risk and make it more vulnerable to economic downturns or changes in interest rates. Additionally, companies that rely heavily on debt financing may face challenges in obtaining new loans or bonds if lenders perceive them as having a high risk of default. This can limit the company's ability to raise additional funds in the future, hindering its growth and expansion prospects. In conclusion, debt financing is an important aspect of financial management that enables companies to raise funds by borrowing money or issuing bonds. It offers advantages such as maintaining ownership and control, tax benefits, and flexibility in funding strategic initiatives. However, it also poses risks related to debt levels and access to future financing. Therefore, companies must carefully assess and manage their debt financing strategies to ensure long-term financial stability and growth.

Debt Ratio

The debt ratio is a financial management metric used to measure the proportion of a company's total liabilities to its total assets. It indicates the degree of financial leverage or the extent to which a company relies on debt to finance its operations and investments. The formula to calculate the debt ratio is: Debt Ratio = Total Liabilities / Total Assets A higher debt ratio indicates a greater reliance on debt, while a lower debt ratio suggests a more conservative financial structure with a higher proportion of equity financing. The debt ratio is important for several reasons: 1. Financial Risk Assessment: The debt ratio helps stakeholders, including lenders, investors, and analysts, assess the financial risk associated with a company. A higher debt ratio implies a higher risk of default, as a significant portion of the company's assets is financed through debt. 2. Solvency and Liquidity Analysis: The debt ratio provides insights into a company's ability to meet its long-term obligations. A high debt ratio may indicate a company's inability to generate sufficient cash flow to repay its debt, potentially leading to liquidity issues and solvency concerns. 3. Capital Structure Evaluation: The debt ratio is a key determinant of a company's capital structure. It helps assess the balance between debt and equity financing, influencing the company's financial stability and flexibility. Companies with high debt ratios may be more vulnerable to economic downturns or fluctuations in interest rates. It is important to note that the optimal debt ratio varies across industries and depends on factors such as the company's growth prospects, cash flow generation, and industry norms. Comparing a company's debt ratio with industry peers and historical data can provide a more meaningful analysis. In conclusion, the debt ratio is a crucial financial management tool that helps evaluate a company's leverage, financial risk, solvency, and capital structure. A comprehensive understanding of the debt ratio is essential for making informed financial decisions and assessing a company's financial health.

Debt Service Coverage Ratio (DSCR)

The Debt Service Coverage Ratio (DSCR) is a measure used in financial management to determine the ability of a company or individual to meet its debt obligations. It is calculated by dividing the company's net operating income by its total debt service obligations. To calculate the DSCR, the net operating income is determined by subtracting all operating expenses, including but not limited to interest, taxes, and depreciation, from the company's total revenue. The total debt service obligations include all debt payments, such as interest and principal payments, due during a given period. The DSCR is expressed as a ratio, typically ranging from 0 to 2 or higher. A DSCR below 1 indicates that the company's net operating income is insufficient to cover its debt obligations, thereby indicating a higher risk of default. Conversely, a DSCR above 1 signifies that the company's net operating income is healthy enough to cover its debt payments, indicating a lower risk of default. The DSCR is an important financial metric used by lenders and investors to assess the creditworthiness and financial health of a company or individual. It provides insight into the company's ability to generate sufficient income to service its debt and indicates the level of risk associated with lending or investing in the company. Lenders often have minimum DSCR requirements that borrowers must meet to secure financing. A high DSCR is generally preferred, as it indicates a lower risk of default and a greater ability to repay the debt. A low DSCR, on the other hand, may limit the borrower's access to credit or result in higher interest rates to compensate for the increased risk. In conclusion, the Debt Service Coverage Ratio (DSCR) is a critical financial metric used to assess the ability of a company or individual to cover its debt obligations. It provides valuable information to lenders and investors and helps determine the level of risk associated with lending or investing in a particular entity.

Debt Service

Debt service refers to the regular and timely payment of principal and interest on outstanding debt. It encompasses the financial obligation that an entity has to meet its debt obligations over a specified period. Debt service is a crucial aspect of financial management as it directly impacts an organization's ability to borrow funds and maintain a favorable credit rating. The debt service schedule outlines the specific amounts and dates of payment for both principal and interest. This schedule is typically established when the debt is incurred and is essential for accurately budgeting and forecasting future cash flows. Debt service obligations are either short-term or long-term, depending on the repayment period. For businesses, debt service is primarily managed through cash flow generated from operations. Adequate cash flow is necessary to fulfill debt obligations while also covering other operational expenses. The ability to service debt strategically and efficiently is often a key consideration for lenders and investors when evaluating an organization's financial health and creditworthiness. In the context of personal finance, debt service refers to the repayment of personal debts, such as mortgages, student loans, and credit card balances. Individuals must budget their income and expenses to ensure they can consistently meet these debt repayments on time. Failure to meet debt service obligations can result in late fees, increased interest rates, and damage to one's credit score. Debt service ratios are frequently used to assess an entity's ability to service its debt. The debt service coverage ratio (DSCR) measures the availability of cash flow to cover debt payments. A higher DSCR indicates a greater capacity to service debt, while a lower ratio may indicate financial stress or difficulty meeting obligations. In conclusion, debt service refers to the regular payment of principal and interest on outstanding debt. It plays a critical role in financial management, impacting an organization's creditworthiness. Proper debt service management is crucial for both businesses and individuals to maintain a healthy financial position and fulfill their financial obligations.

Debtor-In-Possession (DIP) Financing

Debtor-in-Possession (DIP) financing is a type of financing arrangement that is used in the context of financial management when a company files for bankruptcy under Chapter 11 of the United States Bankruptcy Code. In this situation, the company is allowed to continue operating and managing its assets and business operations while it undergoes a reorganization process. During a Chapter 11 bankruptcy, the company becomes what is known as a "debtor-in-possession," meaning it retains control over its assets and operations. This is in contrast to other types of bankruptcy, such as Chapter 7, where a trustee is appointed to oversee the liquidation of the company's assets.

Default Premium

Default premium, in the context of financial management, refers to the additional interest or return expected by investors to compensate them for the risk associated with investing in securities issued by entities with a higher probability of defaulting on their financial obligations. When investors purchase securities, such as bonds or stocks, from entities with a higher risk of default, they demand a higher return on their investment to compensate for the increased likelihood of not receiving the expected payments or returns. This additional return is known as the default premium. It reflects the market's assessment of the entity's creditworthiness and the risks associated with investing in its securities.

Default Risk Premium

The default risk premium refers to the additional return that investors require as compensation for the uncertainty associated with default risk. In financial management, default risk refers to the possibility that a borrower will fail to make timely interest or principal payments on their debt obligations.In other words, when investors lend money to individuals, companies, or governments, there is always a chance that the borrower will default on their loan and fail to repay the borrowed amount. This default risk is influenced by various factors such as the borrower's creditworthiness, financial stability, and the economic and industry conditions in which they operate.The default risk premium is the difference between the interest rate offered on a risk-free investment, such as U.S. Treasury securities, and the interest rate on a particular debt instrument that incorporates the default risk. For example, if the risk-free rate is 3% and the interest rate on a corporate bond is 6%, the default risk premium would be 3%.This premium serves as compensation for the potential losses that investors may incur if the borrower defaults. It reflects the market's perception of the likelihood of default and the severity of potential losses. Higher default risk premiums are associated with higher levels of default risk and, therefore, require higher returns on investment to compensate for the increased uncertainty.Financial managers use the default risk premium as a crucial factor in their decision-making processes. When evaluating investment opportunities, they consider the default risk premium to determine whether the potential return justifies the level of risk. This helps them assess the attractiveness of different investment options and make informed decisions based on their risk tolerance and return objectives.

Default Risk

Default risk refers to the possibility that a borrower or debtor will not be able to meet its financial obligations, resulting in a default on their loan or debt repayment. In financial management, default risk is a critical concept as it highlights the potential for loss faced by lenders and investors when providing funds or extending credit to borrowers. Default risk is influenced by various factors, including the creditworthiness and financial stability of the borrower, the level of debt, the industry and economic conditions, as well as the specific terms and conditions of the loan or debt agreement. Lenders and investors assess default risk by analyzing a range of quantitative and qualitative factors.

Default

The term "financial management" refers to the process of planning, organizing, directing, and controlling the financial activities of an organization. It involves the strategic allocation of resources and the strategic management of the financial functions within the organization. Financial management entails various activities, including financial planning, budgeting, resource allocation, financial analysis, and financial reporting. These activities are crucial for the success and sustainability of any organization, whether it is a business entity or a nonprofit organization.

Defensive Stock

A defensive stock is a type of investment that is considered relatively safe and stable in times of economic downturn or market volatility. It is typically associated with companies that provide essential goods or services, such as utilities, healthcare, or consumer staples, which are less influenced by changes in the overall economy. Defensive stocks are often sought by investors who have a conservative investment strategy and prioritize capital preservation over high returns. These stocks tend to have predictable cash flows and stable earnings, making them less susceptible to major fluctuations in the market. As a result, they are often seen as a reliable source of income and a way to mitigate risk in a portfolio.

Deferred Annuity

A deferred annuity is a financial instrument that allows individuals to save money for retirement and receive regular income payments at a later date. It is a contract between the individual, known as the annuitant, and an insurance company or other financial institution. With a deferred annuity, the annuitant deposits money into the contract over a period of time, known as the accumulation phase. During this phase, the funds grow tax-deferred, meaning that the annuitant does not have to pay taxes on any gains until they start receiving income payments. Once the annuitant reaches a certain age, typically around 59½, they can choose to start receiving income payments from the annuity. This is known as the annuitization phase. The annuitant can select from various payment options, such as receiving a fixed amount each month for a specified period or receiving payments for the remainder of their life. One of the main benefits of a deferred annuity is the ability to accumulate funds over time without being taxed on the gains. This can be advantageous for individuals who are looking to save for retirement and want to maximize their savings potential. Deferred annuities also offer some degree of flexibility. The annuitant can typically make additional contributions to the annuity, which can help increase the overall value of the contract. Additionally, some annuities allow for partial withdrawals or lump sum withdrawals in case of emergencies or unexpected expenses. However, it is important to note that there are some drawbacks to deferred annuities as well. One downside is the potential for surrender charges or penalties if the annuitant decides to withdraw funds before a certain period of time. These charges can vary depending on the specific annuity contract and may reduce the overall value of the annuity. In conclusion, a deferred annuity is a savings and income vehicle that allows individuals to save for retirement and receive regular income payments at a later date. It provides tax-deferred growth and offers flexibility in terms of contributions and withdrawal options. However, it is important to carefully consider the terms and fees associated with the annuity before making a decision.

Deferred Tax Asset

A deferred tax asset is an accounting concept used in the field of financial management that represents a potential reduction in future tax liabilities. It arises when the amount of taxes paid or payable in the current financial year, as determined by tax authorities, is higher than the amount of taxes recognized in the books of a company or individual for that same period. The recognition of a deferred tax asset allows the entity to offset the difference between the tax reported in the financial statements and the tax payable to the tax authorities, resulting in a reduction of future tax expenses. The asset is only recorded if it is probable that the entity will have sufficient future taxable income against which the deferred tax asset can be offset. It is important to note that the realization of the deferred tax asset depends on the company's ability to generate taxable income in the future. The main reason behind the existence of deferred tax assets is the difference in timing between when expenses or losses are recognized for financial accounting purposes and when they are recognized for tax purposes. This is due to the different set of rules and regulations that govern financial accounting and taxation. For example, certain expenses may be deducted in the financial statements immediately, but the tax authorities may only allow them to be deducted over a period of several years. A deferred tax asset can also arise from the utilization of tax credits or carryforwards, which are incentives provided by tax authorities to encourage specific behaviors or investments. These tax benefits can be carried forward to future years when they are expected to result in tax savings. For example, a research and development tax credit or a net operating loss carryforward can create a deferred tax asset.

Deflation

Deflation in the context of Financial Management refers to a sustained decrease in the general price level of goods and services in an economy over a period of time. This is characterized by a negative inflation rate, meaning that prices are falling rather than rising. Deflation is the opposite of inflation and can have significant implications for various aspects of financial management. Deflation can occur due to various factors, such as a decrease in demand for goods and services, increased productivity and efficiency, technological advancements, or a decrease in the money supply. When the general price level falls, consumers may postpone purchases as they anticipate further price declines. This can lead to a decrease in consumer spending, which can negatively impact businesses and overall economic growth.

Degree Of Operating Leverage (DOL)

The Degree of Operating Leverage (DOL) is a financial metric that measures the sensitivity of operating income to changes in sales volume. It reveals the percentage change in operating income resulting from a given percentage change in sales. In other words, DOL quantifies the impact of sales variations on a company's profitability. DOL is computed by dividing the percentage change in operating income by the percentage change in sales. It is commonly expressed as a ratio or a decimal value. A high DOL indicates a higher degree of operating leverage, which means that a small change in sales volume will have a significant effect on operating income, while a low DOL implies a lower sensitivity to sales fluctuations.

Delphi Method

The Delphi method is a structured and iterative approach used in financial management to obtain a consensus from a group of experts or participants on a specific issue or problem, especially when there is a lack of complete information or uncertainty surrounding the topic. This method involves a series of questionnaires or surveys that are administered to the participants anonymously. The purpose is to gather individual opinions, judgments, and insights without any bias or influence from other participants. The responses are collected, analyzed, and summarized by a facilitator or researcher who then provides a feedback report to the participants. The Delphi method fosters a systematic and controlled process of information exchange and feedback, which allows for multiple rounds of iteration. It encourages participants to reevaluate and revise their initial responses in light of the collective group's opinion, thereby promoting convergence towards a consensus or agreement. The anonymity of the participants and the absence of face-to-face interaction reduce the potential for dominant individuals or group dynamics to unduly influence the outcome. This approach mitigates the impact of hierarchical or power differentials within the group and encourages unbiased and independent thinking. The Delphi method also incorporates statistical techniques and feedback mechanisms to ensure the quality and reliability of the results. The facilitator reviews and summarizes the responses, identifies areas of agreement or disagreement, and provides a range of perspectives to the participants in subsequent rounds. By utilizing the Delphi method in financial management, organizations can tap into the collective intelligence and expertise of a diverse set of individuals, including industry professionals, financial analysts, researchers, and academics. It is particularly useful in situations involving strategic decision-making, forecasting, risk assessment, and policy development. In conclusion, the Delphi method facilitates the systematic gathering and synthesis of expert opinions in financial management. It enables organizations to make informed and robust decisions by leveraging the wisdom of the crowd while minimizing biases and uncertainties associated with complex financial issues.

Depreciation Expense

Depreciation Expense refers to the allocation of an asset's cost over its useful life. It represents the decrease in value or the wear and tear that an asset experiences as it is used in the production process or in generating revenue. It is a critical concept in financial management as it allows businesses to accurately account for the reduction in value of their assets over time. Depreciation Expense is a non-cash expense, meaning it does not involve the actual outflow of cash. Instead, it is a way to properly match the cost of an asset with the revenue it helps generate. By recognizing the expense over the asset's useful life, the company can spread the cost of the asset over the period during which it is used, rather than having to deduct the full cost in the year of purchase.

Depreciation Method

Depreciation Method refers to the systematic allocation of the cost of an asset over its useful life. It is a financial management concept that allows companies to spread the cost of an asset over the periods in which it provides economic benefits. Depreciation is an accounting technique used to reflect the gradual reduction in the value of an asset over time due to wear and tear, obsolescence, or other factors. By expensing a portion of the asset's cost each accounting period, companies can accurately reflect the asset's declining value on their financial statements.

Depreciation Recapture

Depreciation recapture in financial management refers to the process of reclaiming tax deductions previously taken for depreciating assets. When a business or individual sells an asset that has been depreciated for tax purposes, the tax code requires them to recapture a portion of the previously claimed depreciation as taxable income. This recapture is necessary because depreciation deductions allow businesses and individuals to reduce their taxable income in order to defer paying taxes on the asset's value over its useful life. However, when the asset is sold, the recapture rule ensures that the tax advantage gained from the depreciation deductions is not completely permanent.

Depreciation Schedule

A depreciation schedule is a financial tool used by businesses to allocate the cost of an asset over its useful life. It is a detailed record that outlines the annual depreciation expense of an asset, typically for accounting and tax purposes. The schedule is prepared based on various depreciation methods such as straight-line, declining balance, or units of production method, which determine how the asset's value will be distributed over time. The purpose of a depreciation schedule is to accurately reflect the reduction in value of an asset as it ages or becomes less efficient. By spreading out the cost of an asset over its useful life, businesses can match the expense with the revenue generated by the asset, resulting in more accurate financial statements. The schedule usually includes information such as the asset's initial cost, expected useful life, salvage value, and the chosen depreciation method. It also provides a breakdown of the depreciation expense for each year, allowing businesses to track the asset's decreasing value and estimate its remaining book value. In addition to aiding in financial reporting, depreciation schedules also play a crucial role in tax planning. Depending on the jurisdiction and applicable tax laws, businesses may be able to deduct the depreciation expense from their taxable income, reducing their overall tax liability. By regularly updating and maintaining an accurate depreciation schedule, businesses can ensure compliance with accounting standards and tax regulations. It also allows them to make informed decisions regarding asset repairs, replacements, or upgrades, as they can assess the asset's remaining useful life and cost-effectiveness. In conclusion, a depreciation schedule is an essential financial management tool that helps businesses allocate the cost of an asset over its useful life. It provides a detailed record of the asset's decreasing value and aids in financial reporting and tax planning. By accurately accounting for depreciation, businesses can make informed decisions and improve their overall financial management.

Depreciation

Depreciation is a financial concept used in the field of management accounting to account for the decrease in value of an asset over time. It is an allocation method that reflects the systematic consumption, wear and tear, or obsolescence of an asset's economic benefits." When an asset is acquired, it is expected to provide economic benefits to the organization over its useful life. However, as the asset is utilized or becomes outdated, its value gradually diminishes. In order to accurately reflect the true worth of the asset on the balance sheet, depreciation is used to allocate the cost of the asset over its useful life.

Derivative

A derivative is a financial instrument that derives its value from an underlying asset or set of assets. It is a contract between two parties, typically a buyer and a seller, where they agree to exchange cash flows or ownership rights based on the performance of the underlying asset(s). The value of a derivative is derived from the changes in the value of the underlying asset. This can include commodities, currencies, stocks, bonds, interest rates, or other financial variables. Derivatives can be categorized into four main types: options, futures, forwards, and swaps. Options give the buyer the right, but not the obligation, to buy or sell the underlying asset at a specific price within a specified period. Futures contracts specify the purchase or sale of the underlying asset at a predetermined price and future date. Forwards are similar to futures but are customized agreements between two parties. Swaps involve the exchange of cash flows or liabilities based on variables such as interest rates or exchange rates. Derivatives serve various purposes in financial management. They can be used for hedging, which is the practice of reducing or eliminating financial risks. For example, a company may use a futures contract to hedge against the risk of price fluctuations in a commodity it needs for production. Derivatives can also be used for speculation, where investors bet on the future price movements of the underlying assets to generate profits. It is essential to note that while derivatives can provide opportunities for profit or risk management, they also carry inherent risks. One of the major risks associated with derivatives is the possibility of losing more than the initial investment. Market volatility and unexpected events can impact the value of the underlying asset and, consequently, the value of the derivative. Financial institutions and investors often use derivatives to manage their portfolios and optimize their risk-return trade-offs. They help in diversifying portfolios, managing interest rate risk, currency risk, and other market-related risks. However, the complexity and potential risks involved in derivative transactions require thorough understanding and analysis to ensure effective financial management.

Diluted Earnings Per Share (Diluted EPS)

Diluted Earnings Per Share (Diluted EPS) is a financial metric that indicates the amount of a company's earnings available to each outstanding share of common stock after taking into account the potential dilution from various sources, such as stock options, convertible securities, and other potential common stock. It is an important measure used by investors and analysts to assess the true earning power of a company and its ability to generate profits from its operations. Diluted EPS is calculated by dividing the net income (after deducting preferred dividends) by the weighted average number of common shares outstanding, including the potential dilutive effect of stock options, convertible securities, and other potential common stock.

Dilution

Dilution, in the context of financial management, refers to the reduction of ownership or control of existing shareholders in a company as a result of the issuance of new shares or securities. When a company decides to raise additional capital through equity financing, it often issues new shares to investors. This process, known as a primary offering, can result in dilution for existing shareholders. Dilution occurs because the total number of shares outstanding increases, thereby reducing the proportional ownership and control of existing shareholders.

Direct Costs

Direct costs, in the context of financial management, refer to the expenses that can be directly attributed to the production or provision of a specific product or service. These costs are incurred as a result of the direct labor, materials, or other inputs that are directly used in the production process. Direct costs are often categorized as either direct labor costs or direct material costs. Direct labor costs include the wages or salaries paid to the workers who are directly involved in the production process. These costs can include the wages of assembly line workers, machine operators, or other personnel directly involved in the production process. Direct material costs, on the other hand, include the cost of the materials or components that are directly used in the production process. These costs can include the cost of raw materials, components, or other inputs that are directly used to create the final product. Direct costs are important for financial management because they provide an accurate picture of the costs directly associated with the production or provision of a specific product or service. By understanding and tracking direct costs, companies can make informed decisions regarding pricing, profitability, and resource allocation. For example, companies can use direct costs to determine the cost per unit of a product, which can then be compared to the sales price to determine profitability. Direct costs can also be used to identify areas of inefficiency or waste in the production process, allowing companies to make adjustments and improve overall cost-effectiveness. In summary, direct costs are the expenses that are directly incurred as a result of the production or provision of a specific product or service. These costs include direct labor costs, such as wages or salaries paid to workers involved in the production process, and direct material costs, such as the cost of raw materials or components used in the production process. Understanding and tracking direct costs is essential for financial management, as it provides valuable information for pricing, profitability analysis, and resource allocation decisions.

Discount Broker

A discount broker, in the context of financial management, refers to a type of brokerage firm that provides clients with the ability to buy and sell securities at a significantly lower cost compared to full-service brokers. Unlike full-service brokers, discount brokers typically offer minimal or no investment advice or personalized service. They primarily focus on executing trades on behalf of clients, providing basic investment tools, and facilitating transactions in the financial markets.

Discount Rate

The discount rate, in the context of Financial Management, refers to the interest rate used to determine the present value of future cash flows. It represents the rate of return required by an investor or company in order to invest in a particular project or asset. Essentially, the discount rate takes into consideration the time value of money, which is the concept that money available today is worth more than the same amount of money in the future due to its potential earning capacity. By discounting future cash flows to their present value, the discount rate accounts for this difference in worth over time.

Discounted Cash Flow (DCF) Analysis

Discounted Cash Flow (DCF) Analysis is a financial management technique used to evaluate the value of an investment or a company by examining the cash flows it is expected to generate in the future. This analysis takes into account the time value of money, recognizing that a dollar received in the future is worth less than a dollar received today. The DCF analysis involves forecasting the cash flows expected to be generated by the investment or company over a certain period of time, typically several years. These cash flows include both operating cash flows, such as revenue and expenses, as well as financing cash flows, such as debt payments and capital expenditures. The cash flows are then discounted back to the present using a discount rate to account for the time value of money. The discount rate used in the DCF analysis represents the opportunity cost of investing in the investment or company under evaluation. It reflects the return an investor could earn by investing in an alternative investment with a similar level of risk. The discount rate is typically determined by considering factors such as the required rate of return, the risk-free rate of return, and the company's cost of capital. The key assumption in the DCF analysis is that the value of an investment or company is equal to the present value of the expected future cash flows it will generate. By discounting the future cash flows back to the present, the DCF analysis provides an estimate of the value of the investment or company. If the estimated value is higher than the current market price, the investment or company may be considered undervalued and a potential buying opportunity. On the other hand, if the estimated value is lower than the current market price, the investment or company may be considered overvalued and a potential selling opportunity. The DCF analysis has its limitations, as it relies on assumptions and forecasts that may be subject to error. It also requires the selection of an appropriate discount rate, which can be subjective and vary based on individual or market perceptions of risk. However, despite these limitations, the DCF analysis is a widely used and accepted tool in financial management for assessing the value of investments and companies.

Discounted Cash Flow (DCF)

Discounted Cash Flow (DCF) is a financial management method used to evaluate the value of an investment or business project by estimating its future cash flows and discounting them back to their present value. The DCF analysis takes into account the time value of money, which states that a dollar received in the future is worth less than a dollar received today. The concept is based on the principle that money has potential earning capacity and can be invested to earn returns over time. To perform a DCF analysis, future cash flows are projected over a specified time period, usually using financial forecasts and assumptions. These cash flows represent the inflows and outflows of money that the investment or project is expected to generate. The accuracy and reliability of the cash flow projections are crucial for the accuracy of the DCF valuation. Once the cash flows are estimated, they are discounted back to their present value using a discount rate. The discount rate is a rate of return that reflects the cost of capital and the risk associated with the investment or project. It represents the rate at which future cash flows are brought back to their present value. The higher the discount rate, the lower the present value of the cash flows. The DCF valuation is calculated by summing the present value of all projected cash flows, including the initial investment and any terminal value. The terminal value represents the value of the investment or project at the end of the projected period. It is usually estimated using a multiple of the final year cash flow or by applying a perpetuity formula. DCF analysis is commonly used in financial management to make investment decisions, evaluate business projects, and value companies. It is a widely accepted method because it takes into account the time value of money and provides a more accurate estimate of the true value of an investment or project. However, it is important to note that the DCF analysis relies heavily on the accuracy and reasonableness of the assumptions and projections made, and small changes in these inputs can significantly impact the valuation result.

Discounted Payback Period

The discounted payback period is a financial management metric used to evaluate the length of time it takes for a project to generate enough cash flows to recoup its initial investment, while also taking into account the time value of money. Specifically, it calculates the number of years required for the present value of the project's cash inflows to equal or exceed the initial investment. To calculate the discounted payback period, the future cash flows of the project are discounted back to their present value using an appropriate discount rate, which reflects the opportunity cost of capital. The present value of each cash flow is calculated by dividing the cash flow by $(1 + \text{discount rate})^n$, where n represents the number of years from the present. The discounted cash flows are then cumulatively added up until the cumulative sum becomes equal to or greater than the initial investment. The discounted payback period offers several advantages over the traditional payback period. Firstly, it considers the time value of money, which recognizes the fact that a dollar received in the future is worth less than a dollar received today due to inflation and other factors. Secondly, it incorporates the cost of the capital used to fund the project, which provides a more realistic assessment of its profitability. Lastly, it helps prioritize projects by identifying those with shorter payback periods, enabling management to allocate resources more efficiently. However, the discounted payback period also has some limitations. It does not account for cash flows that occur after the payback period, which can lead to projects being incorrectly excluded or undervalued. Additionally, it relies on the accuracy of the discount rate, which can be challenging to estimate. Furthermore, it does not incorporate qualitative factors such as risk, market conditions, and strategic alignment, which are crucial for comprehensive project evaluation. In conclusion, the discounted payback period is a valuable tool in financial management for assessing the time it takes for a project to recover its initial investment while considering the time value of money. It provides a more accurate representation of a project's profitability and helps in the prioritization of investment opportunities. However, it is important to consider its limitations and supplement it with other financial metrics and qualitative analysis to make well-informed decisions.

Diversifiable Risk

Diversifiable risk, also known as unsystematic risk or specific risk, refers to the portion of an investment's risk that can be eliminated through diversification. It is a type of risk that is specific to individual assets or a particular industry, and is not related to the overall movements of the market or the economy as a whole. Diversifiable risk arises due to factors that are unique to a particular company or sector, such as company-specific events or industry-specific trends. These risks can be mitigated or reduced by investing in a diversified portfolio that includes a variety of different assets across various industries and sectors.

Diversification Benefit

The diversification benefit refers to the principle in financial management where an investor can reduce their overall risk by constructing a portfolio of investments that is comprised of a variety of different assets. By including assets that are not highly correlated with each other in the portfolio, the investor can potentially increase their return while at the same time decreasing the overall volatility. When considering the diversification benefit, it is important to understand the difference between systematic risk and unsystematic risk. Systematic risk, also known as market risk, is the risk that is inherent in the entire market or economy and cannot be eliminated through diversification. Unsystematic risk, on the other hand, is the risk that is specific to individual assets or industries and can be reduced through diversification. The goal of diversification is to reduce unsystematic risk by spreading investments across different asset classes, industries, and regions. By doing so, any negative events or downturns that affect one particular asset or industry are less likely to have a significant impact on the entire portfolio. For example, if an investor were to have a portfolio consisting solely of stocks in the technology sector, they would be highly exposed to any negative events or market downturns that affect that specific industry. However, if the investor also includes investments in other sectors such as healthcare, consumer goods, or real estate, the impact of any negative events on the technology sector would be lessened. The diversification benefit is not limited to just different asset classes or industries, but can also be achieved through geographical diversification. By including investments from different regions or countries, an investor can further decrease the overall risk of their portfolio. This is because different regions or countries may have different economic cycles or market trends, and by investing in a variety of different regions, the investor can potentially benefit from the growth or stability of one region even if another region is experiencing a downturn. Overall, the diversification benefit is an essential principle in financial management that allows investors to reduce risk by constructing a portfolio of assets that are not highly correlated with each other. By including investments from different asset classes, industries, and regions, investors can potentially increase their return while lowering the overall volatility of their portfolio.

Diversification

Diversification, in the context of financial management, refers to the strategy of spreading investment funds across various assets and asset classes to reduce overall risk. The primary objective of diversification is to create a well-balanced portfolio that can potentially mitigate the impact of adverse events on individual investments or sectors within the portfolio. By diversifying investments, individuals or organizations increase the likelihood of achieving more consistent returns over time. This is because different assets and asset classes tend to have varying levels of sensitivity to economic, market, and political conditions. When some investments perform poorly due to unfavorable conditions, others may perform well, thus offsetting the losses. There are several ways to achieve diversification in a portfolio. One common approach is to invest in different asset classes, such as stocks, bonds, real estate, and commodities. Each asset class has its own risk and return characteristics, and by combining them, investors can potentially benefit from their different performance patterns over time. Additionally, within each asset class, diversification can be achieved by investing in a range of securities. For example, in the stock market, investors can diversify by purchasing stocks from different industries or regions. Similarly, in the bond market, diversification can be achieved by investing in bonds with varied maturities, credit ratings, and issuers. Another way to diversify a portfolio is by including investments with different levels of risk. This includes both conservative investments with low-risk and lower returns, such as government bonds, as well as more aggressive investments with higher risk and potential for higher returns, such as small-cap stocks or emerging market equities. It is important to note that diversification does not guarantee profits or protect against losses, but it can help mitigate risk. This is because diversification cannot completely eliminate the possibility of loss, particularly in the event of a systemic market downturn. However, by spreading investments, diversification aims to reduce the impact of any single investment's poor performance on the overall portfolio.

Diversified Portfolio

A diversified portfolio is a financial management strategy that involves investing in a wide variety of assets across different classes, sectors, and geographies to minimize risk and maximize returns. The main objective of a diversified portfolio is to spread out investments across different areas in order to reduce the impact of any losses that may occur in a particular investment or asset class. This strategy is based on the belief that different investments will perform differently over time, and by diversifying, an investor can reduce the overall risk of their portfolio. A diversified portfolio typically includes a mix of stocks, bonds, mutual funds, real estate, commodities, and other investment vehicles. By having a mix of different asset classes, the portfolio is less susceptible to fluctuations in any one market or sector. For example, if there is a downturn in the stock market, the investor's exposure to other asset classes such as bonds or real estate may help offset those losses. Furthermore, a diversified portfolio may also include investments in different sectors or industries. This is done to mitigate the risk associated with any one sector. For instance, if an investor has a significant portion of their portfolio invested in technology stocks and there is a sudden decline in the tech sector, the impact on the overall portfolio will be reduced if there are other sectors performing well. In addition to diversification by asset class and sector, a diversified portfolio may also include investments in different geographies. By investing in different countries or regions, the portfolio is less exposed to risks that are specific to a particular country or region. This can include political instability, regulatory changes, or economic uncertainties. While diversification can reduce risk, it does not guarantee profits or protect against losses. Certain risks, such as systemic risks or unforeseen economic events, can affect all investments regardless of diversification. Therefore, it is important for investors to regularly review and rebalance their diversified portfolios to ensure they align with their financial goals and risk tolerance.

Dividend Aristocrat

A Dividend Aristocrat refers to a company that has consistently increased its dividend payment to shareholders for at least 25 consecutive years. It is a prestigious and highly sought-after designation within the financial management field, indicating the company's financial stability and ability to generate consistent cash flows. To be classified as a Dividend Aristocrat, a company must meet certain criteria and follow strict dividend policies. The primary requirement is a track record of increasing dividends for a minimum of 25 years, which demonstrates the company's commitment to sharing its profits with shareholders. This consistent dividend growth signals the company's financial strength, as it reflects the ability to generate sustainable earnings over the long term. Dividend Aristocrats are typically large, well-established companies with a solid market reputation. They often operate in mature industries with stable demand and have a history of delivering consistent financial performance. These companies possess strong competitive advantages, allowing them to generate robust cash flows even in challenging economic conditions. The Dividend Aristocrat designation is highly regarded by investors as it signifies a company's commitment to returning value to shareholders. Dividends are a crucial component of total return in investment, and a consistent dividend growth track record indicates a company's ability to create wealth for its shareholders. Investors often consider Dividend Aristocrats as attractive investment opportunities due to their ability to provide a regular income stream and potential capital appreciation. Moreover, their consistent dividend growth can act as a hedge against inflation, ensuring that shareholders' returns keep pace with the rising cost of living. It is important to note that not all dividend-paying companies are Dividend Aristocrats. The designation is specific to companies that meet the strict criteria of consistent dividend growth for at least 25 years. Investors interested in Dividend Aristocrats should conduct thorough research and analysis before making investment decisions.

Dividend Aristocrats

Dividend Aristocrats are a select group of companies that have consistently increased their dividends for at least 25 consecutive years. This designation is a testament to a company's financial stability, profitability, and commitment to returning value to their shareholders. To be considered a Dividend Aristocrat, a company must meet certain criteria. Firstly, it must be a member of the S&P 500 index, which comprises the largest publicly traded companies in the United States. Secondly, it must have a track record of increasing its dividend payout every year for a minimum of 25 years. Companies that fail to meet these requirements are not eligible for the Dividend Aristocrat status. The ability to consistently raise dividends for such an extended period is an indication of a company's strong financial position and sustainable growth. Dividend Aristocrats typically exhibit characteristics such as stable cash flows, solid management, and a competitive advantage in their respective industries. These companies have managed to navigate various economic and market cycles while still rewarding their shareholders with consistent dividend increases. Being a Dividend Aristocrat has several implications for both investors and the company itself. For investors, these companies offer the potential for a reliable and growing income stream. Dividend payments can provide a steady source of cash flow, particularly for income-oriented investors who rely on dividend income to cover their expenses or reinvest in other investments. For the companies themselves, the Dividend Aristocrat status can enhance their reputation and attract long-term investors. It demonstrates a commitment to shareholder value and signals financial stability and consistency. Dividend Aristocrats tend to have a lower cost of capital as they enjoy favorable borrowing terms and easier access to capital markets.

Dividend Cover

Dividend cover is a financial ratio used in financial management that measures how many times a company's earnings can cover the payment of dividends to its shareholders. It is also known as the dividend coverage ratio. Dividend cover is calculated by dividing the company's earnings per share (EPS) by its dividend per share (DPS). The formula for dividend cover is: Dividend cover = EPS / DPS A higher dividend cover ratio indicates that a company has sufficient earnings to cover its dividend payments. This is generally seen as a positive sign for investors, as it suggests that the company is generating enough profits to support its dividend policy. On the other hand, a lower dividend cover ratio may indicate that a company's earnings are not enough to cover its dividend payments. This could be a cause for concern, as it may suggest that the company is dipping into its reserves or borrowing money to fund its dividend payments, which could be unsustainable in the long run. Dividend cover is an important ratio for both investors and management. For investors, it provides insight into the company's ability to generate profits and sustain its dividend payments. A high dividend cover ratio is generally seen as a positive signal that the company is financially healthy and capable of distributing dividends. On the other hand, a low dividend cover ratio may indicate financial difficulties and raise doubts about the sustainability of the dividend policy. For management, dividend cover is used as a tool to evaluate the appropriateness of dividend payments. They can use the ratio to assess if the company's earnings are sufficient to cover the expected dividend payments and adjust the dividend policy accordingly. It can also be used as a benchmark to compare the company's dividend policy with industry peers and competitors.

Dividend Coverage Ratio

The dividend coverage ratio is a financial metric used in the field of financial management to assess a company's ability to pay dividends to its shareholders. It measures the company's capacity to generate enough cash from its operations to cover the dividend payments, ensuring that the dividends are sustainable and not at risk of being cut in the future. The formula to calculate the dividend coverage ratio is: Dividend Coverage Ratio = (Net Income - Preferred Dividends) / Dividends In this formula, the key components are: - Net Income: This refers to the company's total earnings after subtracting all expenses, taxes, and interest. It is a measure of profitability. - Preferred Dividends: This refers to any dividend payments made to preferred shareholders, usually at a fixed rate. - Dividends: This represents the total amount of dividends paid to common shareholders. The primary purpose of the dividend coverage ratio is to evaluate whether a company has sufficient earnings to sustain its dividend policy. A ratio above 1 indicates that the company has generated enough net income to cover the dividend payments, suggesting that it is financially healthy and able to fulfill its dividend obligations. On the other hand, a ratio below 1 may indicate that the company's earnings are not enough to support the dividend payments, which could be a signal of potential financial challenges or an unsustainable dividend policy. Financial managers and investors use the dividend coverage ratio to make informed decisions regarding dividend payments and investments in dividend-paying stocks. A high dividend coverage ratio is generally considered favorable, as it suggests that the company has a stable income stream and can continue to provide reliable dividend payments. Conversely, a low ratio may raise concerns about the company's ability to sustain its dividend policy in the long term and could result in a lower stock valuation.

Dividend Discount Model (DDM)

The Dividend Discount Model (DDM) is a financial model used in financial management to estimate the value of a company's stock based on the present value of its future dividends. It assumes that the intrinsic value of a stock is equal to the present value of all the future dividends that the stock is expected to generate. The DDM calculates the value of a stock by discounting its expected dividends back to the present at an appropriate discount rate. The discount rate used in the model is typically determined by the company's cost of equity, which is the return required by investors to hold the stock. The model assumes that dividends grow at a constant rate, known as the dividend growth rate, and this growth rate is used to estimate the future dividends of the stock. In order to use the DDM, financial managers need to make several assumptions. They need to estimate the future dividends that the company is expected to pay, the dividend growth rate, and the appropriate discount rate. These assumptions are based on the company's historical financial data, industry trends, and other relevant factors. The DDM is most commonly used for valuing stocks of companies that pay regular dividends, as the model heavily relies on the estimation of these dividends. One limitation of the DDM is that it does not account for factors such as changes in the company's risk profile or fluctuations in the market. It assumes that the company's dividend growth rate will remain constant indefinitely, which may not always be the case. Additionally, the accuracy of the model heavily depends on the accuracy of the assumptions made by financial managers. Small deviations in these assumptions can lead to significant deviations in the estimated value of the stock.

Dividend Growth Model

The Dividend Growth Model is a financial management tool used to estimate the value of a company's stock based on its dividend payments and the expected growth rate of those dividends. It assumes that the value of a stock is equal to the present value of all future dividends that it will pay to investors. The model is based on the principle that investors buy stocks primarily for the income they generate through dividend payments. By analyzing the company's historical dividend payments and its projected growth rate, investors can determine the intrinsic value of the stock.

Dividend Growth Rate

The dividend growth rate, in the context of financial management, refers to the annual rate of increase in a company's dividend payments to its shareholders over a specified period of time. It is a key measure used in evaluating the attractiveness of an investment in dividend-paying stocks. Calculating the dividend growth rate involves comparing the dividends paid out by a company in different years. The formula for determining the dividend growth rate is: (Ending Dividend - Beginning Dividend) / Beginning Dividend x 100 Where the "Ending Dividend" represents the most recent dividend payment, and the "Beginning Dividend" represents the dividend payment from the previous period. A higher dividend growth rate is generally seen as more favorable for investors. It indicates that the company is increasing its dividend payments at a rapid pace, which can result in higher returns for shareholders. On the other hand, a lower or negative dividend growth rate may suggest that the company is experiencing financial difficulties or is prioritizing other uses of its earnings. Investors often consider the dividend growth rate along with other factors, such as the company's financial stability, industry trends, and future earnings prospects, to make informed investment decisions. The dividend growth rate can help investors gauge the potential long-term profitability of an investment and can be used to compare different stocks within the same industry or sector. Additionally, the dividend growth rate can also be used to estimate the future potential income from an investment. By assuming a steady growth rate, investors can project the potential future income they may receive from dividend payments. However, it is important to note that the dividend growth rate is not a guarantee of future performance, as market conditions and company factors can impact a company's ability to sustain or increase its dividend payments.

Dividend Irrelevance Theory

The dividend irrelevance theory is a concept in financial management that suggests that a firm's dividend policy has no impact on its value and therefore, it is irrelevant for investors in determining the value of a company. Proposed by Modigliani and Miller in the 1960s, this theory contradicts the traditional belief that the payment of dividends affects the overall worth of a firm. According to the dividend irrelevance theory, the value of a company is determined by its income-generating potential and the risk associated with its future earnings, rather than the amount of dividends it pays. In other words, investors are primarily concerned with the expected cash flows from their investment and are indifferent to whether those cash flows come in the form of dividends or capital gains. This theory is based on several assumptions. Firstly, it assumes that investors have access to the same information and possess rational behavior, allowing them to accurately assess the future earnings potential of a company. Additionally, it assumes that capital markets are efficient and free from any trading restrictions or taxes. Lastly, it assumes that the investment decisions of a company are not affected by its dividend policy. The dividend irrelevance theory has important implications for both investors and managers. For investors, it means that they should focus on the fundamental characteristics of a company, such as its profitability and growth prospects, rather than its dividend policy when making investment decisions. On the other hand, for managers, it suggests that they have flexibility in designing their dividend policies, as it will not directly impact the value of the firm. However, it is important to note that while the dividend irrelevance theory may hold true in theory, in practice, the payment of dividends can have signaling effects. For example, a company that consistently increases its dividends may signal to the market that it has confidence in its future prospects, leading to an increase in its stock price. Similarly, a decrease in dividends may signal financial distress or lack of growth opportunities, leading to a decrease in the stock price. In conclusion, the dividend irrelevance theory posits that a firm's dividend policy has no bearing on its overall value. Investors are primarily concerned with the future cash flows generated by a company rather than the dividends it pays. While this theory holds true in theory, in practice, dividend payments can have signaling effects that impact a company's stock price.

Dividend Payout Ratio

The dividend payout ratio is a financial metric used by companies to determine the proportion of earnings that are distributed to shareholders in the form of dividends. It is a measure of how much of a company's net income is being paid out to shareholders rather than being reinvested back into the business. The formula for calculating the dividend payout ratio is: Dividend Payout Ratio = Dividends Paid / Net Income Typically, the dividend payout ratio is expressed as a percentage. A higher payout ratio indicates that a larger proportion of a company's earnings is being distributed to shareholders, while a lower payout ratio suggests that more of the earnings are being retained by the company for future growth opportunities. There are several factors that can influence a company's dividend payout ratio. These can include the company's growth prospects, financial stability, cash flow position, and its dividend policy. It is important for companies to strike a balance between paying dividends to shareholders and retaining earnings for reinvestment, as it can impact the company's ability to finance future growth initiatives. Investors use the dividend payout ratio as one of the metrics to evaluate a company's dividend-paying ability. Companies that have a long history of paying consistent dividends, along with a high dividend payout ratio, are often viewed favorably by income-seeking investors. On the other hand, companies with low or no dividends may be more attractive to growth-focused investors who prefer that the company reinvest its earnings back into the business. It is important to note that the dividend payout ratio should not be analyzed in isolation. It should be compared to industry peers and historical trends to gain a better understanding of a company's dividend policy and sustainability. Additionally, companies should consider other financial factors, such as debt levels and capital expenditures, when determining an appropriate dividend payout ratio.

Dividend Policy

A dividend policy is a strategic decision made by a company's management team regarding the amount and frequency of dividend payments to its shareholders. This decision determines the portion of the company's earnings that will be distributed to shareholders as dividends, as opposed to being retained for reinvestment in future projects or other uses. Dividend policy is an important aspect of financial management as it affects both the company's shareholders and its overall financial health. The key elements of a dividend policy include the dividend payout ratio, dividend stability, and dividend growth.

Dividend Reinvestment Plan (DRIP)

A Dividend Reinvestment Plan (DRIP) is a program offered by certain companies to allow shareholders to automatically reinvest their cash dividends into additional shares of the company's stock. The main purpose of a DRIP is to provide shareholders with a convenient and cost-effective way to build their investment in the company over time. Under a DRIP, shareholders who participate in the program will receive additional shares of stock instead of cash dividends. These additional shares are typically purchased directly from the company at current market prices, without any fees or commissions. The number of additional shares received will be based on the amount of the dividend payment and the current market price of the stock.

Dividend Yield Ratio

The dividend yield ratio is a financial ratio used in financial management to evaluate the return on investment provided by a company's dividend payments to its shareholders. It measures the percentage return an investor can expect to receive from holding the company's shares in the form of dividends. The formula to calculate the dividend yield ratio is: Dividend Yield Ratio = Dividends per Share / Market Price per Share The dividends per share represent the total amount of dividends paid out by the company to its shareholders divided by the total number of outstanding shares. This figure reflects the cash return the investors receive in the form of dividends for each share they hold. The market price per share is the current price at which the company's shares are traded in the stock market. It represents the price that investors are willing to pay for one share of the company's stock. The dividend yield ratio is expressed as a percentage and indicates the annual return on investment through dividend payments. A higher dividend yield ratio signifies a higher return on investment through dividends, while a lower ratio indicates a lower return. Investors use the dividend yield ratio as a tool for comparing the dividend-paying capacity of different companies within the same industry or sector. It helps investors assess the attractiveness of investing in a particular company's stock based on the potential income it can provide through dividends. However, it is important to note that a high dividend yield ratio does not necessarily imply a good investment opportunity. It may indicate that the company's stock price has fallen significantly, resulting in a higher yield. Therefore, investors should consider other factors such as the company's financial health, growth prospects, and dividend stability before making investment decisions solely based on the dividend yield ratio.

Dividend Yield

Dividend yield is a financial metric used in the field of financial management to determine the return on investment (ROI) that an investor can expect to earn from a dividend-paying stock. It is calculated by dividing the annual dividend per share by the current market price per share and is usually expressed as a percentage. The formula to calculate dividend yield is as follows: Dividend Yield = (Annual Dividend per Share / Current Market Price per Share) x 100 Dividend yield provides insight into the income generated by an investment in a dividend-paying stock. It is particularly useful for income-focused investors who rely on regular dividend payments to generate a steady stream of income. By comparing the dividend yield of different stocks, investors can assess the relative attractiveness of these investments based on their potential to generate income. A high dividend yield may indicate that a stock is undervalued or that the company has a generous dividend policy. Conversely, a low dividend yield may suggest that a stock is overvalued or that the company does not prioritize dividend payments. It is important to note that dividend yield should not be the sole criterion for investment decision-making, as it does not take into account other factors such as the company's financial health, growth prospects, and overall market conditions. Dividend yield can also be used to compare the income generated by dividend-paying stocks to the yields offered by other investment options, such as bonds or savings accounts. For example, if the dividend yield of a stock is higher than the interest rate on a savings account, it may be more attractive for an investor seeking income. In summary, dividend yield is a financial measure used in financial management to assess the return on investment from a dividend-paying stock. It is calculated by dividing the annual dividend per share by the current market price per share and is expressed as a percentage. It helps investors evaluate the income potential of different stocks and compare them to other investment options.

Dividend

A dividend is a sum of money that is paid to shareholders of a company out of its earnings or profits. It represents the return earned by shareholders for their investment in the company. Dividends are usually distributed periodically, such as quarterly or annually, and can be in the form of cash or additional shares of stock. In financial management, dividends play a crucial role in determining the value of a company's stock and the overall return on investment for shareholders. Companies typically pay out dividends as a way to share their profits with investors and attract more investors to the company.

Dodd-Frank Wall Street Reform Act

The Dodd-Frank Wall Street Reform and Consumer Protection Act, commonly referred to as the Dodd-Frank Act, is a piece of legislation enacted in 2010 to address the shortcomings in the regulatory framework that contributed to the financial crisis of 2008. Its primary objective is to promote financial stability and protect consumers from abusive financial practices. The Dodd-Frank Act introduced a wide range of reforms aimed at strengthening the oversight and regulation of the financial industry. It established new regulatory bodies and enhanced the authority of existing ones to monitor and control various aspects of the financial system. Some of the key provisions of the act include: The creation of the Financial Stability Oversight Council (FSOC), which is responsible for identifying and mitigating systemic risks that could threaten the stability of the financial system as a whole. The FSOC is composed of representatives from various regulatory agencies and is tasked with coordinating efforts to monitor and respond to emerging risks. The establishment of the Consumer Financial Protection Bureau (CFPB), an independent agency focused on protecting consumers from unfair, deceptive, or abusive practices by financial institutions. The CFPB has the authority to enforce consumer protection regulations and to implement rules to ensure transparency and fairness in the financial marketplace. The implementation of the Volcker Rule, which restricts banks from engaging in proprietary trading and from certain types of investment activities that could pose excessive risks to their own financial stability. The rule aims to separate traditional banking activities from riskier speculative activities, reducing the likelihood of another financial crisis. In addition to these provisions, the Dodd-Frank Act also introduced measures to enhance the transparency and accountability of financial institutions, such as increased capital and liquidity requirements, improved risk management practices, and stricter regulation of derivatives and credit rating agencies. The Dodd-Frank Wall Street Reform and Consumer Protection Act represents a comprehensive effort to prevent a repeat of the financial crisis by addressing the root causes of the meltdown. It aims to instill greater stability, fairness, and transparency in the financial system, while also protecting consumers from harmful practices. The act has had a profound impact on the financial industry and continues to shape the regulatory landscape for banks, lenders, and other financial institutions.

Dodd-Frank Wall Street Reform And Consumer Protection Act

The Dodd-Frank Wall Street Reform and Consumer Protection Act, also known as Dodd-Frank Act or simply Dodd-Frank, is a piece of legislation enacted in the United States in 2010. This act was designed to address the issues that led to the financial crisis of 2008 and aimed to establish a more stable and transparent financial system by implementing various reforms and regulations. Dodd-Frank Act introduced significant changes in the financial industry, including enhanced regulatory oversight, increased accountability, and consumer protection measures. The act created several new regulatory agencies and enforced stricter rules for banks, investment firms, and other financial institutions.

Dollar Roll

A dollar roll is a financial transaction that involves the sale and repurchase of mortgage-backed securities (MBS) for a specific period at a predetermined price. It is commonly used by financial institutions and investors to finance or manage their short-term cash needs. In a dollar roll transaction, the seller agrees to sell MBS to the buyer and simultaneously enter into a forward contract to repurchase the same or similar MBS at a later date. The repurchase price is typically higher than the sale price, reflecting the interest earned on the funds advanced by the buyer. The underlying MBS in a dollar roll transaction are usually issued by government-sponsored enterprises (GSEs) such as Fannie Mae or Freddie Mac. These securities represent pools of mortgages and are guaranteed by the GSEs, making them relatively safe investments. The MBS used in dollar roll transactions are typically "to-be-announced" (TBA) contracts, meaning that the specific pool of mortgages backing the securities has not yet been identified. Instead, the seller agrees to deliver MBS with certain characteristics (e.g., coupon rate, maturity) at a later date. Financial institutions and investors use dollar rolls for various purposes. One common use is to finance their MBS holdings without selling the securities outright. For example, if a financial institution owns a portfolio of MBS but needs short-term cash, it can enter into a dollar roll transaction to temporarily obtain the cash it needs, with the intention of repurchasing the MBS at a later date. This allows the institution to meet its liquidity needs while maintaining exposure to the MBS market. Dollar rolls can also be used as a hedging tool to manage interest rate risk. By entering into a dollar roll, an investor can effectively lock in a future MBS purchase price, protecting against potential price increases caused by interest rate changes. This can be particularly useful in a rising interest rate environment, as it allows investors to mitigate potential losses on their MBS holdings.

Dollar-Cost Averaging (DCA)

Dollar-Cost Averaging (DCA) is a financial management strategy that involves investing a fixed dollar amount at regular intervals over a long period of time, regardless of the price or market conditions. This approach aims to reduce the impact of market volatility on the overall investment. With DCA, an investor purchases a fixed dollar amount of a particular investment, such as stocks or mutual funds, at regular intervals, usually monthly or quarterly. The amount invested remains constant, no matter whether the market price of the investment is high or low. As a result, the investor ends up buying more shares when prices are low and fewer shares when prices are high.

Double Entry Accounting

Double entry accounting is a fundamental concept in financial management that involves recording and classifying financial transactions in a systematic and accurate manner. It is based on the principle that every transaction has two aspects: a debit and a credit. Each transaction affects at least two accounts, ensuring that the accounting equation (Assets = Liabilities + Equity) remains in balance. The process of double entry accounting begins with identifying and analyzing the financial transactions that occur within an organization. These transactions can be related to the purchase or sale of goods, payment of expenses, borrowing or lending of money, or any other economic event that has a monetary impact. Once the transactions have been identified, they are recorded in the general journal, which serves as the primary book of original entry. In the general journal, each transaction is recorded by debiting one account and crediting another. The choice of accounts to be debited or credited is determined by the nature of the transaction. For example, when cash is received from a customer, the cash account is debited (increased) and the account receivable is credited (decreased), reflecting the decrease in the amount owed by the customer. Similarly, when goods are purchased on credit, the inventory account is debited (increased) and the accounts payable account is credited (increased), indicating an increase in inventory and a corresponding increase in the amount owed to the supplier. Once the transactions have been recorded in the general journal, they are posted to the respective accounts in the general ledger. The general ledger contains a separate account for each component of the accounting equation, such as cash, accounts receivable, accounts payable, and equity. The postings in the general ledger are organized in a systematic manner, allowing for easy retrieval and analysis of financial data. Double entry accounting provides numerous benefits for businesses and organizations. It ensures accuracy and completeness in financial records, as every transaction is recorded in two separate accounts. It allows for the preparation of accurate financial statements, such as the income statement and balance sheet, which are essential for decision-making, internal control, and external reporting. Additionally, double entry accounting facilitates the identification and resolution of errors and inconsistencies, as any discrepancy in the accounting equation indicates an error in recording or classifying transactions.

Dow Jones Industrial Average (DJIA)

The Dow Jones Industrial Average (DJIA) is a stock market index that represents the performance of 30 large, publicly-traded companies listed on stock exchanges in the United States. It is one of the most widely cited measures of the overall health of the US stock market and is often used as a benchmark for the performance of individual stocks and mutual funds. The DJIA was created in 1896 by Charles Dow and is based on the stock prices of its constituent companies. The index is calculated using a price-weighted methodology, where the stock prices of the 30 companies are added together and divided by a divisor to determine the average value of the index. The divisor is adjusted periodically to account for stock splits, mergers, and other structural changes in the constituent companies. The 30 companies that make up the DJIA are a representative sample of the US economy and include companies from various sectors such as technology, healthcare, finance, consumer goods, and industrials. Some well-known companies included in the index are Apple, Microsoft, Boeing, Coca-Cola, and Goldman Sachs. The DJIA is considered a leading indicator of economic performance and investor sentiment. When the index rises, it generally indicates positive economic conditions and investor confidence, while a decline in the index suggests the opposite. Financial managers and investors often use the DJIA as a barometer to gauge overall market trends and make investment decisions. While the DJIA is widely followed, it has its limitations. The index represents only a small fraction of the thousands of stocks listed on US exchanges and does not reflect the performance of the broader market. Additionally, the price-weighted methodology gives more weight to higher-priced stocks, which can skew the index's performance. In conclusion, the DJIA is a stock market index that tracks the performance of 30 large US companies. It is used as a benchmark to assess overall market trends and is considered a leading indicator of economic performance. However, it has limitations and should be interpreted in conjunction with other market indicators.

Duration Matching

Duration matching is a risk management strategy employed in financial management to align the duration of assets and liabilities within a portfolio. Duration refers to the weighted average time it takes for cash flows from an investment to be recovered. Assets and liabilities with longer durations are more sensitive to changes in interest rates, which can result in financial losses.

The aim of duration matching is to minimize the potential negative impact of interest rate changes by ensuring that the duration of assets matches the duration of liabilities. This is done by selecting investments with durations that closely match the expected duration of the liabilities. By doing so, the value of the assets and liabilities will respond similarly to changes in interest rates, offsetting the impact on the overall portfolio.

Duration Risk

Duration risk, in the context of financial management, refers to the potential for a change in interest rates to affect the price or value of a fixed-income investment. It is commonly used to measure the sensitivity of the price of a bond or bond portfolio to changes in interest rates. The concept of duration risk is based on the understanding that the price of a fixed-income security is inversely related to changes in interest rates. When interest rates rise, the price of existing fixed-income securities tends to fall, and vice versa. This is because investors demand higher yields on their investments when interest rates are higher, making existing bonds with lower yields less attractive and causing their prices to decrease. Duration risk helps investors and managers assess the potential impact of these interest rate changes on the value of their fixed-income investments. It measures the weighted average time it takes to receive the cash flows from a bond or bond portfolio, including both coupon payments and the final principal repayment. A higher duration indicates a longer average time to receive the cash flows and therefore a greater sensitivity to changes in interest rates. By understanding and managing duration risk, investors and managers can make informed decisions to mitigate the impact of interest rate changes on their fixed-income investments. For example, if an investor expects interest rates to rise, they may choose to invest in shorter duration bonds or reduce their exposure to fixed-income securities altogether. Conversely, if interest rates are expected to decline, investors may seek to increase their exposure to longer duration bonds to capture potential capital gains. In summary, duration risk is a critical consideration in financial management, especially when dealing with fixed-income investments. It helps investors and managers assess the potential impact of interest rate changes on the value of their bond portfolios and make informed decisions to manage this risk effectively.

Earnings Before Interest And Taxes (EBIT)

Earnings Before Interest and Taxes (EBIT) is a measure used in financial management to assess a company's operating profitability before considering the effects of interest expenses and income taxes. It represents the earnings generated by a company's core operations, excluding the costs associated with debt financing and tax obligations. In essence, EBIT provides insights into a company's ability to generate profit from its primary business activities. By excluding interest expenses and income taxes, it allows for a clearer assessment of the company's operational efficiency and profitability, independent of financial strategies and tax policies.

Earnings Before Interest, Taxes, Depreciation, And Amortization (EBITDA)

Earnings Before Interest, Taxes, Depreciation, and Amortization (EBITDA) is a financial metric commonly used in financial management to assess a company's operating performance and profitability. It represents the company's earnings before deducting interest expenses, taxes, and non-cash expenses such as depreciation and amortization. EBITDA is calculated by adding back interest, taxes, depreciation, and amortization to the net income. The formula for calculating EBITDA is: EBITDA = Net Income + Interest Expense + Tax Expense + Depreciation Expense + Amortization Expense EBITDA serves as a useful tool for financial analysts and investors to evaluate a company's ability to generate operating income and cash flow from its core operations. By excluding interest, taxes, depreciation, and amortization, EBITDA provides a clearer picture of a company's underlying profitability. One of the main benefits of using EBITDA in financial analysis is that it helps to eliminate the impact of non-operating factors such as financing decisions and tax rates, allowing for better comparability between companies in the same industry or across different industries. EBITDA is especially relevant for industries or companies with high levels of debt or significant differences in tax rates. For instance, companies with large capital expenditures, such as manufacturing companies or telecommunications providers, often have significant depreciation and amortization expenses. By excluding these non-cash expenses, EBITDA provides a more accurate reflection of their operational performance. However, it is important to note that EBITDA has its limitations and should not be the only metric used to evaluate a company's financial health. EBITDA does not take into account changes in working capital, capital expenditures, or debt repayments, which are important factors in assessing a company's ability to generate free cash flow. In conclusion, Earnings Before Interest, Taxes, Depreciation, and Amortization (EBITDA) is a financial metric that allows for a clearer assessment of a company's operating performance and profitability by excluding interest, taxes, depreciation, and amortization expenses. It provides a useful tool for financial analysis, particularly in industries with high levels of debt or significant differences in tax rates. However, EBITDA should be used in conjunction with other financial metrics to gain a comprehensive understanding of a company's financial health.

Earnings Per Share (EPS)

Earnings per share (EPS) is a financial ratio that represents the portion of a company's profit allocated to each outstanding share of common stock. It is an important measure used by investors to assess a company's profitability and determine its worth in the market. To calculate EPS, the net income of a company is divided by the total number of outstanding shares. Net income is the company's total revenue minus all expenses, taxes, and interest. The resulting value is the amount of profit available to be distributed to shareholders. EPS provides insight into a company's profitability on a per-share basis. It is commonly used by investors to compare the earning potential of different companies in the same industry or to track a company's performance over time. A higher EPS indicates that a company is generating more profit per share, which is generally seen as positive for investors. EPS is also an essential metric for valuation purposes. It is used in various financial ratios and valuation models, such as the price-to-earnings (P/E) ratio. The P/E ratio compares a company's stock price to its EPS, providing insight into how much investors are willing to pay for each dollar of earnings. A higher P/E ratio suggests that investors have higher expectations for future earnings growth. Investors should consider EPS in conjunction with other financial indicators and ratios to get a comprehensive view of a company's financial health. It is important to compare EPS with industry peers and analyze trends over time to identify potential risks and opportunities.

Economic Indicators

Economic indicators are statistical data that provide information about the overall health and performance of an economy. These indicators are used by financial managers to analyze and assess the current and future economic conditions, as well as to make informed decisions regarding their financial strategies and investments. There are various types of economic indicators, each providing a different perspective on the state of the economy. These indicators can be broadly categorized into three main categories: leading indicators, lagging indicators, and coincident indicators. Leading indicators are used to predict the future direction of the economy. They are considered to be precursors of economic trends and changes. Examples of leading indicators include stock market performance, building permits, new orders for durable goods, and consumer confidence index. Lagging indicators, on the other hand, confirm the economic conditions that have already occurred. They reflect changes that have already taken place and are used to confirm or validate the direction of the economy. Examples of lagging indicators include unemployment rate, inflation rate, corporate profits, and interest rates. Coincident indicators provide real-time information about the current state of the economy. They indicate the current economic conditions and the overall health of the economy. Examples of coincident indicators include GDP growth rate, retail sales, industrial production, and personal income. Financial managers use economic indicators to analyze the overall economic health, identify trends and patterns, and assess the risks and opportunities in the market. By understanding these indicators, financial managers can make informed decisions regarding their investment strategies, asset allocation, and financial planning. Economic indicators also help financial managers in assessing the impact of various economic factors on their business operations, profitability, and cash flow. By monitoring these indicators, financial managers can identify potential risks and prepare contingency plans to mitigate the impact of adverse economic conditions.

Economic Order Quantity (EOQ)

Economic Order Quantity (EOQ) is a financial management concept that helps organizations determine the most cost-effective quantity of inventory to order at a given time. It is the optimal balance between ordering costs and holding costs. EOQ considers three main components: demand, ordering costs, and holding costs. Demand refers to the quantity of a product or material that an organization expects to use or sell during a specific time period. Ordering costs include expenses associated with placing an order, such as processing paperwork and transportation costs. Holding costs consist of expenses incurred for storing inventory, such as warehouse space, insurance, and obsolescence. The formula to calculate EOQ is: EOQ = √((2 * demand * ordering costs) / holding costs) By using this formula, organizations can determine the optimal quantity to order that minimizes total costs. When the EOQ is reached, the holding costs and ordering costs are balanced, resulting in the lowest total cost. There are a few assumptions made in the EOQ model. It assumes that demand is constant and known with certainty, ordering costs remain constant regardless of the order quantity, and holding costs are incurred based on the average inventory level during a time period. EOQ provides numerous benefits to organizations. It helps minimize inventory costs by reducing excess inventory and avoiding stockouts. By ordering the optimal quantity, organizations optimize their cash flow and working capital. EOQ also assists in streamlining the procurement process, ensuring efficient inventory management. However, it is important to note that EOQ has some limitations. It assumes a deterministic demand and does not consider demand variations or uncertainties. It also assumes that holding costs and ordering costs are the only relevant costs to consider, neglecting other factors such as stockouts and lost sales. Overall, EOQ is a valuable financial management tool to determine the optimal order quantity that minimizes total costs associated with ordering and holding inventory. By striking the right balance, organizations can achieve cost savings, improve cash flow, and enhance overall operational efficiency.

Economic Value Added (EVA)

Economic Value Added (EVA) is a financial performance measure used in financial management to evaluate the value created by a company above its cost of capital. It is a profitability metric that indicates whether a company has generated excess returns for its investors. EVA is calculated by deducting the company's cost of capital from its net operating profit after taxes (NOPAT). The cost of capital represents the opportunity cost of investors' capital employed in the business and is calculated by multiplying the weighted average cost of capital (WACC) by the company's invested capital. If a company's EVA is positive, it means that it has generated returns above its cost of capital, signaling that it has created value for its shareholders. Conversely, a negative EVA indicates that the company has not generated sufficient returns to cover its cost of capital, implying value destruction. EVA provides a comprehensive assessment of a company's financial performance by considering both its operating income and the cost of capital. Unlike traditional accounting measures, such as net income or earnings per share, EVA takes into account the true economic cost of all sources of capital, including equity and debt. Managers use EVA to evaluate the effectiveness of their business strategies and to identify areas for improvement. By focusing on generating positive EVA, managers can align their operational decisions with the goal of maximizing shareholder value. EVA can also be used to compare the performance of different business units within a company or to benchmark against competitors. Overall, EVA provides a valuable tool for measuring and managing the financial performance of a company. It helps identify whether a company is creating value for its shareholders and provides insights into how to improve profitability and increase shareholder wealth.

Effective Annual Rate (EAR)

The Effective Annual Rate (EAR), also known as the Annual Equivalent Rate (AER), is a financial metric used to compare the annual interest rates of different investment options or loans with different compounding periods. It represents the true annual rate of return or cost of borrowing, taking into account the effect of compounding. The EAR is calculated by adjusting the nominal interest rate to account for the compounding frequency. It reflects the total amount of interest earned or paid over a one-year period when compounding occurs more than once per year. It is expressed as a percentage and provides a standardized way to compare investment opportunities or loan options on an annual basis. When compounding occurs more frequently than once a year, the nominal interest rate is divided by the number of compounding periods, and the resulting figure is raised to the power of the number of compounding periods per year. The EAR is then calculated by subtracting 1 from this value, multiplying by 100, and rounding to

93

the nearest decimal place. The significance of using the EAR in financial management is that it allows individuals or businesses to accurately compare investment options or loan offers with different compounding frequencies. By considering the EAR rather than the nominal rate, investors can make informed decisions about where to invest their money or which loan option offers the most favorable terms. For example, if an individual is comparing two savings accounts with a nominal interest rate of 5%, but one compounds interest quarterly and the other compounds interest monthly, the EAR for the quarterly compounding account will be lower than that of the monthly compounding account. This means that the quarterly compounding account will provide a lower annual return compared to the monthly compounding account, even though both have the same nominal interest rate. Therefore, the EAR is an essential tool in financial management for accurately evaluating the annual returns or costs associated with different investment or borrowing opportunities, taking into account the effect of compounding.

Effective Interest Rate (EIR)

The Effective Interest Rate (EIR) is a key concept in financial management that represents the true cost or return of a financial transaction or investment over a specified period of time. It takes into account both the nominal interest rate and the compounding frequency to provide a more accurate measure of the overall cost or return. The EIR is used in various financial calculations, such as determining the annual percentage rate (APR) on loans, assessing the profitability of investments, and comparing different financial products. It helps individuals and businesses make informed decisions by considering the time value of money and providing a standardized measure to compare different financial options.

Effective Tax Rate

The effective tax rate is a financial metric used in financial management to calculate the average rate at which a company or individual pays taxes relative to their taxable income. It is expressed as a percentage and is a key indicator of the overall tax liability of the entity. The effective tax rate is calculated by dividing the total tax paid by the taxable income. The taxable income is the income after deducting allowable tax deductions, exemptions, and credits. The total tax paid includes income taxes, payroll taxes, and any other taxes owed to the government. The effective tax rate provides a more accurate measure of the tax burden compared to the nominal tax rate, which is the statutory tax rate set by the government. The nominal tax rate does not consider the impact of deductions and credits, and therefore does not reflect the actual tax burden faced by the entity. By analyzing the effective tax rate, financial managers can assess the efficiency of the company's tax planning strategies and identify areas for potential tax savings. A lower effective tax rate indicates that the entity is successfully minimizing its tax liability, while a higher effective tax rate may signal inefficiencies or unfavorable tax treatment. The effective tax rate is also commonly used for benchmarking purposes and to compare the tax performance of different entities within the same industry or sector. It allows financial managers to evaluate the competitiveness of the entity's tax position and identify opportunities for improvements or adjustments in tax planning strategies.

Efficient Frontier

The efficient frontier is a concept in financial management that represents the combination of investment portfolios that provide the highest possible expected return for a given level of risk, or the lowest possible risk for a given level of expected return. It is a key tool used in modern portfolio theory to help investors optimize their portfolio allocations. The efficient frontier is derived from the expected returns and risk (usually measured by standard deviation) of various asset classes or securities. By plotting these data points on a graph, with expected returns on the y-axis and risk on the x-axis, a curved line is formed that represents all possible combinations of portfolios. Each point on this curve represents a unique portfolio that offers a specific level of risk and expected return. Portfolios that lie below the efficient frontier are considered sub-optimal because they either have higher risk for the same expected return or lower expected return for the same level of risk compared to portfolios on the efficient frontier. Portfolios that lie on the efficient frontier are considered efficient because they offer the best risk-return tradeoff. Investors can use the efficient frontier to determine their optimal asset allocation by selecting a portfolio that lies on the efficient frontier that aligns with their risk tolerance and investment objectives. Depending on individual preferences, an investor may choose a more aggressive portfolio with higher expected returns and higher risk, or a more conservative portfolio with lower expected returns and lower risk. The efficient frontier is not a static concept and can shift based on changes in the expected returns and risks of the underlying assets or securities. As new information becomes available or market conditions change, the efficient frontier can provide guidance on reallocating or rebalancing a portfolio to maintain its efficiency.

Efficient Market Hypothesis (EMH)

The Efficient Market Hypothesis (EMH) is a theory in financial management that states that financial markets are highly efficient and that it is nearly impossible to consistently achieve above-average returns by using any information available in the market. The EMH is based on the assumption that all market participants are rational and have access to the same information. It suggests that any new information regarding a stock or any other financial asset is quickly and accurately reflected in its price. Therefore, it is not possible to consistently outperform the market by trading based on information that is already known to all market participants.

Efficient Portfolio

An efficient portfolio in the context of financial management refers to a combination of assets that provides the highest possible return for a given level of risk or the lowest possible risk for a given level of return. It is an optimal portfolio that maximizes returns or minimizes risk based on the investor's preferences and tolerance for risk. The concept of an efficient portfolio is derived from the principles of modern portfolio theory (MPT) developed by Harry Markowitz. MPT suggests that investors can optimize their investment returns by diversifying their portfolios across different assets with varying levels of risk and return. By combining assets with different risk and return characteristics, investors can reduce the overall risk of their portfolio without sacrificing potential returns. The risk and return characteristics of individual assets are measured using statistical techniques such as standard deviation and expected returns. These metrics provide insights into the assets' historical volatility and potential future performance. An efficient portfolio is constructed by selecting assets that have low or negative correlations with each other, as this reduces the overall risk of the portfolio. When assets are negatively correlated, they tend to move in opposite directions, providing a natural hedge against market fluctuations. To identify the efficient frontier, which represents the set of all efficient portfolios, the investor must consider their risk tolerance and financial goals. The efficient frontier is a graph that shows the optimal portfolios that provide the maximum return for a given level of risk or the minimum risk for a given level of return. The investor can then select a portfolio from the efficient frontier that aligns with their risk preferences.

Elasticity

Elasticity is a measure of the sensitivity of one variable to changes in another variable. In the context of financial management, elasticity refers to the responsiveness of a financial metric or indicator to changes in the underlying factors that drive it. Financial managers use elasticity to analyze the relationships between inputs and outputs in various financial scenarios. It helps them understand how changes in variables such as price, demand, interest rates, or costs impact the overall financial performance of a company.

Employee Stock Ownership Plan (ESOP)

An Employee Stock Ownership Plan (ESOP) is a type of employee benefit plan that allows employees to become owners of the company they work for. Under an ESOP, the company sets up a trust fund and contributes shares of its stock or cash to the fund on behalf of the employees. The shares are allocated to individual employee accounts, and the employees are able to accumulate ownership in the company over time. The main purpose of an ESOP is to provide employees with a financial stake in the company and give them an incentive to work towards its success. By becoming owners, employees have a vested interest in the company's performance and are more likely to work hard to improve its profitability and share price. This can lead to increased productivity and loyalty among employees, as well as a greater sense of job security. ESOPs can be used as a tool for succession planning, as they allow owners of closely held businesses a way to sell their shares and transition ownership to employees. It can

95

also be used to attract and retain top talent, as it provides employees with an additional form of compensation and a long-term investment opportunity. From a financial management perspective, ESOPs can have several advantages. First, they can be a tax-efficient way for owners to sell their shares, as contributions to the ESOP are tax-deductible and the distributions to employees can be tax-free if certain conditions are met. Second, they can help to improve the company's balance sheet by reducing its debt burden, as cash contributions to the ESOP can be used to repay loans or fund capital expenditures. Finally, ESOPs can be a way to increase employee motivation and engagement, which can lead to improved financial performance and shareholder value. However, ESOPs also have some potential drawbacks. They can be complex and costly to set up and administer, requiring legal and financial expertise. Additionally, there can be restrictions on the sale of ESOP shares, limiting employees' ability to diversify their investment portfolios. Finally, the value of ESOP shares can be highly dependent on the performance of the company's stock, which can be volatile and subject to market fluctuations.

Enterprise Value (EV)

Enterprise Value (EV) is a financial metric used in the field of financial management to determine the total value of a company. It is a measure of a company's total worth, taking into account both its market capitalization and its debt. EV represents the value that an investor would have to pay to acquire the entire business, including its liabilities. To calculate the enterprise value, several factors are considered. The most significant components are a company's market capitalization and its outstanding debt. Market capitalization is the total value of a company's outstanding shares of stock, calculated by multiplying the share price by the number of shares. Debt, on the other hand, includes both short-term and long-term obligations, such as loans, bonds, or lines of credit. By including debt in the calculation, EV provides a more comprehensive picture of a company's value than market capitalization alone. This is because debt represents a claim on a company's assets and future cash flows, and needs to be considered when assessing its overall worth. Excluding debt from the valuation would not give a complete understanding of the company's financial health and potential risks. Enterprise value is especially useful in financial management for comparing companies and determining their relative value. It allows investors to compare companies of different sizes and capital structures on an equal basis. For example, two companies might have similar market capitalizations, but if one has a significant amount of debt, its enterprise value would be higher. EV is also a key component in financial ratios such as the EV/EBITDA (Enterprise Value/Earnings Before Interest, Taxes, Depreciation, and Amortization) ratio. This ratio is often used to assess a company's valuation relative to its operating performance and can provide insight into a company's profitability and potential for growth.

Equity Financing

Equity financing refers to the method of raising capital for a company by issuing shares of stock to investors in exchange for their investment. It is a common practice in financial management, allowing businesses to secure funds for various purposes such as expansion, research and development, or debt repayment.Equity financing is essentially a form of long-term financing, as the investors become part owners of the company and hold a stake in its future profits and growth. In return for their investment, shareholders receive ownership rights, voting rights, and the potential for dividends.One of the main advantages of equity financing is that it does not require the repayment of borrowed funds. Unlike debt financing, which involves interest payments and the obligation to pay back the principal amount, equity financing supplies funds without adding any debt to the company's balance sheet. This can be particularly beneficial for start-ups or companies with limited cash flow, as it reduces the financial burden and allows them to allocate resources to other areas of the business.Equity financing also offers some degree of flexibility and stability to the company's capital structure. Since equity does not have a fixed repayment schedule, the company has more freedom in managing its cash flows and investing in growth opportunities. Additionally, equity investors typically have a vested interest in the company's success, which can provide access to valuable expertise, networks, and strategic guidance.Nevertheless, there are also some drawbacks to consider. By issuing shares, the company dilutes its ownership, reducing the proportion of ownership held by existing shareholders. This can result in a loss of control and decision-making power for the original founders or majority shareholders. Moreover, unlike debt financing, equity financing does not offer tax advantages such as deductibility of interest payments.In conclusion, equity financing is a method of raising funds for a company by issuing shares to investors. It offers advantages such as no repayment obligation, flexibility in cash flow management, and access to expertise, but may also result in dilution of ownership and loss of control.

Equity Multiplier

The Equity Multiplier is a financial ratio that measures the proportion of a firm's total assets that are financed by shareholders' equity. It is an important indicator in financial management as it provides insight into a company's financial leverage and its ability to generate returns for its shareholders. The formula to calculate the Equity Multiplier is: Equity Multiplier = Total Assets / Shareholders' Equity This ratio helps determine the extent to which a company relies on debt financing to fund its operations. A higher equity multiplier indicates a higher level of financial leverage, which means that a larger portion of the company's assets is financed by debt. On the other hand, a lower equity multiplier suggests a lower reliance on debt and a higher proportion of assets being financed by equity. The Equity Multiplier is useful for investors and financial analysts when evaluating a company's financial health and risk. A higher equity multiplier may indicate a higher level of risk, as the company's profitability and cash flow may be more sensitive to changes in interest rates or economic conditions. It also implies a higher level of debt that needs to be serviced, which can increase the company's financial risk. Conversely, a lower equity multiplier suggests a lower level of financial risk, as the company has a larger portion of its assets financed by equity. This indicates a stronger financial position and a higher ability to weather economic downturns or other financial challenges. Overall, the Equity Multiplier is a valuable tool in financial management that helps assess a company's reliance on debt financing and its financial risk. It aids investors and financial analysts in understanding the capital structure of a company and its potential for generating returns for shareholders.

Equity Risk Premium

The equity risk premium refers to the additional return that investors demand for investing in stocks as compared to risk-free investments, such as government bonds. It is a key concept in financial management as it helps investors and analysts assess the potential risks and rewards associated with investing in equity securities. In the context of financial management, the equity risk premium can be calculated using various approaches. One commonly used method is the historical approach, which involves looking at historical data and determining the average excess return of stocks over risk-free investments over a certain period of time. This historical data can provide insights into the past performance of equity markets and help investors make informed decisions about potential future returns. Another approach to estimating the equity risk premium is the implied approach, which involves analyzing market prices and implied volatility to determine the market's expectation of future equity returns. This approach takes into account the current market environment and investor sentiment to provide a more forward-looking estimate of the equity risk premium. The equity risk premium plays a crucial role in financial management as it influences investment decisions and asset allocation strategies. Investors typically require a higher return for taking on the additional risk associated with equity investments. A higher equity risk premium implies that investors perceive a higher level of risk in the stock market, which may lead to a lower valuation and potentially lower stock prices. Financial managers use the equity risk premium to determine the appropriate expected return on equity investments and to assess the relative attractiveness of different investment opportunities. It helps them evaluate the risk-reward trade-off and make decisions that align with their investment objectives and risk tolerance. Understanding the equity risk premium also allows financial managers to quantify the risk premium and incorporate it into their investment models and valuation techniques.

Equity Risk

Equity risk is a concept in financial management that refers to the potential for an investment in company stocks or shares to experience losses or fluctuation in value due to various factors. It is inherently tied to the volatility and uncertainty of the stock market and is a critical consideration for investors and financial managers. Equity risk can arise from multiple sources and can have diverse impacts on investments. One primary source of equity risk is the general performance of the stock market. Stock prices can fluctuate significantly based on various economic factors, such as interest rates, inflation, and economic indicators. Changes in these factors can directly affect the profitability and financial condition of companies, which, in turn, impact the value of their stocks. Another source of equity risk is company-specific factors. These include factors such as management decisions, competitive landscape, technological advancements, market demand, and regulatory changes. Poor or unfavorable developments in any of these areas can negatively impact a company's financial performance and, consequently, its stock price. Equity risk is widely recognized as an integral part of investing in stocks and is often quantified using measures such as beta. Beta is a statistical metric that measures the sensitivity of a stock's price movements in relation to the overall market movements. Stocks with a beta greater than 1 are considered riskier than the overall market, while those with a beta less than 1 are considered less risky. Effective management of equity risk involves various strategies, including diversification, hedging, and investment in different asset classes. Diversification refers to spreading investments across a range of stocks or industries to reduce the impact of a potential decline in any one investment. Hedging involves using derivative products, such as options or futures contracts, to protect against potential losses in stock values. Additionally, investors may also choose to invest in other asset classes, such as bonds or real estate, which have different risk-return characteristics compared to equities. In summary, equity risk is the potential for investment in stocks or shares to experience losses or fluctuations in value due to factors such as overall market performance and company-specific factors. It is a fundamental consideration in financial management and requires careful analysis and management to mitigate risks and maximize returns.

Equity Swap

An equity swap is a financial arrangement between two parties that involves the exchange of the cash flows derived from the ownership of a specified equity instrument or a basket of equity instruments. In this agreement, the parties agree to exchange the returns or cash flows generated by the equity instruments for a predefined period. In an equity swap, one party, known as the equity receiver or the equity payer, agrees to pay the other party, known as the equity provider or the equity hedger, the return on a specific equity instrument. The return can be in the form of dividends, capital gains, or any other cash flow generated by the equity instrument. The equity swap allows both parties to achieve their respective financial objectives. The equity receiver may want exposure to the returns generated by the specified equity instrument without actually owning it, which can be due to various reasons such as avoiding direct investment costs, regulatory restrictions, or tax considerations. On the other hand, the equity provider may have surplus exposure to the specified equity instrument and seeks to diversify their portfolio or hedge their risk. Equity swaps are commonly used by financial institutions, such as investment banks, to gain exposure to a specific equity market or sector without taking ownership of the underlying equities. This allows them to manage their risk and provide additional investment options to their clients. In an equity swap, the parties agree to a notional principal amount, which represents the value of the equity instrument or basket of equity instruments. The notional principal amount serves as the basis for calculating the cash flows exchanged between the parties. These cash flows can be fixed, floating, or a combination of both, depending on the terms of the agreement. Equity swaps can be structured as either single-stock swaps or index swaps. In a single-stock swap, the equity instrument is a specific stock, while in an index swap, the equity instrument is a broad-based index, such as the S&P 500 or the FTSE 100. Overall, equity swaps are versatile financial instruments that allow parties to gain exposure to the returns of specific equity instruments without owning them. They provide flexibility, risk management, and diversification opportunities to market participants.

Equity

Equity, in the context of financial management, refers to the ownership interest that shareholders hold in a company. It represents the residual interest in the assets of the company after deducting liabilities. Equity represents a claim on the company's assets and earnings, and shareholders are considered the owners of the company's equity. Equity can be categorized into two main types: common equity and preferred equity. Common equity refers to the ordinary shares of the company, which entitle the shareholders to participate in the company's profits and to vote in certain matters affecting the company. Preferred equity, on the other hand, represents a class of shares that have certain preferential rights and privileges compared to common equity. These rights may include a fixed dividend rate, priority in receiving dividends, and priority in the distribution of assets in the event of liquidation. The value of equity is influenced by various factors, including the company's financial performance, market conditions, industry dynamics, and investor sentiment. The value of equity is typically measured through the market capitalization of the company, which is the total value of all outstanding shares of common equity. Market capitalization is calculated by multiplying the current market price per share by the number of outstanding shares. Equity plays a crucial role in financial management as it represents the shareholders' stake in the company and provides a source of financing for the company's operations and growth. Equity financing involves raising funds by issuing new shares of common equity or preferred equity, which dilutes the ownership of existing shareholders. This form of financing enables companies to raise capital without incurring debt obligations and interest expenses. However, it also gives rise to the expectation of future returns to shareholders in the form of dividends or capital gains. In summary, equity in financial management refers to the ownership interest that shareholders have in a company. It represents a claim on the company's assets and earnings and plays a crucial role in financing the company's operations and growth. Understanding and managing equity is essential for shareholders, management, and investors to evaluate the value and performance of a company.

Eurobond

Eurobond refers to a type of bond that is issued and traded outside the jurisdiction of the country in whose currency it is denominated. It is a debt instrument that enables large multinational companies and governments to borrow funds on an international scale. Eurobonds are typically issued in major international currencies such as the euro or the US dollar. Unlike domestic bonds, Eurobonds are not subject to regulations and restrictions imposed by a specific country or its regulatory authorities. This allows the issuers to have greater flexibility in terms of maturity, coupon rate, and overall structure. Eurobonds are typically offered to investors in multiple countries and are traded in international financial markets.

Event Risk

Event risk refers to the possibility of an unexpected event occurring that can have a significant impact on a company's financial position and operations. These events can arise from various sources, such as economic, political, environmental, or technological factors, and can substantially disrupt the normal course of business. In financial management, event risk is an important consideration as it can lead to financial losses, increased volatility, and overall uncertainty in the market. It is essential for companies to anticipate and mitigate event risk to protect their financial well-being and achieve their strategic objectives.

Ex-Dividend Date

An ex-dividend date is a crucial term used in financial management that refers to the date on or after which a security, such as a stock or a bond, starts trading without the entitlement to the most recently declared dividend or interest payment. This means that an investor who purchases the security on or after the ex-dividend date will not receive the upcoming dividend payment. The ex-dividend date is set by the stock exchange or market where the security is traded, typically a few days before the record date. The record date is the date on which the company determines the shareholders who are entitled to receive the dividend payment. The time gap between the ex-dividend date and the record date allows for the settlement of transactions and ensures that only those investors who were shareholders on the record date receive the dividend.

Excess Return

Excess Return, also known as the abnormal or alpha return, is a financial metric used in the field of financial management to measure the additional return generated by an investment or portfolio over and above the return that would be expected based on its risk profile. It is a measure of the value added by the investment manager through active management and stock selection. Excess return is calculated by subtracting the risk-free rate of return from the actual return of the investment. The risk-free rate of return represents the return on an investment with zero risk, typically the yield on a government bond or a similar low-risk investment. By subtracting the risk-free rate, excess return isolates the additional return generated by the investment that is not attributable to the overall market movement.

Exchange Rate

An exchange rate, in the context of financial management, refers to the rate at which one currency can be exchanged for another. It represents the value of one currency in terms of another currency. Exchange rates play a crucial role in international trade and investment, as they determine the purchasing power of one currency in another country. The exchange rate is determined by various factors including interest rates, inflation rates, political stability, and market forces of supply and demand. Generally, exchange rates are determined in the foreign exchange market, which is the global marketplace for trading currencies. In this market, banks, financial institutions, corporations, and individual traders participate in buying and selling different currencies. Exchange rates can be classified into two categories: fixed exchange rates and floating exchange rates. Under a fixed exchange rate system, the value of a currency is fixed against a specific reference currency or a basket of currencies. Governments or central banks usually maintain fixed exchange rates by intervening in the foreign exchange market to keep the exchange rate within a certain range. On the other hand, a floating exchange rate system allows the value of a currency to fluctuate freely based on market forces. Exchange rate fluctuations can have significant impacts on businesses and economies. They can affect the profitability of businesses engaged in international trade, as the cost of importing and exporting goods and services is influenced by exchange rates. Exchange rate movements can also affect the competitiveness of domestic industries in international markets. For example, a depreciation of a country's currency can make its exports more competitive, while an appreciation can make its imports cheaper. Furthermore, exchange rates have implications for investors and portfolio managers. International investors must consider exchange rate risk when investing in foreign assets, as fluctuations in exchange rates can affect the returns on their investments. Portfolio managers also need to consider exchange rate movements when diversifying investments across different currencies to manage risk.

Exposure

Exposure indicates the degree of risk to which a financial entity, such as a company or individual, is exposed due to various factors in the financial market. It represents the vulnerability of an entity to market fluctuations, changes in interest rates, foreign exchange rates, credit risks, and other variables that can impact its financial health and stability. Exposure can be categorized into different types based on specific financial risks: 1. Credit Exposure: This refers to the potential loss a financial entity may incur if a borrower fails to repay the principal or interest of a loan. It includes both direct exposure (such as loans and credit facilities extended by the entity) and indirect exposure (such as investments in debt instruments). 2. Market Exposure: Also known as price risk, market exposure refers to the potential loss an entity may incur due to adverse movements in financial markets. It includes exposure to equity prices, interest rates, commodity prices, and foreign exchange rates. Market exposure is commonly managed through various hedging techniques, such as derivatives and options. 3. Liquidity Exposure: This represents the risk that arises when an entity does not have sufficient cash or liquid assets to meet its financial obligations in a timely manner. Liquidity exposure can result from unforeseen events, changes in market conditions, or poor cash management practices. Effective liquidity risk management is crucial to ensure the entity can meet its short-term obligations without significant disruptions. 4. Operational Exposure: Operational exposure refers to the potential impact of operational risks on the financial position of an entity. These risks include factors such as system failures, human error, legal and regulatory compliance, and supply chain disruptions. Managing operational exposure involves implementing robust risk management frameworks and ensuring effective internal controls. 5. Country/Political Exposure: This type of exposure reflects the potential risks associated with operating in a specific country or region. It includes risks related to political instability, changes in government policies or regulations, economic conditions, and currency exchange restrictions. Country exposure is crucial for entities with international operations, as it can significantly impact their financial performance and sustainability. In summary, exposure in the context of financial management refers to the quantification and assessment of risks faced by an entity in relation to various financial factors. Understanding and managing exposure is essential for making informed financial decisions, mitigating risks, and preserving the entity's financial well-being.

Face Value

Face value is a term commonly used in financial management to refer to the nominal or stated value of a financial instrument, such as a bond or a share of stock. It represents the initial value assigned to the instrument at the time of issuance. In the context of bonds, face value is the amount that the bond issuer promises to repay to the bondholder upon maturity. It is also known as the par value or principal amount. Bonds are typically issued with a fixed face value, which is used to calculate the periodic interest payments, known as coupon payments, that the bondholder will receive over the life of the bond. At maturity, the bondholder will receive the face value as the final payment. Similarly, in the case of shares of stock, face value represents the nominal value assigned to each share at the time of issuance. The face value of a share has no direct relation to its market value or the price at which it is currently traded. Instead, it is used to determine the legal capital of the company, which is the minimum capital required to be maintained by law. The face value of shares is typically set very low, such as $0.01 per share, to allow flexibility in pricing and trading. It is important to note that face value may not reflect the true value or market price of a financial instrument. Market forces such as supply and demand, interest rates, and investor sentiment can cause the market price of a bond or share to deviate significantly from its face value. Investors and financial managers need to consider the current market price, as well as other factors such as the issuer's creditworthiness and the instrument's yield, when making investment decisions.

Fair Market Value (FMV)

Fair Market Value (FMV) is a financial term used to determine the worth or value of an asset or property in a transaction between a willing buyer and a willing seller, both of whom are knowledgeable, informed, and not under any compulsion to buy or sell. The FMV is the estimated price at which an asset or property would be exchanged on the open market, taking into consideration various factors such as supply and demand, prevailing market conditions, and the characteristics of the asset or property itself. It represents the fair and reasonable price that would be agreed upon by two parties in a voluntary and arm's-length transaction.

Fair Value Accounting

Fair Value Accounting is a method of valuing assets and liabilities based on their current market price or an estimate of their current market price. It is used in Financial Management to determine the true economic value of an asset or liability and to reflect this value in financial statements. Under fair value accounting, assets and liabilities are recorded at their fair market value on the balance sheet. This means that the value of the assets and liabilities is based on what they could be sold for in the current market, rather than the historical cost or book value. One of the main advantages of fair value accounting is that it provides more relevant and timely information to investors and stakeholders. By valuing assets and liabilities at their fair market value, it reflects their current worth and gives a more accurate picture of a company's financial position. However, fair value accounting can also be subject to volatility and uncertainty, especially in times of market instability. The market prices of assets and liabilities can fluctuate greatly, which can result in significant changes in reported financial results. Fair value accounting is used for a wide range of financial instruments and assets, including stocks, bonds, derivatives, and real estate. It is also used for certain liabilities, such as financial obligations or contingent liabilities. Overall, fair value accounting is an important tool in financial management that provides a more accurate and relevant representation of a company's financial position. It helps investors, analysts, and stakeholders make more informed decisions based on current market conditions.

Federal Funds Rate

The Federal Funds Rate is the interest rate at which depository institutions, such as commercial banks and credit unions, lend funds held at the Federal Reserve to other banks on an overnight basis. It is one of the most significant tools used by the Federal Reserve to control monetary policy and influence the economy. The Federal Funds Rate serves as a benchmark for short-term interest rates in the financial markets. It directly affects borrowing costs for consumers and businesses, influencing investment decisions, spending patterns, and overall economic activity. The Federal Reserve manages the Federal Funds Rate by buying or selling government securities in the open market, thereby affecting the supply of and demand for reserves in the banking system.

Federal Open Market Committee (FOMC)

The Federal Open Market Committee (FOMC) is a key financial management institution in the United States that is responsible for making decisions related to monetary policy. It is made up of members from the Board of Governors of the Federal Reserve System and the presidents of the Federal Reserve Banks. The primary objective of the FOMC is to promote price stability and maximum employment. To achieve this, the committee regularly meets to assess the current state of the economy, evaluate risks, and determine the appropriate course of action for monetary policy. These decisions play a crucial role in influencing interest rates, which in turn affect borrowing costs, investment decisions, and overall economic activity.

Federal Reserve System (The Fed)

The Federal Reserve System (also known as the Fed) is the central banking system of the United States. It serves as the nation's central bank and is responsible for implementing monetary policy, providing financial services to depository institutions, and maintaining the stability of the financial system. As the central bank, the Federal Reserve System plays a crucial role in managing the country's money supply and interest rates. It is tasked with the responsibility of conducting monetary policy to promote stable prices and maximum sustainable economic growth. This is achieved through the control of the money supply and influencing interest rates, which in turn affects the borrowing costs for individuals, businesses, and governments. The Federal Reserve System also acts as a bank for banks, providing financial services and oversight to depository institutions. It helps ensure the stability and efficiency of the banking system by supervising and regulating banks and other financial institutions. It also provides them with essential services, such as processing payments, storing cash reserves, and facilitating the transfer of funds between banks. In addition to its role in monetary policy and banking supervision, the Fed plays a vital role in maintaining the stability of the financial system. It monitors and assesses risks within the financial system, taking steps to mitigate potential threats to the economy. It provides liquidity to the financial markets during times of stress, acting as a lender of last resort to prevent financial crises. The Federal Reserve System is composed of several entities, including the Board of Governors, the Federal Open Market Committee (FOMC), and 12 regional Federal Reserve Banks. The Board of Governors is the central decision-making body responsible for formulating monetary policy and overseeing the system's activities. The FOMC is responsible for setting the target federal funds rate, which influences short-term interest rates. In conclusion, the Federal Reserve System is the central banking system of the United States, responsible for managing monetary policy, providing financial services to banks, and maintaining financial stability. Its actions and decisions have significant impacts on the economy and the financial well-being of individuals, businesses, and governments.

Fiduciary

A fiduciary is a person or entity who is entrusted with the responsibility of managing the financial affairs of another individual or entity, known as the beneficiary. This relationship is based on trust, and the fiduciary is legally obligated to act in the best interests of the beneficiary, putting their interests before their own. As part of their role, fiduciaries must exercise a high standard of care, skill, and diligence in managing the financial matters entrusted to them. They are required to make informed decisions, considering the specific needs and objectives of the beneficiary. This includes the obligation to avoid conflicts of interest and act impartially, ensuring that personal interests do not influence their decision-making process or compromise the beneficiary's financial well-being.

Financial Analysis

Financial Analysis is a critical process in financial management that involves assessing the financial health and performance of a company or organization. It encompasses the evaluation of various financial statements, such as income statements, balance sheets, and cash flow statements, to gain insights into the company's profitability, liquidity, solvency, and efficiency. The primary objective of financial analysis is to provide meaningful and accurate information to stakeholders, including investors, creditors, managers, and regulatory bodies, to aid in decision-making processes. By analyzing financial data, stakeholders can assess the company's performance, determine its ability to generate profits and cash flows, evaluate its risk profile, and make informed investment or lending decisions. Financial analysis involves a range of techniques and methods to interpret and analyze financial data effectively. Some commonly used tools include ratio analysis, trend analysis, benchmarking, and financial modeling. Ratio analysis involves the computation and interpretation of various financial ratios, such as liquidity ratios, profitability ratios, and leverage ratios, to assess the company's financial position and performance in relation to industry norms or previous periods. Trend analysis compares financial data over multiple periods to identify patterns or trends, highlighting areas of growth or deterioration. Benchmarking involves comparing a company's financial performance with its competitors or industry standards to determine its relative performance and identify areas for improvement. In addition to the examination of financial statements, financial analysis may also involve the consideration of qualitative factors, such as industry trends, market conditions, and management quality. These qualitative factors provide context and further insights into the company's financial performance and prospects. Overall, financial analysis plays a crucial role in financial management by providing objective and evidence-based information about a company's financial health and performance. It helps stakeholders in making informed decisions, identifying areas for improvement, and assessing the risks and opportunities associated with the company's financial operations.

Financial Crisis

A financial crisis can be defined as a severe disruption in a country's financial system, characterized by a sharp decline in asset prices, tightening of credit conditions, and widespread panic and uncertainty among investors and consumers. It often leads to a deep recession, high unemployment rates, and significant losses for businesses and individuals. Financial crises typically arise due to a combination of factors, including unsustainable economic policies, excessive debt levels, speculative bubbles, and poor risk management practices. These factors can create vulnerabilities and imbalances within the financial system, which eventually trigger a crisis when they become unsustainable. During a financial crisis, banks and other financial institutions face significant liquidity and solvency problems. They struggle to meet their short-term funding needs, leading to a credit crunch where lending to businesses and consumers becomes scarce and expensive. This hampers economic activity and can result in bankruptcies and job layoffs. One of the key features of a financial crisis is the collapse in asset prices, such as stocks, real estate, and commodities. This sudden decline erodes the wealth of individuals and businesses, leading to a negative wealth effect. As a result, consumer spending and business investment decline, further exacerbating the economic downturn. Financial crises can have severe and long-lasting impacts on an economy. Governments and central banks often intervene to stabilize the financial system and mitigate the negative effects. They may provide liquidity support to banks, implement monetary stimulus measures, and enact regulatory reforms to prevent future crises. In conclusion, a financial crisis refers to a severe disruption in a country's financial system, characterized by a sharp decline in asset prices, tightening of credit conditions, and widespread panic and uncertainty. It can have devastating effects on the economy, leading to a recession, high unemployment rates, and significant losses for businesses and individuals.

Financial Distress

Financial distress, in the context of financial management, is a state in which a company or individual is unable to meet their financial obligations and is at risk of insolvency or bankruptcy. It is characterized by a lack of sufficient cash flow to cover debt payments and ongoing expenses. Financial distress can be caused by various factors, including poor financial management practices, economic downturns, industry disruptions, or unexpected events such as natural disasters. It is often a result of excessive borrowing, high debt levels, or inadequate revenue generation.

Financial Engineering

Financial Engineering is a multidisciplinary field that combines financial theory, mathematics, and computer technology to create innovative financial products and solutions. It involves the application of quantitative techniques and risk management strategies to solve complex financial problems. The primary objective of financial engineering is to design and structure financial products that maximize returns while minimizing risk. This is achieved through the use of mathematical models and algorithms that analyze and predict market behavior, investment performance, and risk exposure. Financial engineers use their expertise in finance, mathematics, and programming to develop sophisticated financial models and investment strategies.

Financial Forecasting

Financial forecasting is the process of making educated predictions about a company's future financial performance based on historical data, market trends, and industry analysis. It involves projecting future revenues, expenses, and cash flows to anticipate potential outcomes and make informed decisions. Financial forecasting plays a crucial role in financial management as it helps organizations plan and allocate resources effectively, assess their financial health, and evaluate the feasibility of business strategies. By providing insights into future financial performance, forecasting enables businesses to make informed decisions about investments, pricing strategies, cost management, and budgeting.

Financial Institution

A financial institution can be defined as an establishment that conducts financial transactions, such as loans, investments, and deposits, with customers. These institutions play a vital role in the financial system by providing various services to individuals, businesses, and governments. Financial institutions can be categorized into different types, including commercial banks, credit unions, investment banks, insurance companies, and mutual funds. Commercial banks are the most common type of financial institution and are responsible for accepting deposits, lending money, and providing other financial services to customers. Credit unions, on the other hand, are member-owned financial institutions that offer similar services but with a focus on serving a specific group of individuals, such as employees of a particular company or members of a certain organization. Investment banks are primarily involved in providing advisory services to corporations, governments, and other institutions regarding mergers, acquisitions, and other financial transactions. They also facilitate the issuance of securities, such as stocks and bonds, to raise capital for their clients. Insurance companies, as the name suggests, offer various insurance products, such as life insurance, property insurance, and health insurance, to protect individuals and businesses against financial loss. Mutual funds are financial institutions that pool money from multiple investors and invest it in a diversified portfolio of securities, such as stocks and bonds. By pooling resources, individuals can gain access to a professionally managed investment portfolio that may not have been feasible for them individually. In addition to these traditional financial institutions, the rise of technology has given rise to newer players in the financial industry known as fintech companies. These companies leverage technology to provide innovative financial products and services, such as mobile banking apps, peer-to-peer lending platforms, and digital wallets. Overall, financial institutions provide a wide range of services and play a critical role in the financial system. They ensure the smooth functioning of the economy by facilitating the flow of funds between savers and borrowers, managing risks, and providing financial services to meet the needs of individuals, businesses, and governments.

Financial Intermediary

A financial intermediary is a type of financial institution that acts as an intermediary between savers and borrowers. Its main role is to channel funds from those who have excess savings to those who need funds for various purposes, such as investing in businesses or purchasing personal assets. Financial intermediaries play a crucial role in the financial system by facilitating the flow of funds in the economy. They provide a variety of services that help match the needs of savers and borrowers while reducing the risks associated with lending and borrowing.

Financial Leverage

Financial leverage refers to the use of borrowed funds or debt to finance investments or assets, with the aim of increasing potential returns to shareholders. It is a measure of the degree to which a company relies on debt to finance its operations and growth. Financial leverage can be calculated using the debt-to-equity ratio, which compares a company's total debt to its total equity. A high debt-to-equity ratio indicates that a company has a large amount of debt relative to its equity, while a low ratio indicates the opposite.

Financial Market Integration

Financial market integration refers to the process of linking and harmonizing different financial markets, such as stock markets, bond markets, and foreign exchange markets, into a single unified market or platform. This integration allows for the free flow of capital, resources, and investment opportunities across different regions and countries. Financial market integration is a key aspect of global financial management, aiming to create more efficient and effective financial systems. It is facilitated by advancements in technology, communications, and market liberalization policies, which have significantly reduced barriers to entry and the costs of trading and investing in different markets.

Financial Market

A financial market refers to a platform or system where individuals, corporations, and governments can trade financial assets such as stocks, bonds, currencies, and commodities. It serves as a venue for the buying and selling of various financial instruments, enabling participants to raise capital, invest funds, hedge risks, and speculate on market movements. Financial markets encompass a wide range of activities, structures, and intermediaries that facilitate the exchange and transfer of financial assets. These markets include the primary market, where new securities are issued through initial public offerings (IPOs) or private placements, and the secondary market, where existing securities are traded among investors. Secondary markets, represented by stock exchanges, over-the-counter markets, and electronic trading platforms, provide liquidity and enable investors to buy or sell securities after their initial issuance. Furthermore, financial markets can be categorized based on the types of assets being traded. Equity markets focus on the issuance, trading, and valuation of equity securities, such as stocks and shares, which represent ownership in a company. Debt markets, on the other hand, enable the trading of debt instruments such as government bonds, corporate bonds, and loans. Foreign exchange markets facilitate the exchange of different currencies, allowing individuals and businesses to conduct international trade. Commodity markets deal with buying and selling physical goods, such as oil, gold, wheat, and coffee. Financial markets are crucial components of the economy, as they play a vital role in allocating capital and determining prices. They provide opportunities for individuals and organizations to invest their savings, drive economic growth, and mobilize resources for productive purposes. The efficiency and effectiveness of financial markets depend on factors such as transparency, regulation, information dissemination, market integrity, and investor protection.

Financial Markets

Financial markets refer to the platforms or systems where various financial products, such as stocks, bonds, currencies, and commodities, are traded, bought, and sold. These markets facilitate the flow of capital between investors, borrowers, and lenders. Moreover, they play a crucial role in determining the prices of financial assets and the allocation of resources within an economy. Financial markets are essential for efficient allocation of capital, and they are structured in various ways to cater to different types of financial instruments and participants. The major types of financial markets include the stock market, bond market, foreign exchange market, and commodity market. The stock market is a marketplace where shares of publicly traded companies are bought and sold. It provides a platform for companies to raise capital by selling shares and for investors to invest in the potential growth of those companies. Stock markets also enable the trading of derivatives such as stock options and futures contracts. The bond market, on the other hand, is where debt securities, such as government bonds and corporate bonds, are bought and sold. This market allows governments and companies to raise funds by issuing debt instruments, while investors can buy these bonds to generate income from periodic interest payments and the final repayment of principal. The foreign exchange market is responsible for the trading of currencies. It enables participants to exchange one currency for another, facilitating international trade and investment. This market operates 24 hours a day, five days a week, and involves a wide range of participants, including banks, corporations, governments, and speculators. The commodity market deals with the buying and selling of raw materials or primary products, such as gold, oil, wheat, and natural gas. It facilitates price discovery and hedging for producers, consumers, and investors in these commodities. Financial markets are highly influenced by a range of factors, including economic indicators, political events, and investor sentiment. These factors can cause fluctuations in asset prices, making financial markets dynamic and constantly changing. In conclusion, financial markets are crucial for the efficient allocation of capital and the facilitation of economic activity. They provide a platform for buying and selling financial instruments, determine asset prices, and play a vital role in the overall functioning of an economy.

Financial Ratios

Financial ratios are quantitative tools used in financial management to analyze and assess the financial performance and health of a company. These ratios are calculated by comparing different financial variables such as revenue, assets, liabilities, and equity. They provide valuable insights into various aspects of a company's financial position, profitability, efficiency, liquidity, and solvency. Financial ratios are used by investors, creditors, and analysts to make informed decisions regarding investment, lending, and overall business performance evaluation. These ratios help in assessing a company's ability to generate profits, manage its assets and liabilities, and meet its financial obligations.

Financial Risk Management

Financial Risk Management refers to the process of identifying, evaluating, and mitigating potential threats that may adversely impact an organization's financial stability and profitability. It involves implementing strategies and measures to minimize the impact of risks and ensure the company's ability to achieve its financial goals. Risk management plays a crucial role in the field of financial management as it helps businesses anticipate and handle uncertainties related to market fluctuations, credit defaults, liquidity crises, and other financial risks. By identifying these risks in advance, organizations can develop effective strategies, policies, and procedures to minimize their negative impact on business operations and financial performance. The first step in financial risk management is to identify and assess the various types of risks an organization may face. These risks can be categorized into different areas, such as market risk, credit risk, operational risk, liquidity risk, and legal risk. Market risk encompasses the potential losses resulting from changes in market variables, such as interest rates, exchange rates, and commodity prices. Credit risk refers to the risk of default by borrowers or counterparties, while operational risk pertains to risks associated with internal processes, systems, and human error. Once the risks have been identified, the next step is to evaluate their potential impact and likelihood of occurrence. This involves analyzing historical data, conducting risk assessments, and using statistical models and forecasting techniques to estimate the magnitude and probability of different risks. By quantifying the risks, organizations can prioritize their response strategies and allocate resources accordingly. Finally, financial risk management involves implementing risk mitigation measures and monitoring their effectiveness. This may include buying insurance policies, diversifying investments, establishing contingency plans, improving internal controls, and regularly monitoring and reviewing risk exposures. By actively managing and monitoring risks, organizations can minimize the likelihood and impact of adverse events and enhance their ability to achieve their financial objectives. In conclusion, financial risk management is a critical component of financial management that encompasses the identification, evaluation, and mitigation of potential threats to an organization's financial stability and profitability. By effectively managing risks, businesses can reduce uncertainties and increase their resilience and competitiveness in the dynamic and unpredictable financial landscape.

Financial Statement Analysis

A financial statement analysis is a process in financial management that involves evaluating and interpreting the financial information presented in a company's financial statements. The purpose of this analysis is to assess the financial health and performance of a company, as well as to provide insights into its past and future operations. There are three main financial statements that are typically analyzed: the balance sheet, the income statement, and the cash flow statement. The balance sheet provides a snapshot of a company's financial position at a specific point in time, while the income statement shows the company's revenue, expenses, and profitability over a specific period of time. The cash flow statement, on the other hand, shows the cash inflows and outflows of a company during a specific period. Financial statement analysis involves using various techniques and ratios to analyze and interpret the financial data. These techniques include horizontal analysis, vertical analysis, ratio analysis, and trend analysis. Horizontal analysis compares financial data over multiple periods to identify trends and changes, while vertical analysis compares different items within a financial statement to assess their

106

proportionate contribution to the overall financial position of the company. Ratio analysis is an important aspect of financial statement analysis, as it provides insights into a company's liquidity, solvency, efficiency, and profitability. Common ratios used in financial statement analysis include liquidity ratios (such as the current ratio and quick ratio), solvency ratios (such as the debt-to-equity ratio and interest coverage ratio), efficiency ratios (such as the asset turnover ratio and inventory turnover ratio), and profitability ratios (such as the return on assets and return on equity). Trend analysis involves analyzing the financial data over a period of time to identify patterns, changes, and outliers. It helps in identifying the company's historical performance, as well as predicting its future performance. Financial statement analysis also involves comparing a company's financial data with industry averages or benchmark data to assess its relative performance and position within the industry. In conclusion, financial statement analysis is a critical tool in financial management that enables investors, creditors, and other stakeholders to assess the financial health, performance, and prospects of a company. It provides important insights into a company's ability to generate profits, manage its assets and liabilities, and generate cash flows. By analyzing and interpreting the financial statements, stakeholders can make informed decisions regarding their investments, lending, and other financial dealings with the company.

Financial Statement Footnotes

Financial statement footnotes refer to additional information or explanations provided in the footnotes section of a company's financial statements. These footnotes provide important details that enhance the understanding and interpretation of the financial statements. The footnotes section is an integral part of the financial statements, providing clarity and context to the numbers presented in the statements. It is usually placed at the end of the financial statements, following the balance sheet, income statement, and cash flow statement. One of the key purposes of financial statement footnotes is to disclose accounting policies and significant accounting estimates. This information helps users of financial statements understand the basis on which the financial statements have been prepared and the judgments made by management. For example, footnotes may disclose the methods used to value inventory, recognize revenue, or account for long-term assets. Footnotes also provide information about contingencies and commitments that may impact the financial position of the company. This can include legal disputes, warranty obligations, or lease commitments that may have a future financial impact. By disclosing these contingencies and commitments, companies allow users of financial statements to assess the potential risks and uncertainties associated with the company's operations. Furthermore, financial statement footnotes often provide details about related party transactions. These transactions involve the company and its affiliates, shareholders, directors, or key management personnel. Disclosing these transactions is crucial as they may carry a risk of conflicts of interest or may be conducted on terms that are not arm's length. Footnotes also provide information about subsequent events that occur between the end of the reporting period and the date when the financial statements are approved for issuance. These events may include mergers and acquisitions, significant litigation settlements, or changes in accounting policies. By providing this information, companies ensure that users of financial statements have the most up-to-date information available to make informed decisions. Overall, financial statement footnotes play a vital role in enhancing the transparency and usefulness of financial statements. They provide additional context, explanations, and information that are essential for interpreting the numbers in the statements. By disclosing accounting policies, contingencies, related party transactions, and subsequent events, footnotes help users of financial statements understand the company's financial position, performance, and risks more comprehensively. In conclusion, financial statement footnotes are an integral part of the financial reporting process. They provide additional information and explanations that enhance the understanding and interpretation of the financial statements. By disclosing accounting policies, contingencies, related party transactions, and subsequent events, footnotes provide users of financial statements with crucial insights into the company's financial position, performance, and risks.

Fiscal Policy

Fiscal policy refers to the use of government spending and taxation measures to influence the overall economy. It involves the government's decisions on how to allocate its resources and manage its budget in order to achieve desired economic outcomes. One objective of fiscal policy is to stabilize the economy by managing aggregate demand. During periods of recession or economic slowdown, the government may increase its spending or reduce taxes to stimulate demand and encourage economic activity. Conversely, during periods of inflation or economic overheating, the government may decrease its spending or increase taxes to reduce demand and cool down the economy.

Fiscal Year

A fiscal year, in the context of financial management, refers to a period of twelve consecutive months that an organization uses for accounting and financial reporting purposes. It is a predefined time frame that helps businesses and other entities manage and assess their financial performance. The fiscal year is not necessarily the same as the calendar year and can start and end on any date. Many businesses choose to align their fiscal year with the calendar year for simplicity. However, some organizations, especially those in sectors with distinct seasonal patterns, may select different start and end dates to better reflect their operational cycle. During the fiscal year, an entity tracks and records all its financial transactions, including revenue, expenses, assets, and liabilities. This information is used to prepare financial statements, such as the income statement, balance sheet, and cash flow statement, which provide insight into the organization's financial health and performance. By using a fiscal year, businesses can effectively monitor their financial activities and implement strategic planning. It allows them to assess the profitability and growth of their operations, make informed decisions regarding resource allocation, and measure their financial performance against set targets and objectives. Another important aspect of the fiscal year is budgeting. Organizations typically create annual budgets that align with their fiscal year. This budget represents the expected income and expenses for the twelve-month period and serves as a financial roadmap for the entity. In summary, a fiscal year is a predetermined twelve-month period used for financial management and reporting purposes. It allows organizations to track and analyze their financial performance, make informed decisions, and create budgets. By aligning the fiscal year with their operational cycle, businesses can gain a better understanding of their financial health and plan for future growth and success.

Fixed Annuity

A fixed annuity is a financial product that provides a guaranteed income stream to the annuity holder for a specified period of time or for life. It is an agreement between an individual and an insurance company, where the individual makes a lump sum payment or a series of payments to the insurance company in exchange for regular fixed payments in the future. Unlike variable annuities, which are tied to the performance of underlying investments, a fixed annuity offers a fixed rate of return on the investment. This means that the annuity holder knows exactly how much income they will receive each month, regardless of market fluctuations or changes in interest rates. Fixed annuities are often used as a retirement planning tool, as they provide a reliable source of income during retirement. The annuity holder can choose to receive payments for a fixed number of years (e.g., 10 or 20 years) or for the rest of their life. If the annuity holder selects the latter option, the insurance company assumes the risk of outliving the annuity, providing a valuable safeguard against longevity risk. In addition to the fixed rate of return, another advantage of fixed annuities is that they offer tax-deferred growth. This means that any interest earned on the annuity is not taxed until it is withdrawn. This can be particularly beneficial for individuals in higher tax brackets, as it allows them to defer taxes on their annuity earnings until they may be in a lower tax bracket during retirement. However, it's important to note that fixed annuities do have some limitations. One major limitation is that they may not keep pace with inflation. Since the rate of return on a fixed annuity is fixed, it may not provide enough income to maintain the annuity holder's purchasing power over time. Additionally, unlike other investment vehicles, such as stocks or bonds, fixed annuities typically do not offer the potential for capital appreciation. In conclusion, a fixed annuity is a financial product that offers a guaranteed income stream for a specific period of time or for life. It provides a fixed rate of return and tax-deferred growth, which can be advantageous for retirement planning. However, it may not keep pace with inflation and typically does not offer the potential for capital appreciation.

Fixed Asset

A fixed asset is a tangible or intangible resource owned or controlled by a company that is expected to provide future economic benefits and is held for the purpose of producing goods or services, for rental to others, or for administrative purposes. These assets are typically used for a prolonged period of time, usually exceeding one year, and include properties such as land, buildings, machinery, vehicles, office equipment, patents, copyrights, and trademarks. Fixed assets hold value over time, and their acquisition is capital-intensive, involving significant expenditure and long-term commitment. In financial management, fixed assets are considered a vital component of a company's balance sheet, representing the long-term investment made by the organization. They are reported at historical cost, which includes the purchase price and any directly attributable costs of bringing the asset into use, such as transportation and installation fees. The value of fixed assets is subject to depreciation, which is the systematic allocation of the asset's cost over its useful life. Depreciation reflects the gradual consumption, obsolescence, wear and tear, and technological advancements that reduce the asset's value over time. The depreciation expense is recorded in the company's income statement to match the cost of the fixed asset to the revenue it helps generate during its useful life. Fixed assets are vital for the efficient operation of a business and contribute to its production capacity, revenue generation, and competitive advantage. Additionally, they often serve as collateral for loans and can be sold or leased to generate additional income. However, managing fixed assets requires proper tracking, maintenance, and periodic reassessment to ensure their continued usefulness and accurate valuation.

Fixed Charge Coverage Ratio

The Fixed Charge Coverage Ratio is a financial management tool used to assess a company's ability to meet its fixed financial obligations. It calculates the company's ability to pay interest and principal on its debt, lease payments, and other fixed charges using its earnings before interest, taxes, depreciation, and amortization (EBITDA). The formula for calculating the Fixed Charge Coverage Ratio is as follows: Fixed Charge Coverage Ratio = (EBITDA + Fixed Charges) / (Fixed Charges + Interest Expense) Fixed Charges include lease payments, insurance premiums, and other fixed expenses, while Interest Expense refers to the cost of borrowing money. By comparing the company's earnings to its fixed financial obligations, the Fixed Charge Coverage Ratio provides insight into its financial health and ability to service its debts. A ratio of less than 1 suggests that the company may have difficulty meeting its fixed financial obligations with its current earnings. This could indicate financial distress or potential insolvency. On the other hand, a ratio of more than 1 indicates that the company's earnings are sufficient to cover its fixed charges, providing confidence to lenders and creditors. The Fixed Charge Coverage Ratio is commonly used by lenders, creditors, and investors when evaluating a company's creditworthiness and financial stability. It provides an indication of the company's ability to generate enough cash flow to meet its fixed financial obligations, which is crucial for maintaining solvency and avoiding default on loans. However, it's important to remember that the Fixed Charge Coverage Ratio should not be used as the sole determinant of a company's financial health. It should be considered alongside other financial ratios and factors, such as liquidity, profitability, and market conditions, to gain a comprehensive understanding of the company's financial position and future prospects.

Fixed Cost

A fixed cost is a cost that does not change with changes in the level of production or sales. It remains constant regardless of the volume of output or the level of activity within a business. In financial management, fixed costs refer to the expenses that a company incurs regardless of its production or sales volume. These costs are incurred to maintain the basic operational capabilities of a business, such as rent, insurance, salaries, and equipment maintenance. Unlike variable costs, which change based on production or sales levels, fixed costs are fixed and do not vary. They can be considered as the foundational expenses needed to keep a business running, even if there are no sales or production activities occurring. Fixed costs are an essential component of a company's cost structure. They need to be carefully managed and accounted for in the financial planning and budgeting process. Since they are independent of the level of activity, they play a crucial role in determining a company's breakeven point, which is the point at which total revenue equals total costs. For example, let's consider a manufacturing company that has a monthly rent expense of $5,000, regardless of how many units it produces. This rent expense is a fixed cost. Whether the company produces 100 units or 1,000 units, the rent expense remains the same. It is important for the company to understand this fixed cost and ensure that its pricing strategy and sales volume are sufficient to cover this expense. In summary, fixed costs are the expenses that remain constant regardless of the level of production or sales. They are critical in determining a company's breakeven point and need to be carefully managed in financial planning and budgeting processes.

Fixed Costs

Fixed costs are expenses that do not change with the level of production or sales volume. In financial management, fixed costs refer to the predetermined expenses that remain constant regardless of the level of activity or sales. These costs are incurred regularly, and their amounts remain unchanged within a specific time period, usually within a fiscal year. In businesses, fixed costs are crucial for budgeting and financial planning purposes because they provide stability to the overall cost structure. Examples of fixed costs include rent or lease payments for office or manufacturing space, insurance premiums, property taxes, salaries of permanent employees, and annual subscription fees for software or equipment maintenance. Fixed costs are different from variable costs, which fluctuate in direct proportion to the level of activity or sales volume. While variable costs increase or decrease based on changes in production or sales levels, fixed costs remain constant. This means that even if there is no production or sales activity, fixed costs still need to be paid. Understanding fixed costs is essential for financial decision-making as they directly impact a company's profitability. By identifying and analyzing fixed costs, companies can assess their breakeven point and determine the minimum level of activity or sales needed to cover these expenses. Additionally, fixed costs play a significant role in determining the company's cost structure and pricing strategies. One challenge with fixed costs is that they are difficult to reduce in the short term. Since these costs are contractual or essential to business operations, they cannot be easily adjusted based on changes in production or sales volumes. However, long-term strategic decisions can be made to minimize fixed costs, such as renegotiating lease agreements, downsizing office space, or implementing cost-saving measures in employee salaries and benefits. To effectively manage fixed costs, financial managers need to carefully analyze and plan their allocation. By accurately tracking and monitoring fixed costs, companies can control their spending and make informed decisions regarding their cost structure. This can lead to improved profitability and financial stability. Overall, fixed costs are predetermined expenses that remain constant regardless of changes in production or sales volume. Understanding and managing these costs are crucial for financial management, as they directly impact a company's profitability and cost structure. By employing effective cost control strategies and financial planning, companies can optimize their fixed cost allocation and achieve financial success.

Fixed Rate Mortgage

A fixed rate mortgage is a type of mortgage loan that has a fixed interest rate for the entire duration of the loan. In other words, the interest rate does not change over time, providing borrowers with predictable monthly payments. With a fixed rate mortgage, the interest rate is set at the time of borrowing and remains constant for the term of the loan, which can typically range from 15 to 30 years. This means that regardless of how the market interest rates fluctuate during this period, the borrower's interest rate stays the same. As a result, borrowers are shielded from potential increases in interest rates, providing them with stability and peace of mind when budgeting for their monthly mortgage payment. Fixed rate mortgages are popular among borrowers who prefer a consistent and stable payment schedule. This makes them particularly attractive to individuals and families who plan to stay in their homes for a longer period of time and want to avoid the uncertainty associated with adjustable rate mortgages, which have interest rates that can change periodically. In addition to predictable monthly payments, fixed rate mortgages also offer other advantages. They give borrowers the opportunity to lock in historically low interest rates, reducing the risk of future increases. This can result in significant savings over the life of the loan. Furthermore, fixed rate mortgages simplify financial planning as borrowers know exactly how much of their monthly payment will go towards principal and interest, facilitating long-term budgeting. While fixed rate mortgages provide stability and peace of mind, they may not always be the best option for every borrower. For instance, individuals who plan to sell their property in the near future or expect to refinance their mortgage before the loan term ends may not benefit as much from the predictability of a fixed rate mortgage. Additionally, borrowers who believe that interest rates will significantly decrease in the future might find adjustable rate mortgages more appealing. In conclusion, a fixed rate mortgage is a type of mortgage loan that offers borrowers a predictable interest rate and monthly payment, which remains constant throughout the term of the loan. It provides stability and peace of mind for borrowers who want to avoid the uncertainty associated with fluctuating interest rates, making it an attractive choice for individuals and families planning to stay in their homes for the long term.

Fixed-Income Investments

Fixed-Income Investments are financial instruments that provide a fixed return over a specified period of time. These investments typically take the form of bonds or similar debt securities issued by governments, municipalities, corporations, or other entities. The fixed return is typically in the form of interest payments, known as coupon payments, made regularly to the investor until the maturity date of the bond. Fixed-Income Investments are considered less risky than equity investments because the return and the repayment of principal are contractual obligations of the issuer. The fixed return provides a predictable cash flow for investors, making these investments attractive for those seeking a stable income stream. Furthermore, fixed-income investments are often seen as a valuable diversification tool, as they tend to have a low correlation with equities and other asset classes. There are several types of fixed-income investments, including government bonds, corporate bonds, municipal bonds, and mortgage-backed securities. Government bonds are issued by national governments and are typically considered the least risky fixed-income investments, as they are backed by the full faith and credit of the issuing government. Corporate bonds are issued by corporations to finance their operations or expansion, and their risk depends on the creditworthiness of the issuer. Municipal bonds are issued by local governments to fund public infrastructure projects, and they offer tax advantages to investors. Mortgage-backed securities are created by pooling together a large number of mortgage loans and selling them as a bond-like investment. The price and yield of fixed-income investments are inversely related. When interest rates rise, the price of existing fixed-income securities decreases, as their fixed coupons become less attractive compared to new issues with higher coupons. On the other hand, when interest rates decline, the price of existing fixed-income securities increases, as their fixed coupons become more attractive. This inverse relationship between interest rates and fixed-income prices is known as interest rate risk. In conclusion, fixed-income investments are financial instruments that provide a fixed return over a specified period of time, typically in the form of interest payments. They are considered less risky than equity investments, provide a stable income stream, and offer diversification benefits. The main types of fixed-income investments include government bonds, corporate bonds, municipal bonds, and mortgage-backed securities. The price of fixed-income investments is influenced by changes in interest rates.

Fixed-Income Securities

Fixed-income securities are financial instruments that pay a fixed amount of income over a specific period of time. These securities are issued by governments, municipalities, corporations, and other entities to finance their operations and projects. They are commonly known as "bonds" or "debt securities." Fixed-income securities are considered safer than equity securities because they provide a fixed and predictable income stream. The income can be in the form of periodic interest payments or a lump sum payment at maturity. The fixed income is usually determined by the coupon rate, which is the annual interest rate stated on the face of the bond. There are various types of fixed-income securities, including government bonds, corporate bonds, municipal bonds, mortgage-backed securities, and certificates of deposit. Government bonds are issued by national governments and are considered to be the safest. Corporate bonds are issued by companies to raise capital, and their risk and return depend on the creditworthiness of the issuer. Municipal bonds are issued by state and local governments to fund public projects, and they offer tax advantages to investors. Mortgage-backed securities are created by pooling together mortgages and offering them as investment products. Certificates of deposit are time deposits offered by banks with fixed interest rates and maturity dates. Fixed-income securities are traded in the bond market, where investors buy and sell these securities. The price of a fixed-income security is influenced by various factors, including interest rates, inflation, credit ratings, and market demand. When interest rates rise, the prices of existing fixed-income securities typically fall, as investors can earn higher returns with new bonds offering higher interest rates. Conversely, when interest rates fall, the prices of existing fixed-income securities usually rise, as they provide more attractive yields compared to new bonds. Investors in fixed-income securities typically seek a stable income stream and capital preservation. They are often preferred by risk-averse investors who value the security and predictability of fixed returns. However, it is important to note that fixed-income securities still carry risks, including credit risk, interest rate risk, inflation risk, and liquidity risk. It is essential for investors to carefully evaluate these risks and consider their investment objectives and risk tolerance before investing in fixed-income securities.

Floating-Rate Note (FRN)

A Floating-Rate Note (FRN) is a type of debt instrument that has a variable interest rate. The interest rate on an FRN is typically tied to a benchmark interest rate, such as LIBOR (London Interbank Offered Rate) or the Prime Rate. As the benchmark interest rate changes, the interest rate on the FRN adjusts accordingly. FRNs are commonly issued by governments, corporations, and financial institutions as a way to raise capital. They are often used to manage interest rate risk, as the variable interest rate allows the issuer to align the coupon payments with the prevailing market rates.

Foreign Direct Investment (FDI)

Foreign Direct Investment (FDI) refers to the investment made by individuals, businesses, or governments of one country into the economies of another country. It involves the establishment of new businesses, the acquisition of existing businesses, or the expansion of operations in a foreign country. FDI plays a crucial role in financial management as it can provide various benefits to both the investing country and the host country. For the investing country, FDI allows companies to access new markets, exploit comparative advantages, and benefit from lower production costs. It also enables companies to diversify their operations and reduce risks associated with economic uncertainties in their home country. Furthermore, FDI enables companies to gain new knowledge, technologies, and management skills from the host country, leading to improved competitiveness and innovation. For the host country, FDI can contribute to economic growth, employment creation, and infrastructure development. It can attract foreign capital, which can be used to finance domestic investments and reduce the reliance on domestic savings. FDI can also enhance productivity and technological capabilities by introducing advanced production techniques and management practices. Additionally, FDI can stimulate competition, promote trade integration, and transfer new skills and knowledge to the local workforce. However, FDI also poses certain challenges and risks. It can lead to the outflow of profits and the repatriation of funds to the investing country, which may have adverse effects on the balance of payments and foreign exchange reserves of the host country. Additionally, FDI can create dependency on foreign investors and result in the exploitation of natural resources and labor. It can also lead to market concentration and the displacement of local firms, particularly in sectors where foreign companies have a competitive advantage. Overall, FDI is an important aspect of financial management as it influences economic development, international trade, and global competitiveness. It requires careful consideration of the potential benefits and risks involved, as well as effective policies and regulations to promote a favorable investment climate and ensure the maximum benefits for both investing and host countries.

Foreign Exchange Exposure

Foreign Exchange Exposure refers to the risk faced by a company or individual due to changes in exchange rates. It is a measure of the extent to which a company's financial position and cash flows are affected by fluctuations in foreign exchange rates. A company's exposure to foreign exchange risk can arise from various sources, such as imports and exports, foreign borrowings, investments in foreign subsidiaries, or foreign currency transactions. When a company engages in business activities denominated in a foreign currency, it becomes exposed to the risk of exchange rate fluctuations. There are three types of foreign exchange exposure: 1. Transaction Exposure: This type of exposure relates to the risk faced by a company due to changes in exchange rates between the time a transaction is entered into and the time it is settled. If a company has outstanding foreign currency-denominated receivables or payables, a change in exchange rates can affect the value of these receivables or payables when they are settled. This can impact the company's cash flows and profitability. 2. Translation Exposure: Also known as accounting exposure, translation exposure refers to the impact of exchange rate fluctuations on a company's financial statements when the functional currency of its foreign subsidiaries is

112

different from the reporting currency. The translation of financial statements from the subsidiary's currency to the reporting currency can result in gains or losses due to changes in exchange rates. 3. Economic Exposure: Economic exposure is the long-term impact of exchange rate changes on a company's competitive position, future cash flows, and market value. It reflects the vulnerability of a company's profitability to changes in exchange rates. Economic exposure is difficult to measure and manage as it involves factors such as changes in market demand, pricing power, and competition in foreign markets. Managing foreign exchange exposure is an important aspect of financial management. Companies may use various strategies to mitigate the impact of exchange rate fluctuations, such as hedging through forward contracts, options, or futures contracts. Additionally, companies may also diversify their operations and revenue streams across different countries to reduce their exposure to a single currency or market.

Foreign Exchange Hedging

Foreign Exchange Hedging refers to the practice of using financial instruments or strategies to minimize or mitigate the risks associated with fluctuations in foreign exchange rates. It is a risk management technique employed by companies or individuals who engage in international trade or investments. The primary purpose of foreign exchange hedging is to protect against potential losses that may arise due to changes in exchange rates. When a company or individual is involved in cross-border transactions, they are exposed to currency risk, which is the risk of adverse movements in exchange rates that could adversely affect the value of their assets or liabilities denominated in foreign currencies. Companies that engage in foreign exchange hedging usually do so to reduce their exposure to currency risk and to stabilize cash flows. They may enter into various types of hedging transactions or use financial instruments such as forward contracts, futures contracts, options, or swaps to lock in exchange rates or to limit the impact of adverse currency movements on their business operations. By hedging their foreign exchange exposure, companies can protect themselves against unexpected currency fluctuations and budget or plan their expenses and revenues more accurately. A favorable exchange rate can result in cost savings or increased profitability, while an unfavorable exchange rate can lead to higher costs or reduced revenues. Foreign exchange hedging is particularly important for companies that have significant foreign currency exposures or operate in volatile currency markets. It allows them to manage their foreign exchange risk and focus on their core business activities without being overly influenced by unpredictable currency movements. In conclusion, foreign exchange hedging is a crucial aspect of financial management for companies or individuals involved in international trade or investments. It helps them mitigate currency risk, protect against potential losses, and manage their cash flows more effectively. By utilizing hedging techniques and financial instruments, entities can minimize the uncertainties and challenges associated with foreign exchange fluctuations.

Foreign Exchange Market (Forex)

The foreign exchange market, also known as the forex market, is a decentralized global marketplace where participants trade currencies. It serves as a platform for the exchange of one currency for another, enabling international trade and investment by facilitating currency conversion. The forex market operates 24 hours a day, five days a week, across different time zones, and involves a vast network of buyers, sellers, and intermediaries such as banks, financial institutions, and currency traders. It is the largest and most liquid financial market in the world, with an average daily trading volume exceeding trillions of dollars.

Foreign Exchange Market

Foreign Exchange Market is a global decentralized marketplace where currencies are traded. It is a fundamental component of the global financial system and plays a crucial role in facilitating international trade and investment. The Foreign Exchange Market operates through a network of financial institutions, such as banks, that act as intermediaries between buyers and sellers. In this market, currencies are traded in pairs, with one currency being exchanged for another. The value of one currency is determined relative to another currency, and this exchange rate is influenced by various factors, including economic indicators, geopolitical events, and government policies. The exchange rates fluctuate continuously throughout the trading day, providing opportunities for traders to profit from the price movements. The main participants in the Foreign Exchange Market are commercial banks, central banks, multinational corporations, investment firms, and retail traders. These participants engage in currency trading to meet various needs, such as hedging currency risk, facilitating international transactions, and speculating on currency movements. There are several ways to trade currencies in the Foreign Exchange Market. The most common method is spot trading, where currencies are bought and sold for immediate delivery. Another method is forward contracts, where parties agree to exchange currencies at a predetermined future date and exchange rate. Additionally, traders can use derivative products, such as options and futures, to speculate or hedge against currency movements. The Foreign Exchange Market operates 24 hours a day, five days a week, allowing participants to trade currencies at any time. The market is decentralized, meaning that there is no physical location where all transactions take place. Instead, trading occurs electronically through a network of computers, ensuring continuous access and liquidity. One of the key features of the Foreign Exchange Market is its high liquidity. It is the largest financial market in the world, with trillions of dollars' worth of currencies being traded daily. This high liquidity ensures that traders can easily enter and exit positions at competitive prices. In conclusion, the Foreign Exchange Market is a global decentralized marketplace where currencies are traded. It plays a vital role in facilitating international trade and investment and provides opportunities for traders to profit from currency movements. The market operates 24/5 and offers various trading methods and high liquidity.

Foreign Exchange Rate

A foreign exchange rate, also known as a forex rate or FX rate, is the rate at which one currency can be exchanged for another currency. It represents the value of one currency in terms of another currency. This rate is determined by the foreign exchange market, where currencies are traded. Foreign exchange rates play a crucial role in financial management as they affect international trade, investment, and business operations. They are influenced by various factors, including economic indicators, government policies, interest rates, inflation rates, and market expectations.

Forward Contract

A forward contract is a financial instrument that allows two parties to agree on a price today for the future delivery of an asset or a commodity. It is an agreement between a buyer and a seller to exchange a specific quantity of an underlying asset at a predetermined price, on a future date. The contract specifies the terms and conditions of the transaction, including the quantity, quality, delivery date, and price of the asset. Forward contracts are typically used to hedge against future price fluctuations or to speculate on the future movement of prices. The buyer of the contract, known as the long position, agrees to purchase the underlying asset at the specified price at the agreed-upon date. The seller of the contract, known as the short position, agrees to deliver the asset to the buyer at the specified price on the agreed-upon date. One key characteristic of a forward contract is that it is a legally binding agreement. Both the buyer and the seller are obligated to fulfill the terms of the contract, regardless of the market conditions at the time of maturity. This means that both parties bear the risk of adverse price movements. The absence of a centralized exchange for forward contracts differentiates them from other financial derivatives, such as futures contracts. As a result, forward contracts are generally traded over-the-counter (OTC), meaning they are privately negotiated between the two parties involved. This allows for greater flexibility in terms of contract customization to meet specific needs. Forward contracts are prevalent in various industries, including agriculture, commodities, currencies, and interest rates. They are particularly useful for businesses and individuals who want to mitigate the risks associated with future price fluctuations. By locking in a future price, participants in a forward contract can protect themselves from potential losses or secure a favorable price for the asset. In summary, a forward contract is a financial agreement between a buyer and a seller to exchange an asset at a specified price on a predetermined future date. It is a binding contract that helps to manage price risks and allows parties to take advantage of favorable price movements.

Forward Rate Agreement (FRA)

A Forward Rate Agreement (FRA) is a financial contract between two parties who wish to hedge against future fluctuations in interest rates. It is commonly used in the financial management to mitigate the risk associated with interest rate changes. In a FRA, one party agrees to pay a fixed interest rate on a notional principal amount at a specified future date, while the other party agrees to pay a floating interest rate based on a reference rate, such as LIBOR, over the same period. The specified future date is referred to as the settlement date, and the period between the settlement date and the start date of the contract is known as the forward period. The purpose of a FRA is to lock in an interest rate for future borrowing or lending in order to manage the exposure to interest rate fluctuations. For example, a company may enter into a FRA to protect itself against an increase in interest rates, ensuring that it will pay a fixed rate that is lower than the expected market rate. On the other hand, a financial institution may enter into a FRA to protect itself against a decrease in interest rates, guaranteeing a minimum return on its lending activities. When the settlement date arrives, the party whose interest rate is lower than the agreed fixed rate on the FRA will make a payment to the other party. The payment is calculated based on the difference between the fixed rate and the floating rate multiplied by the notional principal amount and the length of the forward period. FRAs are typically traded in the over-the-counter market, allowing parties to customize the terms of the agreement to suit their specific needs. They are widely used by financial institutions, corporations, and fund managers to manage their interest rate exposure and protect against market volatility.

Freddie Mac (Federal Home Loan Mortgage Corporation)

Freddie Mac, also known as the Federal Home Loan Mortgage Corporation, is a government-sponsored enterprise (GSE) established in 1970. It operates in the secondary mortgage market, providing liquidity for mortgage lenders and facilitating the availability of affordable housing for American families. As a GSE, Freddie Mac plays a vital role in the financial system by purchasing residential mortgages from lenders and packaging them into mortgage-backed securities (MBS). These MBS are then sold to investors in the global capital markets. By doing so, it transfers the risk associated with the mortgages from the original lenders to the investors who purchase the MBS. This process helps lenders free up their capital so that they can make more mortgages and extend credit to potential homebuyers. Freddie Mac operates under a government charter and is supervised by the Federal Housing Finance Agency (FHFA). Its mission is to provide stability, liquidity, and affordability to the housing market. The corporation achieves this by buying primarily conforming mortgages, which meet specific criteria set by Freddie Mac, such as loan size, credit quality, and borrower income. By establishing these standards, Freddie Mac aims to reduce the risk of defaults on the mortgages it purchases, ensuring stability in the housing market. In addition to purchasing mortgages, Freddie Mac also guarantees certain mortgage-related securities issued by other entities. This guarantee provides investors with an additional level of assurance regarding the creditworthiness of the underlying mortgages. Through its guarantee programs, Freddie Mac helps promote confidence in the mortgage market by enhancing the liquidity and marketability of the securities. Financial management at Freddie Mac involves various activities related to risk management, capital allocation, and financial reporting. The corporation carefully manages the risks associated with its mortgage portfolio, including interest rate risk, credit risk, and market risk. It also regularly assesses its capital needs and ensures it maintains sufficient capital levels to support its operations and fulfill its mission. Freddie Mac's financial management practices are subject to oversight and regulation to ensure the safety and soundness of the corporation and the stability of the housing market. Its financial statements are prepared in accordance with generally accepted accounting principles (GAAP) and are audited by an independent public accounting firm. The corporation regularly reports its financial performance to shareholders, stakeholders, and government authorities to maintain transparency and accountability.

Free Cash Flow (FCF)

Free Cash Flow (FCF) is a financial metric used by organizations to measure the amount of cash generated from its operations after accounting for capital expenditures required to maintain and expand its business. It provides valuable insights into a company's ability to generate cash and indicates its potential for growth, investor returns, debt repayment, and future investments. FCF can be calculated as the difference between the cash inflows from operating activities and the cash outflows from investing activities. Operating activities include cash flows from core business operations such as sales revenue, cost of goods sold, and operating expenses. Investing activities include cash flows related to the purchase or sale of long-term assets like property, plant, and equipment or investments in other businesses. A positive FCF indicates that a company has generated cash from its operations that can be used for various purposes such as paying dividends to shareholders, reducing debt, repurchasing shares, or reinvesting in the business. It signifies the company's ability to fund its growth and meet its financial obligations without relying on external financing. On the other hand, a negative FCF suggests that the company is spending more cash on investments and operations than it is generating from its core business activities. This may require the company to rely on external funding sources such as debt or equity to meet its financial obligations or fund future growth. Negative FCF can also indicate inefficiencies in managing working capital or excessive capital expenditures. Analysts and investors often use FCF as a key metric to evaluate the financial health and performance of a company. It helps assess the company's ability to generate sustainable cash flows, its efficiency in managing working capital, its capital allocation decisions, and its potential for future growth. Comparing FCF of different companies in the same industry can provide insights into their relative financial strength and operational efficiency.

Free Cash Flow To Equity (FCFE)

The Free Cash Flow to Equity (FCFE) is a measure of the financial performance of a company, specifically its ability to generate cash flow available to be distributed to equity investors. It represents the cash flows that are available to the company's shareholders after all operating expenses, taxes, and reinvestment needs have been met. FCFE is calculated by subtracting capital expenditures and working capital investment from the company's operating cash flow. FCFE is an important metric in financial management as it provides insights into the amount of cash that is available for distribution to shareholders, such as dividends or share buybacks. It is particularly useful for equity investors, as it helps them evaluate the potential returns they can expect from their investment in the company. By analyzing FCFE, financial managers can assess the company's ability to generate returns for its shareholders. A positive FCFE indicates that the company has generated more cash than it needs to reinvest in the business or pay off debt obligations. This surplus cash can be distributed to equity investors, enhancing shareholder value. Conversely, a negative FCFE suggests that the company is not generating enough cash to meet its obligations and may need to rely on external financing. Financial managers can also use FCFE to assess a company's growth prospects. A company with a consistently positive FCFE demonstrates its ability to generate cash from its operations, which can be used for future investments or expansion. On the other hand, a company with a declining or negative FCFE may indicate a lack of growth opportunities or inefficient capital allocation. In summary, FCFE is a valuable metric in financial management that measures the cash flow available to equity investors. It helps evaluate the company's ability to generate returns, assess its growth prospects, and make informed investment decisions. Understanding FCFE allows financial managers to effectively manage the company's cash flow and allocate resources to maximize shareholder value.

Full Disclosure Principle

The Full Disclosure Principle is a fundamental accounting principle that requires a company to provide all necessary information and disclosures in its financial statements and related footnotes. This principle aims to ensure that users of financial statements have access to all relevant information needed to make well-informed decisions. Under this principle, a company must disclose any information that could impact the judgment or decision-making process of its users. This includes but is not limited to information about the company's accounting policies, significant accounting estimates, contingent liabilities, lawsuits, related party transactions, and changes in accounting principles or methods. The company must provide sufficient details and explanations, allowing users to understand the nature and implications of these items. The Full Disclosure Principle contributes to the transparency of financial reporting, as it promotes the disclosure of important information beyond what is included in the basic financial statements. It helps to prevent the omission of relevant facts or the use of misleading information that could potentially mislead financial statement users. By adhering to the Full Disclosure Principle, a company enhances its financial reporting credibility and ensures that users have access to a complete and accurate picture of its financial position, performance, and cash flows. This principle is especially important for potential investors, creditors, and other stakeholders who rely on financial statements to assess the company's financial health and make informed decisions. Moreover, the Full Disclosure Principle is essential for compliance with applicable accounting standards and regulatory requirements. These standards often dictate specific disclosure requirements for certain transactions, events, or circumstances, which companies must adhere to when preparing their financial statements. In summary, the Full Disclosure Principle in financial management requires companies to provide all necessary information and disclosures in their financial statements and related footnotes. This principle ensures transparency, prevents the omission of relevant facts, and provides users with a complete and accurate understanding of a company's financial position, performance, and cash flows.

Full Faith And Credit

Full Faith and Credit refers to the guarantee that a government or organization will honor its financial obligations by repaying its debts in a timely manner. It is a fundamental concept in the field of financial management, particularly in the context of lending and borrowing. When a government or organization seeks to borrow funds, it does so by issuing debt instruments such as bonds or loans. These debt instruments represent a promise to repay the lender at a future date, usually with interest. The lender, in turn, provides funds to the borrower based on the belief that the borrower's promise will be fulfilled.

Fund Manager

A fund manager is a professional who is responsible for managing and overseeing the investment operations of a mutual fund or other types of investment funds. The primary role of a fund manager is to make investment decisions that align with the overall investment objectives and strategies of the fund. This includes conducting research, analyzing financial data, and monitoring market trends to identify potential investment opportunities. In addition to researching and selecting investments, fund managers are also responsible for determining the appropriate investment allocation for the fund's portfolio. This involves considering factors such as risk tolerance, asset class diversification, and the fund's investment horizon. The fund manager's goal is to achieve the highest possible returns for the fund's investors while managing risk effectively. Fund managers are often highly experienced professionals with a deep understanding of financial markets and investment strategies. They typically work closely with a team of analysts and researchers to gather information and evaluate potential investment opportunities. Communication is also a crucial aspect of a fund manager's role. They must effectively communicate investment decisions and strategies to stakeholders, such as fund investors and senior management. Regular reporting and updates on the fund's performance and market outlook are essential in maintaining transparency and trust with investors. Furthermore, fund managers must stay informed about regulatory requirements and industry best practices. They are responsible for ensuring that the fund's operations comply with applicable laws and regulations, including disclosure and reporting obligations. In conclusion, a fund manager plays a vital role in the financial management of investment funds. Their responsibilities range from conducting research and analysis, making investment decisions, managing the fund's portfolio, communicating with stakeholders, and staying up-to-date with regulatory requirements. Through their expertise and guidance, fund managers strive to maximize returns for their investors while balancing risk.

Fundamental Analysis

Fundamental analysis is a key component of financial management that involves evaluating the intrinsic value of a security by analyzing various factors related to the company's financial health, industry dynamics, and macroeconomic environment. It is a method used by investors and financial professionals to assess the fundamental strength and potential future performance of a company before making investment decisions. In fundamental analysis, the focus is on studying the underlying factors that drive the value of a company's stock or bond. This includes analyzing financial statements, such as the balance sheet, income statement, and cash flow statement, to assess the company's profitability, liquidity, and financial stability. Ratios such as earnings per share (EPS), price-to-earnings (P/E) ratio, and return on equity (ROE) are commonly used to gauge a company's financial performance and compare it with industry peers and benchmarks. Moreover, fundamental analysis takes into account qualitative factors such as the company's management team, industry trends, competitive positioning, and regulatory environment. By assessing these factors, analysts can determine the company's competitive advantage, growth potential, and overall feasibility. Furthermore, fundamental analysis is not limited to assessing individual companies but also involves analyzing the broader economic environment and industry conditions. This includes evaluating macroeconomic factors such as interest rates, inflation rates, government policies, and consumer behavior, which can have a significant impact on a company's performance and future prospects. Overall, the goal of fundamental analysis is to determine the intrinsic value of a security and compare it with its market price to identify potential investment opportunities. By conducting a thorough analysis of a company's financials, industry dynamics, and macroeconomic environment, investors can make informed decisions and achieve long-term financial objectives.

Future Value (FV)

Future value (FV) is a financial concept used in the field of financial management to determine the value of an investment or cash flow at a specified point in the future. It is a measure of the expected worth of an asset or investment after accruing interest or experiencing growth over a specific period of time. The calculation of future value takes into account various factors such as the initial amount invested, the rate of return or interest rate, and the time period over which the investment is held. It is based on the principle of compound interest, which means that the interest earned in each period is added to the principal, and subsequent interest is then earned on the new total. This compounding effect allows the value of an investment to grow exponentially over time. In essence, future value is a way to quantify the potential value of an investment or cash flow in the future. It helps investors and financial managers evaluate the attractiveness of different investment opportunities and make informed decisions about where to allocate their resources. The calculation of future value involves the use of a formula, which can be expressed as: $FV = PV \times (1 + r)^n$ Where: - FV = Future value - PV = Present value or initial investment - r = Rate of return or interest rate - n = Number of periods or time periods This formula allows for the determination of the future value of an investment by multiplying the present value by the growth factor, which is equal to $(1 + r)$ raised to the power of n. The growth factor represents the rate at which the investment is expected to grow over time, taking into account the compounding effect of earning interest on interest. By calculating the future value of an investment, financial managers can assess the potential returns and risks associated with different investment options. It provides a quantitative measure that helps inform decision-making and allows for the comparison of alternative investment opportunities. Future value is a fundamental concept in financial management that aids in the evaluation and analysis of investments and cash flows.

Futures Contract

A futures contract is a standardized agreement between two parties to buy or sell a specified asset, such as commodities, currencies, or financial instruments, at a predetermined price and date in the future. It is a financial derivative that allows investors to speculate on the price movement of the underlying asset without owning the asset itself. The basic structure of a futures contract includes the quantity of the underlying asset, the delivery or settlement date, and the agreed price. The two parties involved in the contract are known as the buyer (long position) and the seller (short position). The buyer agrees to purchase the asset at the specified maturity date, while the seller agrees to sell the asset at that same date. One distinctive feature of futures contracts is the margin requirement. Both the buyer and the seller are required to deposit an initial margin with a clearinghouse to ensure their ability to fulfill the contract obligations. This margin acts as collateral and provides a certain level of protection against potential default. As the value of the underlying asset fluctuates, the margin balance is adjusted to reflect the mark-to-market value of the contract. The main purposes of futures contracts are hedging and speculation. Hedging involves using futures contracts to offset the price risk associated with the underlying asset. For example, a corn farmer can sell corn futures to protect against potential price declines, ensuring a certain level of income regardless of market fluctuations. Speculators, on the other hand, engage in futures contracts to profit from price movements without the intention of taking physical delivery of the asset. Trading futures contracts takes place on regulated exchanges, where standardized contracts are traded in a centralized marketplace. These exchanges provide transparency, liquidity, and price discovery for futures contracts, ensuring fair and efficient trading. They also enforce strict rules and regulations to prevent market manipulation and protect participants. In conclusion, futures contracts are essential financial tools that provide investors with the opportunity to trade, hedge, and speculate on the price fluctuation of various assets in a standardized and regulated manner. They enable market participants to manage risk, diversify portfolios, and potentially profit from future price movements.

118

Futures Market

A futures market, in the context of financial management, refers to a centralized marketplace where standardized contracts for the future delivery of commodities, assets, or financial instruments are bought and sold. It is a derivative market that enables participants to hedge risks or speculate on future price movements. Participants in a futures market typically include producers, consumers, and investors who seek to manage or profit from price fluctuations. These markets provide a mechanism for these individuals or entities to establish a binding agreement to buy or sell a specified quantity of a particular asset on a future date at a predetermined price.

General Partner

A general partner refers to a member of a business partnership or a limited partnership who bears unlimited personal liability for the debts and obligations of the partnership. They are active participants in the management and decision-making processes of the partnership, responsible for overseeing day-to-day operations and making strategic decisions. As a general partner, individuals contribute capital to the partnership and are entitled to a share of the partnership's profits. They also share the responsibility for any losses incurred by the partnership. General partners have the authority to enter into contracts on behalf of the partnership, and their actions bind the partnership legally. They have fiduciary duties towards the partnership, meaning they must act in the best interests of the partnership and its partners.

Geometric Brownian Motion (GBM)

Geometric Brownian Motion (GBM) is a mathematical model commonly used in financial management to describe the behavior of an asset price over time. It is particularly applicable to assets whose returns exhibit log-normal distribution and have constant volatility. GBM assumes that the price of an asset follows a stochastic process, where the future price depends on both the current price and a random component. It is characterized by two main parameters: the drift, which represents the average rate of return, and the volatility, which measures the standard deviation of the returns. The GBM equation is expressed as: $S(t) = S(0) * exp[(\mu - (\sigma^2/2)) * t + \sigma * W(t)]$ Where: - $S(t)$ is the price of the asset at time t - $S(0)$ is the initial price of the asset - μ is the expected return or drift rate - σ is the standard deviation or volatility of the asset's returns - t is the time period - $W(t)$ is a standard Brownian motion or Wiener process Using GBM, financial managers can forecast the future price movements of an asset based on its historical data. By estimating the drift and volatility, they can simulate various scenarios to evaluate investment opportunities, calculate risk measures, and make informed decisions regarding portfolio management, pricing derivatives, and hedging strategies. However, it is important to note that GBM has its limitations. The model assumes that asset prices follow a continuous and smooth path, whereas in reality, they can be subject to sudden jumps or discontinuities. Additionally, GBM assumes that the variance of prices is constant over time, which might not always hold true in real-world situations.

Geometric Mean Return

The geometric mean return is a measure used in financial management to calculate the average rate of return of an investment over multiple periods, taking into account the compounding effect. It is often used to assess the performance of investment portfolios, funds, or individual assets.Unlike the arithmetic mean return, which simply calculates the average of the individual period returns, the geometric mean return demonstrates the compound growth rate of an investment. It reflects the compounding effect that occurs when the returns of an investment are reinvested.

Gini Coefficient

The Gini Coefficient is a statistical measure used in the field of Financial Management to assess income inequality within a given population or economy. It provides a quantitative measure of the distribution of wealth or income among individuals or households. This coefficient is derived from the Lorenz Curve, which is a graphical representation of the cumulative distribution of income. The curve plots the cumulative percentage of the population on the horizontal axis against the cumulative percentage of total income on the vertical axis. A perfectly equal distribution of income would result in a 45-degree line, while a highly unequal distribution would result in a curve that deviates significantly from this line. The Gini Coefficient itself is a ratio that ranges between 0 and 1, where 0 represents perfect equality (all individuals or households have the same income) and 1 represents maximum inequality (one individual or household has all the income while the rest have none). A higher coefficient indicates a greater level of income inequality within the population. The Gini Coefficient is calculated by dividing the area between the Lorenz Curve and the 45-degree line by the total area below the 45-degree line. This can be interpreted as the proportion of income that would need to be redistributed in order to achieve perfect equality. In financial management, the Gini Coefficient is used to evaluate the fairness and efficiency of income distribution within an economy. It helps policymakers and economists understand the social and economic implications of income inequality and inform decision-making related to taxation, social programs, and wealth redistribution. While the Gini Coefficient provides valuable insights into income inequality, it is important to interpret and use it in conjunction with other socioeconomic indicators to gain a comprehensive understanding of the underlying factors contributing to inequality and to develop effective policies for addressing the issue.

Global Depository Receipt (GDR)

A Global Depository Receipt (GDR) is a financial instrument that represents an ownership interest in shares of a foreign company. It is issued by a depositary bank, typically in a country other than where the company is based, to enable international investors to trade the company's shares on a foreign stock exchange. When a company decides to issue GDRs, it appoints a depositary bank that will be responsible for the issuance and custody of the GDRs. The bank will create a pool of the company's shares, known as the underlying shares, and issue GDRs against this pool. Each GDR represents a certain number of underlying shares, which can vary depending on the company's preference. GDRs can be listed on one or more foreign stock exchanges, such as the London Stock Exchange or the New York Stock Exchange. This allows international investors to buy and sell GDRs in their local currency, without the need to directly trade in the company's shares on its home stock exchange. The GDRs are quoted and traded in the same way as ordinary shares, with their prices determined by supply and demand in the market. Investors who hold GDRs are entitled to the same dividends, capital gains, and other benefits as shareholders who hold the underlying shares directly. The depositary bank acts as an intermediary between the company and the GDR holders, collecting dividends and distributing them to GDR holders in their local currency. GDR holders also have the right to convert their GDRs into the underlying shares, subject to certain conditions and procedures specified by the company and the depositary bank. GDRs provide several benefits for both companies and investors. For companies, GDRs offer an avenue to raise capital from international markets and increase their global visibility. GDR issuances can attract a broader range of investors and potentially lead to a higher valuation for the company. For investors, GDRs provide an opportunity to gain exposure to foreign companies and diversify their investment portfolio without the need for extensive knowledge of foreign markets or currencies.

Going Concern

A going concern is a term used in financial management to describe a business entity that is expected to continue its operations for the foreseeable future. When evaluating the financial statements of a company, it is important to assess whether the company is a going concern. This assessment provides valuable information on the company's ability to generate sufficient cash flows to meet its obligations and sustain its operations in the long term.

Gold Standard

The gold standard is a monetary system in which the value of a country's currency is directly linked to a specific amount of gold. Under this system, each unit of currency represents a certain amount of gold. The gold standard establishes a fixed exchange rate between gold and currency, ensuring stability and predictability in international trade and finance. In a gold standard system, a country's currency can be freely converted into gold at a fixed price. This means that the currency's value is determined by the amount of gold it can be exchanged for. The fixed exchange rate discourages excessive inflation and prevents governments from manipulating the value of their currency to their advantage. The gold standard has been used throughout history, with various countries adopting and abandoning it at different times. It was most widely used during the late 19th and early 20th centuries, particularly among major economies such as the United States and the United Kingdom. One of the key benefits of the gold standard is its ability to provide a stable and reliable medium of exchange. By linking currency to a tangible asset like gold, the risk of currency devaluation or hyperinflation is minimized, fostering confidence among individuals and businesses. This stability promotes international trade by providing a uniform standard of value that can be trusted by all parties involved. However, the gold standard also has its limitations and drawbacks. The fixed exchange rate can constrain a government's ability to implement monetary policies to address economic fluctuations. It can also limit the flexibility of governments to respond to financial crises or recessions by adjusting their currency's value. Additionally, the availability of gold reserves can become a limiting factor for a country's economic growth. Despite its limitations, the gold standard played a crucial role in shaping the modern financial system. Its emphasis on stability and predictability set a precedent for future monetary systems and influenced the development of central banking practices. Although no longer widely practiced, the gold standard remains a significant concept in the study of financial management and the history of international finance.

Golden Parachute

A golden parachute, in the context of financial management, refers to a pre-arranged financial arrangement or compensation package provided to top executives or key personnel of a company in the event of a change in control or ownership of the company, such as a merger or acquisition. The primary purpose of a golden parachute is to provide financial protection and additional incentives for executives in the event of a change in control that may result in their termination or displacement from their position. It is intended to ensure that executives are adequately compensated for their contributions to the company, regardless of the circumstances surrounding their departure.

Goodwill Impairment

Goodwill impairment refers to a reduction in the value of a company's goodwill asset that occurs when the estimated fair value of the asset falls below its carrying value. Goodwill represents the excess of the purchase price of an acquired business over the fair value of its identifiable net assets. It is recorded as an intangible asset on the balance sheet. Under financial management, goodwill impairment is a significant consideration as it directly impacts a company's financial statements and can affect its overall financial health. When a company acquires another business, it pays a premium above the identifiable net assets to gain access to intangible assets such as brand recognition, customer relationships, and intellectual property. This premium is recorded as goodwill on the acquiring company's balance sheet. The accounting for goodwill requires regular testing for impairment. Impairment tests are carried out at least annually or whenever certain triggering events occur that may suggest a potential decline in value. Triggering events include a significant adverse change in the economic climate, a downturn in the company's financial performance, or a change in management strategy. To determine if goodwill is impaired, the company compares the fair value of the reporting unit to its carrying value. The reporting unit is the lowest level of an entity that is evaluated for goodwill impairment. If the fair value is lower than the carrying value, an impairment loss is recognized. This loss is recorded as a non-cash expense on the income statement, reducing the net income and the overall value of the company. Goodwill impairment impacts the financial management of a company in several ways. Firstly, it directly affects the company's profitability and financial performance by reducing the reported net income. This can result in decreased shareholder value, lower earnings per share, and reduced dividends. Secondly, goodwill impairment triggers a reassessment of the company's assets and liabilities, leading to potential adjustments in valuations and financial ratios. It may necessitate a reassessment of debt covenants or impact the company's ability to obtain financing at favorable terms. In conclusion, goodwill impairment is an essential concept in financial management involving the reduction in the value of a company's goodwill asset. Regular testing for impairment is necessary to ensure the accurate representation of a company's financial position and performance, as well as compliance with accounting standards.

Goodwill

121

Goodwill, in the context of financial management, refers to an intangible asset that represents the value of a business beyond its tangible assets and liabilities. It arises when a company is purchased for a price higher than the fair market value of its net assets, including tangible assets such as property, equipment, and inventory, as well as liabilities such as debt and accounts payable. Goodwill is calculated by subtracting the fair market value of a company's net identifiable assets from the purchase price. These net identifiable assets include tangible assets, liabilities, and intangible assets such as patents, trademarks, and customer relationships that can be separately identified and valued. The difference between the purchase price and the net identifiable assets is considered goodwill.

Gordon Growth Model

The Gordon Growth Model, also known as the Gordon Dividend Model or the Gordon Growth Dividend Discount Model, is a financial valuation tool used in the field of financial management. It is named after Myron J. Gordon, the economist who first proposed the model in 1959. The Gordon Growth Model is used to determine the intrinsic value of a company's stock by estimating its dividends and the rate at which those dividends are expected to grow over time. It is based on the assumption that the value of a stock is equal to the present value of its expected future dividends.

Government Bond

A government bond refers to a fixed income security issued by the government to finance its activities and projects. It is a debt instrument that enables the government to borrow money from investors for a specific duration, known as the bond's maturity period. Governments issue bonds to raise funds for various purposes, including infrastructure development, welfare programs, and budgetary requirements. Investors who purchase government bonds become lenders to the government and are entitled to receive regular interest payments, known as coupon payments, throughout the bond's tenure. At the bond's maturity, the investor receives the bond's face value, which represents the initial investment amount. Government bonds are considered low-risk investments as they are backed by the full faith and credit of the issuing government. This means that governments are generally reliable in repaying their debts. Consequently, government bonds are often regarded as safe havens for investors seeking stability and steady returns. The interest rates on government bonds are determined through auctions, where investors place bids stating the price they are willing to pay for the bond and the yield they expect to receive. The government then sets the coupon rate based on the demand and prevailing market rates. These rates can be fixed or variable, depending on the type of bond issued. Government bonds are classified into different categories based on various factors. These include the maturity period, such as short-term (usually less than one year), medium-term (one to ten years), or long-term (more than ten years). Additionally, they may be categorised based on whether they are inflation-indexed bonds, zero-coupon bonds, or callable bonds, among others. Investors in government bonds should carefully consider their investment objectives, risk tolerance, and liquidity needs before investing. While government bonds are relatively safe, they are not entirely risk-free. Factors such as changes in interest rates, inflation, and political stability can impact the value of government bonds in the secondary market.

Green Bonds

Green Bonds are financial instruments issued by governments, municipalities, corporations, and other entities to raise capital for projects that have a positive and measurable environmental impact. These bonds are specifically designed to fund projects that promote sustainability, combat climate change, and protect the environment. Unlike traditional bonds, which are used to finance general corporate purposes or infrastructure projects, Green Bonds are dedicated to funding activities and initiatives aimed at achieving environmental objectives. The projects eligible for Green Bond financing can include the development of renewable energy facilities, energy-efficient building constructions, waste management systems, sustainable agriculture, and initiatives for the conservation of natural resources.

Gross Domestic Product (GDP)

Gross Domestic Product (GDP) is a key measure of economic activity and performance within a country. It represents the total monetary value of all goods and services produced within a specific geographic region, typically a country, over a given period of time, usually a year. GDP is an important indicator for financial management as it provides a snapshot of the overall health and growth of an economy. It is used by governments, policymakers, and businesses to inform decision-making and assess economic performance.

Gross Margin

Gross margin is a financial metric used in financial management to analyze and evaluate a company's profitability and overall financial health. It represents the difference between a company's total revenue and its cost of goods sold (COGS). Gross margin is expressed as a percentage and provides important insights into a company's ability to generate a profit from its core business operations. The formula to calculate gross margin is as follows: Gross Margin = (Total Revenue - COGS) / Total Revenue * 100 Gross margin is a key indicator of a company's profitability because it reveals the amount of profit generated for each dollar of sales after deducting the direct costs associated with producing or acquiring the goods or services sold by the company. A higher gross margin indicates that the company is able to generate more profit from each sale, while a lower gross margin suggests that the company's cost of production or acquisition is higher relative to its revenue. Gross margin is particularly useful in comparing the financial performance of companies within the same industry or sector. By analyzing the gross margins of different companies, investors and financial analysts can gain insights into the relative cost efficiency and pricing power of these companies. A company with a higher gross margin compared to its peers may indicate superior operational efficiency or a competitive advantage in pricing its products or services. Changes in gross margin over time can also provide valuable information about a company's financial performance and operational efficiency. A consistent or increasing gross margin indicates that the company is effectively managing its costs and maintaining or improving its pricing strategy. Conversely, a declining gross margin may suggest that the company is facing challenges such as increasing costs or pricing pressure. In summary, gross margin is a key financial metric used in financial management to assess a company's profitability and cost efficiency. It provides insights into the company's ability to generate profit from its core business operations and is a useful tool for comparing the financial performance of companies within the same industry or sector. Changes in gross margin over time can indicate trends in a company's financial performance and operational efficiency.

Gross Profit Margin

The Gross Profit Margin, also known as the Gross Margin, is a financial metric used in the field of financial management to assess a company's profitability. It measures the proportion of revenue that remains after deducting the cost of goods sold (COGS) and is expressed as a percentage. This metric is vital for understanding a company's ability to generate profit from its core business activities. By analyzing the gross profit margin, financial managers can evaluate the efficiency of a company's production and pricing strategies. To calculate the gross profit margin, one must subtract the COGS from the total revenue and divide the result by the total revenue. The formula can be expressed as: Gross Profit Margin = (Total Revenue - Cost of Goods Sold) / Total Revenue A higher gross profit margin indicates that a company is generating more profit from each dollar of revenue. It implies that the company has effective cost control measures, efficient production processes, and can potentially withstand price fluctuations in the market. On the other hand, a lower gross profit margin suggests that a company's production costs are relatively high compared to its revenue, which can be a cause for concern. It may indicate pricing issues, poor inventory management, or excessive production expenses. Comparing the gross profit margin of a company with its competitors in the same industry can provide valuable insights. Understanding why a company has a higher or lower gross profit margin compared to its peers can help identify strategic advantages or areas for improvement. In conclusion, the gross profit margin is a crucial financial metric used in financial management to evaluate a company's profitability. It provides valuable information about a company's ability to generate profit from its core operations and can aid in identifying areas of strength or weakness. By calculating and analyzing this metric, financial managers can make informed decisions regarding pricing strategies, cost control, and overall business performance.

Hedge Fund Manager

A hedge fund manager is a professional who oversees the management and investment strategies of a hedge fund. Hedge funds are private investment vehicles that pool capital from accredited investors and institutional investors to generate high returns. The hedge fund manager is responsible for making investment decisions, executing trades, and managing the fund's portfolio. The primary goal of a hedge fund manager is to generate alpha, which refers to the excess return earned above the fund's benchmark. To achieve this, the manager employs various investment strategies, such as long-short equity, global macro, event-driven, and quantitative strategies. These strategies aim to exploit market inefficiencies, price discrepancies, and other opportunities to outperform the market. As the person in charge, the hedge fund manager collaborates with a team of analysts and researchers to identify investment opportunities and develop trading strategies. They conduct thorough research and analysis of financial markets, economic trends, and individual securities to make informed investment decisions. The manager also monitors the fund's performance, risk exposure, and compliance with regulatory requirements. In addition to investment management, the hedge fund manager also plays a critical role in investor relations. They communicate with investors, providing regular updates on the fund's performance and addressing any questions or concerns. The manager may also participate in fundraising efforts, seeking to attract new investors and grow the fund's assets under management. Overall, a hedge fund manager is a skilled and experienced professional who navigates the complex world of financial markets to generate superior returns for the fund's investors. They possess a deep understanding of investment strategies, risk management, and financial analysis. Additionally, they demonstrate strong leadership and communication skills to effectively manage a team and engage with investors.

Hedge Fund

Hedge fund refers to a type of investment fund that pools capital from accredited individuals or institutional investors and employs various investment strategies to generate high returns. The fundamental characteristic of a hedge fund is its ability to use a wide range of investment techniques that are not typically available to other investment vehicles such as mutual funds.These investment strategies can include taking both long and short positions in different types of assets, employing leverage, using derivatives, and participating in complex transactions in order to profit from market inefficiencies or specific events. Hedge funds often aim to generate absolute returns, meaning they seek to achieve positive returns regardless of the direction of the overall market.

Hedge Ratio

Hedge Ratio in the context of Financial Management refers to the relationship between the quantities of a financial asset and its corresponding hedging instrument that are needed to neutralize the risk associated with the asset. The hedge ratio is typically calculated by dividing the change in the value of the asset by the change in the value of the hedging instrument. This ratio helps determine the amount of the hedging instrument that should be held to offset the potential losses or gains in the value of the asset.

Hedging Strategies

Hedging strategies in the context of financial management refer to the various tactics and techniques employed by individuals and organizations to mitigate or offset potential financial risk. These strategies are used to minimize the negative impact of unpredictable or adverse events on financial positions, investments, or transactions. One commonly used hedging strategy is diversification, which involves spreading investments across a variety of assets or sectors. By diversifying their portfolio, investors can reduce their exposure to risk associated with a specific company, industry, or market. This strategy helps ensure that losses in one area can be offset by gains in another, thus potentially reducing overall volatility.

Hedging Strategy

A hedging strategy refers to a risk management technique employed by businesses and investors to mitigate the potential impact of adverse price movements in financial markets. The primary objective of a hedging strategy is to create a protective position that can offset potential losses resulting from market volatility. Hedging involves taking an offsetting position in a related security or financial instrument in order to reduce or eliminate the risk of price fluctuations. This is typically done by using derivatives such as options, futures, or swaps. By entering into these derivative contracts, investors are able to lock in a certain price or establish a limit on potential losses. There are various types of hedging strategies that can be utilized depending on the specific risk exposure and financial objectives of the business or investor. Some common hedging strategies include: 1. Long and short positions: This strategy involves taking both a long position (buying) and a short position (selling) on the same or related assets. By doing so, any potential losses from one position can be offset by gains in the other, thereby reducing overall risk exposure. 2. Options hedging: This strategy involves using options contracts to hedge against potential price fluctuations. By purchasing options, investors have the right, but not the obligation, to buy or sell an underlying asset at a predetermined price within a specified period of time. This provides protection against adverse price movements while allowing for potential gains if the market moves in their favor. 3. Futures hedging: In this strategy, investors use futures contracts to hedge against future price movements. Futures contracts specify the future delivery of an underlying asset at a predetermined price. By entering into a futures contract, investors can lock in a price and protect themselves against potential losses resulting from unexpected price fluctuations. Hedging strategies are widely used in financial management to manage risk and protect against potential losses. By implementing effective hedging strategies, businesses and investors can safeguard their portfolios and minimize the impact of adverse market movements on their financial performance.

Hedging Transaction

A hedging transaction in the context of financial management refers to a strategy used by individuals or companies to minimize or eliminate the potential risks associated with the price fluctuations of an asset or investment. It involves taking an offsetting position in a related security or financial instrument, with the intention of protecting against adverse movements in the value of the initial investment The purpose of a hedging transaction is not to generate profits, but rather to mitigate potential losses that may arise from changes in market conditions. By taking a hedging position, the investor or company aims to neutralize or reduce the impact of price fluctuations on their overall portfolio or specific investments. There are various types of hedging transactions, including but not limited to: 1. Futures Contracts: These are financial derivatives that obligate the buyer to purchase an asset or the seller to sell an asset at a predetermined future date and price. By entering into a futures contract, an investor can protect against future price changes by locking in a specific price in advance. 2. Options Contracts: Options give the buyer the right, but not the obligation, to buy (call option) or sell (put option) a specific asset at a predetermined price within a specified period. By purchasing options contracts, investors can protect against potential losses while still retaining the opportunity to participate in favorable market movements. 3. Forward Contracts: Similar to futures contracts, forward contracts are customized agreements between two parties to buy or sell an asset at a specified future date and price. They are typically used for non-standardized transactions and can be tailored to specific needs and requirements. Hedging transactions can be utilized by both individuals and businesses across various asset classes, including stocks, commodities, currencies, and interest rates. The specific hedging strategy employed will depend on the investor's risk tolerance, investment objectives, and the nature of the underlying asset or investment. Overall, hedging transactions serve as a risk management tool, allowing investors and businesses to protect against adverse market movements and reduce the potential impact of unpredictable events. By implementing appropriate hedging strategies, individuals and companies can safeguard their financial positions and enhance the stability of their portfolios.

Hedging

Hedging in the context of Financial Management refers to a risk management strategy employed by individuals and organizations to mitigate or offset potential losses or fluctuations in the value of an asset or investment. It involves taking positions or adopting strategies that act as a counterbalance to the risks associated with certain financial exposures. The primary purpose of hedging is to protect against adverse market movements, uncertainty, and volatility. By implementing hedging techniques, investors aim to minimize the potential impact of undesirable events on their portfolio or financial position. This strategy can be applied to various financial instruments, including stocks, bonds, commodities, currencies, and derivatives. Hedging involves establishing offsetting positions or employing financial instruments that have a negative correlation to the underlying assets. By doing so, investors can potentially reduce or eliminate the risk of large losses resulting from adverse price movements. The most commonly used hedging instruments include options, futures contracts, forwards, and swaps. Options, for instance, provide the buyer with the right, but not the obligation, to buy (call option) or sell (put option) a specific asset at a predetermined price within a specified period. By buying put options, investors can protect themselves from potential declines in the value of the asset. Conversely, call options can be purchased to hedge against potential increases in the asset's value. Futures contracts, on the other hand, enable investors to lock in the price at which an asset will be bought or sold in the future. By entering into a futures contract, investors can protect themselves against potential price fluctuations. This is particularly useful when dealing with commodities or foreign currencies, where price volatility is common. Overall, hedging plays a crucial role in managing risk and protecting investments in the field of Financial Management. It allows individuals and organizations to reduce their exposure to unwanted risks by employing various techniques and instruments. By hedging, investors can gain a certain level of confidence and stability in their portfolios, even in unpredictable market conditions.

High-Frequency Trading (HFT)

High-Frequency Trading (HFT) is a computerized trading strategy that involves the rapid execution of a large number of trades within very short time intervals. Using powerful algorithms and cutting-edge technology, HFT aims to profit from small price discrepancies in financial markets. HFT traders use sophisticated computer systems to analyze market data and execute trades in a matter of milliseconds. They rely on high-speed connections and co-located servers to gain a competitive advantage over traditional traders. By being able to react to market movements faster than human traders can, HFT seeks to exploit fleeting market inefficiencies and capitalize on small price differentials. HFT strategies are typically based on mathematical models and statistical arbitrage techniques. These models analyze vast amounts of data in real-time to identify patterns and trends that may indicate profitable trading opportunities. HFT traders may employ various strategies, such as market making, arbitrage, and statistical arbitrage, to generate profits. One key characteristic of HFT is its high trading frequency. HFT algorithms can execute thousands of trades per second, accounting for a significant portion of the overall trading volume in many financial markets. This high trading frequency allows HFT traders to quickly enter and exit positions, often taking advantage of small price movements that may go unnoticed by traditional traders. HFT has revolutionized the financial markets, bringing both benefits and challenges. On the positive side, HFT has increased market liquidity, narrowed bid-ask spreads, and facilitated price discovery. However, critics argue that HFT can create market instability and exacerbate market volatility, particularly during times of stress. Additionally, concerns have been raised about the potential for unfair advantages and the impact of HFT on market integrity. Overall, High-Frequency Trading is a computerized trading strategy that relies on powerful algorithms and high-speed technology to execute a large number of trades within very short time intervals. With its ability to quickly identify and exploit small market inefficiencies, HFT has become a significant player in the global financial markets.

High-Yield Bond

A high-yield bond, also known as a junk bond, is a type of bond that offers a higher yield or return compared to other traditional fixed-income securities. These bonds are generally issued by companies with below-average credit ratings, making them riskier investments. High-yield bonds are characterized by their lower credit ratings, typically below investment grade, which indicates a higher probability of default. As a result, these bonds are considered speculative investments and are accompanied by higher risk and potential volatility.

Holding Period Return (HPR)

Holding Period Return (HPR) is defined as the total return on an investment over a specific period of time, taking into account both capital gains and income generated from dividends or interest. HPR is a commonly used measure in financial management to evaluate the performance of an investment over a given time frame. It allows investors to assess the profitability of their investment and compare it to other available options. It is calculated by dividing the ending value of the investment by the beginning value, subtracting 1, and then multiplying by 100 to express the return as a percentage.

Hurdle Rate

The hurdle rate, also known as the required rate of return, is a key concept in financial management. It is the minimum rate of return that an investment or project must achieve in order to be considered acceptable and to create value for the company or investor. The hurdle rate is used as a benchmark to evaluate whether the potential return on an investment or project is high enough to compensate for the risk involved. It takes into account factors such as the cost of capital, the opportunity cost of investing in alternative projects, and the specific risks associated with the investment or project.

IPO (Initial Public Offering)

IPO, which stands for Initial Public Offering, is a significant event in the field of Financial Management. It refers to the process by which a private company offers its shares to the public for the first time, thereby transitioning from a privately held company to a publicly traded one. In this process, the company issues new shares of stock and sells them to institutional investors and retail investors, who become shareholders in the company. Before conducting an IPO, a company typically needs to meet certain requirements set by regulatory bodies, such as the Securities and Exchange Commission (SEC) in the United States. These requirements might include a certain size and profitability threshold, as well as having an established track record. The company also needs to appoint an investment bank or a group of underwriters to manage the IPO process and assist with offering the shares to the public. The main purpose of an IPO is to raise capital for the company. By going public, the company can access the equity markets to secure funding for various purposes such as expanding operations, investing in research and development, paying off debt, or acquiring other companies. In addition, an IPO can also enhance the company's public image and improve its recognition and credibility in the marketplace. However, conducting an IPO also involves certain challenges and considerations. The company needs to navigate through complex legal and financial regulations, disclose detailed financial information to the public, and comply with ongoing reporting requirements. Moreover, the process can be costly in terms of fees paid to investment banks and legal advisors. Additionally, once a company goes public, it becomes subject to increased scrutiny from shareholders, analysts, and the public, which can bring about added pressure for transparency and financial performance.

Illiquid Asset

An illiquid asset refers to an asset that cannot be easily converted into cash without incurring significant costs or experiencing a substantial loss in value. These assets tend to have limited trading activity in the market, making it difficult to find buyers or sellers, and they often have longer settlement periods compared to liquid assets. Illiquidity can arise due to various reasons, such as the nature of the asset itself, market conditions, or legal and regulatory restrictions. Examples of illiquid assets include real estate properties, private equity investments, certain types of debt securities, and certain alternative investments like hedge funds or venture capital funds.

Implied Volatility

Implied volatility is a key concept in financial management that measures the expected magnitude of price changes in a financial asset, such as stocks, bonds, or options. It is derived from the market price of the asset's options and reflects the market's expectations of future volatility. In essence, implied volatility is the market's estimate of how much an asset's price will fluctuate over a specific time period. It is often expressed as a percentage and is used to calculate the price of options. Higher implied volatility indicates a greater expected range of price movements, while lower implied volatility suggests a more stable or predictable price pattern. This information is crucial for investors and traders who depend on options strategies to manage risk and seek profit.

In-Kind Distribution

In financial management, in-kind distribution refers to the process of distributing goods or services instead of cash as a form of payment or transfer. This type of distribution is commonly used in various contexts, such as humanitarian aid, government programs, and nonprofit organizations. When an in-kind distribution occurs, the recipient receives specific goods or services instead of monetary funds. These goods or services can range from basic necessities like food, clothing, or shelter to more specialized items like medical supplies or educational materials. In-kind distributions can also include services such as medical care, educational programs, or vocational training.

Incentive Stock Option (ISO)

An Incentive Stock Option (ISO) is a type of stock option granted to employees by their employer as an incentive and reward for their performance and loyalty. It is one of the many tools used by companies to attract and retain talented employees. ISOs are governed by specific rules and regulations set forth by the Internal Revenue Service (IRS) in the United States. ISOs provide employees with the right to purchase company stock at a predetermined price, known as the exercise price or strike price. This price is usually lower than the current market price of the stock, making it an attractive benefit for employees to participate in. The exercise price is fixed at the time the ISO is granted and remains unchanged throughout the life of the option. One of the key advantages of ISOs is that they offer preferential tax treatment to the employee. When the employee exercises the option and sells the stock, any gains are generally taxed as long-term capital gains instead of ordinary income. This can result in significant tax savings for the employee, as long-term capital gains tax rates are typically lower than ordinary income tax rates. There are certain eligibility criteria that employees must meet in order to receive ISOs. These criteria include being an employee of the company issuing the options, working for the company for a certain period of time, and being employed on a full-time basis. Additionally, the maximum number of ISOs that an employee can receive in a given year is limited by the IRS. ISOs come with certain restrictions and conditions. For instance, there is usually a waiting period, known as the vesting period, during which the employee must remain with the company in order to exercise the options. Furthermore, ISOs usually have an expiration date, after which they become worthless if not exercised. In summary, ISOs are a valuable tool for companies to motivate and reward their employees. They provide employees with the opportunity to purchase company stock at a discounted price and benefit from potential capital gains tax advantages. However, it is important for employees to understand the rules and restrictions associated with ISOs to maximize their benefits and avoid any potential pitfalls.

Income Investing

Income investing is a financial management strategy that focuses on generating a steady stream of income from investments. It involves investing in assets that provide regular cash flows, such as bonds, dividend-paying stocks, and real estate investment trusts (REITs). The goal of income investing is to generate a consistent and reliable income stream that can be used to cover living expenses, reinvest in additional income-generating assets, or save for future needs. It is particularly attractive to individuals who are seeking a source of passive income or retirees who rely on investment income to fund their retirement lifestyle.

Income Statement

An income statement is a financial statement that provides an overview of a company's revenues, expenses, and net income or loss over a specific period of time. Also known as a profit and loss statement or statement of operations, the income statement is one of the key financial statements used in financial management. It helps to assess the profitability and financial performance of a company. The income statement follows a specific format and is divided into several sections. The top section of the income statement lists the company's revenue or sales. This includes all the income generated from the company's primary business activities, such as the sale of goods or services. The revenue section also includes any other non-operating income, such as interest income or gains from the sale of assets. The next section of the income statement is the cost of goods sold (COGS) or cost of sales. This represents the direct costs associated with producing or delivering the company's products or services. It includes expenses such as raw materials, labor, and manufacturing overhead. By subtracting the COGS from the revenue, the company can calculate its gross profit. After the gross profit, the income statement includes other operating expenses. This section lists all the expenses incurred in the course of the company's normal operations, such as salaries, rent, utilities, marketing, and research and development expenses. These expenses are subtracted from the gross profit to determine the operating profit. The income statement also includes non-operating expenses, such as interest expense or losses from the sale of assets. These expenses are deducted from the operating profit to arrive at the net income before taxes. Finally, taxes are deducted from the net income before taxes to calculate the net income or net loss for the period. Overall, the income statement provides a snapshot of a company's financial performance and helps stakeholders and financial managers assess its profitability and efficiency. By analyzing the different sections of the income statement, financial managers can identify areas for improvement, make informed decisions, and evaluate the company's overall financial health.

Income Tax Expense

Income Tax Expense is a crucial component of financial management that refers to the amount of taxes a business or individual is required to pay to the government based on their taxable income. It represents an expense that reduces the net income or profit of an entity and is recorded on the income statement. Income tax is a mandatory payment imposed by the government on individuals and businesses to fund public services and programs. The amount of income tax expense is determined by applying the applicable tax rate to the taxable income earned during a specific financial period.

Income Tax Return

An Income Tax Return is a formal document that individuals or businesses are required to file with the tax authorities, such as the Internal Revenue Service (IRS), at the end of each tax year. It provides a comprehensive summary of the taxpayer's financial activities and serves as the basis for calculating and paying the income tax owed to the government. The purpose of filing an Income Tax Return is to report all sources of income, deductions, credits, and exemptions to determine the tax liability or the amount of tax that the taxpayer owes. It ensures that taxpayers are fulfilling their tax obligations and enables the government to assess and collect taxes fairly and accurately.

Inflation Rate

Inflation Rate is a key concept in financial management that measures the percentage increase in the general price level of goods and services over a specified time period. It is generally expressed as an annualized percentage rate. Inflation is caused by various factors, including increased demand for goods and services, increased production costs, changes in government policies, and fluctuations in the value of currency. When prices rise, the purchasing power of money decreases, and individuals and businesses have to spend more to buy the same quantity of goods and services.

Inflation-Adjusted Return

Inflation-adjusted return is a financial indicator used in financial management to evaluate the performance of an investment after accounting for inflation. It provides a more accurate assessment of the real value of an investment by adjusting the nominal return for the impact of inflation. When evaluating the performance of an investment, it is important to consider the purchasing power of the returns. Inflation erodes the value of money over time, as it reduces the purchasing power of each dollar. Therefore, the nominal return alone does not provide an accurate picture of the investment's actual performance. The inflation-adjusted return is calculated by subtracting the inflation rate from the nominal return. The resulting figure represents the real rate of return, which reflects the investment's true growth in purchasing power. To calculate the inflation-adjusted return, the following formula is typically used: Inflation-Adjusted Return = (1 + Nominal Return) / (1 + Inflation Rate) - 1 For example, if an investment generated a nominal return of 8% over a period when inflation was 2%, the inflation-adjusted return can be calculated as follows: Inflation-Adjusted Return = (1 + 0.08) / (1 + 0.02) - 1 = 0.0588 or 5.88% This means that the investment's purchasing power increased by approximately 5.88% after adjusting for inflation. The inflation-adjusted return is a valuable metric for investors as it provides a more accurate measure of the investment's performance. It allows investors to compare the real returns of different investments and make more informed decisions based on their financial goals and risk tolerance.

129

Inflation-Protected Securities (TIPS)

Inflation-Protected Securities (TIPS) are financial instruments issued by the U.S. Department of the Treasury as a means to protect investors from the erosive effects of inflation. TIPS are specifically designed to provide investors with a hedge against inflation by adjusting their principal value in line with changes in the Consumer Price Index (CPI). TIPS can play an important role in financial management by helping investors preserve the purchasing power of their investments. Unlike traditional fixed-income securities, TIPS provide investors with a guaranteed real rate of return that adjusts for changes in inflation. This makes TIPS particularly attractive for risk-averse investors who seek protection against inflation.

Inflation

Inflation refers to the sustained increase in the general price level of goods and services in an economy over a period of time. It is typically measured by the inflation rate, which represents the annual percentage change in the Consumer Price Index (CPI) or other price indices. When inflation occurs, each unit of currency buys fewer goods and services compared to previous periods. In other words, inflation erodes the purchasing power of money. This means that individuals and businesses need to spend more to maintain the same standard of living or level of production.

Initial Margin

Initial Margin is a term used in the field of Financial Management to refer to the initial deposit or collateral required by a broker or exchange in order to initiate a transaction, such as buying or selling a financial instrument like stocks, commodities, or derivatives. It acts as a form of security that protects the broker or exchange from potential losses if the transaction is not successfully completed. When an investor or trader wants to engage in a transaction, they are required to deposit a certain amount of money or assets as the initial margin. This amount is determined by the broker or exchange based on factors such as the volatility of the financial instrument being traded, market conditions, and the investor's creditworthiness. The initial margin helps ensure that the investor has enough capital to cover any potential losses that may arise from the transaction.

Initial Public Offering (IPO)

An initial public offering (IPO) refers to the process of a private company making its shares available to the public for the first time, thus becoming a publicly traded company. It is a significant milestone in the life cycle of a company and can have a profound impact on its financial management. Through an IPO, a company offers a portion of its ownership to public investors in the form of shares. These shares can be bought and sold on stock exchanges, allowing individuals and institutional investors to become shareholders and have a stake in the company's future performance. The IPO process usually involves several stages, including selecting underwriters, preparing an offering prospectus, conducting due diligence, setting a price range, and marketing the offering to potential investors. From a financial management perspective, an IPO can provide several benefits to a company. Firstly, it offers the opportunity to raise significant capital, which can be used for various purposes such as expanding operations, developing new products, paying off debts, or making acquisitions. By going public, a company gains access to a broader investor base and can attract institutional investors, who can provide long-term capital and expertise. Moreover, an IPO can enhance a company's visibility and reputation, which can be advantageous for attracting customers, partners, and talented employees. Going public can also increase a company's credibility and transparency, as it becomes subject to stricter regulatory and reporting requirements. This can instill trust in investors and help to establish a positive relationship with the financial markets. However, going public also comes with challenges and considerations for financial management. The IPO process can be complex, time-consuming, and expensive. Companies must carefully evaluate their readiness for going public, ensuring that their financial systems, internal controls, and corporate governance practices are in place to meet the demands of being a public company. Furthermore, once a company is public, it faces increased scrutiny from investors, analysts, and regulators. Financial management must be diligent in meeting reporting obligations, managing investor expectations, and demonstrating consistent performance. The company's financial strategy and decision-making may also be influenced by the need to balance short-term shareholder demands with long-term value creation. In conclusion, an initial public offering is the process of a private company becoming a publicly traded company by offering shares to the public for the first time. It can provide opportunities for capital raising, visibility, and credibility but also requires careful financial management to navigate the complexities and expectations of being a public company.

Institutional Investor

Institutional Investor refers to a financial entity, including pension funds, insurance companies, mutual funds, and endowments, that invests large amounts of capital on behalf of its clients or members. These institutions pool together funds from multiple individual investors or businesses to create a substantial amount of capital, which is then professionally managed by their investment teams. Such investors are known for their ability to make significant long-term investments and have the financial capacity to take on larger risks compared to individual investors. They typically have a diverse investment portfolio, which includes various asset classes, such as stocks, bonds, real estate, commodities, and alternative investments. Institutional investors play a crucial role in the financial markets, as they have the power to influence the prices, liquidity, and overall stability of the securities they invest in. Their large-scale investments can impact the supply and demand dynamics of these securities, thus affecting market movements. Institutional investors often have access to extensive research resources and employ experienced professionals to analyze investment opportunities and manage their portfolios effectively. These investors often prioritize long-term investment strategies, aiming to generate consistent returns and mitigate risks over time. They may also engage in active or passive investing approaches, depending on their investment objectives and philosophies. Active investing involves actively managing portfolios by continually monitoring markets and making investment decisions based on market trends, economic conditions, and company-specific information. Passive investing, on the other hand, involves investing in index funds or exchange-traded funds (ETFs) that mirror the performance of a specific market index or sector. Institutional investors often engage in various strategies to optimize their returns, including diversification, asset allocation, and risk management. They may also utilize different investment vehicles, such as hedge funds, private equity, and venture capital funds, to further enhance their portfolio's performance and capture additional opportunities. Furthermore, institutional investors are subject to regulatory and reporting requirements to ensure transparency and accountability to their clients or members. In summary, institutional investors are financial entities that invest significant amounts of capital on behalf of their clients or members. They play a vital role in the financial markets, influencing prices and stability. These investors have the ability to take on larger risks and manage diverse portfolios, often employing long-term investment strategies.

Institutional Ownership

Institutional ownership refers to the percentage of a company's shares that are held by institutional investors, such as mutual funds, pension funds, and insurance companies. It is an important metric in financial management as it provides insight into the level of confidence and interest that professional investors have in a particular company. Institutional ownership is a reflection of the overall market sentiment towards a company. When institutional investors own a significant portion of a company's shares, it suggests that these professional investors believe in the company's growth potential and profitability. This can be seen as a positive sign for individual investors and can increase the company's credibility in the market. One of the main advantages of high institutional ownership is the stability it brings to the stock price. Institutions tend to be long-term investors and are less likely to make impulsive trading decisions based on short-term market fluctuations. Their presence in the market provides liquidity and reduces the volatility of a company's stock, which can be beneficial for individual investors. Furthermore, institutional investors often have access to extensive research and resources, allowing them to make informed investment decisions based on detailed analysis. Their expertise and knowledge can help drive the growth and success of the companies they invest in. However, it is important to note that high institutional ownership can also have some drawbacks. When institutions own a large percentage of a company's shares, it can lead to a loss of control for individual investors and potentially influence corporate decision-making. Additionally, if institutions decide to sell off their holdings, it can create significant downward pressure on the stock price. In conclusion, institutional ownership plays a crucial role in financial management as it indicates the level of confidence and interest professional investors have in a company. It can provide stability to stock prices and bring expertise and resources to support a company's growth. However, it also has the potential to impact control and create volatility in the market.

Interest Coverage Ratio (ICR)

The Interest Coverage Ratio (ICR) is a financial ratio used in financial management to assess a company's ability to pay its interest expenses on its outstanding debt. It measures the company's ability to generate enough operating income to cover the interest obligations of its debt obligations. The ICR is calculated by dividing the company's earnings before interest and taxes (EBIT) by its interest expenses. The resulting ratio indicates how many times the company's operating income can cover its interest payments. A higher ICR indicates a stronger ability to meet the interest payments, while a lower ICR suggests a higher risk of defaulting on debt obligations.

Interest Rate Parity (IRP)

The interest rate parity (IRP) is a financial concept that describes the relationship between exchange rates and interest rates in different countries. It suggests that the difference in interest rates between two countries should be offset by the changes in the exchange rate between their currencies. In other words, the expected return on an investment in one currency should be equalized by the anticipated change in the exchange rate. IRP is based on the principle of arbitrage, which assumes that investors will seek to exploit any opportunities for risk-free profits. If there is a discrepancy between the interest rates and exchange rates of two countries, investors can take advantage of this imbalance by borrowing in the country with the lower interest rate, converting the funds into the currency of the country with the higher interest rate, and investing in securities or other assets that yield a higher return. Under IRP, the forward exchange rate should reflect the interest rate differentials between two countries. The forward exchange rate is the rate at which one currency can be exchanged for another at a future date. According to IRP, the forward exchange rate should be calculated by multiplying the spot exchange rate by the ratio of the interest rates in the two countries. If IRP does not hold, it would create an opportunity for risk-free profits through currency arbitrage. Speculators would borrow in the currency with the lower interest rate, convert it into the currency with the higher interest rate, invest in the higher-yielding assets, and then convert back to the original currency at maturity. This would lead to an increase in demand for the higher-yielding currency, causing its value to appreciate and the lower-yielding currency to depreciate, until IRP is restored. IRP is an important concept for financial management as it helps determine the fair value of currencies and interest rates. It enables investors and businesses to make informed decisions about international investments, hedging strategies, and capital allocation. By understanding the relationship between interest rates and exchange rates, financial managers can assess the potential risks and returns associated with international transactions, and adjust their strategies accordingly to maximize value and minimize exposure to currency fluctuations.

Interest Rate Parity

Interest Rate Parity is a financial concept that states that the difference in interest rates between two countries is equal to the percentage difference between the forward exchange rate and the spot exchange rate. It is a fundamental principle in financial management that helps determine exchange rates and interest rate differentials between countries. The basic idea behind interest rate parity is that in an efficient and competitive market, investors should not be able to earn risk-free profits by exploiting differences in interest rates between countries. If there is a difference in interest rates between two countries, investors will transfer their funds to the country with the higher interest rate, leading to an increase in demand for that country's currency. This increased demand for the currency will cause its value to appreciate and its exchange rate to rise. Interest rate parity is commonly used in the foreign exchange market to determine the forward exchange rate. The forward exchange rate is the rate at which one currency can be exchanged for another at a future date. According to interest rate parity, the forward exchange rate should incorporate the interest rate differential between the two currencies. If the forward exchange rate does not reflect this interest rate differential, there will be an opportunity for arbitrage – the simultaneous buying and selling of currencies to take advantage of the discrepancy in exchange rates. The interest rate parity equation can be expressed as follows: Forward exchange rate / Spot exchange rate = (1 + Interest rate of the foreign country) / (1 + Interest rate of the domestic country) This equation suggests that the forward exchange rate should equal the spot exchange rate adjusted for the interest rate differential between the two countries. If the forward exchange rate is higher than the spot exchange rate, it implies that the interest rate in the foreign country is higher than the domestic country. Conversely, if the forward exchange rate is lower than the spot exchange rate, it suggests that the interest rate in the domestic country is higher than the foreign country.

Interest Rate Risk

Interest rate risk refers to the potential impact of changes in interest rates on the value of an investment or a financial instrument. It is a crucial concept in financial management as it directly affects the profitability and overall financial health of a company. When interest rates fluctuate, the value of fixed-income securities, such as bonds or loans, can change. This change in value is caused by the inverse relationship between interest rates and bond prices. As interest rates rise, the prices of existing bonds decline, and vice versa. This means that an investor or a company that holds fixed-income securities may experience losses if they need to sell those securities when the interest rates have increased.

Interest Rate Swap (IRS)

An Interest Rate Swap (IRS) is a financial derivative that involves the exchange of interest payments between two parties, often referred to as the "fixed rate payer" and the "floating rate payer." The purpose of an IRS is to manage interest rate risk or to speculate on interest rate movements. In an IRS, the two parties agree to exchange interest payments based on a notional principal amount. The notional principal is an imaginary amount that serves as the basis for calculating the interest payments. No actual principal amount is exchanged between the parties. The fixed rate payer agrees to pay a fixed rate of interest on the notional principal, while the floating rate payer agrees to pay a variable rate of interest that is linked to a specified reference rate, such as LIBOR or a government bond yield. The reference rate is typically adjusted periodically, such as every three or six months. The interest payments are calculated by applying the agreed-upon fixed or floating rate to the notional principal amount. The fixed rate payer pays the fixed rate multiplied by the notional principal, while the floating rate payer pays the floating rate multiplied by the notional principal. At the start of the IRS, the present value of the fixed rate payments is usually equal to the present value of the floating rate payments. This makes the IRS a fair contract with no upfront cost. However, as interest rates change over time, the present value of the fixed and floating rate payments may diverge, creating a potential profit or loss for one of the parties. An IRS can be used for various purposes in financial management. It allows firms to manage interest rate risk by converting variable rate debt into fixed rate debt or vice versa. This can help protect against adverse interest rate movements and provide certainty in interest payments. IRS can also be used by investors to speculate on interest rate movements. For example, if an investor expects interest rates to rise, they can enter into an IRS as the floating rate payer, expecting to pay lower interest payments in the future as rates increase. In conclusion, an Interest Rate Swap is a financial instrument that allows two parties to exchange interest payments based on a notional principal. It helps manage interest rate risk and can be used for speculation purposes in financial management.

Interest Rate Swap

An interest rate swap is a financial contract between two parties to exchange interest rate payments for a specified period of time. The purpose of the swap is to manage or hedge the interest rate risk associated with borrowing or investing. The two parties involved in an interest rate swap are typically referred to as the "fixed-rate payer" and the "floating-rate payer." The fixed-rate payer agrees to make fixed interest rate payments to the floating-rate payer, while the floating-rate payer agrees to make floating interest rate payments to the fixed-rate payer. The interest rate payments are based on a notional principal amount, which is the agreed-upon amount used to calculate the payments. The notional principal is not actually exchanged between the two parties, but serves as a benchmark for determining the payment amounts. The fixed interest rate is predetermined and remains constant throughout the life of the swap. It is typically based on a benchmark interest rate, such as the LIBOR (London Interbank Offered

133

Rate), plus a spread. The floating interest rate, on the other hand, is based on a reference rate, such as the LIBOR, that changes periodically. The payment amounts are calculated by multiplying the notional principal by the respective interest rate and time period. Interest rate swaps can be used for various purposes, depending on the needs of the parties involved. For example, a company with a variable-rate loan may enter into an interest rate swap agreement to convert the variable interest payments into fixed payments, thereby reducing the uncertainty and risk associated with fluctuating interest rates. Interest rate swaps can also be used by investors to speculate on interest rate movements. For instance, an investor who believes that interest rates will decrease may enter into a swap agreement to receive fixed interest payments and pay floating interest payments. If interest rates do indeed decrease, the investor will profit from the swap. In conclusion, an interest rate swap is a financial contract used to manage interest rate risk by exchanging fixed and floating interest rate payments between two parties. It provides a way to convert variable interest payments into fixed payments or to speculate on interest rate movements.

Interest Rate

Interest Rate - The interest rate refers to the amount charged by a lender to a borrower for the use of borrowed funds. It is typically expressed as a percentage and is a key component in financial management. The interest rate plays a significant role in various aspects of financial decision-making, including borrowing, saving, investing, and budgeting. In the context of financial management, the interest rate directly impacts the cost of borrowing for individuals, businesses, and governments. When individuals or entities borrow money, they are obliged to pay back the principal amount along with interest, which is the cost of borrowing. The interest rate determines how much additional money a borrower has to pay back to the lender. For borrowers, the interest rate represents the cost of financing. A higher interest rate leads to higher borrowing costs, which can reduce the affordability of loans and impact the ability of individuals and businesses to invest and grow. On the other hand, lower interest rates can stimulate borrowing and encourage economic activity. For lenders, the interest rate represents the return on investment. Lenders earn interest income by lending money to borrowers, and the interest rate determines the amount of return they will receive. Higher interest rates can attract more lenders and investors who are seeking higher returns, while lower interest rates may discourage lenders and lead to reduced investments. Besides its impact on borrowing and lending, the interest rate also influences saving and investing decisions. When interest rates are high, individuals may choose to save their money in interest-bearing accounts or invest in fixed-income securities that offer attractive returns. Conversely, when interest rates are low, individuals may be more inclined to spend or invest in assets with potentially higher returns. In summary, the interest rate is a key concept in financial management as it affects the cost of borrowing and lending, the return on investment, and saving and investing decisions. Understanding the interest rate and its impact is crucial for individuals, businesses, and governments to make informed financial decisions and manage their resources effectively.

Internal Rate Of Return (IRR)

The Internal Rate of Return (IRR) is a financial metric used to evaluate the profitability of an investment. It is the rate at which the net present value (NPV) of an investment becomes zero. In other words, it is the discount rate that makes the present value of the investment's cash inflows equal to the present value of its cash outflows. To understand the concept further, let's break down the definition: The net present value (NPV) is a measure that calculates the difference between the present value of cash inflows and the present value of cash outflows. The present value of future cash flows is determined by discounting them using a specific discount rate or required rate of return. The NPV is positive if the present value of cash inflows is greater than the present value of cash outflows, indicating a profitable investment. The IRR, on the other hand, is the discount rate that sets the NPV of the investment to zero. It represents the breakeven point for the investment, where the expected return equals the initial outlay. If the IRR is higher than the required rate of return, the investment is considered profitable. Conversely, if the IRR is lower than the required rate of return, the investment is deemed unprofitable. The IRR is commonly used in capital budgeting decisions to assess the feasibility of potential investments. It allows businesses to compare different investment opportunities and select the most lucrative option. By evaluating the IRR of each investment, decision-makers can determine which projects are expected to generate the highest return and add the most value to the company. It is important to note that the IRR may have limitations in certain scenarios, such as projects with unconventional cash flow patterns or multiple IRRs. However, it remains a valuable tool in financial management for evaluating the profitability and attractiveness of investment opportunities.

Intrinsic Value

In financial management, intrinsic value refers to the perceived or estimated value of an asset, investment, or company based on its fundamental characteristics and potential future earnings. It is an evaluation of the true worth of the asset, rather than its current market value. The intrinsic value is determined by analyzing various factors such as the financial performance, growth prospects, industry outlook, competitive position, and other relevant information about the asset or company. It aims to assess the underlying value that can be realized over time and provide an estimate of its future potential. Unlike market value, which is determined by supply and demand dynamics in the market and can fluctuate based on sentiment and irrational behavior, intrinsic value focuses on the long-term fundamentals of an asset. It is a more rational and objective approach to valuing investments. There are different methods and models used to calculate or estimate the intrinsic value of an asset or company. Some commonly used methods include discounted cash flow (DCF) analysis, comparable company analysis, relative valuation multiples, and asset-based approaches. DCF analysis involves forecasting the future cash flows generated by the asset or company and discounting them back to the present value using an appropriate discount rate. This method takes into account the time value of money and reflects the worth of expected future cash flows in today's terms. Comparable company analysis compares the financial and operating metrics of the target asset or company with those of similar companies in the same industry or sector. By assessing the relative valuation multiples such as price-to-earnings (P/E) ratio, price-to-sales (P/S) ratio, or price-to-book (P/B) ratio, the intrinsic value can be estimated. Overall, intrinsic value is an important concept in financial management as it helps investors and analysts make informed investment decisions based on a rational and fundamental assessment of an asset's worth. By understanding the intrinsic value of an asset, investors can determine whether it is undervalued or overvalued in the market, and potentially capitalize on investment opportunities.

Inventory Turnover

Inventory turnover is a financial ratio that measures the efficiency of a company in managing its inventory. It indicates how quickly a company sells its inventory and replaces it with new stock. The ratio is calculated by dividing the cost of goods sold by the average inventory during a specific period. The inventory turnover ratio helps in evaluating the effectiveness of a company's inventory management. A higher inventory turnover ratio generally suggests that a company is selling its goods at a faster rate, which is beneficial as it reduces the risk of inventory obsolescence and decreases holding costs. On the other hand, a lower inventory turnover ratio may indicate potential issues like slow sales, overstocking, or inefficient inventory management. The formula to calculate inventory turnover is: Inventory Turnover Ratio = Cost of Goods Sold / Average Inventory Where: Cost of Goods Sold includes the direct costs related to the production or purchase of goods that are sold by the company. It typically includes the cost of raw materials, labor, and other production costs. Average Inventory is calculated by adding the beginning inventory and ending inventory for a specific period and dividing it by 2. It represents the average value of inventory held by the company during that period. It is important to use average inventory instead of only considering the ending inventory because the ending inventory might not accurately reflect the average inventory level throughout the period. Using average inventory provides a more representative value for calculating the inventory turnover ratio. The inventory turnover ratio is industry-specific, meaning that what is considered a good or bad ratio can vary depending on the type of industry. It is important to compare the inventory turnover ratio of a company with industry benchmarks or competitors to gain valuable insights into the company's inventory management performance. In conclusion, the inventory turnover ratio is a crucial financial metric that helps assess a company's effectiveness in managing inventory. A higher ratio is generally favorable, indicating efficient inventory management and faster sales. However, it is essential to consider industry norms and benchmarks when analyzing this ratio.

Inventory Valuation Methods

Inventory valuation methods refer to the various techniques used by businesses to value their inventories for financial reporting purposes. These methods are crucial for accurately determining the value of inventory on a company's balance sheet and determining the cost of goods sold on the income statement. One commonly used inventory valuation method is the FIFO (First-In, First-Out) method. Under this method, it is assumed that the first items of inventory purchased or produced are the first ones sold. The cost of the oldest inventory is matched with the revenue from the earliest sales, while the cost of the most recent inventory is matched with the revenue from the most recent sales. This method is often preferred in industries where the cost of inventory tends to rise over time, as it results in the lowest cost of goods sold and the highest ending inventory value.

Investment Bank

An investment bank is a financial institution that provides a range of services to individuals, corporations, and governments regarding their financial needs, specifically in the areas of capital raising, mergers and acquisitions, and financial advisory. Investment banks play a crucial role in the global financial market by acting as intermediaries between issuers and investors. They facilitate the flow of capital by assisting businesses in raising funds through underwriting and distributing securities in primary markets. This involves conducting due diligence, pricing the securities, and marketing them to potential investors. In addition to capital raising, investment banks also offer advisory services for mergers, acquisitions, and restructuring activities. They carefully analyze the financial situation and future prospects of companies, providing strategic advice to clients aiming to expand or optimize their businesses. This can involve conducting financial valuation, negotiating deals, and structuring transactions to maximize shareholder value. Moreover, investment banks are involved in the trading of financial instruments, such as stocks, bonds, and derivatives, in the secondary market. They act as market makers, ensuring liquidity and facilitating efficient trading for investors. They also provide research and analysis on various industries and companies to help investors make informed decisions about their portfolios. To carry out these services, investment banks employ a wide range of professionals, including investment bankers, salespeople, traders, analysts, and researchers. These individuals possess expertise in various financial disciplines, such as corporate finance, capital markets, risk management, and regulatory compliance. It is important to note that investment banks operate in a highly regulated environment, subject to scrutiny from regulatory authorities to ensure the stability and integrity of the financial system. They are required to comply with strict regulatory standards, such as capital adequacy requirements, risk management guidelines, and reporting obligations. In conclusion, investment banks are financial institutions that provide comprehensive financial services to clients, focusing on capital raising, mergers and acquisitions, and financial advisory. They play a vital role in the global financial system, facilitating the flow of capital, offering strategic advice, and ensuring efficient trading in financial markets.

Investment Banker

An investment banker is a financial professional who provides a range of services to clients such as corporations, governments, and individuals, with the goal of helping them raise capital, make strategic financial decisions, and execute complex financial transactions. As part of their role, investment bankers serve as intermediaries between companies seeking to secure funds for various purposes, such as expanding their operations or financing mergers and acquisitions, and investors looking for opportunities to deploy their capital. They help bridge the gap between these two parties by assessing the financial needs of the clients, identifying potential investors, and structuring financial deals that align with the objectives of all parties involved. One of the key functions of investment bankers is underwriting, where they assist companies in issuing securities, such as stocks or bonds, to raise funds. They analyze the financial health and prospects of the issuing firm, determine an appropriate pricing strategy for the securities, and then purchase the securities themselves or find buyers in the market. By doing so, investment bankers take on the risk associated with these securities and ensure that the issuing company receives the desired amount of capital. In addition to underwriting, investment bankers also provide advisory services to clients, offering guidance on matters such as mergers and acquisitions, divestitures, and corporate restructuring. They conduct extensive financial analysis, assess the valuation of companies involved in these transactions, and help negotiate favorable terms for their clients. Through their expertise in financial markets and deal structuring, investment bankers play a crucial role in ensuring the success and efficiency of these transactions. Furthermore, investment bankers engage in activities such as corporate finance, where they work closely with companies to optimize their capital structure, manage their debt, and evaluate investment opportunities. They assist clients in formulating financial strategies that align with their long-term goals and provide them with the necessary financial tools to execute these strategies effectively. In summary, an investment banker is a financial professional who plays a vital role in facilitating the flow of capital between investors and companies. Through services such as underwriting, advisory, and corporate finance, they help clients raise capital, make informed financial decisions, and execute complex transactions, ultimately contributing to the efficient functioning of financial markets.

Investment Banking

Investment Banking is a financial management service that helps corporations, governments, and other entities raise capital by underwriting and issuing securities. It involves assisting clients in various financial activities, such as mergers and acquisitions, initial public offerings (IPOs), and private placements. Primarily, investment banks act as intermediaries between companies in need of funds and investors looking to invest their capital. They play a crucial role in the capital markets, facilitating the flow of money from investors to those who require it. This process involves extensive analysis, risk evaluation, and strategic advice to ensure the successful execution of financial transactions.

Investment Grade

An Investment Grade is a rating assigned by credit rating agencies to indicate the creditworthiness of a borrower or a debt instrument. It is a measure used in financial management to assess the risk associated with investing in a particular bond, loan, or other debt product. Investment grade ratings are typically given to borrowers or debt instruments that have a relatively low risk of defaulting on their payments. The ratings are based on various factors such as the borrower's financial stability, credit history, and ability to generate sufficient cash flows to meet their debt obligations.

Investment Horizon

The investment horizon refers to the length of time that an investor plans to hold an investment before selling it or realizing its value. It is an important concept in financial management as the investment horizon affects the investment strategy and risk tolerance of an investor. The decision to hold an investment for a short-term, medium-term, or long-term period can have significant implications on the potential returns and level of risk associated with the investment.

Joint Venture (JV)

A Joint Venture (JV) is a strategic partnership or collaboration between two or more entities, typically businesses, to achieve a specific objective. In the context of Financial Management, a Joint Venture is a financial arrangement where two or more companies come together to form a separate legal entity to pursue a mutually beneficial project, investment, or business opportunity. In a Joint Venture, each participating entity contributes resources such as capital, expertise, technology, or other assets, and shares the risks, costs, profits, and losses associated with the venture according to the agreed upon terms and conditions. The joint venture partners maintain their separate legal structures and continue to operate as independent entities outside of the joint venture. The purpose of forming a Joint Venture in Financial Management can vary. It may be undertaken to combine complementary strengths, resources, or capabilities of the participating entities to achieve synergistic benefits that individually they couldn't attain. This collaboration enables companies to leverage each other's strengths, expand market reach, access new technology or markets, reduce costs, share risks, and gain a competitive advantage. The structure and governance of a Joint Venture are typically defined by a legal agreement or contract between the participating entities. This agreement outlines the objectives, funding arrangements, profit-sharing mechanisms, decision-making processes, and other key aspects of the joint venture. The partners must agree on important matters such as investment ratios, voting rights, distribution of profits, exit strategies, dispute resolution mechanisms, and the duration of the joint venture. Joint Ventures can be beneficial in various financial management scenarios. They can be used for large-scale infrastructure projects, international business operations, research and development ventures, market entry strategies, production and manufacturing collaborations, and many other business initiatives that require significant financial resources, expertise, or access to new markets.

Joint Venture

A joint venture is a business arrangement between two or more companies that agree to combine their resources and expertise to undertake a specific project or achieve a common goal. It involves the creation of a separate legal entity, typically in the form of a new company, in which the partnering companies own a share and share in the risks, rewards, and control of the venture. Financial management plays a crucial role in the success of a joint venture. It involves the efficient utilization of financial resources, proper allocation of costs and revenues, and the management of financial risks. The financial manager in a joint venture is responsible for overseeing the financial aspects of the partnership, ensuring the financial stability of the venture, and maximizing the return on investment for the participating companies.

Junk Bond

A junk bond, also known as a high-yield bond or speculative bond, is a type of debt security that carries a higher risk of default compared to investment-grade bonds. Junk bonds are typically issued by companies or governments with a lower credit rating or a higher level of financial leverage. Unlike investment-grade bonds, which are considered low-risk investments, junk bonds have a higher risk of default due to their lower credit ratings. Credit ratings are assigned by credit rating agencies based on the issuer's ability to meet its financial obligations. Issuers of junk bonds offer higher interest rates to compensate investors for taking on additional risk. The higher interest rates reflect the increased probability of default and the lower market demand for such bonds. As a result, junk bonds have a higher yield compared to investment-grade bonds. Junk bonds are often issued by companies that have a high degree of financial leverage or operate in volatile industries. These companies may have limited cash flows or may be facing financial difficulties, making it more challenging for them to repay their debts. Additionally, governments may issue junk bonds to fund infrastructure projects or to finance budget deficits. Investing in junk bonds can be attractive for investors seeking higher returns, as the higher interest rates can result in greater yield compared to other fixed-income investments. However, the increased risk of default means that investors need to assess the creditworthiness of the issuer before investing in junk bonds. It is important for investors to analyze the financial health of the issuer, market conditions, and other factors that may impact the issuer's ability to meet its debt obligations. In summary, junk bonds are debt securities that are considered to have a higher risk of default compared to investment-grade bonds. They are issued by companies or governments with lower credit ratings or higher levels of financial leverage. Junk bonds offer higher interest rates to compensate investors for taking on additional risk, but investors need to carefully assess the creditworthiness of the issuer before investing in these bonds.

Laffer Curve

The Laffer Curve is a theoretical concept in financial management that demonstrates the relationship between tax rates and tax revenue. It suggests that there exists an optimal tax rate that maximizes government revenue, beyond which increasing tax rates actually lead to a decrease in revenue. The Laffer Curve is named after economist Arthur Laffer, who presented the idea in the 1970s as a way to illustrate the potential negative effects of excessive taxation. The curve is represented graphically, with tax revenue on the vertical axis and tax rate on the horizontal axis. According to the Laffer Curve, at very low tax rates, government revenue is also low because there is not enough tax being collected. As tax rates increase, revenue initially increases as well due to the fact that the government is collecting more from each taxpayer. However, as tax rates continue to rise, individuals and businesses may start to change their behavior in response to the higher taxes. At some point, increasing tax rates further will have a negative effect on government revenue because taxpayers will be less inclined to work, invest, or engage in economic activities that generate taxable income. This behavior is known as the "disincentive effect" of high taxation. As tax rates become excessively high, people may choose to work less, evade taxes, or move their businesses to lower-tax jurisdictions, resulting in a decrease in taxable income and thus a decrease in government revenue. The Laffer Curve suggests that there is a tipping point where the negative effects of higher tax rates outweigh the positive effects of collecting more tax revenue. Finding this optimal tax rate is crucial for governments in order to balance the need for revenue generation with economic growth and individual incentives to work and invest. However, it is important to note that the shape of the Laffer Curve is subject to debate and can vary depending on various factors such as the structure of the economy, taxpayer behavior, and the types of taxes being considered.

Lead Underwriter

A Lead Underwriter is a financial professional who takes the primary responsibility for managing the underwriting process of a securities offering. The underwriting process involves assessing the risk and determining the terms and conditions of the issuance of securities by a company or government entity. The lead underwriter plays a crucial role in the successful completion of the offering by coordinating with other underwriters and ensuring compliance with regulatory requirements. The primary tasks of a lead underwriter include evaluating the financial condition and performance of the issuer, analyzing market conditions, and establishing the appropriate pricing and allocation of the securities to investors. They work closely with the issuer to prepare the necessary documents, such as the prospectus, which provides detailed information about the securities being offered. The lead underwriter also plays a key role in marketing and promoting the offering to potential investors. During the underwriting process, the lead underwriter also manages the syndicate of underwriters, which consists of multiple financial institutions collaborating to underwrite the securities offering. They coordinate the activities of the syndicate members and allocate responsibilities among them. The lead underwriter ensures that each member of the syndicate fulfills its obligations and performs due diligence to mitigate risks associated with the offering. In addition to managing the underwriting process, the lead underwriter is responsible for liaising with regulatory bodies, such as the Securities and Exchange Commission (SEC), to ensure compliance with applicable laws and regulations. They need to have a comprehensive understanding of the relevant legal and regulatory requirements to ensure that the offering meets all necessary guidelines and standards. The role of a lead underwriter requires strong analytical and financial skills, as well as excellent communication and negotiation abilities. They need to have a deep understanding of the financial markets and be able to assess the risks and opportunities associated with different types of securities offerings. The lead underwriter also needs to build and maintain relationships with institutional investors and other key stakeholders to ensure a successful offering.

Leverage Buyout (LBO)

A Leveraged Buyout (LBO) is a financial strategy in which a company is acquired using a significant amount of borrowed funds or debt. The acquired company's assets are used as collateral for the borrowed funds, and the debt is repaid using the future cash flows generated by the company. In an LBO transaction, the buyer typically invests a smaller amount of equity and relies on the target company's assets and cash flows to generate the necessary returns. LBOs are often used by private equity firms to acquire control of a target company. These firms seek to maximize their returns by leveraging the target company's assets and cash flows. Typically, the target company is publicly traded, but it can also be a private company. By acquiring a controlling stake in the target company, the private equity firm aims to improve its operational and financial performance and eventually sell it for a higher price, thereby generating a significant return on its initial investment.

Leverage Ratio

A leverage ratio is a financial metric that measures the level of debt a company has relative to its equity or other measures of financial resources. It provides insight into the company's ability to meet its financial obligations and to withstand financial distress or economic downturns. The leverage ratio is calculated by dividing the company's total debt by its equity or assets. The numerator of the ratio represents the amount of debt the company has, including both short-term and long-term liabilities. The denominator represents the company's equity, which includes shareholders' equity and retained earnings, or its total assets.

Leverage

Leverage, in the context of financial management, refers to the use of borrowed funds or debt to increase the potential return on investment. It involves utilizing debt financing to magnify the returns generated by the investments made by a company or individual. Leverage is typically employed to increase the profitability or to acquire assets that would not have been affordable with only equity financing. When an individual or a company takes on debt to finance their operations or investments, it allows them to utilize their own capital or equity in a more efficient manner. By using leverage, the potential returns on their investments are amplified, as the profits earned are calculated on the total investment (including borrowed funds) rather than the equity invested.

Leveraged Buyout (LBO)

A Leveraged Buyout (LBO) refers to a financial transaction in which a company or a group of investors acquires another company by using a significant amount of borrowed money, typically in the form of debt, to finance the purchase. The debt is secured by the assets of the acquired company, and the assets often serve as collateral for the loan. One of the key characteristics of an LBO is the high level of financial leverage used in the transaction. This means that the acquirer invests a relatively small amount of equity capital and finances the majority of the purchase price with debt. The goal of an LBO is to generate a return on investment that exceeds the cost of the debt used to finance the acquisition, thereby increasing the equity value of the acquiring company.

Liability Insurance

Liability insurance is a form of insurance that protects an individual or entity from being held responsible for financial obligations resulting from property damage or bodily injury to another party. It is a key component of risk management in financial management. Liability insurance works by providing coverage for legal claims made against the insured party in the event of an accident or mishap. This type of insurance is particularly important for businesses that may face significant financial losses if they are found liable for injuries or damages caused by their products, services, or operations. There are various types of liability insurance, including general liability, professional liability, and product liability insurance. General liability insurance covers a wide range of risks associated with a business's operations, such as slip and fall accidents or property damage. Professional liability insurance, also known as errors and omissions insurance, protects professionals, such as doctors, lawyers, and consultants, from claims arising from mistakes or negligence in their professional services. Product liability insurance covers businesses that manufacture or sell products, protecting them from claims related to defective products causing harm to consumers. Liability insurance policies typically have coverage limits, which represent the maximum amount the insurance company will pay out for claims made against the insured party. The insured party is responsible for paying any costs above these limits. The cost of liability insurance premiums is influenced by various factors, including the industry in which the insured operates, the size of their business, and their claims history. Insurance companies may also require the insured to meet certain risk management standards or take specific measures to mitigate risks. In conclusion, liability insurance is a critical component of financial management as it protects individuals and entities from potential financial losses associated with legal claims made against them. By transferring the risk of liability to an insurance company, businesses and individuals can focus on their operations with peace of mind, knowing that they are protected in the event of accidents or damages that may result in costly legal proceedings.

Liability Management

Liability management is a financial management strategy that focuses on the management and control of a company's liabilities in order to optimize its financial structure and minimize risk. It involves the proactive planning and implementation of various techniques to manage both short-term and long-term liabilities to ensure the financial stability and sustainability of the company. The primary goal of liability management is to strike a balance between the company's assets and liabilities, with the aim of maximizing shareholder value and minimizing the cost of borrowing. This involves carefully analyzing and monitoring the company's liabilities, including debt obligations, credit facilities, lease agreements, and other financial commitments.

Liability

Liability refers to a financial obligation or debt that a company or individual owes to another entity. It represents the amount of money that needs to be paid back, either in the form of cash or other assets, to fulfill the commitment or settlement of a specific financial obligation. Liabilities are recorded on the balance sheet of a company and are categorized into current and long-term liabilities. Current liabilities are short-term obligations that are expected to be settled within one year or the normal operating cycle of a business. Examples of current liabilities include accounts payable, accrued expenses, short-term loans, and credit card debt. These obligations are usually settled by using current assets or by creating new current liabilities. Long-term liabilities, on the other hand, are debts or obligations that are due beyond one year or the normal operating cycle of a business. They typically include long-term loans, bonds payable, lease obligations, and pension liabilities. Unlike current liabilities, long-term liabilities are not expected to be settled in the near future but over an extended period of time. Liabilities are crucial in financial management as they represent the sources of a company's financing and determine its solvency. Understanding the types and amount of liabilities is essential for assessing the financial health and stability of a business. It helps the management make informed decisions regarding borrowing, investing, and managing cash flows. Furthermore, liabilities play a significant role in financial analysis by calculating various ratios like the debt-to-equity ratio, current ratio, and interest coverage ratio. These ratios assist in evaluating a company's ability to pay off its debts, its leverage, liquidity, and overall financial risk.

Lien

Lien is a legal right or claim, typically in the form of a security interest, over a specific asset or property that is granted to a creditor as collateral for a loan or other financial obligation. This right allows the creditor to obtain ownership or possession of the asset if the debtor fails to fulfill their financial obligations. In the context of Financial Management, a lien serves as a safeguard for lenders to protect their interests and ensure the repayment of debt. It creates a legal mechanism through which creditors can enforce their claim on a debtor's assets in the event of default. Once a lien is established, the creditor has the right to seize and sell the property or asset to recover the amount owed. There are different types of liens, including voluntary and involuntary liens. Voluntary liens are created by the debtor as part of a contractual agreement, such as when an individual takes out a mortgage to purchase a property. In this case, the lender has the right to foreclose on the property if the borrower fails to make the required loan payments. Involuntary liens, on the other hand, are created by statutory laws or court judgments. Examples of involuntary liens include tax liens imposed by the government or judgment liens resulting from a legal dispute. Lenders typically conduct a lien search before extending credit to a borrower or granting a loan. This search helps determine if there are existing liens on the borrower's assets, which may affect the creditor's ability to collect their debt. In cases where multiple liens exist on a single asset, priority is usually determined by the date of creation, with earlier liens having priority over later liens. In summary, a lien is a legal right or claim granted to a creditor over a specific asset as collateral. It provides the creditor with the ability to enforce their claim and recover the debt owed in the event of default. Through the establishment of liens, lenders can mitigate the risks associated with lending and ensure the repayment of loans or other financial obligations.

Lienholder

A lienholder, in the context of Financial Management, refers to an individual or entity that holds a legal claim or interest on an asset owned by another party until a debt or financial obligation is fulfilled. This party has the right to possess and potentially sell the asset to recover the outstanding debt or obligation if the borrower defaults on their payment. A lien is a legal right granted to the lienholder as security or collateral for a loan or debt. It provides the lienholder with a legal claim against the property or asset, which acts as a guarantee that they will be repaid. The lienholder can place a lien on various types of assets, such as real estate, vehicles, or even personal property, depending on the nature of the debt. The lienholder's role is essential in managing financial risk and protecting their investment. They often work in conjunction with lenders, such as banks, financial institutions, or individuals who have provided funds to the borrower. By holding the lien, the lienholder has priority over other creditors or claimants in case of default or bankruptcy. When a borrower fails to fulfill their financial obligations, the lienholder can initiate legal actions to enforce their rights. This may include foreclosing on a property, repossessing a vehicle, or seizing other assets covered by the lien. The lienholder can typically sell the asset to recover the outstanding debt, along with any associated fees or costs. To protect their interests, lienholders often require specific terms and conditions when providing loans or financing. These may include higher interest rates, shorter repayment periods, or additional collateral. By doing so, they mitigate the risk of non-payment and increase the likelihood of recovering their funds. In summary, a lienholder is an individual or entity that holds a legal claim or interest on an asset until a debt or financial obligation is fulfilled. They play a crucial role in managing financial risk and protecting their investment by enforcing their rights if the borrower defaults on their payment.

Liquid Asset

Liquid Asset: A liquid asset is a type of asset that can be easily converted into cash or cash equivalents without a significant loss in value. In the context of financial management, liquid assets play a critical role in ensuring the liquidity and financial stability of an entity. Having a sufficient amount of liquid assets is important for both individuals and organizations, as they provide a cushion in times of financial difficulty or unforeseen expenses. These assets can be readily accessed and used to meet immediate financial obligations, such as paying bills or settling debts. Examples of liquid assets include cash, bank deposits, Treasury bills, money market funds, and short-term government bonds. These assets are considered highly liquid because their value is easily determinable and they can be quickly converted into cash without much transaction cost. In financial management, liquidity is a key measure of an entity's ability to meet its short-term financial obligations. Liquid assets are an essential component of liquidity management as they provide the necessary liquidity buffer, ensuring that the entity can meet its ongoing expenses and obligations in a timely manner. It is also important to maintain a balanced liquidity position, ensuring that the entity holds a sufficient amount of liquid assets without compromising its long-term financial goals. Holding too many liquid assets may result in underutilization of capital and lower returns, whereas holding too few liquid assets may expose the entity to financial risks and difficulties in meeting its obligations. Financial managers closely monitor the level and composition of liquid assets to effectively manage the entity's liquidity position. By regularly analyzing and projecting cash inflows and outflows, financial managers can determine the optimal level of liquid assets needed to ensure the entity's financial stability and operational continuity. In conclusion, liquid assets are assets that can be easily converted into cash or cash equivalents without a significant loss in value. They are crucial for maintaining liquidity and financial stability, allowing entities to meet their immediate financial obligations effectively.

Liquidation Value

Liquidation value refers to the estimated worth of a company's assets if it were to be sold or liquidated. This value is typically lower than the fair market value of the assets, as it takes into account the potential costs and losses associated with a forced sale. In financial management, the liquidation value is an important concept used to assess the potential value of an investment. The liquidation value is calculated by determining the net amount that would be realized if all the company's assets were sold and all its liabilities were paid off. This value is often used as a conservative estimate of the company's worth in cases where a quick sale is necessary or when the company is experiencing financial distress. The liquidation value can be estimated using a variety of approaches, depending on the nature of the company's assets. For tangible assets such as inventory, equipment, and real estate, an appraisal may be conducted to determine their current market value. Intangible assets such as patents, trademarks, and brand names may be valued based on their potential future earnings or the cost of their development. Liabilities, including outstanding debt and other obligations, are subtracted from the total asset value to arrive at the net liquidation value. Investors and creditors use the liquidation value as an important benchmark when evaluating a company's financial health and potential return on investment. For investors, the liquidation value provides a sense of security, as it represents the minimum amount of value that can be recovered in the event of a company's failure. Creditors may use the liquidation value to assess the likelihood of recovering their loans or investments in case of default. In conclusion, the liquidation value is a key concept in financial management that represents the estimated worth of a company's assets if it were to be sold or liquidated. It is an important measure used by investors and creditors to evaluate the potential value and risks associated with an investment.

Liquidity Crisis

Liquidity crisis refers to a situation wherein a company or an individual faces a severe shortage of cash or liquid assets to meet its short-term obligations, such as paying immediate debts or covering operational expenses. It occurs when the cash inflows of an entity are inadequate to meet its liquidity needs, creating an imbalance between its liabilities due for immediate payment and its available cash reserves. A liquidity crisis is often characterized by the inability of the concerned entity to quickly convert its assets into cash or obtain additional funding from external sources. This lack of liquidity can result in severe financial distress and can potentially lead to bankruptcy or insolvency if not promptly addressed. There are various factors that can contribute to the occurrence of a liquidity crisis. Poor cash flow management, excessive reliance on short-term debt, unexpected changes in the economic environment, or a sudden decline in the value of assets can all lead to a shortage of available cash. Additionally, factors such as economic recessions, market volatility, and unforeseen events like natural disasters or pandemics can exacerbate the liquidity challenges faced by companies or individuals. In order to mitigate the impact of a liquidity crisis, proactive measures need to be taken. This may involve implementing effective cash flow management strategies, such as maintaining adequate cash reserves, optimizing working capital, and reducing unnecessary expenses. It may also involve exploring alternative financing options, such as securing lines of credit or obtaining short-term loans to bridge the gap between cash inflows and outflows. Furthermore, closely monitoring the financial health of the entity and regularly conducting cash flow projections can help uncover any potential liquidity challenges in advance. Timely identification of liquidity issues allows for prompt action and enables the implementation of appropriate measures to avoid a full-blown crisis.

Liquidity Preference Theory

Liquidity preference theory, also known as the liquidity trap theory, is a theory in financial management that explains the relationship between interest rates and the demand for money. Developed by John Maynard Keynes in the 1930s, this theory suggests that people have a preference for holding liquid assets, such as money, rather than illiquid assets, such as bonds or stocks. According to the liquidity preference theory, the demand for money is influenced by three motives: the transaction motive, the precautionary motive, and the speculative motive. The transaction motive refers to the demand for money to meet day-to-day expenses and carry out transactions. It is influenced by factors such as income level, price level, and the speed of circulation of money. When income and price levels increase, the demand for money for transactions also increases. The precautionary motive relates to the demand for money to have a financial buffer for unexpected expenses or emergencies. People prefer to hold liquid assets to avoid the risk of not having enough funds in case of unforeseen circumstances. This motive is influenced by factors such as the level of uncertainty and the stability of income. The speculative motive is associated with the demand for money as an investment opportunity. When people expect interest rates to fall in the future, they may choose to hold their money in liquid form rather than investing in long-term assets. This motive is influenced by factors such as expected changes in interest rates, expected returns on investments, and market conditions. The liquidity preference theory suggests that the demand for money is inversely related to interest rates. As interest rates rise, the cost of holding money increases, leading to a decrease in money demand. Conversely, when interest rates decline, the cost of holding money decreases, resulting in an increase in money demand. This inverse relationship between interest rates and the demand for money is often depicted graphically as a downward-sloping curve known as the liquidity preference curve. In summary, the liquidity preference theory explains how individuals' preferences for liquidity influence the demand for money. It recognizes the transaction, precautionary, and speculative motives driving the demand for money and highlights the inverse relationship between interest rates and money demand. This theory is significant in financial management as it helps understand the dynamics of interest rates, money markets, and investors' decision-making processes.

Liquidity Premium

Liquidity premium is a concept used in financial management to assess the additional return investors require on an investment that is less liquid compared to a more liquid investment of similar risk. It accounts for the additional compensation investors demand for bearing the risk associated with an illiquid investment. Illiquid investments are those that cannot be easily converted into cash without incurring significant costs or potential loss in value. Investors typically demand a higher return on illiquid investments to compensate for the lack of immediate access to their funds. This additional return, known as the liquidity premium, forms a crucial component of the expected total return on an investment.

Liquidity Ratio

The liquidity ratio is a financial management metric that measures a company's ability to meet short-term obligations by assessing its ability to convert current assets into cash to cover current liabilities. It indicates the company's liquidity position and its ability to maintain its financial stability in the short run. The liquidity ratio is calculated by dividing current assets by current liabilities. Current assets include cash, marketable securities, accounts receivable, and inventory that can be easily converted into cash within one year. Current liabilities include accounts payable, accrued expenses, short-term debt, and other obligations that are due within one year. The resulting ratio indicates the number of times the current assets can cover the current liabilities. A higher liquidity ratio indicates better short-term financial health and indicates that the company has a strong ability to meet its current obligations. This is important for businesses as it provides assurance to creditors, suppliers, and other stakeholders that the company can manage and pay off its debts in a timely manner. It also allows the company to take advantage of potential business opportunities, such as acquiring new assets or investing in growth initiatives. On the other hand, a lower liquidity ratio may raise concerns about a company's ability to meet its short-term obligations. This may indicate that the company has insufficient liquid assets to cover its liabilities or that it relies heavily on short-term financing. A low liquidity ratio can expose the company to financial difficulties if it encounters unexpected expenses, economic downturns, or difficulties in generating cash flow. It is important to note that while a higher liquidity ratio may indicate greater financial stability, excessively high liquidity ratios may suggest an inefficient use of capital. Holding too much cash or inventory can tie up resources that could have been used for more productive purposes, such as investing in long-term assets or research and development. In conclusion, the liquidity ratio is a crucial measure in financial management that assesses a company's ability to meet short-term obligations. It provides insights into the company's liquidity position and its ability to maintain financial stability in the short run. A higher liquidity ratio indicates better financial health, while a lower ratio may raise concerns about the company's ability to meet its obligations. Striking the right balance is essential to ensure efficient use of capital while maintaining financial stability.

Liquidity Risk

Liquidity risk refers to the potential for a company or financial institution to encounter difficulty in meeting its short-term obligations and needs for cash. It arises when a firm is unable to sell or convert its assets into cash quickly and at a reasonable price, resulting in a liquidity shortfall that can lead to financial instability or even insolvency. Liquidity risk is a critical aspect of financial management as it affects the ability of an organization to fund its operations, meet its financial obligations, and respond to unexpected cash requirements. It can arise from various factors, including changes in market conditions, economic downturns, regulatory actions, or internal issues within the firm. There are two types of liquidity risk: funding liquidity risk and market liquidity risk. Funding liquidity risk refers to the potential inability of a firm to obtain sufficient funding to meet its obligations. It can occur when there is a sudden loss of confidence in the firm's ability to repay its debts or access additional financing. Market liquidity risk, on the other hand, refers to the potential difficulty in buying or selling an asset quickly and at its fair value. This risk is particularly relevant for firms that hold illiquid assets or operate in markets with limited trading activities. Liquidity risk can have severe consequences for a firm. In the short term, it can result in increased borrowing costs, difficulty in obtaining credit, and constrained investment opportunities. In the long term, it can lead to financial distress, loss of reputation, and even bankruptcy. To manage liquidity risk effectively, organizations employ various strategies and techniques. These may include maintaining adequate cash reserves, diversifying funding sources, establishing lines of credit, developing contingency plans, and regularly monitoring and stress-testing liquidity levels. In conclusion, liquidity risk is a critical aspect of financial management that refers to the potential for a firm to face difficulties in meeting its short-term cash needs and obligations. It can arise from various factors and can have severe consequences for the stability and viability of an organization. Effective liquidity risk management is essential for ensuring the financial health and resilience of a firm.

Liquidity Trap

A liquidity trap refers to a situation in which monetary policy becomes ineffective and fails to stimulate economic growth and investment due to extremely low interest rates or a decrease in aggregate demand. In financial management, a liquidity trap can have a significant impact on the availability and circulation of money within an economy. During a liquidity trap, there is a high preference for holding money rather than spending or investing it. As a result, even if central banks reduce interest rates to stimulate borrowing and spending, individuals and businesses may remain unwilling to take on additional debt or make new investments. This creates a situation where monetary policy loses its effectiveness in boosting economic activity.

Liquidity

Liquidity refers to the ability of a company to convert its assets into cash quickly and easily, without incurring a significant loss in value. It measures the short-term solvency of a business and its ability to meet its immediate financial obligations. A high level of liquidity is important for businesses as it ensures that they have sufficient cash on hand to cover unexpected expenses, pay off short-term debts, and take advantage of investment opportunities. Conversely, a low level of liquidity can lead to financial difficulties and potentially bankruptcy.

Loan Covenant

A loan covenant is a financial agreement between a borrower and a lender that establishes certain conditions and restrictions the borrower must adhere to while the loan is outstanding. These conditions are designed to protect the financial interests of the lender and ensure that the borrower maintains certain financial ratios or meets specific operational requirements. Loan covenants are an integral part of financial management as they provide lenders with a means to monitor the financial health and performance of the borrower. They act as safeguards to minimize the risk of default and protect the lender's investment. By imposing these conditions, lenders can mitigate potential risks that may arise during the loan term.

Long-Term Debt

Long-Term Debt refers to the financial obligations or liabilities that are expected to be paid off over a period exceeding one year. It is a form of borrowing that helps businesses or individuals finance their long-term investments or capital requirements. Long-term debt usually takes the form of loans or bonds, which are contractual agreements between the borrower and the lender. These obligations are typically repaid with interest over an extended period of time. The interest rate on long-term debt is often fixed, allowing for a predictable payment schedule. One common example of long-term debt is a mortgage, which is a loan taken out to purchase real estate. The repayment period for a mortgage is typically 10 to 30 years, making it a long-term financial commitment. Another example is corporate bonds, which are issued by companies to raise capital for business expansion or other financing needs. The maturity period for corporate bonds can range from 5 to 30 years. Long-term debt plays a crucial role in Financial Management as it can provide businesses with the necessary capital to invest in growth opportunities. By securing long-term debt, companies can fund capital projects, acquire assets, or expand their operations. However, managing long-term debt requires careful consideration and analysis. When evaluating long-term debt, financial managers assess several factors such as the interest rate, repayment terms, and the impact on the company's cash flow. It is important to ensure that the cost of borrowing does not exceed the potential return on investment. Additionally, financial managers must consider the company's ability to generate sufficient cash flow to meet interest and principal payment obligations. Long-term debt is a critical component of a company's capital structure, affecting its overall financial health and creditworthiness. Too much long-term debt can increase a company's financial risk and decrease its ability to handle unexpected financial challenges. On the other hand, a moderate level of long-term debt can be beneficial by leveraging the company's assets and enhancing its return on equity. In summary, long-term debt is a form of borrowing that extends beyond one year and is typically used to finance investments or capital needs. Financial managers must carefully assess the terms and impact of long-term debt to ensure it aligns with the company's financial goals and ability to repay.

Long-Term Liabilities

Long-Term Liabilities are financial obligations or debts that a company is expected to pay off or fulfill over a period of more than one year from the date of the financial statement. These liabilities are classified on the company's balance sheet as obligations that are not expected to be settled within the operating cycle, which is typically one year. Instead, they are considered long-term financial obligations that extend beyond the current accounting period. Long-Term Liabilities are an essential aspect of a company's financial management as they indicate the company's long-term financial health and potential risks. They represent claims against the company's assets by external parties and often require periodic interest payments. These liabilities can include long-term debt, bonds payable, mortgages, pension liabilities, lease obligations, deferred tax liabilities, and other long-term financial obligations. Long-term debt is a common type of long-term liability, usually consisting of loans or bonds with a maturity period of more than one year. These loans can be obtained from banks or financial institutions and are usually used to fund large-scale investments or expansions that cannot be funded by the company's existing resources or short-term borrowing. Bonds payable are another example of long-term liabilities, representing the company's obligations to repay the principal amount borrowed plus any interest to bondholders. Bonds are typically issued to raise capital from investors and have a predetermined maturity date. Mortgages are long-term loans secured by real estate properties, often used to finance the purchase or construction of buildings or land for business purposes. The company is obligated to make periodic payments, including principal and interest, over the term of the mortgage. Pension liabilities arise when a company provides retirement benefits to its employees, such as pensions or post-employment healthcare. These obligations represent the present value of future expected payments to retired employees and are typically funded over the employees' working years. Lease obligations are long-term contracts in which a company rents a property, equipment, or vehicles for an extended period. These leases often require periodic rental payments and are considered long-term liabilities as they extend beyond the current accounting period. Deferred tax liabilities arise when there is a temporary difference between taxable income and accounting income. These liabilities represent the future tax obligations that the company will incur when the temporary difference reverses. Long-Term Liabilities are crucial to monitor in financial management as they can impact a company's profitability, liquidity, and overall financial stability. It is essential for a company to manage these obligations effectively to ensure it can meet its long-term financial obligations as they become due. Failing to do so may lead to financial distress or even bankruptcy.

Macroeconomics

Macroeconomics is the branch of economics that deals with the overall performance and behavior of the economy as a whole. It focuses on aggregate variables such as GDP, inflation, unemployment, and interest rates to understand how different sectors of the economy interact and influence each other. At its core, macroeconomics seeks to analyze the economy's key drivers and their impact on national income, economic growth, and stabilization policies. It encompasses various theories, models, and empirical studies to understand and predict the behavior of major economic aggregates and phenomena.

Maintenance Margin

The maintenance margin, in the context of financial management, refers to the minimum amount of equity or funds that a trader must maintain in their margin account to avoid a margin call. A margin account is a type of brokerage account that allows investors to borrow money to purchase securities. When an investor borrows funds from their broker to make investments, they need to maintain a certain level of equity in their account, known as the initial margin requirement. This initial margin requirement is typically set by the broker and is a percentage of the total value of the securities being purchased. However, the maintenance margin is a lower percentage of the total value of the securities and represents the minimum level of equity that the trader must maintain in their account. If the equity in the account falls below this maintenance margin level, the trader will receive a margin call from their broker. A margin call is a demand from the broker for the trader to deposit additional funds into their account to bring the equity level back up to the maintenance margin. If the trader fails to meet this margin call, the broker has the right to sell the securities in the account to recover the borrowed funds. Maintenance margin requirements are put in place to protect both the trader and the broker. By ensuring that traders maintain a minimum level of equity in their accounts, brokers can reduce the risk of default and the potential loss of borrowed funds. Furthermore, maintenance margins also serve as a risk management tool for traders themselves. By maintaining a certain level of equity in their accounts, traders can mitigate the risk of significant losses in price fluctuations and market downturns.

Margin Account

A margin account is a type of brokerage account that allows investors to borrow money from their broker to buy securities. This borrowing is done against the collateral of the assets already held in the account, such as stocks, bonds, or mutual funds. When opening a margin account, the investor agrees to a margin agreement, which outlines the terms and conditions of borrowing money. The margin agreement lays out the interest rate charged on the loan, the loan-to-value ratio, and any other requirements or restrictions imposed by the broker. One of the key features of a margin account is the ability to leverage investments. By using borrowed funds, investors can potentially increase their buying power and magnify potential gains. However, this also means that losses can be amplified, and investors may be required to deposit additional funds or sell securities to meet margin calls if the value of their investments decreases. Margin accounts offer flexibility and the potential for increased returns, but they also carry higher risk compared to cash accounts. Due to the leverage involved, investors with margin accounts need to carefully monitor their positions and be prepared to act quickly in response to market fluctuations. Margin accounts also require the payment of interest on the borrowed funds. The interest rates charged on margin loans can vary and are typically based on prevailing market rates. It is essential for investors to be aware of the interest costs associated with margin borrowing and factor them into their investment decisions. In addition to interest charges, margin accounts are subject to certain regulations and maintenance requirements. The Federal Reserve Board and the Financial Industry Regulatory Authority (FINRA) impose rules on margin accounts to protect investors and maintain the stability of the financial markets. In summary, a margin account is a form of borrowing that allows investors to leverage their existing assets to potentially increase their investment returns. However, the use of borrowed funds introduces higher risk, and investors must carefully manage their positions and be mindful of interest costs and regulatory requirements.

Margin Call

A margin call is a notification from a broker to a client, indicating that additional funds must be deposited into an account to meet minimum margin requirements. It typically occurs when the value of the securities held by the client drops below a certain threshold, thus reducing the equity in the account. When an investor uses leverage to make investments, they borrow money from a broker to increase their purchasing power. The borrowed funds are referred to as margin. However, brokers require investors to maintain a minimum level of equity in their accounts, known as the margin requirement. The margin requirement is usually expressed as a percentage of the total value of the securities held in the account. If the value of the securities in the account declines, the equity in the account decreases as well. When the equity falls below the margin requirement, the broker issues a margin call to the investor. The margin call serves as a warning that additional funds must be deposited into the account to bring the equity back up to the required level. Failure to meet the margin call may result in the broker liquidating securities in the account to cover the outstanding loan. Margin calls are an integral part of risk management in financial markets. They are designed to protect both the investor and the broker from excessive losses. By requiring investors to maintain a minimum level of equity, brokers can ensure that they have sufficient collateral to cover potential losses if the value of the securities in the account declines significantly. Margin calls are most common in margin trading, where investors borrow funds to trade stocks, options, or futures. They are less common in cash accounts, where investors use only their own funds to make trades.

Margin Trading

Margin trading refers to a financial strategy in which an investor borrows funds from a broker to buy securities. It involves the use of leverage or borrowed money to increase the potential return on investment. The investor puts up a portion of their own capital, known as the initial margin, and the broker lends the remaining funds. Margin trading allows investors to take larger positions in the market with relatively less capital. By borrowing funds, investors can amplify their purchasing power, which can potentially lead to higher profits. However, it also increases the risk and potential losses if the investment does not perform as expected. When engaging in margin trading, investors must maintain a minimum level of equity in their investment account, known as the maintenance margin. If the value of the securities falls below this threshold, the investor may be required to deposit additional funds or face a margin call from the broker. Margin trading is commonly used in the stock market, futures markets, and the foreign exchange market. It allows traders to speculate on the price movements of various assets without needing to have the full amount of funds required for the transaction. One of the key advantages of margin trading is the potential for higher returns. By leveraging borrowed funds, investors can multiply their gains if the investment performs well. However, it is important to note that margin trading also amplifies losses, and an unsuccessful investment can result in significant financial harm. Margin trading involves a higher level of risk compared to traditional trading. The increased leverage can lead to larger losses if the market moves against the investor's position. It requires careful risk management and thorough analysis of the market conditions. In conclusion, margin trading is a financial strategy that enables investors to borrow funds to increase their investment positions. It offers the potential for higher returns, but also carries increased risks. Proper risk management and careful consideration of market conditions are crucial for successful margin trading.

Mark-To-Market (MTM)

Mark-to-Market (MTM) is a financial management concept used to value and report the fair market value of an asset or liability on a regular basis. It involves updating the recorded value of the asset or liability based on current market conditions. The main purpose of MTM is to provide an accurate representation of the value of an asset or liability in the current market. By updating the recorded value of the asset or liability, it allows financial managers and investors to make more informed decisions about their investments and financial positions.

Market Capitalization Rate

The market capitalization rate, also known as the cap rate, is a financial metric used in the field of financial management that measures the rate of return on an investment based on its market value. It is widely used by investors, analysts, and real estate professionals to evaluate the profitability and risk of an investment. The market capitalization rate is calculated by dividing the net operating income (NOI) of an investment by its market value. The NOI is the income generated by the investment after deducting all expenses, such as taxes, maintenance, and insurance. The market value is the current value of the investment in the market, which is determined by factors such as supply and demand, investor sentiment, and economic conditions. The market capitalization rate is expressed as a percentage and indicates the expected rate of return that an investor can expect to earn from an investment. A higher cap rate suggests a higher return potential, but also implies higher risk. On the other hand, a lower cap rate indicates lower risk, but also implies lower return potential. Investors use the market capitalization rate to compare different investment opportunities and make informed decisions about where to allocate their capital. For example, if an investor is considering two investment properties, they can calculate the cap rate for each property and choose the one with the higher rate, assuming all other factors are equal. This indicates that the property has a higher potential for generating income relative to its market value. However, it is important to note that the market capitalization rate should not be the sole determining factor in investment decisions. Other factors, such as the location, condition, and potential for appreciation, should also be considered. Additionally, the cap rate may vary depending on the type of investment and the market conditions.

Market Capitalization Weighted Index

A market capitalization weighted index, also known as a market cap weighted index, is a type of index that reflects the performance of a group of securities based on their market capitalization. Market capitalization is calculated by multiplying the number of outstanding shares of a company by its current stock price. In a market capitalization weighted index, the weight or influence of each individual security is determined by its market capitalization relative to the total market capitalization of all securities in the index. This means that larger companies with higher market capitalizations have a greater impact on the index's performance compared to smaller companies with lower market capitalizations.

Market Capitalization Weighting

Market capitalization weighting is a financial management strategy that assigns weights to individual securities within a portfolio based on their respective market capitalizations. Market capitalization, often referred to as market cap, is the total value of a company's outstanding shares of stock in the market. In a market capitalization-weighted portfolio, larger companies with higher market caps have a greater influence on the overall performance of the portfolio compared to smaller companies. This is because the weights assigned to each security are proportional to their market caps.

Market Capitalization

Market capitalization, also known as market cap, is a financial metric used to measure the total value of a publicly traded company. It is calculated by multiplying the current share price of the company by the total number of outstanding shares. Market capitalization allows investors to assess the size and value of a company relative to other companies in the market. It is widely considered a fundamental indicator of a company's worth and is often used by investors, analysts, and financial professionals to evaluate investment opportunities and make informed decisions.

Market Efficiency Hypothesis

The market efficiency hypothesis, in the context of financial management refers to the theory that financial markets fully reflect all available information and promptly adjust prices to this information. It suggests that it is impossible to consistently achieve above-average returns by actively trading in the market because prices already incorporate all relevant information. The efficient market hypothesis (EMH) is based on the notion that in a well-functioning market, prices of securities would quickly adjust to any new information that becomes available. This means that stock prices should always accurately reflect the intrinsic value of the underlying company, and it would be virtually impossible to consistently outperform the market through stock selection or market timing strategies. According to the EMH, there are three levels of market efficiency: weak, semi-strong, and strong. The weak form of efficiency asserts that current stock prices fully reflect all past price and volume information, making technical analysis useless for predicting future price movements. In other words, analyzing historical price patterns or trading volume would not enable an investor to consistently beat the market. The semi-strong form of efficiency expands on the weak form by suggesting that stock prices also incorporate all publicly available information, including financial statements, news releases, and analyst reports. As a result, fundamental analysis would be of limited value in consistently identifying undervalued or overvalued stocks. The strong form of efficiency takes into account non-public or insider information, asserting that even this type of information is quickly reflected in the market price of a security. This implies that insider trading would not provide an unfair advantage since the market would adjust before the information becomes public knowledge. In summary, the market efficiency hypothesis posits that financial markets are efficient and that it is difficult for investors to consistently earn above-average returns by actively trading in the market. The hypothesis suggests that prices promptly adjust to all available information, making it challenging to consistently outperform the market through stock selection or timing strategies.

Market Efficiency

Market Efficiency, in the context of Financial Management, refers to the extent to which stock prices reflect all available information and quickly adjust to new information. It suggests that financial markets are efficient in processing information and determining the fair value of securities. According to the Efficient Market Hypothesis (EMH), which is the foundation of market efficiency, it is impossible to consistently achieve higher than average returns by using publicly available information. EMH proposes that all investors have access to the same information and act rationally, quickly incorporating new information into stock prices. As a result, it is difficult to consistently outperform the market by making informed investment decisions. Market efficiency is divided into three forms based on the degree of information incorporated into stock prices: weak form, semi-strong form, and strong form efficiency. In weak form efficiency, stock prices reflect all historical price information, meaning that it is impossible to predict future stock prices based on past price movements. Technical analysis, which involves analyzing historical price patterns, is considered ineffective in generating abnormal returns under weak form efficiency. In semi-strong form efficiency, stock prices reflect all publicly available information, including financial statements, news, and market announcements. Therefore, fundamental analysis, which involves examining a company's financial performance and industry factors, is also considered ineffective in consistently beating the market. Strong form efficiency assumes that stock prices reflect all types of information, including both publicly available and private information. In this form, even insider information is quickly incorporated into stock prices, leaving no room for investors to gain an advantage through access to non-public information. Market efficiency has implications for investment strategies, as it suggests that actively managed portfolios may not consistently outperform passively managed portfolios, such as index funds. It also implies that it is difficult to consistently time the market or identify undervalued or overvalued securities based on publicly available information. In conclusion, market efficiency in Financial Management relates to the speed and accuracy with which financial markets reflect all available information in determining stock prices. It supports the notion that it is challenging to consistently achieve abnormal returns by using publicly available information, as all investors have access to the same information and act rationally in incorporating new information into market prices.

Market Order

A market order is a type of order that an investor places with a brokerage firm to buy or sell a security at the current market price. It is the simplest and most straightforward type of order used in financial management. When an investor places a market order to buy a security, the brokerage firm will execute the order at the best available price in the market. This means that the investor will be buying the security at the current asking price. Conversely, when an investor places a market order to sell a security, the brokerage firm will execute the order at the best available price in the market. This means that the investor will be selling the security at the current bid price. One of the main advantages of using a market order is speed of execution. Market orders are typically executed quickly because they allow for immediate execution at the prevailing market price. However, the exact price at which the trade will be executed may not be known beforehand, especially if the market is volatile or illiquid. This can result in a small difference between the expected price and the actual execution price. Another advantage of market orders is their simplicity and ease of use. Investors do not need to specify a specific price when placing a market order. This makes it easy for investors who want to buy or sell a security quickly without having to closely monitor price fluctuations. It is important to note that market orders are subject to market liquidity. In highly liquid markets, where there are many buyers and sellers, market orders are more likely to be executed at the desired price. However, in illiquid markets, where there are fewer buyers and sellers, market orders may be executed at a less favorable price. Therefore, investors should exercise caution when using market orders in illiquid markets. In conclusion, a market order is a type of order that allows investors to buy or sell a security at the current market price. It is a quick and easy way to execute trades, but investors should be mindful of the potential for slippage, especially in illiquid markets.

Market Risk Premium

The Market Risk Premium is a concept widely used in financial management to assess the potential return on an investment relative to the overall market. It measures the additional return that investors expect to receive for taking on the inherent risk of investing in the stock market compared to risk-free investments, such as government bonds. The Market Risk Premium is calculated by subtracting the risk-free rate of return from the expected rate of return on the market. The risk-free rate is typically determined by the prevailing interest rates on government treasuries, which are considered to have almost no risk of default. The expected rate of return on the market is estimated based on historical data and future expectations of market performance. The Market Risk Premium serves multiple purposes in financial management. It provides investors with a benchmark to assess the attractiveness of potential investments. If the expected return on an investment is significantly higher than the Market Risk Premium, it may indicate a favorable investment opportunity. On the other hand, if the expected return is lower than the Market Risk Premium, it may suggest that the investment is overvalued and not worth pursuing. In addition, the Market Risk Premium is used in the calculation of the cost of equity, which is a key input for determining the appropriate capital structure and discount rate in valuation models, such as the Capital Asset Pricing Model (CAPM). The cost of equity represents the return required by shareholders to compensate for the risk they are exposed to by investing in a company's stock. Overall, the Market Risk Premium plays a crucial role in financial management by helping investors and companies make informed decisions about investment opportunities, as well as determining the appropriate cost of capital for valuation purposes. It reflects the compensation investors expect for bearing the risks associated with investing in the stock market, and serves as a fundamental concept in modern finance.

Market Risk

Market risk is the potential for financial losses that can arise from fluctuations in market prices, such as interest rates, exchange rates, commodity prices, and stock prices. It is a key concept in financial management as it allows businesses and investors to assess the potential risks and uncertainties associated with their investment decisions. Market risk is influenced by a variety of factors including macroeconomic conditions, market sentiment, and geopolitical events. For example, changes in interest rates can affect borrowing costs, bond yields, and the value of fixed-income securities. Exchange rate fluctuations can impact the profitability of exports and imports, as well as the value of foreign investments. Commodity price movements can affect the costs of raw materials and production, while stock market fluctuations can impact the value of equity holdings. Managing market risk is essential for businesses and investors to protect their financial well-being. This involves identifying and assessing potential risks, developing risk mitigation strategies, and implementing risk management tools and techniques. Common methods for managing market risk include diversification, hedging, and the use of derivative contracts. Diversification is the practice of spreading investments across different asset classes, industries, and geographies to reduce dependence on any single investment. By diversifying, investors can minimize the impact of adverse market events on their overall portfolio. Hedging involves using financial instruments, such as options, futures contracts, and swaps, to protect against potential losses in the value of an asset. For example, an exporter might use a currency forward contract to hedge against foreign exchange risk. Derivative contracts, such as options and futures, allow investors to speculate on price movements without directly owning the underlying asset. These contracts can be used to hedge against market fluctuations or to take advantage of market opportunities. In conclusion, market risk is a fundamental concept in financial management that refers to the potential for financial losses due to fluctuations in market prices. Understanding and managing market risk is crucial for businesses and investors to protect their assets and make informed investment decisions.

Market Timing

Market timing is a financial management strategy that involves attempting to predict the future movements of the financial markets in order to make investment decisions. The goal of market timing is to buy assets (such as stocks, bonds, or mutual funds) at a low price and sell them at a high price, thereby generating a profit. Market timing relies on the belief that it is possible to accurately predict market cycles, and to buy and sell assets accordingly. This strategy is based on the notion that markets move in predictable patterns, and that by identifying these patterns, investors can make informed decisions about when to enter or exit the market.

Maturity Date

A maturity date, in the context of financial management, refers to the date on which a financial instrument or investment becomes due for payment or is set to expire. It is an important concept in the management of financial assets and liabilities, as it helps determine the timing of cash flows and the overall financial obligations of an entity. When an individual or organization enters into a financial contract or agreement, such as a loan, bond, or insurance policy, there is usually a specified period within which the investment or liability must be settled. This period is known as the maturity period, and the maturity date marks the end of this period. For example, in the case of a bond, the maturity date is the date on which the issuer of the bond is obligated to repay the bondholder the principal amount invested. Until the maturity date, the bondholder receives periodic interest payments based on the terms of the bond agreement. The maturity date is often specified in the terms and conditions of a financial instrument or investment agreement. It is typically communicated to the parties involved at the time of the transaction, enabling them to have a clear understanding of their financial obligations and the timeline within which those obligations need to be fulfilled. Financial managers use the maturity date to assess the risk and return profile of different investments. Investments with longer maturity dates are generally considered to be riskier, as they are exposed to a higher degree of uncertainty and potential fluctuations in the market. On the other hand, investments with shorter maturity dates are often deemed less risky, as they offer more predictable cash flows in a shorter time frame. In summary, the maturity date is a crucial aspect of financial management that signifies the end of a specified period for a financial instrument or investment. It helps individuals and organizations plan their cash flows, assess their financial obligations, and make informed investment decisions based on the timing and risk associated with different options.

Mean Reversion

Mean Reversion is a concept in financial management that refers to the tendency of a financial instrument or a market's price to move back towards its average or mean level after experiencing a significant deviation. It is based on the idea that prices or values that move too far away from their typical average will eventually revert or return to their average level. This concept is grounded in the belief that financial markets and instruments follow certain patterns and exhibit cyclical behavior over time. Mean Reversion suggests that extreme movements away from the mean are unsustainable and will eventually correct themselves. This correction can occur through various mechanisms, such as investor behavior, market forces, or economic fundamentals.

Merger And Acquisition (M&A)

Mergers and Acquisitions (M&A) can be defined as the consolidation of two or more companies to form a new entity or the acquisition of one company by another. It is a strategic move undertaken by companies to achieve various objectives such as expansion, increased market share, synergies, cost savings, and diversification. In the context of financial management, M&A plays a crucial role in shaping the corporate landscape and driving economic growth. This strategic activity involves a series of complex processes including valuation, negotiation, due diligence, and integration, which require meticulous planning and execution.

Mergers And Acquisitions (M&A)

Mergers and Acquisitions (M&A) refer to the process of combining two or more companies in order to form a single entity or for one company to acquire another company. It is a strategic decision made by companies to achieve various objectives such as expanding market share, diversifying product offerings, entering new markets, gaining access to new technology or resources, reducing competition, or achieving economies of scale.

Microeconomics

Microeconomics is a branch of economics that focuses on the study of individual economic units, such as households, firms, and markets. It examines how these units make decisions regarding the allocation of scarce resources to satisfy their unlimited wants and needs.In the context of financial management, microeconomics plays a crucial role in understanding and analyzing the behavior of individual firms and households. It helps financial managers make informed decisions by examining the economic factors that influence the supply and demand of goods and services, as well as the factors that affect the pricing and profitability of these offerings.

Minimum Wage

Minimum wage refers to the legally mandated lowest hourly rate that employers must pay to their employees for their work. It is set by the government to ensure that workers receive a fair and reasonable compensation for their labor, and to establish a baseline standard for wages in the labor market. The purpose of minimum wage is to protect vulnerable workers and prevent labor exploitation by setting a floor on wages. It aims to ensure that employees are not paid wages that are insufficient to meet their basic needs and maintain a decent standard of living.

Modified Duration

The modified duration is a measure of the price sensitivity of a fixed-income security or portfolio to changes in interest rates. It provides an estimation of the potential percentage change in the price of the security for a one percent change in interest rates. Modified duration is a vital concept in financial management as it helps investors and analysts understand the risks associated with changes in interest rates and make informed investment decisions. Modified duration takes into account the fact that the relationship between a bond's price and its yield (or interest rate) is not linear. As interest rates change, the price of a bond generally moves in the opposite direction. However, this relationship is not one-to-one, and the magnitude of the price change depends on various factors like the bond's coupon rate, maturity, and yield-to-maturity. The formula to calculate modified duration is as follows: Modified Duration = Macaulay Duration / (1 + Yield-to-Maturity) Macaulay Duration measures the weighted average time it takes to receive the bond's cash flows. It considers both the timing and amount of each cash flow, discounting them based on the current yield-to-maturity of the bond. Dividing the Macaulay Duration by 1 plus the yield-to-maturity adjusts for the impact of changes in interest rates on the bond's price. By calculating the modified duration, financial managers can assess the interest rate risk associated with a fixed-income investment. A higher modified duration indicates that the bond's price is more sensitive to changes in interest rates, implying greater risk. On the other hand, a lower modified duration suggests that the bond's price is relatively less affected by interest rate fluctuations. Financial managers can use modified duration to compare different fixed-income securities and select those with the desired level of interest rate risk. It helps them evaluate the potential impact of changes in interest rates on the value of their investment portfolios and make appropriate adjustments to mitigate risks or capitalize on opportunities.

Modified Internal Rate Of Return (MIRR)

The modified internal rate of return (MIRR) is a financial management tool used to evaluate the profitability of an investment or project. It is an improvement over the traditional internal rate of return (IRR) method because it addresses some of the limitations and drawbacks of the IRR. The MIRR takes into account the time value of money by discounting both the cash outflows and inflows of a project to their present values at different rates. Unlike the IRR which assumes that cash inflows are reinvested at the same rate as the initial investment, the MIRR allows for a more realistic assumption that cash inflows can be reinvested at a different rate. The MIRR is calculated by first determining the present value of the cash outflows using the project's cost of capital or required rate of return. Then, the future value of the cash inflows is calculated by compounding the cash inflows at the reinvestment rate. Finally, the MIRR is derived by finding the discount rate that equates the present value of the outflows to the future value of the inflows. The MIRR is considered a more accurate indicator of the profitability of an investment because it accounts for the opportunity cost of capital and the reinvestment rate of cash inflows. It provides a more realistic estimate of the project's rate of return and helps in making more informed investment decisions. One of the benefits of using the MIRR is that it provides a consistent rate of return that can be compared across different projects or investments. It allows for better decision making by considering the time value of money and the reinvestment rate of cash inflows. In conclusion, the MIRR is a valuable tool in financial management for evaluating the profitability of an investment or project. It overcomes the limitations of the IRR method by incorporating the time value of money and making a more realistic assumption about the reinvestment of cash inflows. By using the MIRR, financial managers can make more informed investment decisions and compare the profitability of different projects.

Monetary Base

The monetary base is a key measure used in financial management to denote the total amount of a country's currency that is in circulation, as well as the reserves held by the central bank. It is a critical tool for understanding and analyzing the overall health and stability of an economy. In simple terms, the monetary base can be defined as the sum of currency in circulation and the reserves held by the central bank. Currency in circulation refers to the physical notes and coins that are actively being used by individuals and businesses for transactions. These include the money held by individuals in their wallets, cash registers in stores, and bank vaults. On the other hand, reserves refer to the deposits held by commercial banks at the central bank. The monetary base has a direct impact on the supply of money in the economy. When the central bank wants to increase the money supply, it can inject more currency into circulation or increase the amount of reserves available to commercial banks. This can be done through activities such as open market operations, where the central bank buys government securities from banks, thus increasing their reserves. By increasing the monetary base, the central bank aims to stimulate economic activity and encourage lending and investment. Conversely, when the central bank wants to tighten monetary policy and reduce the money supply, it can decrease the monetary base. This can be achieved by selling government securities to banks or increasing the reserve requirements for commercial banks. By reducing the money supply, the central bank aims to control inflation and maintain price stability. Understanding and monitoring the monetary base is crucial for financial management as it helps policymakers and analysts assess the effectiveness of monetary policy measures. By analyzing changes in the monetary base over time, they can gain insights into the overall economic conditions, inflationary pressures, and the potential impact on interest rates and exchange rates. In summary, the monetary base is a measure of the total amount of currency in circulation and reserves held by the central bank. It is a fundamental tool in financial management for analyzing and managing monetary policy, as well as assessing the overall health of an economy.

Monetary Policy Tools

Monetary policy refers to the actions and measures taken by the central bank or monetary authority of a country to manage and control the money supply and interest rates in order to achieve specific economic objectives. These objectives typically include controlling inflation, promoting economic growth, maintaining price stability, and ensuring financial stability. Monetary policy tools are the various instruments and strategies used by central banks to implement and execute their monetary policy objectives. These tools are designed to influence the money supply, credit availability, and interest rates in the economy, thereby affecting the overall level of economic activity and inflation.

Monetary Policy

Monetary policy refers to the actions and decisions taken by a central bank or monetary authority to manage and control the money supply and interest rates in an economy. It is an essential tool in financial management to achieve key economic objectives such as price stability, full employment, and sustainable economic growth. The central bank executes monetary policy through various measures, primarily focused on influencing the availability and cost of money in the economy. These measures include adjusting the reserve requirements for commercial banks, conducting open market operations, and setting the interest rates at which it lends to commercial banks. One of the key goals of monetary policy is to maintain price stability. By managing the money supply, the central bank aims to control inflation and prevent excessive fluctuations in prices. When inflation is high, the central bank may tighten monetary policy by raising interest rates or increasing reserve requirements, thereby reducing the money supply and curbing spending. On the other hand, during periods of low inflation or deflation, the central bank may implement expansionary monetary policy by lowering interest rates or decreasing reserve requirements to stimulate spending and support economic growth. Another objective of monetary policy is to promote full employment. By influencing the availability and cost of credit, the central bank aims to foster an environment conducive to investment, job creation, and economic expansion. Through expansionary monetary policy, the central bank strives to lower interest rates, making it cheaper for businesses and individuals to borrow, invest, and spend, thereby stimulating economic activity and employment. Furthermore, monetary policy plays a crucial role in maintaining financial stability. By regulating the money supply and interest rates, the central bank seeks to ensure the stability and soundness of the banking system. Through measures such as adjusting reserve requirements, the central bank can influence the liquidity and solvency of commercial banks, mitigating the risk of financial crises and disruptions in the financial markets. In conclusion, monetary policy is a vital tool in financial management that central banks use to manage the money supply, interest rates, and economic conditions in an economy. By pursuing key objectives such as price stability, full employment, and financial stability, the central bank aims to support sustainable economic growth and welfare.

Money Market Account

A money market account is a type of financial account that is offered by banks and other financial institutions. It is designed to provide a safe and convenient way for individuals to save and invest their money while earning a competitive rate of interest. Unlike a traditional savings account, a money market account typically offers a higher interest rate. This is because the funds deposited into a money market account are used by the financial institution to invest in low-risk, short-term instruments such as treasury bills, certificates of deposit, and commercial paper. These investments generate interest income, which is then passed on to the account holder. One of the key features of a money market account is its liquidity. Account holders are allowed to make a limited number of withdrawals each month without incurring any fees or penalties. This makes it a convenient option for individuals who want to have access to their funds in case of emergencies or unexpected expenses. In addition, money market accounts are considered to be relatively safe investments. They are insured by the Federal Deposit Insurance Corporation (FDIC) for up to $250,000 per depositor, per insured bank. This means that even if the financial institution fails, the account holder will not lose their money. Money market accounts are suitable for individuals who have a low risk tolerance and want to earn a higher rate of return compared to a traditional savings account. They are also a good option for short-term savings goals, such as saving for a down payment on a house or a vacation. In summary, a money market account is a type of financial account that offers a competitive interest rate and allows for easy access to funds. It provides a safe and convenient way for individuals to save and invest their money, while enjoying the benefits of liquidity and FDIC insurance.

Money Market Funds (MMFs)

Money Market Funds (MMFs) are a type of mutual fund that invests in short-term, low-risk securities such as Treasury bills, certificates of deposit, and commercial paper issued by banks and corporations. They are considered a safe and liquid investment option for investors looking to preserve capital and earn a modest return. MMFs are typically managed by investment firms and are regulated by the Securities and Exchange Commission (SEC) in the United States. They are required to maintain a stable net asset value (NAV) of $1 per share, which means that investors can buy and sell shares of the fund at this fixed price. This stable NAV is achieved by investing in securities with short maturities and high credit ratings, minimizing the risk of losses.MMFs provide a number of benefits to investors. Firstly, they offer a higher yield compared to traditional savings accounts, making them attractive to individuals and institutions seeking a higher return on their cash holdings. Secondly, MMFs provide daily liquidity, allowing investors to easily buy and sell shares on any business day. This makes them a convenient option for short-term cash management needs.Furthermore, MMFs are considered relatively low-risk investments due to their conservative investment strategy. By focusing on high-quality short-term securities, MMFs aim to minimize the risk of default and market volatility. However, it is important to note that although MMFs are considered low-risk, they are not risk-free. While the chances of losing principal are minimal, there is still a possibility of experiencing a decrease in the NAV due to market fluctuations or credit events.MMFs are commonly used by individuals and corporations for various purposes. Individuals often use MMFs as a short-term investment option for cash reserves, emergency funds, or to hold proceeds from the sale of assets until they decide on a long-term investment strategy. Similarly, corporations use MMFs to manage their short-term cash surpluses, ensuring that funds are easily accessible while earning a return.In conclusion, Money Market Funds are mutual funds that invest in low-risk, short-term securities with the objective of preserving capital and providing liquidity. They are considered a safe and convenient option for investors seeking a higher yield on their cash holdings, but it is important to weigh the potential risks before investing.

Money Multiplier

The money multiplier refers to the ratio of the increase in the money supply to the increase in the monetary base. It is a concept used in financial management to understand and analyze the impact of changes in the monetary base on the overall money supply in an economy. The monetary base, also known as high-powered money, represents the total amount of currency in circulation and reserves held by banks. It consists of the currency held by the public and the reserves held by commercial banks. When the monetary base increases, it provides the initial injection of funds into the economy. The money multiplier is calculated by dividing the change in the money supply by the change in the monetary base. It represents the extent to which the initial injection of funds leads to an increase in the overall money supply through the process of credit creation by commercial banks. The higher the money multiplier, the greater the increase in the money supply for a given change in the monetary base. For instance, let's consider a scenario where the central bank increases the monetary base by $100 million. Due to the fractional reserve system, commercial banks are required to hold only a fraction of the deposits as reserves and can lend out the remaining amount. Assuming a reserve requirement of 10%, the commercial banks can lend out $90 million. This $90 million is then re-deposited into banks, and again, 90% of it can be lent out. This process continues, leading to a further increase in the money supply. The money multiplier is influenced by various factors such as the reserve requirement set by the central bank, the willingness of banks to lend, and the demand for credit in the economy. Changes in any of these factors can affect the magnitude of the money multiplier and, consequently, the money supply in the economy.

Monopoly

Monopoly is a concept in financial management that refers to a market structure in which a single company or entity controls the supply and sale of a particular product or service. This dominance allows the monopolistic firm to dictate market prices and conditions, often resulting in limited competition and barriers to entry for other potential market participants. In a monopoly, the lack of competition enables the firm to maintain higher prices and profit margins, which can result in reduced consumer welfare and allocative efficiency. The monopolistic firm has the power to set the price at a level that maximizes its own profits, often at the expense of consumer surplus.

Moral Hazard

Moral hazard refers to the situation where one party engages in risky behavior because it does not have to bear the full consequences of its actions. In the context of financial management, moral hazard usually arises when a person or entity has the potential to take on excessive risks due to the presence of insurance, guarantees, or other forms of protection against losses. For example, consider a bank that has been bailed out by the government in the past. This bailout creates a moral hazard because the bank knows that if it takes on risky investments and suffers losses, the government is likely to step in and rescue it again. As a result, the bank may engage in riskier lending practices, such as giving loans to borrowers with lower creditworthiness, or investing in high-risk assets with the expectation of higher returns. The bank may also be less diligent in monitoring and managing the risks associated with its lending and investment activities. Moral hazard can also occur in the relationship between shareholders and managers of a company. When shareholders provide managers with stock options or performance-based bonuses, it creates an incentive for the managers to take on excessive risks to boost short-term performance and increase the value of their own compensation. This can lead to a misalignment of interests between shareholders and managers, as shareholders bear the ultimate risk and may suffer financial losses if the company fails due to the excessive risk-taking by managers. In financial markets, moral hazard can arise due to the presence of implicit or explicit government guarantees. For example, if market participants believe that the government will bail out large financial institutions in times of crisis, they may be more willing to invest in or lend to these institutions, assuming that the risks are effectively transferred to the government. This can lead to an underpricing of risk and encourage excessive risk-taking by financial institutions, as they are less concerned about the potential losses from their risky activities.

Mortgage-Backed Securities (MBS)

Mortgage-Backed Securities (MBS) are financial instruments that represent an ownership interest in a pool of mortgage loans. These securities are created by financial institutions known as mortgage originators, which include banks, mortgage lenders, and other entities that make home loans to borrowers. When a homebuyer obtains a mortgage loan, the lender has the option to sell that loan to a third party. Instead of holding onto individual mortgages, lenders often bundle multiple loans together to create a pool. This pool of loans serves as the underlying asset for the creation of MBS. The process of creating MBS involves several steps. First, mortgage originators select a group of mortgage loans with similar characteristics based on factors such as interest rates, loan terms, and credit quality. These loans are then transferred to a special purpose vehicle, typically a trust, which holds the loans on behalf of the MBS investors. Next, the trust issues MBS certificates that represent ownership stakes in the pool of loans.

These certificates are sold to investors in the secondary market, such as institutional investors, government-sponsored entities, and individuals. The value of the MBS certificates is derived from the cash flows generated by the underlying mortgage loans, including principal and interest payments made by the borrowers. Investors in MBS receive periodic interest and principal payments, which are distributed based on the terms of the securities. The interest rates on MBS are typically higher than those on Treasury bonds, reflecting the greater risk associated with mortgage loans. However, the risk of default on MBS is mitigated by the underlying collateral, as the securities are backed by the pool of mortgage loans. The secondary market for MBS is an important component of the financial system, providing liquidity and allowing investors to buy and sell these securities. MBS can be traded on exchanges or privately between investors. The market for MBS is influenced by factors such as interest rates, housing market conditions, and investor demand for fixed-income securities.

Mortgage-Backed Security (MBS)

A Mortgage-Backed Security (MBS) refers to a type of financial instrument that is created by pooling together a group of mortgages. These mortgages are typically residential mortgages, although commercial mortgages can also be included. The purpose of creating an MBS is to provide an investment opportunity for investors to earn income from the interest and principal payments made by homeowners on their mortgages. When an MBS is created, the mortgages are bought from the original lenders, such as banks or mortgage companies. The purchased mortgages are then bundled together and sold as a single security to investors. Each investor in the MBS receives a share of the interest and principal payments made by the homeowners whose mortgages are included in the pool.

Moving Average Convergence Divergence (MACD)

The Moving Average Convergence Divergence (MACD) is a technical analysis tool used in financial management to identify potential buy and sell signals in the price of a security. It consists of three elements: the MACD line, the signal line, and the histogram. The MACD line is calculated by subtracting the 26-day Exponential Moving Average (EMA) from the 12-day EMA. The 12-day EMA is more reactive to short-term price movements, while the 26-day EMA provides a smoother average of the price over a longer period. The MACD line represents the difference between these two moving averages and serves as a measure of the momentum of the price movement. The signal line is a 9-day EMA of the MACD line, and it is used to generate buy and sell signals. When the MACD line crosses above the signal line, it is seen as a bullish signal, indicating a potential buying opportunity. Conversely, when the MACD line crosses below the signal line, it is considered a bearish signal, suggesting a potential selling opportunity. The histogram represents the difference between the MACD line and the signal line. It provides a visual depiction of the convergence or divergence between the two lines. A positive histogram indicates that the MACD line is above the signal line, suggesting bullish momentum. Conversely, a negative histogram signifies that the MACD line is below the signal line, indicating bearish momentum. Traders and investors use the MACD to identify potential trend reversals, confirm the strength of an ongoing trend, or generate signals for entering or exiting positions. Crossovers between the MACD line and the signal line, along with changes in the histogram, can provide valuable insights into the price dynamics of a security. By analyzing the MACD indicators, financial managers can make informed decisions regarding the timing of their trades and investments. The MACD helps them interpret the market sentiment and determine whether to buy, sell, or hold a particular security, improving their ability to maximize profits and manage risks effectively.

Municipal Bond Market

Municipal Bond Market: The municipal bond market refers to the market where state and local governments issue debt securities to finance various public projects and initiatives. Municipal bonds, also known as munis, are fixed-income securities that are issued by government entities such as cities, counties, states, and other local agencies. These bonds are typically used to fund public infrastructure projects such as schools, hospitals, highways, water and sewage systems, and other essential facilities. The proceeds from the issuance of municipal bonds are usually used to finance long-term capital projects or to refinance existing debt obligations. Investors who purchase municipal bonds are essentially lending money to the government entity issuing the bond in exchange for regular interest payments and the return of the principal amount at maturity. The interest paid on municipal bonds is generally exempt from federal income taxes and may also be exempt from state and local taxes if the investor resides in the same jurisdiction as the issuer. Municipal bonds are typically categorized into two main types: general obligation bonds and revenue bonds. General obligation bonds are backed by the full faith and credit of the issuing government entity and are supported by its taxing power. In contrast, revenue bonds are secured by the revenue generated from a specific project or facility, such as toll roads, airports, or utilities. The municipal bond market is an important source of funding for state and local governments, allowing them to finance essential public projects and infrastructure without solely relying on tax revenues. It also provides investors with a relatively safe and tax-efficient investment option. However, like any investment, municipal bonds carry risks, including credit risk, interest rate risk, and inflation risk, which may affect the value and performance of these securities over time.

Municipal Bond

A municipal bond is a type of debt security that is issued by a government entity at the local level, such as a city or a municipality. These bonds are commonly used to fund public infrastructure projects, such as the construction of schools, hospitals, or roads. When a government entity issues a municipal bond, it is essentially borrowing money from investors. In return, the government entity promises to pay back the principal amount of the bond, also known as the face value, at a specified future date, known as the maturity date. Additionally, the government entity agrees to make regular interest payments to bondholders at a fixed rate, often semi-annually or annually. One important characteristic of municipal bonds is that they are typically exempt from federal income taxes. This tax advantage makes municipal bonds particularly attractive to high-income investors who are looking for tax-efficient investments. In some cases, municipal bonds may also be exempt from state and local taxes, depending on the location of the bond issuer and the investor's residence. Municipal bonds come in different forms, including general obligation bonds and revenue bonds. General obligation bonds are backed by the full faith and credit of the issuing government entity and can be repaid using any available resources, such as tax revenues. Revenue bonds, on the other hand, are secured by specific sources of revenue, such as tolls from a bridge or fees from a public utility, and these bonds are repaid using the revenue generated by the project that they finance. Investing in municipal bonds can provide individuals with a stable source of income, as the interest payments are typically fixed and predictable. However, it is important for investors to carefully evaluate the creditworthiness of the bond issuer before investing, as the risk of default can vary among different municipalities. Additionally, municipal bond prices can fluctuate in response to changes in interest rates and market conditions.

Mutual Fund Expense Ratio

A mutual fund expense ratio is a measure of the costs associated with operating a mutual fund. It is expressed as a percentage of the fund's average net assets and represents the amount investors pay to cover the fund's operating expenses. These operating expenses include management fees, administrative costs, custodian fees, distribution and marketing expenses, and other overhead costs. The expense ratio is calculated by dividing the total annual expenses by the average net assets of the fund. Investors need to consider the expense ratio when evaluating mutual funds because it directly affects their investment returns. A high expense ratio can eat into the fund's overall performance and reduce the investor's net return. On the other hand, a low expense ratio can enhance the investor's returns. The expense ratio is an important factor to consider when comparing different mutual funds. However, investors should not solely base their investment decisions on this metric. Other factors such as the fund's investment strategy, historical performance, risk profile, and the quality of the fund manager should also be taken into account. Though the expense ratio is an ongoing cost for investors, it is typically deducted from the fund's assets on a daily basis. This means that investors do not need to manually pay the expense ratio separately; it is automatically deducted from their investment. The expense ratio is disclosed in the fund's prospectus and other regulatory documents. In conclusion, the mutual fund expense ratio is a percentage that represents the cost of operating a mutual fund. It is an important factor to consider when selecting mutual funds as it can impact investment returns. Investors should review the expense ratio along with other factors before making investment decisions.

Mutual Fund Expenses

Mutual fund expenses refer to the various costs associated with investing in a mutual fund. These expenses are borne by the shareholders and are deducted from the fund's assets. The fees and charges associated with mutual funds can vary widely depending on the fund's investment strategy, size, and the services provided by the fund company. There are several types of expenses that investors need to be aware of when considering investing in a mutual fund. One of the most common types of expenses is the management fee, which is charged by the fund company to cover the costs of managing the fund's portfolio. This fee is typically calculated as a percentage of the fund's average net assets and is expressed as an annual percentage. In addition to the management fee, there may be other fees and charges, such as the expense ratio, which includes various operating expenses, including administrative expenses, shareholder services, and marketing expenses. The expense ratio is also expressed as an annual percentage and is deducted from the fund's assets on a daily basis. Another type of expense that investors may encounter is the sales load, which is a commission or fee charged when purchasing or selling shares of a mutual fund. There are two main types of sales loads: front-end loads and back-end loads. Front-end loads are paid when shares are purchased, while back-end loads are paid when shares are sold. Some funds may also have a no-load option, which means there is no sales load charged. It is important for investors to carefully review the prospectus and other relevant documents provided by the mutual fund company to understand the expenses associated with investing in a particular fund. These expenses can have a significant impact on an investor's returns over time, so it is essential to consider them when making investment decisions.

Mutual Fund Load

A mutual fund load refers to a sales charge or commission that investors pay when purchasing or selling shares of a mutual fund. This load is a percentage of the total amount invested and is typically collected by the fund's distributor or salesperson. There are generally two types of loads associated with mutual funds: front-end loads and back-end loads. A front-end load, also known as a sales load or a load fee, is charged at the time of purchase and is deducted from the investor's investment amount. For example, if an investor purchases $10,000 worth of shares with a 5% front-end load, $500 will be deducted as a sales charge, and only $9,500 will be invested in the fund. On the other hand, a back-end load, also referred to as a deferred sales charge or a redemption fee, is imposed when the investor sells or redeems shares. The percentage charged may vary depending on how long the investor has held the shares. Back-end loads usually decrease over time (e.g., decreasing 1% per year) and eventually expire after a specified holding period, such as five or six years. It's important to note that not all mutual funds have loads. Mutual funds that do not charge sales commissions are referred to as no-load funds. In contrast, mutual funds that do charge sales commissions are known as load funds. The purpose of load funds is to compensate financial professionals, such as brokers or financial advisors, for their services and expertise in recommending and managing the fund. Investors should carefully consider the impact of loads on their investment returns. The sales charges reduce the initial investment or the amount received upon redemption, potentially affecting overall returns. However, it's worth noting that the presence of a load does not necessarily imply that one fund is superior to another. Investors should evaluate other factors, such as fees, expenses, performance history, and investment objectives, before making investment decisions.

Mutual Fund

A mutual fund is a professionally managed investment vehicle that pools money from numerous investors to invest in a diversified portfolio of securities, such as stocks, bonds, or money market instruments. The fund is managed by a team of experienced portfolio managers, who make investment decisions on behalf of the investors based on the fund's investment objectives. Investors purchase shares or units in the mutual fund, which represent their proportionate ownership in the fund. The value of these shares or units is determined by the net asset value (NAV) of the mutual fund, which is calculated by dividing the total value of the fund's assets by the number of outstanding shares or units. One of the key advantages of investing in mutual funds is the diversification they offer. By pooling money from multiple investors, mutual funds can invest in a wide range of securities across different sectors and geographies. This diversification helps to reduce the risk associated with investing in individual securities.

Additionally, mutual funds provide access to professional management and expertise, which can be especially beneficial for individual investors who may not have the time or knowledge to manage their own investment portfolio effectively. Mutual funds offer various types of funds, each with its own investment strategy and risk profile. For example, equity funds invest primarily in stocks and are suitable for investors seeking long-term capital appreciation. Bond funds, on the other hand, invest in fixed-income securities and are suitable for investors looking for stable income with moderate risk. There are also balanced funds that invest in a combination of stocks and bonds to achieve both capital appreciation and income. Investing in mutual funds also offers liquidity, as investors can typically buy or sell their shares or units on any business day. This allows investors to easily enter or exit their investment positions when needed. Additionally, mutual funds provide transparency to their investors by regularly reporting the fund's performance, holdings, and expenses. It is important for investors to carefully consider their investment objectives, risk tolerance, and time horizon before investing in mutual funds. They should also review the fund's prospectus, which provides detailed information about the fund's investment strategy, fees, and past performance. By conducting thorough research and selecting the right mutual fund, investors can potentially achieve their financial goals and build wealth over time.

Net Asset Value (NAV) Per Share

Net Asset Value (NAV) per share is a financial metric used in the field of financial management to measure the value of a mutual fund or an investment company on a per-share basis. It represents the net value of the assets held by the fund, minus any liabilities, divided by the total number of shares outstanding. In essence, NAV per share indicates the underlying value of each share in the mutual fund or investment company. The calculation of NAV per share involves determining the total value of the assets held by the mutual fund, which typically includes stocks, bonds, cash, and other securities. This total value is then reduced by any liabilities or expenses incurred by the fund, such as management fees, administrative costs, and taxes. The resulting net value is divided by the total number of shares outstanding to determine the NAV per share. NAV per share is an important metric for investors as it provides insight into the value of their investment. Investors can compare the NAV per share of different mutual funds to assess their relative value and performance. A higher NAV per share suggests that the fund has accumulated more assets and is likely to generate higher returns for investors. Conversely, a lower NAV per share may indicate that the fund's assets have decreased in value or that it has significant liabilities. Additionally, NAV per share is used to calculate the purchase and redemption price of mutual fund shares. When an investor buys or sells shares in a mutual fund, the transaction price is typically based on the NAV per share at the time of the transaction. This ensures that investors are buying or selling shares at their fair market value, as determined by the underlying assets of the fund. In summary, Net Asset Value (NAV) per share is a key metric used in financial management to assess the value of a mutual fund or investment company on a per-share basis. It provides insight into the underlying value of each share and is used to determine transaction prices for buying and selling shares. By comparing NAV per share, investors can evaluate the relative value and performance of different mutual funds.

Net Asset Value (NAV)

Net Asset Value (NAV) refers to the total value of a company's assets minus the total value of its liabilities. It is a commonly used financial metric in the field of financial management. NAV helps investors, analysts, and creditors assess the financial health and investment potential of a company or mutual fund. The calculation of NAV involves taking the current market value of all the company's assets, such as cash, stocks, bonds, real estate, and subtracting the total value of its liabilities, such as loans, mortgages, and other debts. The result is a net value representing the company's equity or the value that would be left to shareholders if all the assets were to be sold and all the liabilities were paid off. NAV is often expressed on a per share basis, which is calculated by dividing the total net asset value by the number of outstanding shares. This allows investors to easily compare the value of a company or mutual fund's investments relative to the number of shares outstanding. NAV is particularly useful in evaluating the performance of mutual funds. Mutual funds pool money from multiple investors to invest in a diversified portfolio of assets. By calculating the NAV per share daily, investors can track the change in the fund's value over time. A rising NAV indicates positive returns, while a declining NAV suggests losses. Investors can use this information to track the performance of their investments and make informed decisions about buying or selling fund shares. NAV is also significant in investment appraisal. When considering investing in a company or mutual fund, investors can use the NAV as a benchmark to assess whether the current market price of the shares is overvalued or undervalued. If the market price is significantly higher than the NAV per share, it may indicate an overvaluation and vice versa. This information can guide investors in determining whether an investment opportunity presents good value for their capital. In conclusion, Net Asset Value (NAV) is a financial metric widely used in financial management to determine the value of a company or mutual fund's assets minus its liabilities. It serves as a crucial tool for investors, analysts, and creditors in evaluating financial health, performance, and investment potential.

Net Present Value (NPV)

Net Present Value (NPV) is a financial metric used in financial management to evaluate the profitability of an investment or project. It represents the difference between the present value of cash inflows and the present value of cash outflows over a specified time period, discounted at a predetermined rate of return. The NPV calculation takes into account the time value of money, recognizing that the value of a dollar received in the future is less than the value of a dollar received today. It provides a measure of the net monetary gain or loss of an investment, taking into consideration the timing of cash flows and the required rate of return. To calculate the NPV, the cash inflows and outflows associated with a project are identified and discounted back to their present value using the predetermined rate of return. The present value of the cash inflows is then subtracted from the present value of the cash outflows to determine the net cash flow. If the NPV is positive, it indicates that the project is expected to generate a net profit. Conversely, a negative NPV indicates a net loss. NPV is a widely used financial analysis tool as it provides a comprehensive assessment of an investment's profitability by considering the entire cash flow stream over the project's lifespan. It enables financial managers to compare different investment opportunities and make informed decisions based on the expected returns. Additionally, NPV allows for the consideration of risk and uncertainty by adjusting the discount rate. A higher discount rate reflects a higher risk, resulting in a lower NPV. By incorporating the time value of money and risk factors, NPV provides a more accurate assessment of an investment's value compared to other metrics such as payback period or accounting rate of return.

Net Working Capital

Net working capital, in the context of financial management, refers to the difference between a company's current assets and its current liabilities. It is a measure of the company's ability to meet its short-term obligations and fund its day-to-day operations. Current assets represent the resources that a company expects to convert into cash or use up within one year. These typically include cash, accounts receivable, inventory, and other liquid assets. Current liabilities, on the other hand, are the company's short-term obligations that are due within one year, such as accounts payable, short-term loans, and other current liabilities. The formula for calculating net working capital is: Net Working Capital = Current Assets - Current Liabilities A positive net working capital indicates that a company has sufficient current assets to cover its current liabilities, which is generally seen as a healthy sign. This means that the company is capable of meeting its short-term obligations and has enough resources to cover its day-to-day expenses. Conversely, a negative net working capital suggests that a company may have difficulties in meeting its short-term obligations. It indicates that the company's current liabilities exceed its current assets, which may indicate potential liquidity issues. This could be a sign that the company is relying heavily on short-term borrowing or facing difficulties in collecting receivables or managing inventory. Net working capital is an important metric for financial managers as it provides insights into a company's short-term liquidity and financial health. By monitoring changes in net working capital over time, financial managers can assess the company's ability to generate cash flows from its operating activities and manage its working capital effectively.

Nominal Exchange Rate

The nominal exchange rate is the rate at which one currency can be exchanged for another. It is the price of one currency in terms of another currency. In other words, it represents the amount of one currency needed to purchase a unit of another currency. The nominal exchange rate is determined by various factors, including supply and demand for currencies, interest rates, inflation rates, and economic and political conditions. Changes in these factors can cause the nominal exchange rate to fluctuate over time.

Nominal Interest Rate

A nominal interest rate is the stated rate of interest on a loan or investment without taking into account factors such as compounding or inflation. It represents the percentage of interest that will be paid or earned on an annual basis. In financial management, the nominal interest rate is an important concept as it allows investors and borrowers to understand the cost of borrowing or the potential return on their investment. It is the starting point for calculating the actual interest payments or earnings.

Non-Cumulative Preferred Stock

Non-cumulative preferred stock refers to a type of preferred stock that does not accumulate any unpaid dividends. It is a financial instrument used by companies to raise capital and attract investors. Non-cumulative preferred stock is considered less risky than common stock but more risky than bonds, making it an attractive option for both investors and issuing companies. Unlike cumulative preferred stock, non-cumulative preferred stock does not carry the right to accumulate any unpaid dividends. This means that if the issuing company fails to pay dividends in any given period, the shareholders of non-cumulative preferred stock do not have the right to claim the unpaid dividends in the future. Instead, the company has no obligation to pay the missed dividends and can choose to pay dividends in future periods at its discretion.

Non-Diversifiable Risk

Non-diversifiable risk, also known as systematic risk or market risk, refers to the type of risk that cannot be eliminated or mitigated through diversification. In financial management, it is the risk associated with the overall market or economy and affects the entire market or a specific industry as a whole, rather than being specific to a particular company or investment. Non-diversifiable risk is caused by factors such as macroeconomic conditions, political events, interest rate changes, inflation, natural disasters, and market fluctuations. These factors impact all investments in the market, making it impossible to avoid or reduce the risk through diversification. Unlike diversifiable risk, which can be managed by holding a diversified portfolio, non-diversifiable risk affects all investments and cannot be eliminated by adding more investments to a portfolio.

Non-Operating Income

Non-operating income, in the context of financial management, refers to the revenue or gains generated by a company's activities that are not directly related to its core operations. It includes income sources that are secondary to the primary business activities of a company and are usually considered to be one-time or non-recurring in nature. Non-operating income can be classified into various categories, including: - Gains from the sale of a company's non-core assets: This includes gains from the sale of land, buildings, equipment, or other assets that are not directly used in the production or delivery of goods and services. - Non-recurring or extraordinary items: These are income sources that arise infrequently and are not expected to occur regularly. Examples include insurance settlements, proceeds from lawsuits, or gains from the sale of investments. - Dividend income: This refers to the income received by a company from its investments in other companies' stocks. It is considered non-operating because it is not derived from the company's core operations. - Interest income: This includes income received from investments in interest-bearing assets such as bonds, loans, or bank deposits. Similar to dividend income, it is considered non-operating because it is not generated from the company's main business activities. - Foreign exchange gains: These are gains resulting from fluctuations in foreign currency exchange rates. Companies that have international operations or engage in foreign currency transactions may earn income from favorable exchange rate movements. Non-operating income is important for financial analysis as it provides insights into a company's overall financial performance beyond its core operations. It is typically reported separately from operating income in the income statement to help investors and stakeholders understand the sources and nature of a company's income. While non-operating income can contribute to a company's profitability, it is important to note that excessive reliance on non-operating income may indicate a lack of sustainability or stability in the company's core business operations.

162

Therefore, financial managers need to carefully analyze and evaluate the impact of non-operating income on the overall financial health of the company.

Non-Performing Asset (NPA)

A Non-Performing Asset (NPA) is a classification used in the field of financial management to refer to a loan or advance that has stopped generating income for the lender, typically a bank or financial institution. The classification of an asset as NPA signifies the borrower's inability or unwillingness to repay the loan within the agreed-upon terms and conditions. An asset is classified as a Non-Performing Asset when the principal or interest installment remains overdue for a specified period, usually 90 days or more. This period is known as the 'default' period, indicating that the borrower has failed to make timely payments for an extended duration. The categorization of an asset as NPA is essential for banks and financial institutions as it helps them identify the health of their loan portfolio and take appropriate actions to mitigate the risk associated with such assets. Once an asset is classified as NPA, the lender applies various measures to recover the outstanding dues, primarily through legal proceedings or by seizing and selling off the underlying collateral. The identification of NPA accounts is a crucial process for financial institutions as it aids in assessing their overall asset quality, profitability, and capital adequacy. It also enables them to distinguish between performing and non-performing loans, which play a vital role in determining the lender's financial strength and ability to provide credit to other borrowers. Moreover, the classification of an asset as NPA requires financial institutions to set aside additional provisions or reserves, reducing their profitability. Banks need to maintain adequate provisions for their NPAs and report them accurately to regulatory bodies to ensure transparency and stability in the financial system.

Non-Recourse Loan

Non-recourse loan refers to a type of loan in which the lender has limited or no recourse to the borrower's other assets in case of default. This means that if the borrower fails to repay the loan, the lender can only seek repayment from the collateral or asset that was used to secure the loan and cannot pursue the borrower's other assets or personal finances. In a non-recourse loan, the lender's ability to recover the loan amount is solely dependent on the value of the collateral. If the value of the collateral is insufficient to cover the outstanding loan balance, the lender bears the loss. Therefore, non-recourse loans are considered to be more risky for lenders compared to recourse loans. Non-recourse loans are commonly used in the context of real estate financing. For example, when purchasing a property, the lender may provide a non-recourse loan where the property itself serves as the collateral. If the borrower defaults on the loan, the lender can seize the property but cannot pursue the borrower's personal assets or income. In some cases, non-recourse loans may include certain provisions that limit the lender's recourse beyond the collateral. These provisions may specify that the lender cannot pursue the borrower for any deficiency balance even if the collateral value is insufficient. This is known as a "no-recourse" loan. Non-recourse loans provide certain advantages for borrowers. They offer protection for personal assets in case of default and reduce personal liability. Additionally, non-recourse loans are often used for high-risk ventures, such as real estate developments, where the borrower may not want to risk personal assets. However, non-recourse loans generally come with higher interest rates and stricter loan terms compared to recourse loans. Lenders may require a higher down payment or additional collateral to mitigate the increased risk. Additionally, non-recourse loans are typically limited to borrowers with strong creditworthiness and substantial collateral. In summary, a non-recourse loan is a type of loan where the lender's ability to recover the loan amount is restricted to the value of the collateral. The lender cannot pursue the borrower's other assets or personal finances in case of default. Non-recourse loans are commonly used in real estate financing and provide protection for borrowers' personal assets. However, they come with higher interest rates and stricter loan terms compared to recourse loans.

Operating Cash Flow (OCF)

Operating Cash Flow (OCF) refers to the amount of cash generated or received from a company's core operating activities during a specific period. It is a key financial measure used in financial management to evaluate the cash-generating capabilities of a business. OCF helps assess a company's ability to generate sufficient cash flow from its operations to cover its operating expenses, repay debt, invest in new projects, and distribute profits to shareholders.

163

OCF is calculated by taking the net income and adjusting it for non-cash expenses and changes in working capital. Non-cash expenses include depreciation and amortization, which are accounting expenses but do not involve cash outflows. Changes in working capital account for the fluctuations in current assets and liabilities, such as accounts receivable, inventory, accounts payable, and accrued expenses. These changes can either result in cash inflows or outflows. A positive OCF indicates that a company's operations are generating cash, which is essential for its survival and growth. It shows that the company can cover its day-to-day expenses, invest in its future growth, and have enough liquidity to meet its financial obligations. On the other hand, a negative OCF suggests that a company's operations are not generating sufficient cash flow to sustain itself, and it may need to rely on external financing or cash reserves to meet its financial obligations. Financial analysts and investors use OCF to evaluate a company's financial health and performance. It provides insights into the company's ability to generate cash, its profitability, and its efficiency in managing working capital. OCF is also compared to other financial metrics, such as net income, to assess the quality of a company's earnings. If a company has low OCF relative to its net income, it may indicate that its earnings are not translating into cash. This can be a warning sign for investors, as it may suggest potential cash flow issues. Furthermore, OCF is crucial for making investment decisions and determining the value of a company. It is used in financial models, such as discounted cash flow (DCF) analysis, to estimate the present value of a company's future cash flows. The OCF generated by a business is considered a fundamental indicator of its long-term value and potential for generating shareholder wealth.

Operating Cycle

The operating cycle is a key concept in financial management that refers to the time it takes for a company to convert its inventory and other resources into cash through the sale of its products or services. It measures the duration of various operational activities, starting from the acquisition of inventory or raw materials, through the production process, to the collection of cash from customers. Understanding and managing the operating cycle is crucial for businesses, as it directly impacts their liquidity, profitability, and overall financial health. By effectively managing the various components of the operating cycle, companies can optimize their working capital and improve their cash flow.

Operating Expense

Operating expenses, also known as OPEX, are the ongoing costs incurred by a company to run its day-to-day operations and generate revenue. These expenses are essential for maintaining the business and keeping it operational. Operating expenses are primarily related to the production and delivery of goods or services sold by the company. Operating expenses can be categorized into various types, including fixed expenses and variable expenses. Fixed expenses are costs that remain constant regardless of the level of production or sales. Examples of fixed expenses include rent, salaries, insurance, and depreciation. Variable expenses, on the other hand, fluctuate with the level of production or sales. Examples of variable expenses include raw materials, direct labor costs, and commissions. Managing operating expenses is crucial for financial management as it directly impacts a company's profitability. By closely monitoring and controlling these expenses, companies can optimize their resources, improve efficiency, and maximize their profit margins. Financial managers use various tools and strategies to control and minimize operating expenses. Cost control measures such as budgeting, cost analysis, and cost reduction techniques are implemented to identify areas of excessive spending and implement measures to reduce costs. This may involve renegotiating contracts with suppliers, finding more cost-effective alternatives, or streamlining business processes to eliminate inefficiencies. In addition to cost control, financial managers also assess the impact of operating expenses on a company's financial performance. Key financial metrics such as gross profit margin, operating profit margin, and net profit margin are monitored to evaluate the efficiency and profitability of the company's operations. These metrics provide insights into the company's ability to generate profits from its operating activities while covering its operating expenses. In summary, operating expenses are the ongoing costs incurred by a company to run its day-to-day operations. Financial managers play a crucial role in managing and controlling these expenses to optimize resources, improve efficiency, and maximize profitability. By closely monitoring and evaluating operating expenses, companies can make informed decisions to drive financial success and sustainability.

Operating Income

Operating Income is a financial metric that represents the amount of profit generated from a company's core operations before taking into account interest and taxes. It is also known as operating profit, operating earnings, or operating income before interest and taxes (EBIT). To calculate operating income, the company's total revenue is subtracted by the cost of goods sold (COGS) and operating expenses. Total revenue includes all sales and inflows of cash from the company's primary activities, while COGS includes the direct production costs necessary to create those products or services. Operating expenses include all other costs associated with running the business, such as marketing expenses, salaries, rent, and utilities. Operating income is a vital metric for financial management as it gives insights into the profitability of a company's core operations. By focusing on operating income, financial managers can assess the efficiency and effectiveness of the company's day-to-day operations without being influenced by external factors such as interest and taxes. Companies with a higher operating income generally have stronger financial positions and are better able to weather economic downturns. It is important to note that operating income only reflects the profitability of a company's core operations and does not take into account interest expenses or taxes. Therefore, it should be used in conjunction with other financial metrics to get a comprehensive understanding of a company's overall financial health.

Operating Leverage

Operating leverage is a financial management concept that measures the degree to which a company's operating income or earnings before interest and taxes (EBIT) will change in response to a change in its sales or revenue. It quantifies the fixed costs and variable costs associated with a company's operations and determines how changes in sales volume will impact the profitability of the business. Operating leverage is determined by the mix of fixed and variable costs in a company's cost structure. Fixed costs are expenses that do not vary with changes in production or sales volume, such as rent, loan payments, salaries, and insurance. Variable costs, on the other hand, are expenses that change in direct proportion to changes in production or sales volume, such as materials, direct labor, and sales commissions. A company with high operating leverage has a higher proportion of fixed costs relative to its variable costs, while a company with low operating leverage has a higher proportion of variable costs. When a company has high operating leverage, a small change in sales volume can have a significant impact on its operating income. This is because the fixed costs remain constant, and any increase in sales will result in a large increase in contribution margin and operating income. However, if sales decline, the fixed costs will still need to be paid, resulting in a larger decline in operating income. On the other hand, a company with low operating leverage has a smaller impact on operating income from changes in sales volume. This is because a larger proportion of its costs are variable, so changes in sales volume are directly reflected in changes in variable costs and contribution margin. While this provides more stability in profitability, it also means that the company may not be able to take advantage of economies of scale or increase its profitability as significantly as a company with high operating leverage.

Operating Margin

Operating Margin is a financial metric used in financial management to measure a company's profitability and efficiency in generating operating income from its primary operations. It is calculated by dividing operating income by net sales or revenue, and then multiplying the result by 100 to express it as a percentage. Operating income represents the income generated by a company from its core operations, excluding any non-operating revenue or expenses such as interest income or expense, taxes, and other extraordinary items. It is also known as operating profit or operating earnings. Operating Margin provides insights into a company's ability to generate profits from its primary activities and how efficiently it is managing its costs. It helps in evaluating the financial health and performance of a company and comparing it with other companies in the same industry. A higher Operating Margin indicates that a company is able to generate greater profits from its core operations, which is a positive sign for investors and stakeholders. It suggests that the company has effective cost controls, pricing strategies, and operational efficiency. On the other hand, a lower Operating Margin may indicate that a company is struggling to generate profits or is facing higher costs, which can raise concerns about its financial viability and competitiveness. Operating Margin is also used in ratio analysis and benchmarking to assess a company's performance over time and against its competitors. It allows for meaningful comparisons between companies of different sizes and industries. It is important to note that Operating Margin can vary significantly across industries, as some industries inherently have higher operating costs or lower profit margins. In conclusion, Operating Margin is a key financial metric that measures a company's profitability and efficiency in generating operating income from its core operations. It is a valuable tool for financial management and analysis, providing insights into a company's financial health and performance.

Operational Risk

Operational risk refers to the potential loss that can occur as a result of inadequate or failed internal processes, people, systems, or external events. It encompasses a wide range of risks that can impact the financial management of an organization, including errors, fraud, regulatory compliance issues, technology failures, and natural disasters. In the context of financial management, operational risk is particularly relevant as it can have a significant impact on the profitability, reputation, and overall stability of a financial institution. Financial institutions are exposed to operational risk in various ways, such as through their lending and investment activities, their payment and settlement systems, and their reliance on complex technology infrastructure. One key aspect of operational risk is the potential for human error. This can occur at all levels within an organization and may stem from inadequate training, lack of oversight, or improper processes and controls. Human error can lead to loss of data, incorrect financial reporting, or failure to comply with regulatory requirements, all of which can have severe consequences for a financial institution. Another significant aspect of operational risk is technology risk. Given the increasing reliance on technology in financial management, technology failures or disruptions can have a profound impact on an organization's operations. This risk can include cyber threats, system failures, data breaches, or inadequate IT infrastructure. Financial institutions need to invest in robust technology systems and implement effective cybersecurity measures to mitigate these risks. Operational risk is not limited to internal factors. External events, such as natural disasters, political instability, or changes in regulatory requirements, can also create operational risk for financial institutions. These events can disrupt operations, cause financial losses, or lead to reputational damage. Financial institutions must implement comprehensive risk management frameworks to identify, assess, and mitigate operational risks. This includes developing robust internal controls, implementing effective risk monitoring and reporting systems, and establishing contingency plans to manage potential disruptions. By effectively managing operational risk, financial institutions can enhance their resilience, protect their stakeholders, and maintain their long-term viability.

Opportunity Cost Of Capital

The opportunity cost of capital refers to the potential return that could have been earned by investing in an alternative investment with similar risk. It represents the return that is forgone when a firm chooses to invest in a particular project or venture. In financial management, the concept of opportunity cost of capital is used to evaluate and make decisions regarding investment opportunities. It helps in determining whether a project or investment is financially worthwhile and whether it can generate returns higher than the cost of capital.

Opportunity Cost

Opportunity cost is a fundamental concept in financial management that refers to the potential benefit or value that is lost when choosing one alternative over another. It represents the next best alternative that could have been chosen instead of the option that was ultimately selected. In financial decision-making, every choice involves a trade-off. When deciding how to allocate resources, such as money, time, or effort, individuals and businesses must consider not only the benefits of the chosen option but also the opportunities that are forgone. The opportunity cost is the value of these forgone opportunities. For example, let's say a company has the option to invest in a new project or allocate the funds towards expanding its existing product line. If the company chooses to invest in the new project, the opportunity cost would be the potential profitability and growth that could have been achieved through expanding the product line. Conversely, if the company chooses to expand the product line, the opportunity cost would be the potential gains from the new project. Opportunity cost is not always directly measurable in monetary terms. It can also encompass intangible factors such as time, reputation, or customer loyalty. For instance, a business owner may have to choose between attending a networking event and working on a new marketing strategy. The opportunity cost of attending the event would be the potential progress and connections that could have been made through working on the marketing strategy. Understanding and considering opportunity cost is crucial in financial management as it helps individuals and businesses make informed decisions. By evaluating the potential benefits and drawbacks of each alternative, decision-makers can assess the true cost and potential impact of their choices. This analysis allows for the prioritization and optimization of resources, ultimately leading to more effective and efficient use of available capital.

Option Premium

Option premium refers to the price that an investor pays to purchase an option contract. This premium represents the cost of acquiring the right, but not the obligation, to buy or sell an underlying asset at a specified price within a certain period of time. Options are derivative instruments that derive their value from the fluctuations in the price of the underlying asset. The premium of an option is determined by various factors, including the current market price of the underlying asset, the strike price of the option, the time remaining until expiration, the volatility of the underlying asset, and prevailing interest rates. These factors collectively influence the level of risk associated with the option, and therefore, impact its value in the market. When an investor purchases a call option, they pay an upfront premium to acquire the right to buy the underlying asset at the specified strike price during the option's lifespan. Conversely, when an investor purchases a put option, they pay a premium to acquire the right to sell the underlying asset at the strike price. The premium serves as compensation to the option seller, who is obligated to fulfill the terms of the contract if the option is exercised. The amount of the premium can vary significantly depending on the characteristics of the underlying asset and market conditions. Generally, options that have a longer time until expiration and a higher level of volatility tend to command higher premiums. Similarly, options with lower strike prices, relative to the current market price of the underlying asset, tend to have higher premiums. The concept of option premium plays a crucial role in options pricing and risk management strategies. Investors and traders analyze the premium of options to assess their potential profitability and to gauge the level of risk associated with their investment. By accurately pricing options premiums, investors can make informed decisions about whether to buy, sell, or hold options contracts, based on their specific investment objectives and risk tolerance.

Option

Financial management is the process of planning, organizing, directing, and controlling the financial activities of an organization in order to achieve its financial objectives. It involves making decisions about the allocation of resources, such as capital, investments, and expenses, to ensure the financial health and success of the organization. The primary goal of financial management is to maximize the value of the organization for its shareholders or owners. This is done by ensuring that the organization has sufficient funds to meet its financial obligations, while also generating profits and growth. Financial management encompasses various activities, including financial planning, budgeting, forecasting, cash flow management, risk analysis, investment decision making, and financial reporting.

Options Pricing Models

Options pricing models are mathematical formulas used to estimate the fair value of options. These models involve various factors such as the underlying asset price, volatility, time to expiration, interest rates, and dividends. The two most widely used options pricing models are the Black-Scholes model and the Binomial model.

Ordinary Share

An ordinary share, also known as common stock, is a type of equity security that represents ownership in a corporation. It is the most basic form of ownership in a company and provides investors with voting rights and a share in the company's profits. As owners of ordinary shares, investors have the right to vote on matters that affect the company's operations and management, such as the election of the board of directors and major corporate decisions. Each ordinary share typically carries one vote, allowing shareholders to have a say in the company's affairs. However, the influence of individual shareholders may be limited in large corporations with millions of outstanding shares. In addition to voting rights, ordinary shares give investors the opportunity to profit from the company's success. When the company performs well and earns profits, it may distribute a portion of those profits as dividends to its shareholders. The dividend payment is often calculated based on the number of ordinary shares held by each shareholder, meaning that shareholders with more shares receive a larger dividend payment. On the other hand, ordinary shares also expose investors to certain risks. Since ordinary shareholders are the last to be paid in case of liquidation, they have a lower priority compared to creditors and holders of preferred shares. Therefore, if a company goes bankrupt, ordinary shareholders may lose their entire investment. Furthermore, the value of ordinary shares is subject to fluctuations in the stock market. Factors such as the company's financial performance, industry trends, and overall market conditions can influence the price of ordinary shares. This means that shareholders may experience gains or losses depending on the performance of their investments. In summary, ordinary shares represent ownership in a corporation and provide investors with voting rights and a share in the company's profits. While they offer the potential for dividends and capital appreciation, they also carry risks and their value can fluctuate in the stock market.

Out-Of-The-Money (OTM) Option

An out-of-the-money (OTM) option is a type of options contract in which the strike price of the option is higher than the current market price for a call option, or lower than the current market price for a put option. In other words, the option does not have any intrinsic value at the time of expiration. For a call option, if the strike price is higher than the current market price of the underlying asset, the option is considered OTM. This means that if the holder of the call option were to exercise their right to buy the underlying asset at the strike price, they would be paying more than what the asset is currently worth in the market. Therefore, it does not make financial sense for the holder to exercise the option, as they could simply buy the asset at a lower price in the open market. Conversely, for a put option, if the strike price is lower than the current market price of the underlying asset, the option is considered OTM. This means that if the holder of the put option were to exercise their right to sell the underlying asset at the strike price, they would be selling it for less than what it is currently worth in the market. Therefore, it does not make financial sense for the holder to exercise the option, as they could simply sell the asset at a higher price in the open market. Because OTM options do not have any intrinsic value, their value is solely based on the probability that the market price of the underlying asset will move in a favorable direction before the option expires. As a result, OTM options are generally less expensive to purchase than in-the-money (ITM) or at-the-money (ATM) options, which have intrinsic value. Traders and investors may choose to buy OTM options as speculative instruments, as they offer the potential for significant returns if the market price of the underlying asset moves in the expected direction. However, due to the inherent risk associated with OTM options, their value can quickly diminish if the market does not move as anticipated. Therefore, purchasing OTM options requires careful analysis and an understanding of the underlying market conditions.

Over-The-Counter (OTC) Market

The Over-the-Counter (OTC) market refers to the decentralized marketplace where financial instruments, such as stocks, bonds, commodities, and derivatives, are traded directly between two parties rather than through a centralized exchange. In contrast to the organized and regulated exchanges, such as the New York Stock Exchange (NYSE) or the London Stock Exchange (LSE), the OTC market operates through a network of dealers and market participants who facilitate the buying and selling of securities. Transactions in the OTC market are typically conducted electronically or over the phone, allowing for greater flexibility and accessibility. One of the key features of the OTC market is that it allows for trading of securities that may not be listed on a formal exchange. This includes smaller companies, start-ups, or securities that don't meet the listing requirements of organized exchanges. As a result, the OTC market provides an alternative platform for investors to access a wider range of securities and investment opportunities. Additionally, the OTC market is known for its flexibility in terms of price negotiations and contract terms. Unlike exchanges with standard bid-ask spreads, prices in the OTC market can be negotiated directly between buyers and sellers. This can be particularly beneficial for institutional investors or large market participants who require customized trading arrangements or have specific hedging needs. However, the OTC market also entails certain risks. Due to its decentralized nature and lack of regulation, the OTC market may be subject to higher levels of counterparty risk, as there is no central authority overseeing the transactions. Additionally, liquidity may be lower compared to exchanges, which can make it more challenging to find a willing buyer or seller for a particular security. Overall, the Over-the-Counter (OTC) market plays a significant role in the financial landscape by providing a platform for direct trading between parties, expanding access to securities, and offering flexibility in terms of price negotiations and contract terms. However, investors need to be aware of the risks associated with engaging in OTC market transactions and should exercise caution when participating in this market.

Overbought

Overbought refers to a situation in financial management where the price of a security or asset has risen to a level that exceeds its intrinsic value or justifies its current market price based on underlying factors. This often occurs when market participants, driven by greed or market optimism, push the price of an asset beyond its fundamental worth or the level that can be sustained by supply and demand dynamics. When a security is deemed to be overbought, it is believed to have reached an unsustainable level and may be due for a corrective downward price movement. The concept of being overbought is frequently used in technical analysis, a methodology that studies historical price patterns and trends to make predictions about future price movements. Technical analysts use various indicators and tools, such as the Relative Strength Index (RSI) or the Moving Average Convergence Divergence (MACD), to identify overbought conditions in a security.

Overhead Cost

Overhead cost refers to the ongoing expenses that are not directly tied to the production of goods or services but are necessary for the overall operation of a business. These costs include expenses such as rent, utilities, insurance, administrative salaries, and office supplies. Overhead costs are typically fixed and incurred on a regular basis, regardless of the level of production or sales. They are essential for maintaining the business infrastructure and enabling the production and delivery of products or services. Unlike direct costs, which are directly attributable to a specific product or service, overhead costs are not easily assignable to a specific cost driver, such as a particular unit of production.

Overhead Costs

Overhead costs refer to the expenses incurred by a business that are not directly linked to the production of goods or services. These costs are incurred as part of the general operations of the company and are essential for the smooth functioning of the organization. Overhead costs can include various expense categories such as rent, utilities, insurance, salaries of non-production employees, office supplies, marketing expenses, and maintenance costs. These costs are necessary for the day-to-day operations and support functions of the business. Unlike direct costs, which can be directly attributed to the production of goods or services, overhead costs are not easily allocable to specific products or services but are necessary for the overall functioning of the company. Managing overhead costs is crucial for the financial health of a business. Keeping these costs under control allows a company to allocate its resources more efficiently, resulting in improved profitability and competitiveness. It is essential for businesses to monitor and analyze their overhead costs regularly to identify areas where efficiencies can be achieved. One way to manage overhead costs is by implementing cost-saving measures such as renegotiating contracts, improving energy efficiency, seeking competitive bids for services, or outsourcing non-essential functions. Companies can also make use of technology to streamline processes and reduce administrative costs. Additionally, implementing effective budgeting and forecasting practices can help keep overhead costs in check. In summary, overhead costs are the necessary expenses incurred by a business in its day-to-day operations that are not directly attributable to the production of goods or services. These costs, although not directly linked to revenue generation, are essential for the overall functioning of the company. Effective management of overhead costs is crucial for maximizing efficiency and profitability in a business.

169

Overhead Rate

The overhead rate is a financial management metric used to determine the allocation of indirect costs to products or services. Indirect costs include expenses such as rent, utilities, and depreciation, which cannot be directly attributed to a specific product or service. The overhead rate is calculated by dividing the total indirect costs by a chosen cost driver, which is typically a measure of the company's activity level or production volume. The cost driver could be the number of labor hours worked, machine hours used, or units produced, depending on the nature of the business. The formula for calculating the overhead rate is as follows: Overhead Rate = Total Indirect Costs / Cost Driver By allocating indirect costs to specific products or services, the overhead rate helps to more accurately determine the true cost of producing each item. This enables management to make informed decisions regarding pricing, production levels, and resource allocation. For example, let's say a manufacturing company has total indirect costs of $200,000 and produces 10,000 units. The chosen cost driver is machine hours, which is 20,000 hours for the period. The overhead rate would then be: Overhead Rate = $200,000 / 20,000 hours = $10 per machine hour This means that for every machine hour used in the production process, an additional $10 should be allocated to cover the indirect costs. If a product requires 5 machine hours to produce, the overhead cost allocated to that product would be $50. It is important for financial managers to regularly monitor and adjust the overhead rate to ensure that costs are allocated properly and reflect the changing dynamics of the business. A too high or too low overhead rate can result in inaccurate product costs, which may lead to poor decision-making.

Overhead Ratio

An overhead ratio, in the context of financial management, is a measure used to evaluate the efficiency and cost-effectiveness of a company's operations. It is a financial metric that provides insight into the company's ability to control and manage its expenses. The overhead ratio is calculated by dividing the total overhead costs of a company by its total sales or revenue. Overhead costs typically include expenses such as rent, utilities, salaries and benefits for non-production staff, depreciation, and other indirect costs that are not directly attributable to the production of goods or services. The formula for calculating the overhead ratio is as follows: Overhead Ratio = Total Overhead Costs / Total Sales or Revenue A lower overhead ratio indicates that a company is operating efficiently and effectively managing its costs. It suggests that the company is able to generate higher profits from its sales or revenue, as a smaller proportion of its income is being consumed by overhead expenses. On the other hand, a higher overhead ratio may indicate inefficiencies or poor cost management within the company. It suggests that a larger proportion of the company's income is being used to cover overhead expenses, resulting in lower profit margins. It is important for companies to monitor and analyze their overhead ratio regularly to identify areas of improvement and make cost-saving decisions. By reducing overhead costs, a company can increase its profitability and improve its overall financial performance. However, it is crucial to maintain a balance between reducing overhead costs and ensuring that the company's operations are not negatively impacted. Cutting costs indiscriminately can lead to a decline in the quality of products or services and may ultimately harm the company's reputation and customer satisfaction. In conclusion, the overhead ratio is a valuable financial metric that helps assess a company's cost management and efficiency. By carefully analyzing and managing overhead costs, companies can strive to achieve optimal financial performance while maintaining the quality of their operations.

P/E Ratio (Price-To-Earnings Ratio)

The P/E Ratio, or Price-to-Earnings Ratio, is a financial metric used in the field of financial management. It is a valuation ratio that represents the ratio of a company's current share price to its earnings per share (EPS).The P/E Ratio is calculated by dividing the market price per share of a company by its earnings per share. The market price per share is the current price at which the company's shares are trading in the market, while the earnings per share is the net income of the company allocated to each outstanding share of common stock.

Par Value

Par value, in the context of financial management, refers to the nominal or face value of a financial instrument, such as a bond or a preferred stock. It is the value at which the instrument is initially issued or can be redeemed at maturity. The par value is determined by the issuer and is typically set at a round number, such as $1,000 for a bond or $100 for a preferred stock. It serves as a reference point for both the issuer and the investor and is often used to calculate certain financial metrics.

Pari Passu

Pari passu is a Latin term used in the context of financial management to describe the equal ranking or treatment of different creditors or investors with respect to their claims on a company's assets or cash flows. It signifies that all parties with pari passu status have an equal right to receive payments or distributions, without any priority or preference given to one over the other. In other words, when creditors or investors hold pari passu status, they are entitled to share the company's available assets or cash flows on a pro-rata basis. This means that each party will receive a proportionate share based on the size of their claim relative to the total claims of all pari passu parties. This principle of pari passu is particularly important in situations where a company is facing financial distress or insolvency. In such cases, the company's assets may be insufficient to fully satisfy the claims of all creditors or investors. The pari passu principle ensures that each party with equal standing is treated fairly and receives a proportional share of the available resources. Pari passu arrangements are commonly found in loan agreements or bond issues, where different lenders or bondholders hold equal priority in receiving repayments. By including pari passu provisions in these agreements, all lenders or bondholders are treated on an equal footing, regardless of when they entered into the financing arrangement.

Passive Income

Passive income refers to the earnings generated from investments or ventures in which the individual has limited or no direct involvement. It is an important concept in the field of financial management as it provides a way to generate income without actively participating in the day-to-day operations of a business or investment activity. The concept of passive income can be understood by contrasting it with active income. Active income is the income that is generated through direct participation in activities such as working a job or running a business. It requires continuous effort and time investment to earn money. In contrast, passive income is earned with minimal effort or involvement beyond the initial setup phase. Passive income can come from various sources, including investments in stocks, bonds, real estate, and businesses. When an individual invests in stocks or bonds, they can earn passive income through dividends or interest payments. Similarly, real estate investments can generate passive income through rental payments. Additionally, individuals can earn passive income by investing in businesses as silent partners or through royalties from creative works such as books or music. The advantages of passive income are significant in the context of financial management. One of the key benefits is that it provides a source of income that is not solely reliant on active work. This diversification of income can be crucial in achieving financial stability and reducing the risk associated with relying solely on active income sources. Passive income also offers the potential for long-term financial growth and wealth accumulation, as the income generated can be reinvested or used to pursue other investment opportunities. In conclusion, passive income refers to the earnings generated through investments or ventures in which the individual has limited or no direct involvement. It is a valuable concept in financial management as it provides a way to earn income with minimal effort and diversify income sources. Understanding and effectively utilizing passive income can offer financial stability, long-term growth, and wealth accumulation opportunities.

Passive Investing

Passive investing, also known as index investing or passive management, is a financial management strategy that aims to mimic the performance of a specific market index or benchmark. It involves investing in a diversified portfolio of securities that replicates the composition and weightings of the chosen index. The objective of passive investing is to generate returns that closely mirror the performance of the broader market. Unlike active investing, where fund managers actively select and trade securities in an attempt to outperform the market, passive investing takes a more hands-off approach. It is based on the belief that, over the long term, the overall market tends to rise, and the returns generated by index funds should reflect this upward trend. Passive investors believe that it is difficult to consistently beat

171

the market and that the costs associated with active management, such as higher fees and trading expenses, can eat away at investment returns. Passive investing typically involves investing in index funds or exchange-traded funds (ETFs) that track a specific index, such as the S&P 500 or the FTSE 100. These funds hold a diversified portfolio of the stocks or bonds that make up the index, and the investment returns of the fund closely match the performance of the index. By investing in a passive strategy, investors can gain exposure to a broad range of securities and benefit from the overall growth of the market without having to pick individual stocks or actively manage their investments. Passive investing is considered a conservative and cost-effective investment approach. It offers diversification, as index funds typically invest in a large number of securities across different industries and sectors. This diversification helps reduce the risk associated with investing in individual securities. Additionally, index funds generally have lower expense ratios compared to actively managed funds, as they require less research and trading activity. As a result, passive investing has gained popularity among individual investors and institutional investors alike.

Passive Investment

A passive investment is a strategy in financial management where an investor aims to replicate the performance of a specific market index or asset class. It involves buying and holding a diversified portfolio of securities that mirror the composition and weightings of the targeted index or asset class. The passive investment approach is based on the belief that markets are efficient and that it is challenging to consistently beat the market over the long term. Therefore, instead of trying to outperform the market through active trading and timing decisions, passive investors seek to capture the overall returns of the market by holding a diversified portfolio that closely reflects the market's composition.

Payback Period

The payback period is a financial management metric that determines the length of time it takes to recover the initial investment made in a project or investment. It is commonly used to assess the risk, profitability, and feasibility of potential projects. The payback period is calculated by dividing the initial investment amount by the expected annual cash inflow or net cash flow. The payback period does not take into account the time value of money, making it a simple and straightforward metric to evaluate investment opportunities.

Payment For Order Flow (PFOF)

Payment for Order Flow (PFOF) is a practice in the financial industry where brokerage firms receive compensation from market makers or other liquidity providers for routing customer orders to them. This practice has gained attention and scrutiny in recent years due to concerns about potential conflicts of interest and the impact on overall market efficiency. Under PFOF, brokerage firms can receive payment in the form of cash or rebates for directing customer orders to specific market makers or liquidity providers. The market makers or liquidity providers benefit from these arrangements by gaining access to a steady flow of orders, which they can then profitably trade against. In return, the brokerage firms receive compensation, which can help offset the costs of executing customer trades or provide an additional revenue stream. Proponents of PFOF argue that it can lead to lower execution costs for retail investors, as market makers and liquidity providers compete to attract order flow by offering more competitive prices. They also contend that PFOF enables brokerage firms to offer commission-free trading to their customers, as the compensation they receive from market makers can help offset the costs of executing trades. However, critics of PFOF raise concerns about its potential negative impact on market integrity. They argue that the practice creates a conflict of interest for brokerage firms, as they may have an incentive to prioritize routing orders to the market makers or liquidity providers that offer the highest compensation, rather than seeking the best execution for their customers. This can result in suboptimal execution prices for retail investors and undermine market fairness and transparency. The Securities and Exchange Commission (SEC) regulates the practice of PFOF and requires brokerage firms to disclose their arrangements and potential conflicts of interest to customers. The SEC also monitors the market to ensure fair and orderly trading and may take enforcement actions against firms that engage in abusive or manipulative practices related to PFOF.

Payment In Kind (PIK) Bond

A Payment in Kind (PIK) Bond is a type of fixed-income security that allows the issuer to pay interest payments in the form of additional bonds rather than cash. Instead of making regular interest payments, the issuer has the option to pay interest by issuing additional bonds at regular intervals. This characteristic differentiates PIK bonds from traditional bonds, where interest payments are made in cash. PIK bonds are typically issued by companies that may not have sufficient cash flows to make regular interest payments, but still want to attract investors. These bonds offer higher yields compared to traditional bonds due to the increased risk associated with the deferred interest payments.

Payment In Kind (PIK)

Payment in Kind (PIK) refers to a type of payment made by a borrower to a lender in the form of additional securities or similar instruments, rather than in cash. It is a method of interest payment that allows the borrower to conserve cash in the short term and to fulfill its obligations to the lender. In this arrangement, the borrower issues new securities or instruments to the lender as a form of interest payment. These securities can be in the form of debt instruments, such as bonds or preferred shares, or equity instruments, such as common shares. The value of these securities is generally based on the prevailing market price at the time of issuance. The key advantage of PIK is that it provides flexibility to the borrower. By using non-cash securities to make interest payments, the borrower can hold onto its cash and use it for other purposes, such as funding operations or making investments. This can be particularly beneficial for companies that are experiencing cash flow constraints or are in a stage of rapid growth where cash is needed for expansion. However, PIK also carries certain risks for both the borrower and the lender. For the borrower, issuing additional securities increases its debt burden, which can lead to higher interest expenses and potential dilution of ownership. Additionally, if the market value of the securities used for PIK declines, it can negatively impact the borrower's financial position. For the lender, PIK introduces credit risk, as the borrower's ability to generate sufficient returns and repay the principal may be dependent on the success of its operations or the appreciation of the securities issued. Moreover, the lender may face liquidity constraints if it cannot readily sell the securities received as payment. Overall, Payment in Kind (PIK) is a mechanism used by borrowers and lenders to manage cash flow and interest payments. It provides flexibility to the borrower but also carries risks for both parties involved. As with any financial arrangement, careful consideration of the potential benefits and risks is essential before entering into a PIK agreement.

Pension Fund

A pension fund is a financial entity specifically created to manage and invest funds on behalf of employees or individuals, with the main objective of providing retirement income. It is a form of pooled investment, where contributions from employees, employers, or both are accumulated and managed over a specified period of time, typically until retirement. The primary purpose of a pension fund is to ensure the long-term financial security of its participants during their retirement years. The fund is invested in a diversified portfolio of assets such as stocks, bonds, real estate, and other financial instruments, aiming to generate returns that will support pension payments and growth over time.

Perpetual Bond

A perpetual bond, also known as a perpetual security or consol, is a type of bond that has no maturity date. This means that the bond does not have a specific repayment period like traditional bonds do. Instead, the bond pays a fixed coupon or interest payment indefinitely until it is redeemed by the issuer. Perpetual bonds are attractive to both issuers and investors for various reasons. For issuers, perpetual bonds provide a long-term source of financing without the need to repay the principal amount. This can be particularly beneficial for companies or governments that require continuous funding for ongoing projects or operations. Furthermore, perpetual bonds may have lower interest rates compared to other types of debt securities, as they offer investors a higher level of security and stability. On the other hand, investors are attracted to perpetual bonds due to their fixed income stream. As the bond pays a constant coupon indefinitely, it can provide a predictable cash flow, making it an appealing option for

173

income-seeking investors. However, investors should consider the risks associated with perpetual bonds. For example, changes in interest rates can impact the value of the bond. If interest rates rise, the value of the perpetual bond may decrease, as investors can potentially earn higher returns from other investments. Therefore, it is important for investors to assess their risk tolerance and evaluate the interest rate environment before investing in perpetual bonds. In conclusion, a perpetual bond is a unique type of bond that does not have a maturity date and pays a fixed coupon indefinitely. It offers issuers a long-term financing option without the need to repay the principal, while providing investors with a predictable income stream. However, investors should be mindful of interest rate changes that can affect the value of perpetual bonds. Overall, perpetual bonds can be a valuable tool for both issuers and investors in the realm of financial management.

Petrodollars

Petrodollars are a term used in financial management to refer to the revenues generated by oil-producing countries through the sale and export of petroleum. These funds are typically denominated in US dollars due to the global preference for this currency in international trade and are a significant factor in the global economy. Oil-producing countries, such as Saudi Arabia, Russia, and the United Arab Emirates, earn substantial revenues from selling oil and petroleum-related products in the global market. These revenues, often referred to as petrodollars, contribute to the wealth and economic growth of these countries. The petrodollar system emerged in the 1970s when the Organization of Petroleum Exporting Countries (OPEC) countries, led by Saudi Arabia, negotiated with oil-importing nations to sell oil exclusively in US dollars. This arrangement was known as the petrodollar system, and it provided OPEC countries with a stable and widely accepted currency for their oil exports. The petrodollar system has significant implications for the global economy. Firstly, it increases the demand for US dollars, as countries need to convert their own currencies into dollars to purchase oil. This creates a constant demand for the US dollar, which strengthens its value in the foreign exchange market and helps maintain its status as the world's primary reserve currency. Secondly, petrodollars have a major influence on global financial markets. Oil-producing countries invest their petrodollar revenues in various financial assets, such as government bonds, stocks, and real estate. These investments can significantly impact asset prices and market trends, as they involve substantial amounts of capital flowing into different markets. Moreover, petrodollars play a crucial role in funding infrastructure development and public services in oil-producing countries. The substantial revenues generated from oil exports allow these nations to invest in projects such as transportation networks, healthcare systems, and educational institutions, which contribute to their economic growth and social development. In conclusion, petrodollars refer to the revenues earned by oil-producing countries from the sale of petroleum, typically denominated in US dollars. The petrodollar system, established in the 1970s, has implications for global currency demand, financial markets, and economic development in oil-producing nations.

Poisson Distribution

The Poisson distribution is a probability distribution that is commonly used in the context of financial management to model the occurrence of events that happen randomly or independently over a fixed interval of time or space. It is particularly useful for analyzing random events that are rare but can have significant impacts on financial outcomes. In financial management, the Poisson distribution is often used to estimate the probability of events such as customer arrivals, equipment failures, product defects, or insurance claims. These events are typically characterized by a low occurrence rate and a random distribution over time. The Poisson distribution provides a mathematical framework to model the probability of these events occurring within a given time period or spatial area.

Ponzi Scheme

A Ponzi scheme is a fraudulent investment operation that pays returns to its investors from their own money or from the money paid by subsequent investors, rather than from any actual profit earned. The scheme attracts new investors by offering returns that are higher than those of other investments, with little or no risk involved. In a Ponzi scheme, the promoter or operator collects money from new investors and uses it to pay the promised returns to earlier investors.

This creates the illusion of a profitable investment opportunity, enticing more people to invest. However, no legitimate investment is actually taking place and no real profits are generated. The scheme collapses when the promoter is unable to attract enough new investors or when a large number of investors try to withdraw their funds at the same time. Without new investments coming in, the operator is unable to fulfill the promised returns and the scheme unravels. At this point, the scheme is exposed as a fraud and many investors lose their money. Ponzi schemes are named after Charles Ponzi, an Italian immigrant who orchestrated one of the most famous and large-scale Ponzi schemes in the 1920s. Ponzi promised investors a 50% return on their investment in just 45 days, or a 100% return in 90 days, by taking advantage of international postal reply coupons. However, Ponzi was not actually engaging in any legitimate postal arbitrage, and instead, was using money from new investors to pay off previous investors. While Ponzi schemes can take many forms, they all share similar characteristics. They rely on a constant influx of new investors to sustain the scheme and use the money from these new investors to pay off earlier investors. This creates a cycle of dependency, where the scheme can only continue as long as new investments keep flowing in. Due to their deceptive nature, Ponzi schemes are illegal and considered a serious financial crime. They prey on investors' greed and lack of knowledge, promising high returns with little risk. It is important for investors to be cautious and skeptical of any investment promising unusually high returns, conduct thorough due diligence, and seek advice from reputable financial professionals.

Portfolio Diversification

Portfolio diversification refers to the strategy of spreading investments across a variety of assets in order to reduce the risk associated with investing in a single asset or asset class. It is a key concept in financial management as it aims to achieve a balance between risk and return. By diversifying a portfolio, an investor can reduce the exposure to individual securities or sectors and mitigate the potential impact of market fluctuations. This is because different assets tend to perform differently under various economic conditions. For example, while stocks may perform well during periods of economic growth, bonds may provide more stability during times of economic uncertainty. There are several benefits to portfolio diversification. Firstly, it can help to reduce the overall risk of a portfolio. By investing in a mix of assets with different risk characteristics, the potential losses from one investment may be offset by gains in others. This can help to smooth out the overall returns of the portfolio and reduce the impact of market volatility. Secondly, portfolio diversification can potentially improve returns. By including assets with different return profiles, such as stocks, bonds, and commodities, an investor can benefit from different sources of potential growth. This can help to capture returns in various market conditions and maximize the opportunity for long-term growth. Additionally, portfolio diversification can provide increased flexibility and liquidity. By investing in different asset classes, an investor can access a broader range of investment opportunities and reduce the reliance on a single investment for liquidity purposes. This can help to improve the overall efficiency of the portfolio and provide more options for capital allocation. In summary, portfolio diversification is a strategy that involves spreading investments across a range of assets to reduce risk and potentially improve returns. It is a fundamental concept in financial management and can help investors achieve their long-term financial goals by balancing risk and reward.

Portfolio Management

Portfolio management refers to the process of managing an individual or institutional investor's investment portfolio to achieve specific financial objectives. It involves making decisions regarding asset allocation, diversification, risk management, and the selection and monitoring of investments. Portfolio managers are responsible for creating and implementing investment strategies that align with the investor's goals and risk tolerance. They evaluate various investment opportunities, analyze their potential risks and returns, and make informed investment decisions to optimize the portfolio's performance while minimizing risk.

Portfolio Manager

A Portfolio Manager is an individual or entity responsible for making investment decisions and managing a portfolio of securities or assets on behalf of clients or investors. The portfolio can include a variety of financial instruments such as stocks, bonds, mutual funds, and other investment products. The primary goal of a Portfolio Manager is to maximize returns while minimizing risk according to the specific investment objectives and requirements set by the clients. The role of a Portfolio Manager involves several key responsibilities. Firstly, they are tasked with conducting thorough research and analysis of potential investment opportunities. This includes assessing the financial health and performance of companies, analyzing market trends and economic indicators, and evaluating various risk factors. Based on this analysis, the Portfolio Manager identifies investment opportunities that align with the clients' objectives and risk tolerance. Once investments are selected, the Portfolio Manager implements the investment strategy by buying and selling securities. This involves executing trades, monitoring market conditions, and staying informed about relevant news and events that may impact the portfolio's performance. They also make necessary adjustments to the portfolio to ensure it remains aligned with the clients' objectives and market conditions. In addition to managing the day-to-day operations of the portfolio, the Portfolio Manager also provides regular communication to clients regarding the performance and progress of their investments. They may prepare reports and presentations, offering insights and recommendations based on their analysis and expertise. The Portfolio Manager also addresses any questions or concerns raised by clients and provides guidance and support in making informed investment decisions. To be successful in the role, a Portfolio Manager must possess a strong understanding of financial markets, investment principles, and risk management techniques. They should stay updated with market trends, regulatory changes, and economic news that may impact the portfolio. Additionally, effective communication and interpersonal skills are essential for building and maintaining strong relationships with clients. Overall, the Portfolio Manager plays a crucial role in helping clients achieve their financial goals by effectively managing their investments.

Preferred Dividend Coverage Ratio

The Preferred Dividend Coverage Ratio is a financial metric used in financial management to assess a company's ability to pay out preferred dividends to its shareholders. It measures the company's earnings available to cover the preferred dividends. The formula to calculate the Preferred Dividend Coverage Ratio is as follows: Preferred Dividend Coverage Ratio = (Net Income - Preferred Dividends) / Preferred Dividends This ratio provides insights into the company's ability to generate sufficient earnings to cover the preferred dividends. A ratio of 1 or higher indicates that the company has enough earnings to cover the preferred dividends, while a ratio below 1 suggests that the company may be facing difficulties in meeting its preferred dividend obligations. For example, let's assume a company has a net income of $10 million and pays preferred dividends of $2 million. Using the formula, we can calculate the Preferred Dividend Coverage Ratio as follows: Preferred Dividend Coverage Ratio = ($10 million - $2 million) / $2 million = 4 In this case, the company has a Preferred Dividend Coverage Ratio of 4, indicating that it generates sufficient earnings to cover the preferred dividends four times over. This suggests a healthy financial position and provides assurance to the preferred shareholders that their dividends will be paid out. Financial managers use the Preferred Dividend Coverage Ratio to assess the company's ability to fulfill preferred dividend obligations and make strategic decisions regarding financing, capital structure, and dividend policy. It helps them determine whether the company can comfortably meet its preferred dividend obligations without jeopardizing its financial stability. In conclusion, the Preferred Dividend Coverage Ratio is a crucial financial metric used in financial management to assess a company's ability to cover its preferred dividends. It indicates the company's ability to generate sufficient earnings to fulfill preferred dividend obligations and plays a significant role in financial decision-making processes.

Preferred Dividend

A preferred dividend is a fixed payment made to the shareholders of preferred stock, which represents their share of the company's profits. Preferred stock is a type of equity security that offers a fixed dividend payment to shareholders before any dividends are distributed to common stockholders. The dividend payment for preferred stock is typically a fixed percentage of the stock's par value or a fixed dollar amount agreed upon at the time of issuance. Preferred dividends are a contractual obligation of the company and must be paid to preferred shareholders before any dividends are distributed to common stockholders. Unlike common stock dividends, which are paid at the discretion of the company's board of directors, preferred dividends are typically required to be paid on a regular basis, either quarterly, semi-annually, or annually.

176

Preferred Stock Dividend

Preferred Stock Dividend is a form of dividend payment that is distributed to shareholders who own preferred stock in a company. Preferred stock is a type of security that represents ownership in a corporation, similar to common stock. However, preferred stockholders have different rights and privileges compared to common stockholders. Unlike common stock, preferred stockholders typically do not have voting rights in the company. However, they have a higher claim on the company's assets and earnings compared to common stockholders. This includes the right to receive dividends before any dividends are distributed to common stockholders. The preferred stock dividend is a regular payment that is made to preferred stockholders based on a predetermined dividend rate or amount. The dividend rate is usually set when the preferred stock is issued and remains fixed throughout the life of the stock. This fixed dividend rate provides preferred stockholders with a predictable income stream. The payment of preferred stock dividends is typically prioritized over the payment of dividends to common stockholders. This means that if a company is facing financial difficulties or needs to conserve cash, it may choose to suspend or reduce the payment of dividends to common stockholders while continuing to pay dividends to preferred stockholders. In some cases, preferred stock dividends may be cumulative. This means that if the company skips a dividend payment or reduces the dividend amount, it will be required to make up for the missed payments in the future before any dividends can be paid to common stockholders. This provides an additional layer of protection for preferred stockholders. Overall, preferred stock dividends are an important aspect of financial management as they provide a return on investment for preferred stockholders and help attract investors to purchase preferred stock. Companies need to carefully manage their dividend payments to ensure they can meet their obligations to both preferred and common stockholders while maintaining financial stability.

Preferred Stock

Preferred stock is a type of stock that grants certain privileges and preferences to its shareholders. It represents ownership in a corporation and is often issued by companies as a way to raise capital. Unlike common stock, which is the most common type of stock, preferred stock usually does not carry voting rights in corporate matters. However, it does have a higher claim on the company's assets and earnings compared to common stock. This means that in the event of liquidation or bankruptcy, preferred shareholders have a priority right to the company's assets before common shareholders are paid. Preferred stock also typically pays a fixed dividend to shareholders, which is predetermined at the time of issuance. This fixed dividend is usually a percentage of the face value or par value of the stock. The dividend payments to preferred shareholders are usually made before any dividends are paid to common shareholders. However, unlike interest payments on debt, the dividend payments to preferred shareholders are not tax-deductible for the issuing company. In addition to these preferences, preferred stock may also have other features such as callability and convertibility. Callability refers to the company's ability to redeem or repurchase the preferred stock from shareholders at a predetermined price within a specified period. Convertibility, on the other hand, allows preferred shareholders to convert their shares into a fixed number of common shares at a predetermined conversion ratio. Preferred stock is often attractive to investors who are seeking a combination of steady income and potential capital appreciation. However, it also carries some risks. If a company is unable to pay dividends to preferred shareholders, it may lead to a decrease in the value of the preferred stock. Additionally, preferred stock is generally considered to be less liquid than common stock, meaning that it may be more difficult to sell or trade.

Present Value (PV)

Present Value (PV) refers to the current value of a future cash flow or a series of future cash flows, discounted at a specific rate of return. It is a fundamental concept in financial management that helps determine the worth of an investment or a stream of payments in today's dollars. PV is based on the concept of the time value of money, which recognizes that the value of money changes over time due to factors such as inflation, interest rates, and risk. By discounting future cash flows, PV takes into account the opportunity cost of tying up capital and provides a way to compare different investment options.

Present Value Of Growth Opportunities (PVGO)

Present Value of Growth Opportunities (PVGO) is a financial metric used in the field of Financial Management to determine the value of a firm's investment in future growth opportunities. It calculates the present value of the expected future cash flows generated by these growth opportunities. In essence, PVGO measures the additional value that a company's future growth prospects add to its overall valuation. It helps investors and financial analysts assess the potential impact of a company's growth initiatives on its stock price.

Price Earnings (P/E) Ratio

The Price Earnings (P/E) Ratio is a financial metric used by investors to assess the valuation of a company's stock. It is calculated by dividing the market price per share by the earnings per share (EPS). The P/E ratio allows investors to gauge how much they are paying for each dollar of earnings generated by the company. A high P/E ratio suggests that investors have high expectations for the company's future earnings, while a low P/E ratio indicates that the market has lower expectations.

Price Earnings To Growth (PEG) Ratio

Price Earnings to Growth (PEG) Ratio is a financial metric used in the field of financial management to assess the value of a company's stock. It measures the relationship between the price-to-earnings (P/E) ratio and the expected earnings growth rate of the company. The P/E ratio is calculated by dividing the market price per share of a company by its earnings per share (EPS). The PEG ratio incorporates the growth rate of the company's earnings in order to provide a more comprehensive valuation of the stock. The formula for calculating the PEG ratio is as follows: PEG Ratio = P/E ratio / Earnings Growth Rate The PEG ratio is considered to be a useful tool for investors as it helps in determining whether a stock is overvalued or undervalued. A PEG ratio of less than 1 suggests that the company's stock may be undervalued, while a PEG ratio of greater than 1 indicates that the stock may be overvalued. A PEG ratio of 1 suggests that the stock is fairly valued. The PEG ratio takes into account both the P/E ratio and the earnings growth rate, providing investors with a more balanced view of the company's valuation. While the P/E ratio alone may not provide a complete picture of the company's value, the PEG ratio adds the important element of the growth rate. The higher the growth rate, the higher the PEG ratio, and vice versa. It is important to note that the PEG ratio is just one of many valuation metrics used by investors and should not be relied upon solely when making investment decisions. Other factors such as the company's financial health, competitive advantage, and industry conditions should also be taken into consideration.

Price Elasticity Of Demand

Price Elasticity of Demand is a measure used in Financial Management to determine the responsiveness of the quantity demanded of a product or service to a change in its price. It is calculated as the percentage change in quantity demanded divided by the percentage change in price. The resulting value indicates how sensitive the demand for a product or service is to changes in its price. Price Elasticity of Demand plays a crucial role in Financial Management as it helps businesses understand the impact of price changes on their revenue and profitability. By knowing the price elasticity of demand for a particular product or service, companies can make informed decisions regarding pricing strategies and forecast how changes in price will affect the demand and overall sales. There are generally three categories for interpreting price elasticity of demand: elastic (where the percentage change in quantity demanded is greater than the percentage change in price), inelastic (where the percentage change in quantity demanded is less than the percentage change in price), and unitary elastic (where the percentage change in quantity demanded is equal to the percentage change in price). Understanding the price elasticity of demand is crucial in determining the optimal price for a product or service. If the demand for a product is elastic, a decrease in price will lead to a proportionately larger increase in quantity demanded, resulting in higher total revenue. On the other hand, if the demand is inelastic, a decrease in price will result in a smaller increase in quantity demanded, implying a potential loss in total revenue. By analyzing the price elasticity of demand, companies can identify the price points at which they can maximize their revenue and profitability.

Price To Book Ratio (P/B Ratio)

The Price to Book Ratio (P/B Ratio) is a financial metric used to evaluate the market value of a company relative to its book value. Book value refers to the net asset value of a company, which is calculated by subtracting its liabilities from its total assets. The formula to calculate the P/B ratio is: P/B Ratio = Market Price per Share / Book Value per Share The market price per share is the current market value of a company's stock, while the book value per share is the net asset value divided by the number of outstanding shares. The resulting P/B ratio provides insight into the market's perception of a company's value. A P/B ratio below 1 suggests that a company's stock is trading at a discount to its book value. This may indicate that the market has a negative view of the company, potentially due to poor financial performance or unfavorable future prospects. On the other hand, a P/B ratio above 1 indicates that the market is valuing the company higher than its book value. This may suggest that investors have a positive outlook on the company, possibly due to strong financial performance or promising growth opportunities. However, it's important to note that the P/B ratio should not be used as the sole criteria for investment decisions. Other factors, such as the company's earnings, cash flow, and industry dynamics, should also be considered in conjunction with the P/B ratio. In summary, the P/B ratio is a financial metric that compares a company's market value to its book value. It provides investors with an indication of how the market values the company relative to its net asset value. A P/B ratio below 1 suggests an undervalued stock, while a P/B ratio above 1 indicates an overvalued stock. The P/B ratio should be used in conjunction with other financial and industry factors to make informed investment decisions.

Price-Earnings Growth (PEG) Ratio

The Price-Earnings Growth (PEG) ratio is a financial metric used in the field of Financial Management to evaluate the attractiveness of a company's stock by considering its earnings growth potential in relation to its current market price. The PEG ratio is calculated by dividing the company's Price-Earnings (P/E) ratio by its projected earnings growth rate. The P/E ratio is a common valuation measure that compares the company's stock price to its earnings per share (EPS). It gives investors an idea of how much they are paying for each dollar of earnings generated by the company. The PEG ratio, by incorporating the earnings growth rate, provides a more comprehensive assessment of the company's value. It helps investors assess whether the stock is overvalued or undervalued, as it takes into account the company's potential for future earnings growth. A PEG ratio below 1 may indicate that the stock is undervalued, while a PEG ratio above 1 may suggest that the stock is overvalued. Investors and financial analysts often use the PEG ratio as a tool for comparing different companies within the same industry or sector. It allows them to identify companies with the most favorable growth prospects relative to their market price. However, it is important to note that the PEG ratio is not a standalone measure and should be used in conjunction with other financial metrics and qualitative analysis. The PEG ratio has its limitations and potential drawbacks. It relies on projected earnings growth rates, which can be uncertain and subject to change. The accuracy of the PEG ratio depends on the quality of these earnings forecasts. Additionally, the PEG ratio does not consider factors such as industry trends, competitive dynamics, or the company's overall financial health. In conclusion, the Price-Earnings Growth (PEG) ratio is a financial metric used in Financial Management to assess the attractiveness of a company's stock by comparing its Price-Earnings (P/E) ratio to its projected earnings growth rate. It helps investors identify stocks that may be overvalued or undervalued based on their growth potential. However, it is important to consider the limitations of the PEG ratio and use it in conjunction with other financial metrics and qualitative analysis.

Price-Earnings To Growth (PEG) Ratio

The Price-Earnings to Growth (PEG) ratio is a financial metric used to evaluate the value of a stock by taking into account its price-to-earnings (P/E) ratio and its expected growth rate. It is often used by investors to determine whether a stock is overvalued or undervalued. The P/E ratio compares the price of a stock to its earnings per share (EPS) and provides an indication of how expensive or cheap a stock is relative to its earnings. A high P/E ratio suggests that the stock is overvalued, while a low P/E ratio suggests that the stock is undervalued. However, the P/E ratio alone does not provide a complete picture of a stock's value. This is where the PEG ratio comes in. The PEG ratio incorporates the expected growth rate of the company's earnings into the analysis, providing a more holistic view of the stock's value. To calculate the PEG ratio, the P/E ratio is divided by the expected earnings growth rate. The expected earnings growth rate is typically estimated by analysts and can be found in financial reports or research reports. A PEG ratio of 1 indicates that the stock is fairly valued, as the P/E ratio is in line with the expected growth rate. A PEG ratio less than 1 suggests that the stock may be undervalued, as the P/E ratio is lower than the expected growth rate. On the other hand, a PEG ratio greater than 1 indicates that the stock may be overvalued, as the P/E ratio is higher than the expected growth rate. It is important to note that the PEG ratio has its limitations. It relies on accurate estimates of the expected earnings growth rate, which can be difficult to obtain. Additionally, the PEG ratio does not take into account other factors that may affect a stock's value, such as industry trends, competitive landscape, and management quality. In conclusion, the Price-Earnings to Growth (PEG) ratio is a financial metric that incorporates the P/E ratio and the expected earnings growth rate to assess the value of a stock. It helps investors determine whether a stock is overvalued, undervalued, or fairly valued. However, it should be used in conjunction with other analysis and factors to make informed investment decisions.

Price-To-Book Ratio (P/B Ratio)

The Price-to-Book Ratio (P/B Ratio) is a financial metric used in the field of financial management to assess the value of a company relative to its net assets. It is calculated by dividing the current market price of a company's shares by its book value per share. Book value per share is derived by dividing the total assets minus total liabilities of a company by the number of outstanding shares. This metric provides insight into the amount per share that shareholders would theoretically receive if the company were to be liquidated.

Prime Rate

Prime Rate is the interest rate that commercial banks charge their most creditworthy borrowers. It serves as a benchmark for various lending products and influences the interest rates on loans and credit cards offered to customers. The Prime Rate is typically determined by banks and is based on the federal funds rate, which is the interest rate at which banks lend reserves to each other overnight. The Prime Rate is generally set at a level above the federal funds rate to account for the additional risk associated with lending to individual borrowers for longer periods of time. The Prime Rate is an important indicator of the overall interest rate environment and is used by banks to price various financial products. It is commonly used as a reference rate for adjustable-rate mortgages, home equity lines of credit, auto loans, and credit cards. The interest rate on these types of loans is often set as Prime Rate plus a certain percentage, known as the margin, which is based on the borrower's creditworthiness and the duration of the loan.

Principal-Agent Problem

The Principal-Agent problem refers to the conflict of interest that arises between a principal and an agent in a financial management context. The principal-agent relationship occurs when one party, the principal, hires another party, the agent, to perform certain tasks or make decisions on their behalf. However, the agent may have their own interests that may not align with those of the principal. This misalignment of interests creates the principal-agent problem. In financial management, the principal-agent problem typically arises when shareholders, who are the principals, hire managers, who are the agents, to run the company. Shareholders expect the managers to act in the best interest of the company and maximize its value. However, managers may prioritize their personal interests, such as job security or bonus incentives, which could conflict with the shareholders' interests. The principal-agent problem can lead to agency costs, which are the costs incurred by the principal in monitoring and controlling the agent's actions to ensure they align with the principal's objectives. These costs can include expenses related to performance evaluation, auditing, and creating incentive systems. Additionally, the principal-agent problem can result in moral hazard and adverse selection issues. Moral hazard occurs when the agent takes on excessive risk because they are not fully bearing the consequences of their actions. For example, managers may engage in risky investment strategies knowing that if they fail, shareholders bear the losses. Adverse selection, on the other hand, refers to the principal selecting an agent who has hidden characteristics or abilities that are detrimental to the principal's interests. For instance, the principal may hire a manager who appears competent but lacks the necessary skills to effectively manage the company. Overall, the principal-agent problem is a fundamental issue in financial management that requires careful monitoring and control to ensure the agent's actions align with the principal's objectives. By addressing this problem effectively, principals can minimize agency costs and improve their company's overall performance.

Private Equity Firm

A private equity firm is a type of financial management company that raises funds from investors and uses those funds to invest in private companies. Unlike other types of investment firms, such as mutual funds or hedge funds, private equity firms focus on investing in companies that are not publicly traded on stock exchanges. Private equity firms raise funds through a variety of sources, including institutional investors such as pension funds, endowments, and insurance companies, as well as high-net-worth individuals and families. These funds are typically pooled together into a single investment vehicle, known as a private equity fund. Once the funds are raised, the private equity firm will identify investment opportunities in private companies that it believes have significant growth potential or are undervalued. The firm will then negotiate and structure a deal to acquire a stake in the company, often taking a majority or controlling interest. Private equity firms typically take an active role in managing and growing the companies in which they invest. This may involve providing strategic guidance and operational expertise, as well as making changes to the company's management team or board of directors. The ultimate goal of the firm is to increase the value of the company and eventually exit the investment at a profit. Private equity firms typically have a predetermined investment period for each fund, typically around 5 to 10 years. During this period, the firm will actively manage its portfolio of investments, seeking to maximize their value through operational improvements, cost reductions, and other financial strategies. At the end of the investment period, the firm will seek to exit its investments through a variety of means, such as selling the company to another investor or taking it public through an initial public offering (IPO). The profits from these exits are then distributed to the investors in the fund, usually in proportion to their initial investment. In summary, a private equity firm is a financial management company that raises funds from investors to invest in private companies with the goal of increasing their value and generating a return for the investors.

Private Equity Fund

A private equity fund is a type of investment vehicle that pools money from high-net-worth individuals and institutional investors to make investments in privately-held companies or acquire controlling stakes in publicly-traded companies and take them private. These funds are typically structured as limited partnerships, with a general partner managing the fund and limited partners providing the capital.Private equity funds invest in a wide range of industries and sectors, including manufacturing, technology, healthcare, and financial services. The primary objective of these funds is to generate attractive returns for their investors by buying companies at a reasonable valuation, implementing strategic changes to improve their operations, and eventually selling them at a higher price.Private equity funds typically have a fixed life cycle, typically ranging from 7 to 10 years. During this period, the fund will invest in various companies and actively manage their operations. The general partner will work closely with the portfolio companies' management teams to identify opportunities for growth and efficiency improvements.At the end of the fund's life cycle, the general partner will seek to exit its investments and generate returns for the limited partners. This could be achieved through an initial public offering (IPO), a sale to another private equity fund or strategic buyer, or a recapitalization of the company.Private equity funds can be attractive for investors seeking higher returns compared to traditional investment options such as stocks and bonds. However, they also come with higher risks and illiquidity, as investments are often held for several years before an exit can be realized.In summary, a private equity fund is an investment vehicle that pools money from investors to acquire and manage companies with the aim of generating attractive returns. These funds play an important role in the financial markets by providing capital and expertise to businesses, facilitating their growth and value creation.

Private Equity

Private Equity refers to a form of alternative investment where funds are raised from institutional investors or high net worth individuals and used to acquire ownership stakes in private companies or publicly traded companies that will be taken private. This form of investment is considered to be long-term and aims to provide investors with a higher return compared to traditional investment options such as stocks and bonds. The process of private equity investment begins with the raising of funds from investors who form a private equity fund. These funds are then used by the private equity firm to acquire ownership stakes in target companies. The private equity firm typically takes a majority stake in the company and works closely with its management to implement strategies that will increase the company's value over time. One common strategy used by private equity firms is to improve the operational efficiency of the company they have invested in. This may involve implementing cost-cutting measures, streamlining business processes, or making strategic acquisitions or divestments. By improving the company's operational performance, the private equity firm aims to increase its profitability and ultimately its value. Private equity investments are typically made over a long-term horizon, usually ranging from five to ten years. During this period, the private equity firm actively monitors the performance of the company and provides guidance and support to its management. The ultimate goal of the private equity firm is to exit the investment at a higher valuation, allowing them to generate substantial returns for their investors. There are several ways in which private equity firms can exit their investments. One common method is through an initial public offering (IPO), where the company's shares are listed on a public stock exchange. Another exit strategy is a sale to another company or a strategic investor. Private equity firms may also sell their stake back to the company's management or to another private equity firm.

Private Placement

Private Placement refers to the process of raising capital by offering securities to a select group of investors, instead of issuing them to the general public. This method of fundraising is typically employed by companies that are not yet ready or eligible to go public or do not wish to incur the costs and regulatory requirements associated with a public offering. Unlike public offerings, where securities are sold through a prospectus and under the supervision of regulatory authorities, private placements involve a direct negotiation between the issuing company and the investors. This allows for a more tailored approach in terms of structuring the terms of the offering and selecting the investors.

Pro Forma Financial Statements

Pro forma financial statements are projected financial statements that are based on certain assumptions and estimations. These statements provide an estimate of the future financial performance of a company, giving insights into its potential profitability and cash flow. Pro forma financial statements are typically prepared for specific purposes, such as financial planning, investment analysis, or mergers and acquisitions. They are also commonly used by startups or companies undergoing significant changes, such as restructuring or expansion, to assess the financial implications of these decisions.

Profit Margin

Profit Margin is the financial metric that measures the profitability of a company. It is calculated by dividing the net income of a company by its total revenue and is expressed as a percentage. The profit margin indicates how much profit a company generates for each dollar of revenue. It is a crucial measure in financial management as it reflects the company's efficiency in controlling costs and managing its operations. A high profit margin indicates that a company is able to generate a significant profit from its sales, while a low profit margin suggests that the company has higher costs or lower revenue relative to its expenses. Profit margin is commonly used by investors, creditors, and analysts to evaluate a company's financial performance and compare it to its industry peers. It helps in assessing the company's profitability, efficiency, and overall financial health. There are different types of profit margins that can be calculated, such as gross profit margin, operating profit margin, and net profit margin. The gross profit margin measures the profitability of a company's core operations by subtracting the cost of goods sold (COGS) from the revenue and dividing it by the revenue. It indicates how well a company can generate profit from its production or provision of goods and services. The operating profit margin measures the profitability of a company's operations after considering both the cost of goods sold and operating expenses, such as administrative expenses and selling expenses. It provides insights into the company's ability to control costs and manage its operating activities. The net profit margin represents the bottom line profitability of a company after deducting all expenses, including taxes, interest, and non-operating expenses. It reflects the company's overall financial

182

performance and indicates how much profit is generated for each dollar of revenue.

Profit And Loss Statement

A Profit and Loss Statement, also known as an income statement or statement of operations, is a financial statement that provides an overview of a company's revenues, expenses, and net income or net loss over a specific period of time. It is a crucial tool in financial management as it helps assess the profitability and performance of a business. The main purpose of a Profit and Loss Statement is to summarize the company's operating results for a particular period, often monthly, quarterly, or annually. It provides a snapshot of the company's ability to generate revenue, manage costs, and ultimately turn a profit. This financial statement follows a standardized format and is divided into several sections that categorize the different sources of revenue and types of expenses. The top section usually includes the company's total revenue or sales, followed by the cost of goods sold (COGS) or direct costs associated with producing the goods or services sold. This section gives insight into the company's gross profit margin or the profit generated before considering any operating expenses. The subsequent sections of the Profit and Loss Statement outline the operating expenses, which are classified into different categories such as selling and marketing expenses, administrative expenses, research and development costs, and other overhead expenses. These expenses are subtracted from the gross profit to calculate the company's operating profit or operating loss. Other items may also be included in the statement, such as interest income or expenses, gains or losses from the sale of assets, and income tax expenses. These items are typically shown separately on the statement to provide a comprehensive view of the company's financial performance. By analyzing the Profit and Loss Statement, financial managers can assess the company's revenue trends, cost structure, and profitability ratios. It enables them to identify areas of strength and weakness, make informed business decisions, and develop strategies for improving the company's financial performance. The statement also helps investors, creditors, and potential stakeholders evaluate the company's profitability and determine its ability to generate a return on investment.

Profitability Index (PI)

The Profitability Index (PI) is a financial metric used in the field of financial management to evaluate the profitability of an investment or project. It is also known as the Profit Investment Ratio (PIR) or the Benefit-Cost Ratio (BCR). The PI measures the relative profitability of an investment by comparing the present value of its cash inflows to the present value of its cash outflows. The formula for calculating the Profitability Index is as follows: PI = PV of Cash Inflows / PV of Cash Outflows Where: - PI represents the Profitability Index - PV refers to the Present Value of the cash inflows and outflows The Profitability Index is used as a decision-making tool in financial management to assess the desirability of an investment or project. A PI greater than 1 indicates that the present value of the cash inflows exceeds the present value of the cash outflows, implying that the investment is expected to generate a positive net present value. In other words, the potential benefits outweigh the costs. On the other hand, a PI less than 1 suggests that the present value of the cash inflows is less than the present value of the cash outflows. This indicates that the investment is expected to generate a negative net present value and may not be financially viable. When evaluating multiple investment or project options, financial managers can use the Profitability Index to compare their relative profitability. The investment or project with the highest PI is considered the most desirable, as it is expected to deliver the greatest value for each dollar invested. However, it is important to note that the Profitability Index should not be solely relied upon as a decision-making tool. It should be used in conjunction with other financial metrics and qualitative factors to make well-informed investment decisions.

Proxy Contest

A proxy contest, in the context of financial management, refers to a corporate event in which shareholders attempt to influence the composition of a company's board of directors. This contest typically arises when shareholders believe that the current board of directors is not acting in their best interests or that changes in the leadership are necessary to enhance corporate performance or maximize shareholder value. During a proxy contest, shareholders seek to persuade other shareholders to vote in favor of their proposed director candidates. They do this by disseminating information, presenting their case, and trying to convince shareholders that their candidates will better represent their interests. Shareholders may utilize various methods to communicate their position, including written materials such as proxy statements, letters, and presentations. The process of a proxy contest involves several stages. First, shareholders must file a notice with the appropriate regulatory body, typically the Securities and Exchange Commission (SEC) in the United States, disclosing their intention to solicit proxies. They must then prepare and distribute proxy materials to shareholders, which can include the names and biographies of their director candidates, their reasons for seeking changes, and details of any proposed corporate governance reforms or strategic plans. Once shareholders have received the proxy materials, they can cast their votes by proxy, granting another individual or entity the authority to vote on their behalf. Typically, shareholders have the option to either vote for the company's slate of director candidates or the dissident shareholders' slate. The outcome of the vote determines the composition of the board of directors, with the winning side gaining control and their candidates being elected or appointed as directors. A successful proxy contest can result in significant changes within a company, such as the replacement of directors, shifts in corporate strategy, or the implementation of specific shareholder proposals. Proxy contests can serve as a mechanism for shareholders to express their dissatisfaction with current management or to advocate for improved corporate governance practices.

Proxy Statement

A Proxy Statement is a document that a company provides to its shareholders to inform them about matters that will be voted on during a shareholders' meeting. The purpose of a Proxy Statement is to help shareholders make informed decisions about the matters being voted on, as well as to provide details about the meeting itself. The Proxy Statement typically includes information such as the date, time, and location of the meeting, as well as instructions on how shareholders can vote on the matters. It also includes information about the company's board of directors, executive compensation, and any potential conflicts of interest that may exist. One of the key components of a Proxy Statement is the Proxy Card. The Proxy Card is a form that shareholders can use to vote on the matters being presented at the meeting. Shareholders can indicate their vote by marking the appropriate box on the card and returning it to the company. In addition to the Proxy Card, the Proxy Statement also includes a proxy statement form. This form allows shareholders to appoint a proxy to vote on their behalf if they are unable to attend the meeting. The appointed proxy then represents the shareholder's vote at the meeting. The Proxy Statement is typically mailed to shareholders prior to the meeting date. It is important for shareholders to carefully review the Proxy Statement and consider the information provided before making their voting decisions. Shareholders may also have the opportunity to ask questions or make comments about the matters being voted on at the meeting. Overall, the Proxy Statement is a crucial document that helps ensure transparency and accountability in the decision-making process of a company. By providing shareholders with key information about the matters being voted on, it empowers them to make informed decisions and participate in the governance of the company.

Public Finance

Public Finance refers to the branch of financial management that deals with the revenue, expenditure, and debt activities of governments at all levels, including central, state, and local governments. It involves the study of government financing, budgeting, taxation, debt management, and resource allocation. Public Finance plays a vital role in the functioning of governments as it helps them to effectively manage their financial resources and meet the demands of their citizens. The main objective of Public Finance is to ensure the efficient and equitable allocation of resources to meet the socio-economic needs and aspirations of the public. Public Finance encompasses various activities, such as revenue generation, which involves the collection of taxes, fees, fines, and other sources of income. Governments utilize these funds to finance public goods and services, such as infrastructure development, healthcare, education, defense, and social welfare programs. Another important aspect of Public Finance is expenditure management. Governments need to carefully allocate their financial resources to different sectors and projects in order to maximize their benefits and minimize wastage. This requires the evaluation of project proposals, cost-benefit analysis, and prioritization based on the needs and priorities of the public. Debt management is another crucial component of Public Finance. Governments often borrow money to fund their expenditures, especially during periods of economic downturns or when faced with large-scale infrastructure development projects. Effective debt management involves determining the appropriate level of borrowing, negotiating favorable loan terms, and ensuring timely repayment to avoid financial instability and excessive debt burden. Furthermore, Public Finance also encompasses the study of taxation policies and their impact on the economy and public welfare. Taxation is an important tool for governments to generate revenue and promote fiscal responsibility. It requires careful consideration of tax rates, tax exemptions, and incentives to encourage economic growth, attract investments, and ensure social equity. In conclusion, Public Finance is a branch of financial management that focuses on the financial activities of governments. It involves revenue generation, expenditure management, debt management, and taxation policies to ensure the efficient and equitable allocation of resources for the benefit of the public.

Public Offering

A public offering, in the context of financial management, refers to the process of offering and selling securities to the general public by a company or government entity. It is a crucial method for raising capital to fund business operations or government projects. During a public offering, a company or government entity issues securities, such as stocks, bonds, or debentures, and offers them for sale to the public. This allows individuals and institutional investors to purchase a stake in the company or provide funding to the government. Public offerings can be conducted through different types of offerings, including initial public offerings (IPOs) or follow-on offerings. An initial public offering (IPO) is the first time a company issues its shares to the public, transitioning from a private to a publicly traded company. IPOs often occur when a company seeks to expand its operations, repay debts, or provide existing shareholders with an opportunity to sell their shares. The process involves hiring an investment bank or underwriter, who assists in determining the offering size, pricing, and timing. Once launched, the IPO is marketed to potential investors, and shares are sold through various channels, such as stock exchanges. Follow-on offerings, on the other hand, are secondary offerings made by companies after their IPOs. These offerings allow companies to raise additional capital while already being publicly traded. The funds generated from follow-on offerings can be used for various purposes, such as expansion, acquisitions, or debt repayment. The shares offered in follow-on offerings are usually issued at a predetermined price based on market conditions and investor demand. Public offerings provide several benefits to companies and governments. They offer a way to access a large pool of potential investors, providing an opportunity for companies to raise substantial funds to support their growth strategies. Additionally, public offerings enhance a company's credibility and visibility in the market, which can lead to increased valuation and a higher market capitalization. For governments, public offerings can be a means to finance infrastructure projects or manage national debt. In conclusion, a public offering is a significant financial event where securities are offered and sold to the general public. It is a valuable tool for companies and governments to raise capital, expand their operations, and achieve their financial objectives.

Put-Call Parity

Put-Call Parity is a fundamental principle in financial management that establishes the relationship between the prices of put options, call options, and the underlying assets. It is based on the assumption that options are correctly priced in the market and that an arbitrage opportunity will not persist. According to the put-call parity principle, the sum of the price of a European call option and the present value of a strike price discounted at the risk-free rate is equal to the sum of the price of a European put option and the current price of the underlying asset. The formula can be stated as: $C + PV(X) = P + S$ Where: C = Price of a European call option P = Price of a European put option $PV(X)$ = Present value of the strike price (X) discounted at the risk-free rate S = Current price of the underlying asset This parity principle implies that if the prices of the options and the underlying asset do not satisfy the put-call parity equation, then an arbitrage opportunity exists. Arbitrage refers to the ability of an investor to make risk-free profits by simultaneously buying and selling related assets at different prices in different markets or at different times. Put-Call Parity is an important concept in options pricing and trading strategies. It can be used to determine the fair value of options, evaluate potential arbitrage opportunities, and create synthetic positions. By understanding the put-call parity relationship, investors and traders can make more informed decisions regarding options trading, hedging, and portfolio management. In conclusion, Put-Call Parity is a principle that establishes the relationship between put options, call options, and the underlying assets. It provides valuable insights into options pricing and trading strategies, helping investors and traders make informed decisions in the financial markets.

Qualified Dividend

Qualified dividends are a specific type of dividend income that is eligible for special tax treatment in the United States. In the context of financial management, the term "qualified dividend" refers to a dividend that meets certain criteria set forth by the Internal Revenue Service (IRS). For a dividend to be considered qualified, it must meet the following requirements:1. The dividend must be paid by a U.S. corporation or a qualified foreign corporation.2. The dividend must be held for a certain period of time. For common stock, the holding period is generally 60 days within the 120-day period that begins 60 days before the ex-dividend date. For preferred stock, the holding period is generally 90 days within the 180-day period that begins 90 days before the ex-dividend date.3. The dividend cannot be from certain types of investments, such as real estate investment trusts (REITs), master limited partnerships (MLPs), or tax-exempt organizations.4. The dividend must be reported by the IRS and included in the taxpayer's income.Qualified dividends are subject to a lower tax rate than ordinary dividends, which are taxed at the individual taxpayer's ordinary income tax rate. The tax rates for qualified dividends depend on the taxpayer's income bracket.For individuals in the 10% to 15% income tax bracket, qualified dividends are taxed at a 0% rate. For individuals in the 25% to 35% income tax bracket, qualified dividends are taxed at a 15% rate. And for individuals in the 39.6% income tax bracket, qualified dividends are taxed at a 20% rate.It is important for taxpayers to understand the distinction between qualified dividends and ordinary dividends, as the tax implications differ. By meeting the criteria outlined by the IRS, individuals can take advantage of the lower tax rates associated with qualified dividends and potentially reduce their overall tax liability.In conclusion, qualified dividends are a specific type of dividend income that satisfies certain requirements set by the IRS. By meeting these requirements, individuals can benefit from a lower tax rate on their dividend income.

Quantitative Analysis

Quantitative analysis is a method used in financial management to analyze and interpret numeric data in order to make informed decisions. It involves the use of mathematical and statistical tools to evaluate financial information, assess risk and return, and support strategic planning and decision-making processes. In the context of financial management, quantitative analysis focuses on the use of quantitative models and techniques to examine financial data and generate insights that can guide financial decision-making. It primarily involves the following steps: 1. Data Collection: Gathering relevant financial information from various sources, such as financial statements, market data, and economic indicators. This data is typically in numerical form, including financial ratios, stock prices, interest rates, and other relevant variables. 2. Data Analysis: Applying statistical methods and mathematical models to analyze the collected data and extract meaningful patterns and relationships. This may include techniques such as regression analysis, time series analysis, correlation analysis, and variance analysis. 3. Risk Assessment: Assessing the potential risks associated with financial decisions by using quantitative techniques, such as probability distributions, Monte Carlo simulations, and value-at-risk (VaR) analysis. This helps financial managers understand the probability and magnitude of potential losses or gains. 4. Forecasting and Projection: Using historical data and statistical models to forecast future financial performance and project the outcomes of different financial strategies. This helps in budgeting, financial planning, and setting realistic goals and targets. 5. Decision Making: Utilizing the insights and findings from quantitative analysis to support decision-making processes in financial management. This may involve evaluating investment opportunities, determining optimal capital structure, pricing financial products, analyzing cost and revenue drivers, and evaluating potential mergers and acquisitions. By employing quantitative analysis techniques, financial managers can enhance their understanding of financial data, identify trends and patterns, quantify risks, and make more informed and objective decisions. It provides a systematic and objective approach to evaluating financial information, facilitating effective financial planning and control, and improving overall organizational performance.

Quantitative Easing (QE)

186

Quantitative Easing (QE) is a monetary policy tool used by central banks to stimulate economic activity and address deflationary pressures in an economy. It involves the purchase of government bonds or other securities by the central bank in order to inject money into the economy and increase the supply of credit. QE is typically implemented when conventional monetary policy measures, such as lowering interest rates, have become ineffective in boosting economic growth or inflation. It is often used as a last resort measure during periods of economic downturn or crisis.

Quick Ratio

The quick ratio is a financial ratio that measures a company's ability to pay off its current liabilities with its most liquid assets. It is also known as the acid-test ratio, indicating the company's ability to meet short-term obligations without relying on the sale of inventory. To calculate the quick ratio, the sum of cash, cash equivalents, short-term investments, and accounts receivable is divided by the current liabilities. The formula is as follows: Quick Ratio = (Cash + Cash Equivalents + Short-term Investments + Accounts Receivable) / Current Liabilities The quick ratio is considered a more conservative liquidity measure compared to the current ratio, as it excludes inventory from the equation. Inventory is generally the least liquid of a company's assets and may take time to sell or convert into cash. By excluding inventory from the calculation, the quick ratio provides a clearer understanding of a company's ability to meet its short-term liabilities. A quick ratio of 1 or greater is typically considered favorable, as it indicates that a company has enough liquid assets to cover its short-term obligations. If the quick ratio is below 1, it suggests that a company may struggle to pay off its current liabilities without relying on selling inventory or borrowing additional funds. However, it is important to note that the ideal quick ratio varies across industries. Some sectors, such as retail, may require higher inventory levels to meet customer demand, resulting in lower quick ratios compared to industries with faster inventory turnover. Therefore, it is essential to compare a company's quick ratio against industry benchmarks and evaluate its liquidity position in the specific context of its business operations.

R-Squared (R2)

R-squared (R2) is a statistical measure that represents the proportion of the variance in the dependent variable that can be explained by the independent variable(s) in a regression model. In the context of financial management, R2 is commonly used to evaluate the goodness of fit of a regression model, which helps determine the predictive power and reliability of the model. Financial managers often use regression analysis to establish relationships between variables and predict future outcomes. In this process, R2 serves as a critical tool to assess how well the independent variables explain the changes in the dependent variable, such as stock returns, revenue growth, or other financial metrics.

Random Walk Theory

The Random Walk Theory in the context of Financial Management is a theory that suggests that the movements of stock prices and other financial variables are random and unpredictable. According to this theory, future price movements cannot be predicted based on past price movements or any other information. Random Walk Theory assumes that stock prices follow a random path where each price change is independent of the previous price changes. This means that the price movement today is not influenced by what happened in the past. In other words, the theory states that stock prices have no memory.

Rate Of Inflation

The rate of inflation is a key measure used in financial management to determine the increase in the general price level of goods and services over a given period of time. It is typically expressed as a percentage and is calculated by comparing the cost of a basket of goods and services in a specific year to the cost of that same basket in a base year, also known as the consumer price index (CPI). The rate of inflation is an important economic indicator that helps individuals, businesses, and governments make informed financial decisions. It affects nearly every aspect of the economy, including savings, investments, borrowing costs, wages, and the overall cost of living. Understanding and monitoring the rate of inflation is crucial for financial managers, as it

187

enables them to forecast the impact of rising prices on various financial activities and adjust their strategies accordingly.

Rate Of Return (ROR)

Rate of Return (ROR) is a financial metric used to measure the profitability of an investment over a specific period of time, expressed as a percentage. It is commonly used in financial management to assess the performance of investments and evaluate the efficiency of capital allocation. The ROR calculation takes into account both the initial investment and the subsequent cash inflows or outflows generated by the investment. The formula for calculating ROR is as follows: ROR = (Ending Value of Investment - Beginning Value of Investment + Cash Inflows) / Beginning Value of Investment By comparing the ROR of different investments, financial managers can make informed decisions regarding the allocation of resources and assess the risk associated with each investment. A higher ROR indicates a more profitable investment, while a lower ROR suggests a less successful outcome. ROR is widely used in financial management because it provides a standardized measure of investment performance that can be used to compare different investments or evaluate the performance of an investment over time. It allows investors and financial managers to assess the return on capital and determine the viability of investment opportunities. However, ROR should not be the sole criterion for investment decision-making. It is important to consider other factors such as risk, liquidity, and market conditions in conjunction with ROR to make well-informed decisions. Additionally, ROR does not account for the time value of money, which can lead to inaccuracies in assessing the true profitability of an investment. In conclusion, Rate of Return (ROR) is a financial metric used in financial management to measure the profitability of an investment. It allows for the evaluation of investment performance and the comparison of different investment opportunities. However, it should be used in conjunction with other factors and considerations to make informed investment decisions.

Real Estate Investment Trust (REIT)

A Real Estate Investment Trust (REIT) is a company that owns, operates, or finances income-generating real estate, often comprising a portfolio of properties. REITs are similar to mutual funds, but instead of investing in stocks and bonds, they invest in real estate assets. REITs were created by Congress in 1960 as a way to provide individual investors with an opportunity to invest in large-scale, income-producing real estate. To qualify as a REIT, a company must meet certain requirements laid out by the Internal Revenue Service (IRS). These requirements include the following: - At least 75% of the REIT's assets must be real estate assets, cash, or government securities. This ensures that the primary focus of the company is on real estate investments. - The REIT must distribute at least 90% of its taxable income to shareholders as dividends. This allows investors to benefit from a steady stream of income generated by the real estate investments. - The REIT must have a minimum of 100 shareholders. This requirement ensures that the benefits of investing in real estate are spread across a diverse group of individuals. - The ownership of the REIT must be transferable. This allows investors to easily buy and sell shares of the company on the stock exchange, providing liquidity. REITs offer investors the opportunity to gain exposure to the real estate market without the need to directly purchase and manage properties. By pooling investor funds, REITs are able to invest in a variety of properties, such as office buildings, shopping centers, apartments, and hotels, which may not be accessible to individual investors. This diversification helps to lower risk and provides investors with a more stable return on their investment. Investing in REITs can provide several benefits. Firstly, they offer the potential for regular income in the form of dividends, making them an attractive investment option for income-focused investors. Additionally, REITs can offer the potential for capital appreciation as the value of the underlying real estate assets increases over time. Lastly, REITs provide investors with a level of liquidity, as shares can be easily bought or sold on the stock exchange.

Real Interest Rate

The real interest rate is a crucial concept in financial management that measures the purchasing power of money over time. It refers to the adjusted interest rate after accounting for the effects of inflation on the nominal interest rate. In simple terms, the real interest rate represents the rate of return on an investment or the cost of borrowing money, adjusted for the impact of inflation. It reflects the true increase in purchasing power that an individual or an organization can expect to earn or pay, considering changes in the general price level. By subtracting the inflation rate from the nominal interest rate, we can calculate the real interest rate. For example, if the nominal interest rate is 5% and the inflation rate is 2%, the real interest rate would be 3%. This means that the investor or borrower would experience a 3% increase in purchasing power after accounting for the effects of inflation. The real interest rate has significant implications for financial decision-making. It helps individuals and businesses evaluate the true cost of borrowing and make informed investment choices. A higher real interest rate implies that the purchasing power of borrowed funds will decrease over time, making borrowing more expensive. On the other hand, a lower real interest rate indicates that the borrowing costs are relatively lower, providing better opportunities for investment and growth. Financial managers carefully monitor changes in the real interest rate to assess the potential profitability of investments and to determine the appropriate cost of capital for borrowing funds. They compare the real interest rate with the expected rate of return on investment projects to make sound financial decisions. Moreover, the real interest rate also impacts various economic factors at the macro level. It influences consumer spending, investment levels, and the overall economic growth rate. Central banks and governments often adjust monetary policies to stabilize the real interest rate and stimulate economic activities.

Realized Gain

Realized gain is a term used in financial management to describe the increase in the value of an investment or asset that has been sold or exchanged for a higher price than its original purchase price. It is a measure of the profit made from the sale of the investment or asset and is often expressed as a percentage or dollar amount. Realized gain is an important concept in financial management as it provides insight into the profitability of an investment decision. It is determined by subtracting the original purchase price of the asset from the sale price, taking into account any transaction fees or costs associated with the sale. The difference between these two values represents the realized gain.

Recapitalization

Recapitalization, in the context of Financial Management, refers to the restructuring of a company's capital structure in order to improve its financial stability, efficiency, or strategic position. It involves changing the composition of a firm's equity and debt to achieve specific objectives and address existing financial challenges or opportunities. One of the main reasons for recapitalization is to optimize the company's capitalization to enhance its financial performance. This may involve reducing excessive debt levels by refinancing existing debt with lower-cost financing options or reducing the overall debt burden. On the other hand, recapitalization may also involve increasing the company's debt component to take advantage of favorable interest rates or to fund growth opportunities. Another objective of recapitalization is to enhance the company's ownership structure, often driven by changing business dynamics or market conditions. This can include issuing new equity shares to raise funds, repurchasing shares to increase the company's ownership by existing shareholders, or adopting various stock-based compensation plans to incentivize and retain key employees. Additionally, recapitalization may be undertaken to consolidate ownership and control of a company. For instance, it may involve a leveraged buyout (LBO) where a company's management or a private equity firm acquires a controlling interest in the company by using significant amounts of debt financing. Furthermore, recapitalization can be employed as a defensive measure to fend off hostile takeovers. By modifying its capital structure, a company may increase its share price, making it less attractive or financially unfeasible for potential acquirers. In summary, recapitalization is a financial management strategy that involves changing a company's capital structure to achieve specific objectives, such as improving financial stability, enhancing ownership structure, funding growth opportunities, or defending against hostile takeovers. It is a critical tool in the arsenal of financial managers to optimize the company's financial performance and position it for future success.

Receivables

Receivables, in the context of financial management, refer to amounts owed to a business by its customers or other parties. These amounts are considered as assets on the company's balance sheet and represent the expected cash inflows from sales on credit or the provision of goods or services. When a business sells its products or services on credit, it allows customers to defer payment until a later date. As a result, the business generates accounts receivable, which represents the right to receive future payments from these customers. This creates a financial obligation on the part of the customers to pay for the goods or services received. Accounts receivable, or simply receivables, are recorded on the balance sheet as current assets since they are expected to be collected within one year. They are typically classified as trade receivables if they arise from normal business operations, or as non-trade receivables if they result from non-operating activities such as loans to employees or advances to suppliers. The management of receivables is essential for ensuring a company's liquidity and financial health. It involves various activities, including determining credit policies, evaluating customer creditworthiness, establishing payment terms, monitoring payment collections, and managing potential bad debts. Effective management of receivables aims to strike a balance between maximizing sales and minimizing associated risks. By granting credit, businesses can attract more customers and increase sales volumes. However, this exposes them to the risk of non-payment or delayed payment, which could impact their cash flow and profitability. Therefore, it is crucial to establish credit limits for customers and regularly assess their creditworthiness using tools such as credit checks and financial analysis. Furthermore, companies need to establish favorable payment terms that encourage prompt payment. This may involve offering discounts for early payment or implementing penalties for late payment. By monitoring payment collections and promptly following up on overdue accounts, businesses can minimize the incidence of bad debts and improve their liquidity position. In conclusion, receivables are amounts owed to a company by customers or other parties. They are considered as assets on the balance sheet and represent the expected cash inflows from credit sales or provision of goods and services. Effective management of receivables involves establishing credit policies, evaluating creditworthiness, setting payment terms, monitoring collections, and managing bad debts.

Recession Resistant

Recession Resistant in the context of financial management refers to businesses or industries that are able to withstand and recover quickly from economic downturns, such as recessions. During a recession, the overall economy experiences a decline in economic activity that can result in decreased consumer spending, reduced business investments, and increased unemployment. This economic downturn can negatively impact businesses, leading to decreased revenues and profitability, and in some cases, business closures and bankruptcies. However, there are certain businesses or industries that are considered recession-resistant due to various factors that enable them to remain relatively stable or even thrive during economic downturns. These recession-resistant businesses tend to continue generating revenue and may even experience growth by offering products or services that are essential or in demand regardless of the economic climate. Typically, recession-resistant businesses operate in sectors that provide essential goods and services, such as healthcare, utilities, and basic consumer goods. In the healthcare sector, for example, hospitals, pharmaceutical companies, and medical equipment manufacturers are generally considered recession-resistant as the demand for healthcare remains constant throughout economic fluctuations. Similarly, utility companies that provide essential services like electricity, water, and gas are also considered recession-resistant as these services are necessary for daily living. In addition to operating in essential sectors, recession-resistant businesses often have certain characteristics that contribute to their ability to weather economic downturns. These characteristics may include strong financial positions, diversified revenue streams, and a focus on cost management and efficiency. Businesses with strong financial positions, such as ample cash reserves and low debt levels, are better equipped to navigate through challenging economic times. Diversification of revenue streams across different products, markets, or customer segments is another characteristic of recession-resistant businesses. By having multiple sources of revenue, these businesses are less vulnerable to a single market or customer segment that may be heavily impacted by a recession. Furthermore, recession-resistant businesses often prioritize cost management and efficiency measures to maintain profitability during economic downturns. These businesses may implement strategies such as cost-cutting initiatives, lean operations, and effective inventory management to minimize expenses and preserve their financial health.

Recession

A recession is a significant decline in economic activity that lasts for a sustained period. It is characterized by a decrease in gross domestic product (GDP), income, employment, and trade. Recession is a natural part of the economic cycle, typically following a period of economic growth. This decline in economic activity can result from various factors such as a decline in consumer spending, investments, government spending, or business activity. During a recession, several negative macroeconomic indicators are observed. GDP, which represents the value of goods and services produced in an economy, declines significantly. This is often accompanied by a decrease in income, as businesses reduce wages or lay off employees. Unemployment rates rise as businesses struggle to maintain profitability and reduce their workforce. Consequently, consumer confidence declines, leading to a decrease in consumer spending, further exacerbating the economic downturn. The impacts of a recession are not limited to the domestic economy but can also have global implications. Reduced trade and investment flows negatively affect countries worldwide. Financial markets tend to suffer during a recession, with stock markets experiencing significant declines and increased volatility. This can further impact both individual and institutional investors, as the value of their investments decline. In response to a recession, governments and central banks often implement contractionary fiscal and monetary policies to stimulate economic growth. These measures may include reducing interest rates, implementing tax cuts, increasing government spending, and providing financial assistance to struggling businesses and individuals. The length and severity of a recession can vary. A recession is typically considered severe if it lasts for an extended period, exceeds two consecutive quarters of negative GDP growth, and significantly affects various economic indicators. The recovery from a recession can also be slow and gradual, as it takes time for businesses and consumers to regain confidence and rebuild the economy.

Red Herring

A red herring, in the context of financial management, refers to a misleading or irrelevant piece of information that distracts or diverts attention from the actual issue or problem at hand. It is commonly used in investment analysis, financial reporting, and corporate decision-making processes. In investment analysis, a red herring may be used by investment managers, brokers, or financial analysts to mislead or divert attention from negative aspects of a particular investment opportunity. By highlighting positive aspects or using exaggerated language, these professionals may try to create a false perception of the investment's potential and profitability.

Redemption Value

Redemption Value refers to the amount of money that an investor receives when they redeem or sell a financial instrument, such as a bond or a mutual fund. It represents the face value or original investment amount plus any additional returns or interest that has been earned on the investment. In the context of financial management, redemption value plays a crucial role in determining the profitability and return on investment of a particular instrument. It is important for investors to understand the redemption value before investing their money, as it helps them assess the potential gains or losses associated with the investment.

Regression Analysis

Regression analysis is a statistical technique used in financial management to identify and quantify the relationship between a dependent variable and one or more independent variables. It is commonly used to forecast future values based on historical data and to understand the impact of changes in the independent variables on the dependent variable. In financial management, regression analysis is used to analyze various aspects of investment, risk assessment, and portfolio management. By examining the relationship between different variables, regression analysis helps financial managers make informed decisions and understand the financial implications of different factors and variables.

Regulatory Capital

Regulatory capital refers to the amount of capital that financial institutions are required by regulators to maintain in order to support their financial stability and mitigate the risks associated with their activities. It is a crucial measure used by regulatory authorities to enhance the financial solvency and ensure the soundness of the banking system. Regulatory capital serves as a cushion for banks and other financial institutions against unexpected losses and acts as a protection for depositors and creditors. It acts as a safeguard to prevent institutions from becoming insolvent and failing to meet their obligations. By imposing capital requirements, regulators aim to maintain the stability and confidence in the financial system, reduce the possibility of bank failures, and minimize the likelihood of a systemic crisis. Regulatory capital is typically classified into two broad categories: Tier 1 capital and Tier 2 capital. Tier 1 capital represents the core capital base of a financial institution and includes common equity, retained earnings, and certain other instruments that possess the highest loss-absorbing capacity. Tier 2 capital, on the other hand, consists of subordinated debt, hybrid instruments, and other supplementary capital instruments that provide additional loss-absorbing capacity but are less permanent than Tier 1 capital. The capital requirements are determined by regulators based on various factors such as the size, complexity, and risk profile of the financial institution. These requirements are usually expressed as a percentage of a bank's risk-weighted assets, which reflect the potential risks associated with different types of loans and investments. The higher the risk, the more capital an institution is required to hold in order to adequately cover the potential losses. In addition to the minimum capital requirements, regulators also establish capital adequacy ratios to assess the overall financial health and stability of banks. The most commonly used ratio is the Basel III framework's Common Equity Tier 1 (CET1) ratio, which measures Tier 1 capital in relation to a bank's risk-weighted assets. Meeting the minimum capital requirements and maintaining sufficient capital ratios are essential for financial institutions to demonstrate their ability to withstand economic shocks, protect depositors, and fulfill their role in the economy.

Reinsurance

Reinsurance is a financial management strategy that involves transferring a portion of an insurance company's risk to another insurance company. The primary purpose of reinsurance is to protect the insurance company from catastrophic events or large losses that may occur. When an insurance company sells policies to individuals or businesses, it assumes the responsibility of paying claims if the insured events occur. However, the insurance company may face significant financial risks if a large number of claims are filed simultaneously, or if the claims are exceptionally high in value. In such cases, reinsurance allows the insurance company to mitigate these risks by transferring a portion of the potential losses to the reinsurer.

Reinvestment Rate

The reinvestment rate, in the context of financial management, refers to the rate at which the cash flows generated from an investment are reinvested back into the same or other investment opportunities. It is a key consideration for investors and businesses as it affects the overall return and growth potential of their investment portfolio. When an investment generates positive cash flows, it provides the investor with the option to either consume the cash flows or reinvest them. The reinvestment rate determines the amount of cash flows that are reinvested and the rate at which they are reinvested. By reinvesting the cash flows, investors can potentially earn additional returns on their original investment.

Reinvestment Risk

Reinvestment risk, in the context of financial management, refers to the potential risk or uncertainty faced by an investor or bondholder when the cash flow generated from an investment or bond is reinvested at a different interest rate than the original investment. This risk arises from the fact that future rates of return on investment are uncertain and may be different from the initial investment rate. When interest rates decline, investors face reinvestment risk because they will have to reinvest their cash flows, such as coupon payments or maturity proceeds, at lower interest rates, potentially leading to a decrease in the overall return of their investment. On the other hand, when interest rates rise, reinvestment risk may result in the need to reinvest at higher rates, making it difficult to achieve the same level of return. Reinvestment risk is particularly relevant for fixed income investments, such as bonds. Bonds typically have a fixed coupon rate and a defined maturity. When the bondholder receives periodic coupon payments, they have the option to reinvest those payments at the prevailing market interest rate. If interest rates have fallen since the original bond purchase, the investor may have to reinvest at a lower rate, resulting in a lower overall return. Similarly, when a bond matures, the investor

192

faces the risk of reinvesting the principal at a lower rate if interest rates have decreased. It is important for investors to consider reinvestment risk when making investment decisions, as it can impact the overall return and risk profile of their portfolios. The extent of reinvestment risk depends on various factors, including the duration or term to maturity of the investment, the magnitude and speed of interest rate changes, and the investor's ability to find suitable alternative investments at a comparable yield. Investors can mitigate reinvestment risk by diversifying their portfolio and considering investments with different maturities or interest rate structures.

Relative Strength Index (RSI)

The Relative Strength Index (RSI) is a technical analysis tool used in the field of financial management to measure the speed and change of price movements in a particular investment. It is a momentum oscillator that compares the magnitude of recent gains to recent losses in an effort to determine overbought or oversold conditions in the market. Developed by J. Welles Wilder, the RSI is calculated using a mathematical formula that takes into account the average gain and average loss of a specified period of time. The RSI ranges from 0 to 100, with readings above 70 generally considered overbought and readings below 30 considered oversold. These thresholds indicate potential reversal points in the price movement, providing traders with signals to buy or sell.

Reserve Requirements

Reserve Requirements, in the context of Financial Management, refer to the mandatory reserves that banks and financial institutions are required to hold with the central bank of a country. These reserves are a percentage of the total deposits held by the bank and act as a safeguard against excessive risk-taking and potential bank failures. Central banks impose reserve requirements on banks as a way to control the money supply and influence the overall economy. By regulating the amount of reserves banks must hold, central banks can affect the ability of banks to extend credit and create new money. This, in turn, has a direct impact on inflation, interest rates, and overall economic stability.

Residual Income

Residual income, in the context of financial management, refers to the amount of income an individual or business has left over after covering all costs and expenses associated with generating that income. It is a measure of financial performance that indicates the profitability and efficiency of an investment or business venture. Unlike traditional income measures that focus on gross income or net income, residual income takes into account the opportunity cost of using capital to generate income. It enables investors and managers to assess the profitability of their investments or business activities by considering the return on capital invested.

Residual Value

Residual value, in the context of financial management, refers to the estimated value of an asset at the end of its useful life or lease term. It is also known as salvage value or scrap value. The residual value is an important concept in financial management as it factors into various financial calculations and decision-making processes. It is particularly relevant in the context of asset depreciation, lease agreements, and asset valuations. It helps in determining the overall profitability, return on investment, and future cash flows associated with an asset or investment.

Retained Earnings

Retained Earnings is a financial term used in the context of financial management. It refers to the portion of a company's net income that is retained or reinvested back into the business after distributing dividends to its shareholders or owners. Retained earnings represent the cumulative profits and losses that a company has accumulated over time and are reported on the company's balance sheet under shareholders' equity. When a company generates a profit, it has a choice to either distribute the earnings to its shareholders in the form of dividends or to retain the earnings for future use within the company. Retaining earnings allows a company to fund its growth, finance capital expenditures, repay debt, and increase its working capital. These retained earnings are accounted for in a separate equity account known as the "retained earnings" account. Retained earnings are calculated by subtracting dividends paid to shareholders from the net profit or net income of the company. The beginning balance of retained earnings is added to the net income, and any dividends paid are then subtracted to arrive at the ending balance of retained earnings. This balance is carried forward to the next accounting period and becomes the beginning balance for that period. Retained earnings play a crucial role in financial management as they represent the historical profits and losses of a company and can be used as a measure of financial strength and stability. Higher retained earnings indicate that a company is generating consistent profits, while lower or negative retained earnings may suggest that a company is struggling financially. Additionally, retained earnings are an important source of internal financing for a company. By retaining earnings, a company can reduce its reliance on external financing options such as debt or equity issuance, which can result in lower financial expenses and improved financial flexibility. In summary, retained earnings represent the portion of a company's earnings that are retained or reinvested back into the business after paying dividends to shareholders. They are an important indicator of a company's financial performance, stability, and ability to finance its own growth and operations.

Return On Assets (ROA)

Return on Assets (ROA) is a financial metric that measures a company's profitability in relation to its total assets. It is a key indicator used by financial managers to assess how effectively a company is utilizing its assets to generate profits. ROA is expressed as a percentage and is calculated by dividing net income by average total assets. ROA is a crucial metric for both investors and financial managers as it provides insights into a company's ability to generate profits from its assets. A higher ROA indicates that a company is effectively utilizing its assets to generate income, while a lower ROA suggests that a company may not be utilizing its assets efficiently.

Return On Capital Employed (ROCE)

Return on Capital Employed (ROCE) is a financial metric used in the field of financial management to measure the profitability and efficiency with which a company utilizes its capital. It provides insights into the company's ability to generate returns on the funds invested in the business, making it a valuable tool for both investors and financial analysts. ROCE is calculated by dividing the company's operating profit (earnings before interest and taxes) by its total capital employed. Total capital employed represents the total investment in the business, which includes both equity and debt. It is calculated by adding the company's shareholders' equity (common stock and retained earnings) to its total long-term debt. ROCE is expressed as a percentage and indicates the return on each unit of capital employed. A higher ROCE indicates greater profitability and efficiency in utilizing capital, while a lower ROCE suggests suboptimal utilization of capital. ROCE is a key financial ratio used to evaluate a company's financial performance and compare it with industry peers. It helps investors and financial analysts assess the company's ability to generate profits from its business operations relative to the capital invested. ROCE is influenced by various factors, such as the company's operating profit, total asset base, and capital structure. A company with a high ROCE implies that it is generating substantial profits relative to the capital invested, indicating strong operational performance and efficient use of resources. Conversely, a low ROCE may indicate weak profitability and underutilization of capital. In conclusion, ROCE is a vital financial metric that provides valuable insights into a company's financial performance and efficiency in utilizing its capital. It helps investors and financial analysts evaluate the profitability and effectiveness of a company's operations, making it an essential tool in financial management.

Return On Capital (ROC)

Return on Capital (ROC) is a financial measure used in financial management to assess the profitability and efficiency of a company's investment in capital. It evaluates how effectively a company is utilizing its capital to generate profits. ROC is calculated by dividing the net operating income (NOI) by the total invested capital of a company. The net operating income represents the earnings before interest and taxes (EBIT) minus the taxes paid, while the invested capital includes both equity and debt. The formula for ROC is as follows: ROC = Net Operating Income / Invested Capital ROC is expressed as a percentage and provides valuable insight into a company's ability to generate returns on its capital investments. It helps stakeholders, such as investors and creditors, evaluate the company's profitability and assess its performance compared to competitors in the same industry.A higher ROC indicates that a company is generating more profits relative to its invested capital. This implies efficient capital allocation and greater potential for growth. Conversely, a lower ROC suggests that the company is not efficiently utilizing its capital, which may indicate suboptimal financial management or operational inefficiencies.ROC is an important metric for financial managers as it enables them to measure the effectiveness of capital investments and make informed decisions regarding resource allocation. By comparing the ROC of different investment projects, financial managers can identify the most profitable opportunities and allocate resources accordingly. They can also use ROC to assess the overall performance of the company and identify areas for improvement.However, it is essential to consider industry-specific benchmarks when evaluating ROC. Different industries have varying levels of capital intensity and profitability expectations, so comparing ROC across industries may not provide an accurate assessment. Financial managers should use industry-specific benchmarks or compare the company's ROC to its historical performance to gain meaningful insights.

Return On Equity (ROE)

The Return on Equity (ROE) is a financial ratio that measures the profitability of a company based on the shareholders' equity. It indicates how efficiently a company uses its equity to generate profits. ROE is calculated by dividing the net income of a company by its average shareholders' equity. The net income represents the total profit earned by the company after deducting all expenses, taxes, and interest. The shareholders' equity is the residual interest in the assets of the company after deducting liabilities. It can also be seen as the company's net assets. ROE is an important measure for shareholders and investors as it indicates how effectively the company is utilizing their investments. A higher ROE suggests that the company is generating more profit with every dollar of equity, which is favourable for shareholders. It also indicates that the company has good financial strength and efficiency in managing its assets and liabilities. ROE can vary across different industries and companies. It is influenced by factors such as profit margins, asset turnover, and leverage. Companies with higher profit margins and asset turnover ratios tend to have higher ROE. However, high leverage can also increase ROE, but it comes with a higher risk for shareholders. Investors use ROE to compare the performance of different companies within the same industry. It helps them assess which companies are more efficient in generating profits and which ones provide better returns on their equity investment. However, it is important to consider other financial ratios and factors when evaluating a company's overall financial health and investment potential. In conclusion, ROE is a financial ratio used to measure the profitability of a company based on its shareholders' equity. It indicates how effectively a company generates profits with its equity and helps investors assess the performance and efficiency of the company. It is an important metric in financial management and investment decision-making.

Return On Investment (ROI)

Return on Investment (ROI) is a widely used financial metric that measures the profitability of an investment relative to its cost. It is a key indicator for evaluating the efficiency and effectiveness of a company's investment decisions. ROI is expressed as a percentage and is calculated by dividing the net profit of an investment by its initial cost, and then multiplying the result by 100. Net profit is the difference between the total revenue generated by an investment and the total expenses incurred. It represents the financial gain or loss from the investment over a specific period of time. The initial cost includes the purchase price of the asset or investment, as well as any associated costs such as transaction fees or installation expenses. ROI is a crucial tool for financial management as it enables companies to assess the profitability and success of their investment initiatives. A higher ROI indicates a more favorable investment, as it demonstrates that the returns generated are greater than the initial cost. Conversely, a lower or negative ROI suggests that the investment is less profitable or even loss-making. ROI is commonly used for comparing the financial performance of different investment options. By calculating the ROI for various investments, companies can determine which option will yield the highest returns. This helps in making informed investment decisions and allocating resources efficiently. ROI is also used to evaluate the performance of specific projects or departments within a company. By comparing the ROI of different projects or departments, management can identify areas that are generating the highest returns and consider reallocating resources accordingly. Furthermore, ROI can be used to assess the success of marketing campaigns or new product launches by measuring the impact on revenue and profitability. It is important to note that ROI should be interpreted in the context of the specific industry or market in which the investment is made. Different industries may have different benchmarks or expectations for ROI due to variations in risk, competition, and market conditions. Therefore, comparing the ROI of investments in different industries may not provide meaningful insights.

Return On Net Assets (RONA)

Return on Net Assets (RONA) is a financial ratio used in financial management to assess the profitability and efficiency of a company's use of its assets. It is calculated by dividing the company's net income by its net assets, and is expressed as a percentage. RONA provides valuable insights into how effectively a company is utilizing its assets to generate profits. It helps in measuring the return generated by each dollar invested in the company's assets. By comparing RONA ratios across different periods or against industry benchmarks, financial managers can evaluate the company's performance and identify areas for improvement.

Revenue Recognition

Revenue recognition is a fundamental concept in financial management that involves the identification and recording of revenue for accounting purposes. It refers to the process of determining when and how revenue should be recognized or recorded in an organization's financial statements, such as the income statement and balance sheet. According to generally accepted accounting principles (GAAP) and International Financial Reporting Standards (IFRS), revenue is recognized when it is both earned and realized or realizable. This means that revenue should be recognized when it has been earned through the delivery of goods or services, and when it is either received in cash or there is a reasonable expectation of receiving it.

Revenue

Revenue refers to the total income generated by a company from its core business operations. It is one of the key financial metrics that indicates the financial performance and sustainability of a business. Revenue is also commonly known as sales or turnover. In financial management, revenue plays a crucial role as it forms the basis for various financial analyses and decision-making processes. It represents the inflow of economic benefits that a company receives from selling its products or services to customers. Revenue can be categorized into different types, depending on the nature of the business. These categories may include sales revenue, service revenue, rental revenue, interest revenue, and dividend revenue, among others. Each category represents a specific source of income for the company. For accurate financial reporting, it is important to distinguish revenue from other types of income, such as capital gains or non-operating income. Revenue is directly related to a company's core business operations and is primarily generated from its regular activities. Revenue is typically reported on the income statement, also known as the profit and loss statement or statement of comprehensive income. This financial statement provides a summary of a company's revenues, expenses, and net income during a specific period. An increase in revenue is generally seen as a positive sign, as it indicates that the company is selling more products or services and generating higher sales. However, it is essential to analyze revenue growth in relation to other financial metrics, such as profit margins and operating expenses, to assess the overall financial health of the company.

Revolving Credit Facility

A revolving credit facility is a type of financing arrangement provided by a financial institution to a borrower, typically a corporation or a business, which allows them to borrow funds up to a specified credit limit. It is a form of short-term borrowing that the borrower can access as needed and repay, similar to a credit card. Unlike a traditional term loan where the borrower receives a lump sum upfront and pays it back in regular installments over a fixed period, a revolving credit facility provides borrowers with flexibility. They can draw funds up to the approved credit limit, repay them, and then borrow again without having to reapply for a new loan. This revolving nature of the facility makes it particularly useful for managing short-term working capital needs and cash flow fluctuations. A revolving credit facility is usually arranged for a specified period, known as the "commitment period," during which the borrower can access the funds. This period is typically renewable, allowing the borrower to continue borrowing and repaying within the agreed terms. The facility also comes with an "interest period" during which the borrower is charged interest on the outstanding balance. The interest rate on a revolving credit facility is often variable, meaning it can fluctuate based on market conditions or a benchmark interest rate, such as LIBOR. This makes the facility more flexible compared to fixed-term loans, where the interest rate is set at the time of borrowing. The borrower is only charged interest on the amount outstanding, providing cost savings when they repay part of the borrowed amount. A revolving credit facility may be secured or unsecured, depending on the borrower's creditworthiness and the lender's requirements. In some cases, the facility may be supported by collateral, such as accounts receivable, inventory, or property, which the lender can seize in case of default. Alternatively, the facility may be unsecured, relying solely on the borrower's creditworthiness. In summary, a revolving credit facility is a flexible form of financing that allows borrowers to access funds up to a specified credit limit, repay them, and borrow again without the need for reapplying. It is particularly useful for managing short-term working capital needs and cash flow fluctuations in businesses.

Risk Management

Risk management in the context of financial management refers to the process of identifying, assessing, and prioritizing potential risks that may affect a company's financial goals and objectives. It involves implementing strategies to mitigate or avoid these risks and monitoring their impact on the company's financial performance. The goal of risk management is to minimize the negative impact of unexpected events or uncertainties on the company's financial stability and profitability. By identifying and understanding potential risks, companies can develop strategies to deal with them effectively, thereby reducing the likelihood of financial loss.

Risk Tolerance

Risk tolerance refers to an investor's ability or willingness to endure fluctuations in the value of their investments or the possibility of potential losses. In the context of financial management, it is a crucial concept as it helps investors determine their investment strategy and portfolio allocation based on their comfort level with risk. An individual's risk tolerance is influenced by a variety of factors, including their financial goals, time horizon, investment knowledge, and their capacity to bear the consequences of potential losses. It is important to note that risk tolerance is subjective and can vary significantly among individuals.

Risk-Adjusted Return

Risk-Adjusted Return refers to the measure of the gain an investment is expected to generate in relation to the amount of risk incurred. It is a financial performance metric that takes into account the level of risk assumed by an investor and adjusts the returns accordingly. When making investment decisions, it is important to consider both the potential return and the associated risk. In general, investments that offer higher returns tend to be accompanied by higher levels of risk. Risk-Adjusted Return allows investors to assess the trade-off between potential gains and the likelihood of incurring losses. The most commonly used method to evaluate Risk-Adjusted Return is the Sharpe Ratio. The Sharpe Ratio compares the excess return of an investment to the volatility of its returns, as measured by its standard deviation. A higher Sharpe Ratio indicates a better risk-adjusted performance, as it suggests that the investment is generating a higher return for the level of risk taken. Another widely utilized measure of Risk-Adjusted Return is the Treynor Ratio. The Treynor Ratio considers the excess return of an investment relative to the risk-free rate, divided by its beta, which measures the investment's sensitivity to market movements. A higher Treynor Ratio suggests a more efficient use of systematic risk by the investment. By using Risk-Adjusted Return measures like the Sharpe Ratio and the Treynor Ratio, investors can compare different investment options and select those that offer the best risk-return trade-off. These metrics help investors make more informed decisions by providing a standardized way to evaluate the relative performance of investments, considering the amount of risk taken into consideration.

Risk-Free Asset

A risk-free asset, in the context of financial management, refers to an investment or asset that has zero risk of default or loss. It is often used as a benchmark or reference point for evaluating the performance of other investments or portfolios. In finance, every investment carries some level of risk. Risk can arise from various factors such as economic conditions, market fluctuations, geopolitical events, or the financial health of the issuer. However, a risk-free asset theoretically eliminates the possibility of any loss or default.

Risk-Free Rate Of Return

The risk-free rate of return, in the context of financial management, refers to the theoretical rate of return on an investment that carries no risk. It serves as a benchmark for evaluating the performance of other investments that do involve risk. The risk-free rate of return is typically associated with investments in Treasury bills or other highly stable and low-risk assets. Investors rely on the risk-free rate of return to determine the minimum return they should expect from an investment. It provides a baseline for comparing the performance and risk of different investment opportunities. If an investment fails to generate a return that exceeds the risk-free rate, it is generally considered to be underperforming or not worth the risk.

Risk-Free Rate

The risk-free rate, in the context of financial management, refers to the theoretical rate of return on an investment that carries zero risk. It represents the minimum return an investor should expect to receive when investing in an asset free of any potential default or fluctuation in value. The risk-free rate serves as a benchmark for evaluating the performance of investments and plays a crucial role in various financial calculations, such as determining the fair value of assets, calculating the cost of capital, and assessing the risk premium of a particular investment. Typically, the risk-free rate is derived from the yield of government bonds or treasury bills, which are considered to have negligible default risk. These securities are backed by the issuing government and are considered a safe haven for investors seeking minimal risk. The interest rate on these government securities reflects the risk-free rate in the financial markets. Investors use the risk-free rate as a fundamental element in the calculation of the required rate of return for an investment. This required rate of return incorporates the risk-free rate and a risk premium that compensates investors for taking on additional risk. The risk-free rate is often considered the "time value of money" and serves as a foundation for pricing other investments based on their perceived level of risk. It is important to note that the risk-free rate is a theoretical construct and may not accurately represent the actual return on any investment. In reality, all investments carry some level of risk, even if minimal. Nevertheless, the risk-free rate provides a standardized benchmark for comparing the relative risk and return of investments within the financial markets.

Secured Loan

A secured loan, in the context of financial management, refers to a type of loan that is backed by collateral or assets provided by the borrower. The collateral is typically an asset of value, such as real estate property, a vehicle, or other valuable possessions. The purpose of providing collateral is to give the lender additional assurance that the loan will be repaid. In the event that the borrower fails to repay the loan as agreed, the lender has the right to seize the collateral and sell it to recover the outstanding debt. This makes secured loans less risky for lenders and, as a result, they often come with lower interest rates compared to unsecured loans.

Securities Exchange Commission (SEC)

The Securities Exchange Commission (SEC) is a regulatory body in the United States that oversees and enforces federal securities laws, aiming to maintain fair and efficient markets and ensure protection for investors. The SEC was established in 1934 under the Securities Exchange Act in response to the stock market crash of 1929 and the subsequent Great Depression. As a result, the SEC was given the responsibility to enforce various securities laws and regulate the activities of participants in the securities market, including corporations, securities exchanges, broker-dealers, investment advisors, and other securities professionals. The primary role of the SEC is to protect investors and maintain the integrity of the securities market. To achieve this, the SEC requires companies that offer securities to the public to provide accurate and comprehensive information to potential investors. These disclosures enable investors to make informed decisions and evaluate the risks associated with their investments. Moreover, the SEC regulates the securities markets by enforcing rules that promote transparency and fair dealing. It monitors and investigates any potential violations of securities laws, such as insider trading, market manipulation, or misleading disclosures. Through these enforcement actions, the SEC aims to maintain a level playing field for all market participants and deter fraudulent practices. Additionally, the SEC plays a crucial role in ensuring the efficiency and stability of the securities market. It oversees the operations of securities exchanges, such as the New York Stock Exchange and the NASDAQ, to ensure they function in a fair and orderly manner. This includes examining the rules and operations of these exchanges, approving new listing standards, and monitoring the trading activities to safeguard market integrity. In summary, the SEC is a regulatory agency that protects investors, maintains market integrity, and ensures efficient and transparent securities markets. Through its enforcement actions, it aims to prevent fraudulent practices and provide a level playing field for all participants. By requiring accurate disclosures, it enables investors to make informed decisions and promotes fair dealing in the securities market.

Securities And Exchange Commission (SEC)

The Securities and Exchange Commission (SEC) is a regulatory agency established by the United States government to oversee and enforce federal securities laws. Its primary goal is to protect investors, maintain fair and efficient markets, and facilitate capital formation. The SEC is responsible for ensuring that companies provide accurate and transparent information to investors so they can make informed decisions. It requires public companies to file periodic reports, such as annual and quarterly reports, which include financial statements, business operations, and other relevant information. These reports are available to the public, allowing investors to evaluate a company's performance and prospects. Another key role of the SEC is to regulate the securities industry, including brokers, dealers, and investment advisors. It sets rules and standards to ensure that these entities operate ethically and provide fair services to their clients. The SEC also oversees securities exchanges, such as the New York Stock Exchange and NASDAQ, to maintain fair and orderly trading environments. In addition to its regulatory functions, the SEC plays a crucial role in enforcing securities laws and combating fraud. It investigates violations of securities laws, such as insider trading, accounting fraud, and market manipulation, and takes legal actions against individuals and companies involved in illegal activities. By holding wrongdoers accountable, the SEC aims to protect investors and maintain the integrity of the financial markets. The SEC also works in collaboration with other domestic and international regulatory bodies to strengthen investor protection and market integrity. It shares information and coordinates enforcement efforts with organizations like the Financial Industry Regulatory Authority (FINRA) and the International Organization of Securities Commissions (IOSCO). In conclusion, the Securities and Exchange Commission is a vital regulatory agency that oversees and enforces securities laws in the United States. By promoting transparency, fair markets, and investor protection, the SEC plays a critical role in maintaining the integrity and stability of the financial system.

Securities

Securities refer to financial instruments that are issued by corporations, governments, or other organizations to raise capital. These instruments represent a claim on the issuer's assets or future cash flows and are used by investors to generate a return on their investment. Securities can take various forms, including stocks, bonds, and derivatives.Stocks, also known as shares or equity, represent ownership in a corporation. When an individual or organization purchases stocks, they become shareholders and have the right to participate in the company's profits through dividends and potential capital appreciation. Stocks provide investors with partial ownership and voting rights in the company.Bonds, on the other hand, are fixed-income securities that represent loans made by investors to the issuer. When an investor purchases a bond, they are essentially lending money to the issuer, which can be a corporation, municipality, or government. In return, the issuer promises to pay fixed or variable interest payments over a specified period and returns the principal amount at maturity.Derivatives are financial contracts whose value is derived from an underlying asset, index, or reference rate. These securities are used to speculate, hedge risks, or lock in future prices. Derivatives include options, futures, swaps, and forwards. Options provide the right, but not the obligation, to buy or sell an asset at a predetermined price and date. Futures contracts dictate the delivery of an asset at a future date for a pre-agreed price. Swaps involve the exchange of cash flows or liabilities between two parties. Forwards are agreements to buy or sell an asset at a predetermined future date and price.

Securitization

Securitization refers to the process of converting illiquid assets into marketable securities. In financial management, it is a technique that allows companies to pool together various assets (such as mortgages, auto loans, credit card receivables, etc.) and transform them into tradable financial instruments known as asset-backed securities (ABS). This process involves three main parties: the originators, the special purpose vehicle (SPV), and the investors. The originators are the companies or financial institutions that possess the underlying assets. They package these assets and transfer them to the SPV, which is created solely for the purpose of securitization. The SPV acquires the assets and issues ABS, which are then purchased by investors.

Selling Short

Selling short is a strategy used in financial management to profit from a decline in the price of a security or asset. In this strategy, an investor borrows and sells the security with the expectation that its price will fall. The investor aims to buy back the security at a lower price and return it to the lender, thereby profiting from the difference between the selling price and the buying price. When an investor decides to sell short, they must first locate a lender who is willing to lend them the security. This could be a brokerage firm or another investor who holds the security in their portfolio. The investor borrows the security and immediately sells it in the market, receiving cash proceeds in return. As the investor expects the price of the security to decline, they monitor the market closely. Once the price reaches the desired target or the investor believes it has reached its bottom, they initiate the buying process. The investor purchases the security at the lower price and returns it to the lender. The profit from selling short is calculated by subtracting the buying price from the selling price, taking into account any transaction costs or fees involved. However, if the price of the security increases instead of decreasing, the investor incurs a loss. In this case, the investor must still repurchase and return the security to the lender at the higher price. Short selling carries inherent risks as there is no limit to how high the price of a security can rise. Selling short allows investors to potentially profit from downward price movements in securities, even in falling markets. It is commonly used by hedge funds, institutional investors, and individual traders to manage risk and generate profits. However, it requires a thorough understanding of the market and careful analysis of the factors influencing the security's price movement.

Sensitivity Analysis

Sensitivity analysis is a financial management technique that involves assessing the impact of variations in input variables or assumptions on the financial results or outcomes of a project, investment, or decision. It is used to evaluate the potential risks and uncertainties associated with these variables and identify the key drivers that have the greatest influence on the financial performance or profitability of a business. The purpose of sensitivity analysis is to understand how changes in input variables affect the financial outputs, such as net present value (NPV), internal rate of return (IRR), cash flow projections, or profitability ratios. By systematically varying one input at a time while keeping other variables constant, sensitivity analysis allows financial managers to assess the sensitivity of the outcomes to changes in different factors. Sensitivity analysis helps financial managers make informed decisions by providing insights into the potential risks and uncertainties associated with a project or investment. It helps identify the critical inputs or assumptions that have the most significant impact on the financial outcomes, enabling managers to focus on these key drivers and develop strategies to mitigate potential risks. Sensitivity analysis also helps in scenario planning and contingency planning, as it allows managers to assess the sensitivity of outcomes under different scenarios and assess the robustness of the financial projections or forecasts. Furthermore, sensitivity analysis aids in assessing the feasibility of a project or investment by identifying the threshold values or critical points at which the financial outcomes change significantly. Managers can use this information to set realistic targets or determine the level of risk tolerance for a particular project. It also helps in evaluating the sensitivity of the project's viability to changes in market conditions, interest rates, exchange rates, or other external factors. In summary, sensitivity analysis is a financial management technique that evaluates the impact of variations in input variables on the financial outcomes of a project or investment. It provides insights into the risks, uncertainties, and key drivers influencing the financial performance and helps in informed decision-making, scenario planning, and risk management.

Shareholder Equity

Shareholder Equity refers to the residual interest in the assets of a company after deducting liabilities. It represents the ownership interest of the shareholders in the company and is a key measure of a company's financial health and net worth. Shareholder Equity is calculated by subtracting total liabilities from total assets. Total assets include both tangible assets, such as property, plant, and equipment, as well as intangible assets, such as patents and trademarks. Liabilities, on the other hand, include both short-term obligations, such as accounts payable and accrued expenses, as well as long-term debt, such as bonds and loans. Shareholder Equity is an important metric for both investors and creditors. It serves as an indicator of the company's solvency, as it shows the extent to which the company's assets are financed by shareholders' investments rather than by borrowing. A higher level of shareholder equity indicates a greater degree of financial stability and lower risk for investors and creditors. Shareholder Equity is also a measure of a company's net worth or book value. It represents the amount of capital that would be left for shareholders if all the company's assets were sold and all its liabilities were paid off. As such, it reflects the underlying value of the company's operations and assets. Shareholder Equity can be affected by various factors, such as changes in the company's profitability, capital injections from shareholders, dividends paid to shareholders, and changes in the value of the company's assets and liabilities. It can increase if the company generates profits and retains a portion of them, and it can decrease if the company incurs losses or distributes dividends. In summary, Shareholder Equity represents the ownership interest of shareholders in a company and is calculated by subtracting total liabilities from total assets. It serves as a measure of financial health, solvency, and net worth, and is important for both investors and creditors.

Sharpe Ratio

The Sharpe Ratio is a financial management metric used to evaluate the risk-adjusted return of an investment or portfolio. It measures the excess return generated per unit of risk taken by considering both the return and volatility of an investment or portfolio. The formula to calculate the Sharpe Ratio is as follows: Sharpe Ratio = (Rp - Rf) / σp Where, Rp is the expected return of the investment or portfolio, Rf is the risk-free rate of return, σp is the standard deviation of the investment or portfolio's excess return.

Short Interest Ratio

The short interest ratio is a financial metric used to evaluate the level of investor interest in a particular security. It is calculated by dividing the total number of shares sold short by the average daily trading volume. The result indicates the number of days it would take for all short sellers to cover their positions based on the average trading volume. A high short interest ratio suggests a significant amount of pessimism or bearish sentiment in the market. It indicates that many investors are betting against the security, expecting its price to decline. This can be seen as a contrarian indicator, as excessively negative sentiment may indicate an oversold condition and potential buying opportunity.

Short Interest

Short interest in the context of financial management refers to the amount of a particular stock or security that investors have sold short but have not yet been covered or bought back. Short selling is a trading strategy where investors borrow shares from a broker and sell them on the market with the expectation that the price will decline. The intention is to buy back the shares at a later time, ideally at a lower price, and return them to the broker. The concept of short interest is used to measure the level of investor sentiment or market expectation for a particular stock. It is typically expressed as a percentage or a ratio of the total number of shares in the market that have been sold short. High short interest indicates that a significant number of investors are bearish on the stock and anticipate a decline in its price. Conversely, low short interest suggests that there is less pessimism and more confidence in the stock's potential for growth.

Short Sale

A short sale refers to a financial transaction where an investor sells borrowed securities with the intention of buying them back at a lower price to return to the lender. This strategy is typically used by investors who believe that the price of a particular security will decline in the future, allowing them to profit from the difference between the sale price and the repurchase price. When executing a short sale, the investor must first borrow the securities they wish to sell from a broker or another investor who owns them. This borrowing is typically facilitated through a margin account, which allows the investor to borrow a certain percentage of the value of the securities. The borrowed securities are then immediately sold in the market at the prevailing market price. The investor's goal is to buy back the borrowed securities at a lower price before the borrowing period ends, which is usually agreed upon with the lender. Once the borrowed securities are repurchased, they are returned to the lender, and the short sale transaction is closed. The investor profits from the difference between the sale price and the repurchase price, minus any borrowing fees or interest charges. Short selling can be a risky strategy since there is no limit to how much the price of a security can rise. If the price of the security increases significantly, the investor may face substantial losses if they are forced to repurchase the securities at a higher price. To manage this risk, short sellers often place stop-loss orders to automatically repurchase the borrowed securities if the price reaches a certain level. In addition to individual investors, short selling is also employed by institutional investors, hedge funds, and speculators. It can be used to speculate on a stock's decline, hedge against long positions in other securities, or arbitrage price differences between related securities.

Short Selling

Short selling is a financial management strategy that allows investors to profit from the decline in the price of a particular security. In this practice, an investor borrows shares of a stock or other financial instrument from a broker and sells them on the open market, with the expectation that the price of the security will decrease. Short selling involves the investor selling borrowed shares, with the obligation to replace those shares at a later date. After selling the borrowed shares, the investor expects the price of the security to drop, at which point they can repurchase the shares at a lower price. The borrowed shares are then returned to the broker, and the investor pockets the difference in price between the sale and repurchase, minus any fees or interest charges incurred during the borrowing period.

Simple Interest

Simple Interest refers to the interest calculated on the initial principal amount or the borrowed amount, without considering compounding. It is a fundamental concept in financial management that helps determine the additional amount to be paid or earned based on the original investment or loaned amount. Simple Interest is usually calculated using the formula: Interest = Principal x Rate x Time. Here, the Principal is the initial amount of money or investment, the Rate is the annual interest rate (expressed as a decimal), and the Time is the duration for which the money is borrowed or invested (in years).

Sinking Fund Provision

A sinking fund provision is a provision included in a bond or loan agreement that requires the borrower to make periodic payments into a separate account, known as a sinking fund, to repay the principal amount of the loan or bonds over time. These payments are usually made at regular intervals, such as annually or semi-annually, and are used to accumulate funds to retire the debt when it matures. The purpose of a sinking fund provision is to ensure that the borrower has sufficient funds set aside to repay the debt when it becomes due. By making regular payments into the sinking fund, the borrower reduces the risk of being unable to meet its repayment obligations at the end of the loan term. This provides additional security to the lender or bondholders, making the investment more attractive to potential buyers and reducing the interest rate that the borrower must pay.

Sinking Fund

A sinking fund is a financial management strategy used by organizations to set aside funds over a period of time to repay a debt or to finance a future capital expenditure. It is a structured savings plan that helps in the systematic accumulation of funds to meet a specific financial obligation or investment requirement. The purpose of a sinking fund is to ensure that there are sufficient funds available when the time comes to make a payment or investment, thus avoiding the need for a sudden financial burden or the use of external financing. Sinking funds are commonly used by businesses, governments, and other organizations to manage their financial obligations more efficiently. By setting aside a predetermined amount of money regularly in a sinking fund, these entities can spread the financial burden of a debt repayment or capital expenditure over a longer period of time. This helps them avoid an immediate strain on their cash flow and reduces the reliance on external borrowings or unplanned withdrawals from other funds.

Socially Responsible Investing (SRI)

Socially Responsible Investing (SRI) refers to the practice of considering social, environmental, and governance factors alongside financial factors when making investment decisions. It is a strategy that aligns investors' financial goals with their ethical and societal values. SRI takes into account various criteria, also known as Environmental, Social, and Governance (ESG) criteria, to assess the impact of an investment on society and the environment. Environmental criteria evaluate a company's performance in areas such as resource usage, pollution, and climate change. Social criteria assess a company's commitment to human rights, labor practices, and community involvement. Governance criteria examine a company's leadership, executive compensation, and transparency.

Solvency Ratio

The solvency ratio is a financial metric used in the field of financial management to assess a company's ability to meet its long-term obligations. It measures the relationship between a company's long-term debt and its assets, providing insight into its overall financial health and stability. By evaluating the solvency ratio, investors, creditors, and other stakeholders can determine whether a company has the resources necessary to repay its debts and continue operating in the long term. The solvency ratio is calculated by dividing a company's total assets by its total liabilities. Total assets include both current and non-current assets, such as cash, inventory, property, plant, and equipment. Total liabilities encompass all forms of debt and obligations, including long-term loans, bonds, and other liabilities. A higher solvency ratio indicates that a company has a greater ability to meet its long-term obligations. This suggests that the company is financially stable and poses less risk to investors and creditors. Conversely, a lower solvency ratio suggests that a company may struggle to repay its debts, potentially indicating financial distress. The solvency ratio is particularly important for investors and creditors who are evaluating a company's creditworthiness. It helps them assess the risk associated with lending money to or investing in a particular company. For investors, a higher solvency ratio may indicate that a company is a safer investment option. On the other hand, creditors may use the solvency ratio to determine the amount of credit they are willing to extend to a company. A company with a lower solvency ratio may be seen as a riskier borrower, thus limiting the amount of credit available to them. In conclusion, the solvency ratio is a key financial measure used in financial management to assess a company's ability to meet its long-term obligations. It provides valuable insights into a company's financial health and stability, allowing investors, creditors, and other stakeholders to make informed decisions regarding their investments or credit offerings. By calculating the solvency ratio, financial analysts can gain a better understanding of a company's financial position and evaluate its long-term viability.

Sovereign Risk

Sovereign risk refers to the risk associated with the possibility of a government defaulting on its financial obligations or failing to meet its debt repayment obligations. It is a critical concept in financial management as it directly affects the stability and creditworthiness of a country. Essentially, sovereign risk is the risk that a government may not be able to honor its financial commitments due to various reasons such as economic instability, political turmoil, mismanagement of public finances, or external shocks. This risk is particularly relevant when it comes to assessing the creditworthiness of a country or when making investment decisions regarding government bonds or other forms of sovereign debt. Investors and lenders consider sovereign risk when evaluating the risk-reward tradeoff of investing in a particular country. Higher sovereign risk typically leads to higher borrowing costs for the government and lower credit ratings, which in turn can have a negative impact on the overall economy. It can also affect foreign direct investment and the availability of international financing for the government and private sector. Thus, managing and mitigating sovereign risk is crucial for maintaining a healthy and stable financial system. To assess the level of sovereign risk, various factors are taken into consideration, including a country's fiscal position, economic indicators, political stability, institutional strength, and external debt levels. Credit rating agencies play a significant role in evaluating and assigning credit ratings to countries, reflecting their assessment of sovereign risk. These ratings not only affect the borrowing costs of the government but also provide valuable information to investors and lenders. Moreover, countries with a history of defaulting on their obligations or experiencing significant financial crises are often perceived to have higher sovereign risk. Examples of sovereign risk events include debt defaults, currency devaluations, bank failures, and political upheavals. These events can have severe consequences for the affected country, leading to economic recessions, higher borrowing costs, and social unrest. Overall, sovereign risk is a crucial aspect of financial management, as it directly impacts the stability of a country's financial system, its ability to access international financing, and its creditworthiness. Understanding and managing this risk is essential for governments, investors, and lenders to make informed decisions and ensure sustainable economic growth.

Special Drawing Rights (SDR)

Special Drawing Rights (SDR) is a type of international reserve asset that is created by the International Monetary Fund (IMF). It was established in 1969 to supplement the existing official reserves of member countries and to provide a stable and secure form of international liquidity. SDRs are not a currency, but rather a potential claim on the freely usable currencies of IMF member countries. The value of SDRs is determined by a basket of five major currencies: the U.S. dollar, the euro, the Chinese renminbi, the Japanese yen, and the British pound sterling. The weightings of these currencies in the SDR basket are reviewed every five years to ensure they reflect the relative importance of each currency in the world economy. SDRs are allocated to IMF member countries in proportion to their quotas, which are based on the size of their economies and their financial contributions to the Fund. Member countries can use their allocated SDRs to settle international transactions, diversify their reserve holdings, and supplement their existing reserves. SDRs can also be exchanged for freely usable currencies at the discretion of IMF member countries. SDRs serve as a supplement to existing reserve assets, such as gold and foreign exchange reserves. They provide countries with an additional means of meeting their balance of payments needs and can help stabilize their currencies during periods of economic and financial instability. SDRs can also promote international cooperation and strengthen the multilateral monetary system. SDRs are not widely used in everyday transactions and are primarily held by central banks and international financial institutions. However, they play an important role in the global financial system and are considered a key component of the international monetary system.

Speculation

Speculation is a financial management strategy that involves making high-risk investments in the hope of generating significant profits. It is a speculative approach that is based on the anticipation of future market trends and price movements. Speculators, also known as traders or investors, take advantage of market inefficiencies and fluctuations to buy and sell financial assets such as stocks, commodities, currencies, and derivatives. They do not have a long-term investment horizon but rather focus on short-term profit opportunities.

Spot Market

A spot market is a financial market where financial instruments, such as stocks, bonds, commodities, and currencies, are traded for immediate settlement and delivery, on the spot. In other words, it is a market where assets are bought and sold for cash and delivered immediately, rather than for future delivery. Participants in the spot market include individuals, corporations, financial institutions, and governments. They trade in various financial instruments based on their investment objectives, risk appetite, and market conditions. One of the key features of the spot market is its liquidity. Since transactions are settled immediately, buyers and sellers can easily enter and exit positions, making it easier to buy and sell assets. This liquidity makes the spot market attractive to investors and traders, as it allows for efficient price discovery and quick execution of trades. Another important characteristic of the spot market is its transparency. Prices are publicly available and determined by the forces of supply and demand. This transparency ensures fair and competitive pricing, reducing the likelihood of market manipulation and providing market participants with equal access to information. The spot market also provides a useful benchmark for valuing financial instruments. For example, the spot price of a commodity, such as gold or oil, is often used as a reference for pricing futures contracts or options. By comparing the current spot price to the price of a futures contract, investors can assess the market's expectations for future price movements. Overall, the spot market plays a crucial role in financial management by providing a platform for the immediate buying and selling of financial instruments, liquidity, transparency, and price discovery. It serves as a foundation for other financial markets, such as the futures market, where participants can enter into contracts for future delivery based on the conditions observed in the spot market.

Spot Rate

A spot rate, in the context of Financial Management, refers to the current exchange rate at which one currency can be exchanged for another currency. It is the rate at which immediate transactions are settled for delivery of currencies in the spot or current market. The spot rate is determined by the foreign exchange market, where currencies are bought and sold. It represents the value of one currency in terms of another currency and is influenced by various factors such as supply and demand, interest rates, inflation, and economic indicators of the respective countries. Spot rates are commonly used in international trade and investment to determine the value of goods and services, as well as to assess the profitability of foreign investments. They play a crucial role in foreign exchange risk management as they provide a benchmark for pricing and hedging currency exposures. Spot rates are quoted for major currency pairs such as USD/EUR, USD/JPY, and GBP/USD. The first currency in the pair is called the base currency, and the second currency is called the quote currency. For example, in the USD/EUR currency pair, the spot rate indicates how many Euros can be obtained per US Dollar. Market participants, such as banks, financial institutions, corporations, and individual traders, closely monitor spot rates to make informed decisions related to foreign exchange transactions. They rely on real-time spot rate information provided by various sources including financial news portals, online trading platforms, and foreign exchange brokers. Spot rates are different from forward rates, which represent the exchange rate for future delivery of currencies. While spot rates reflect the current market conditions, forward rates incorporate interest rate differentials between two currencies and expectations of future exchange rate movements. In summary, the spot rate is the current exchange rate at which currencies are traded in the spot market. It is determined by market forces and is widely used in financial management for international transactions and risk management purposes.

Stakeholder Equity

Stakeholder equity, also known as shareholders' equity or owner's equity, refers to the residual interest in the assets of a company after deducting liabilities. It represents the ownership interest of the shareholders in the company's assets and is a key component of the financial position of the organization. Stakeholder equity can be calculated by subtracting the total liabilities of the company from its total assets. It encompasses the initial investments made by shareholders, as well as any additional capital contributions made over time. It also includes retained earnings, which are the accumulated profits of the company that have not been distributed to shareholders in the form of dividends. Stakeholder equity is an important measure of the financial health and value of a company. It represents the shareholders' claim on the company's assets and shows the net worth of the organization. A higher stakeholder equity indicates a stronger financial position and increases the confidence of investors and lenders in the company. Stakeholder equity is influenced by various factors, such as the profitability of the company, the amount of dividends paid to shareholders, and the issuance or repurchase of company's stock. If the company generates profits, it increases its stakeholder equity, as retained earnings accumulate. Conversely, if the company incurs losses or distributes dividends, stakeholder equity decreases. Stakeholder equity serves as an important metric for evaluating the performance and financial stability of a company. It is often analyzed in conjunction with other financial ratios and indicators to assess the overall value and potential of an organization. Furthermore, stakeholders, including shareholders, creditors, and potential investors, closely monitor changes in stakeholder equity to make informed decisions regarding their involvement in the company.

Standard Deviation

The standard deviation is a statistical measure used in financial management to quantify the volatility or risk associated with an investment or portfolio. It provides a measure of how spread out the returns or prices of an asset or portfolio are relative to the average or expected return. In financial management, standard deviation helps investors and financial managers assess the level of uncertainty or risk that accompanies an investment. It is a key tool for evaluating the risk and return tradeoff of different investments and portfolios. Standard deviation is calculated by taking the square root of the variance, which is the average of the squared deviations from the mean. It is expressed in the same units as the original data, such as percentage for return data or currency for price data. A higher standard deviation indicates a higher degree of variability or dispersion of returns, indicating higher risk, while a lower standard deviation suggests less variability and lower risk. Standard deviation is particularly useful for comparing the risk of multiple investments or portfolios. It allows investors to assess the level of risk associated with different assets or investment options and make more informed decisions based on their risk tolerance and investment objectives. Financial managers also use standard deviation to evaluate the risk and return characteristics of a portfolio. By calculating the standard deviation of a portfolio, managers can understand the level of risk the portfolio is exposed to and make adjustments to achieve the desired risk profile. In summary, the standard deviation is a statistical measure that quantifies the volatility or risk associated with an investment or portfolio. It helps investors and financial managers assess the level of uncertainty and variability in returns, aiding in the evaluation and comparison of different investment options or portfolios.

Statement Of Financial Position

The Statement of Financial Position, also known as the Balance Sheet, is a financial statement that provides a snapshot of an organization's financial health at a specific point in time. It presents the company's assets, liabilities, and shareholders' equity. Assets represent the resources owned or controlled by the organization. These include cash, inventory, property, equipment, investments, and accounts receivable. Assets are classified into current assets, which are expected to be converted into cash within one year, and non-current (or long-term) assets, which have a longer useful life. Liabilities, on the other hand, are the company's obligations or debts, such as loans, accounts payable, and salaries payable. Like assets, liabilities are also classified into current liabilities, which are due within one year, and non-current liabilities, which are due beyond one year. Shareholders' equity represents the residual interest in the assets of the company after deducting liabilities. It includes the issued capital or common stock, retained earnings, and any other reserves or surplus. This amount represents the shareholders' ownership stake in the company. The Statement of Financial Position follows the fundamental accounting equation: Assets = Liabilities + Shareholders' Equity. This equation must always be in balance, as it reflects the company's resources and the claims against those resources. The Statement of Financial Position provides important information for assessing the financial position and performance of a company. It helps stakeholders, including investors, creditors, and regulators, to evaluate the organization's liquidity, solvency, and overall financial stability. By analyzing the different components of the Statement of Financial Position, investors can assess the company's ability to generate future cash flows, its level of debt, and the extent of its ownership by shareholders. Creditors, on the other hand, can determine whether the company has sufficient assets to cover its liabilities and repay its debts. Overall, the Statement of Financial Position is a crucial document that summarizes the financial status of a company and provides valuable insights into its financial health. It allows stakeholders to make informed decisions and evaluate the organization's potential risks and opportunities.

Stochastic Calculus

Stochastic calculus is a branch of mathematics that deals with the modeling and analysis of random processes. In the context of financial management, stochastic calculus is used to understand and quantify the uncertainty associated with financial variables, such as stock prices

206

and interest rates. The key concept in stochastic calculus is the stochastic differential equation (SDE). An SDE is a differential equation driven by a stochastic process, typically represented as Brownian motion or a general stochastic process. The SDE describes the evolution of a financial variable over time, taking into account both deterministic and random components.

Stock Broker

A stock broker is a professional who acts as an intermediary between buyers and sellers of stocks and other securities. They facilitate the buying and selling of financial instruments on behalf of their clients, which may include individual investors, corporations, or institutional investors. Stock brokers play a vital role in the financial markets by providing liquidity and efficiency. They bring together buyers and sellers, matching orders and executing trades. In addition to facilitating transactions, stock brokers also offer a range of other services to their clients, such as investment advice, research, and analysis.

Stock Dividend

A stock dividend is a distribution of additional shares given to existing shareholders of a company based on their ownership of common stock. It is a way for companies to distribute their earnings without utilizing cash resources. When a company declares a stock dividend, it announces a certain percentage or ratio by which the existing shares will be increased. For example, a 10% stock dividend means that for every ten shares held, an investor will receive one additional share. The total number of shares outstanding will increase, but the proportionate ownership remains the same for each shareholder. Stock dividends can be issued by both public and private companies. They are typically issued by companies that want to reward their shareholders without using cash or when they have a surplus of shares available. Companies may also choose to issue stock dividends to maintain their current level of dividends during periods of financial difficulty. Receiving a stock dividend does not change the total value of an investor's holdings in the company. While the number of shares increases, the price per share usually decreases proportionately. The value of the stock dividends received is equal to the value of the additional shares obtained. Stock dividends have accounting implications as well. The value of the stock dividend is transferred from retained earnings to the paid-in capital or common stock account on the balance sheet. This accounting entry reflects the transfer of a portion of the company's retained earnings to the shareholders in the form of additional shares.

Stock Exchange

A stock exchange is a regulated marketplace where securities such as stocks, bonds, and derivatives are bought and sold. It provides a transparent and efficient platform for companies and individuals to raise capital, trade securities, and manage risk. In a stock exchange, buyers and sellers come together and trade securities based on the prevailing market prices. The exchange ensures that the transactions are executed in a fair and orderly manner, with proper adherence to rules and regulations. This helps to maintain confidence and integrity in the market, protecting the interests of investors. One of the primary functions of a stock exchange is to facilitate the initial public offering (IPO) process. When a company decides to go public, it issues shares to the public for the first time. The stock exchange provides a platform for the company to list its shares and raise capital from investors. This aids in the growth and expansion of businesses, as they can access funds for various purposes such as research and development, acquisitions, and debt repayment. Additionally, a stock exchange serves as a secondary market, enabling investors to trade already issued securities. This liquidity factor is crucial for investors as it allows them to buy and sell securities at any time based on their investment objectives. It also provides an avenue for price discovery, where the supply and demand dynamics determine the fair market value of securities. Stock exchanges play a vital role in the overall economy by providing an efficient capital allocation mechanism. They enable savers to invest funds in productive businesses, which in turn drives economic growth and job creation. The exchange also promotes corporate governance principles, ensuring that companies follow transparency, accountability, and disclosure requirements. Overall, a stock exchange serves as a critical infrastructure for financial markets, providing a platform for companies to raise capital and investors to trade securities efficiently. By facilitating the buying and selling of securities in a regulated environment, it helps support economic growth, encourage investment, and foster confidence in the financial system.

Stock Split

A stock split is a corporate action in which a company divides its existing shares into multiple shares. This process increases the number of shares outstanding while reducing the price per share proportionately. The purpose of a stock split is to make shares more affordable and increase liquidity in the market. When a company decides to implement a stock split, it generally chooses a ratio, such as 2-for-1 or 3-for-1, which means that for every existing share, shareholders will receive two or three additional shares, respectively. For example, in a 2-for-1 stock split, if an investor owns 100 shares of a company, they would receive 200 additional shares, resulting in a total of 300 shares. Stock splits have no impact on the overall value of an investor's holdings. Although the number of shares increases, the total value of the shares remains the same. In other words, if an investor owns 1% of a company's shares before a stock split, they will still own 1% of the shares after the split. Stock splits are typically implemented by companies that have seen their share price rise significantly, typically trading at a high nominal value. By reducing the share price, the company aims to attract a wider range of investors who may be deterred by a high price tag. Additionally, the increased liquidity resulting from the higher number of shares can make it easier for investors to buy and sell shares in the market. Overall, stock splits are a way for companies to manage their share price and increase accessibility for investors. By dividing existing shares into multiple shares, companies aim to create a more liquid market and make shares more affordable for a broader range of investors.

Stockbroker

A stockbroker is an individual or a firm that facilitates the buying and selling of securities on behalf of clients. They play a crucial role in financial management by connecting investors with the stock market, allowing them to invest in stocks, bonds, options, and other financial instruments. Stockbrokers are licensed professionals who are knowledgeable about the inner workings of financial markets and are officially registered with regulatory bodies. They act as intermediaries between investors and the stock exchanges, executing trades and providing valuable advice and recommendations to their clients.

Straddle

A straddle is a financial management strategy used by investors to speculate on the future price movement of an underlying asset. It involves the simultaneous purchase or sale of two options contracts with the same expiration date and strike price, but with opposite positions (one call option and one put option). The purpose of a straddle is to profit from a significant price movement in either direction, regardless of the underlying asset's actual movement. If the price of the asset rises above the strike price of the call option, the investor profits from the call option's value increase. Conversely, if the price falls below the strike price of the put option, the investor profits from the put option's value increase.

Strategic Financial Management

Strategic Financial Management refers to the process of making long-term financial decisions that align with an organization's overall goals and objectives. It involves the careful analysis, planning, and control of an organization's financial resources to ensure the creation of value and sustainable growth. In the context of financial management, strategic financial management focuses on the strategic aspects of finance rather than just the operational or transactional aspects. It goes beyond simple budgeting and accounting to consider the broader implications of financial decisions on the organization's competitive position and future prospects. The core objective of strategic financial management is to maximize shareholder value by optimizing the use of financial resources. This is done by identifying and evaluating investment opportunities, determining the optimal capital structure, managing financial risks, and effectively allocating resources across various projects or business units. Strategic financial management involves a systematic approach to financial decision-making, which includes: 1. Financial Analysis: This involves assessing the organization's financial performance, analyzing financial statements, and identifying trends or patterns that can inform strategic decisions. 2. Financial Planning: Once the financial analysis is complete, strategic financial management involves creating a comprehensive financial plan that aligns with the organization's strategic objectives. This plan includes setting financial goals, developing budgets, and forecasting future financial performance. 3. Investment Decisions: Strategic financial management also involves evaluating different investment opportunities, assessing their risks and potential returns, and choosing the ones that create the most value for the organization. 4. Financing Decisions: Another important aspect of strategic financial management is determining the optimal mix of debt and equity financing to fund investments. This includes evaluating different sources of funding, negotiating with lenders or investors, and managing the organization's capital structure. 5. Risk Management: Strategic financial management includes identifying and managing financial risks, such as interest rate risk, currency risk, or commodity price risk. This involves implementing risk mitigation strategies, using hedging techniques, and monitoring market conditions. In summary, strategic financial management is a vital function within an organization that drives value creation and ensures the achievement of long-term financial goals. It involves the strategic allocation of financial resources, rigorous analysis and planning, and effective risk management to maximize shareholder value and support sustainable growth.

Strategic Financial Planning

Strategic financial planning refers to the process of developing and implementing long-term financial strategies that align with an organization's overall goals and objectives. It involves analyzing the current financial position of the organization, identifying potential risks and opportunities, and formulating a plan to optimize financial resources. The primary purpose of strategic financial planning is to ensure the organization's financial stability, profitability, and growth. It involves making informed decisions regarding the allocation of financial resources, including capital budgeting, investment decisions, and funding sources.

Structured Finance

Structured finance is a specialized area of financial management that involves the creation and arrangement of complex financial instruments or securities with customized cash flow arrangements. These instruments are designed to meet specific needs of both issuers and investors by providing tailored risk and return profiles. The main objective of structured finance is to transform illiquid assets or future cash flows into securities that can be traded in the financial markets, thereby increasing liquidity and access to capital for companies or individuals. This process typically involves pooling together a group of similar assets, such as mortgages or loans, and securitizing them into bonds or other tradable instruments. Structured finance transactions often utilize special purpose vehicles (SPVs) or trusts to isolate the financial risks associated with the underlying assets from the issuer's balance sheet. These vehicles serve as legal entities that hold and manage the assets, issuing securities backed by the cash flows generated from those assets. One of the key features of structured finance is the use of tranching, which refers to the division of the cash flows from the underlying assets into different classes or tranches with different levels of risk and return. This allows investors to choose the tranche that matches their risk appetite and investment objectives. Another important aspect of structured finance is the application of various credit enhancement techniques to mitigate risks and improve the creditworthiness of the securities. These techniques can include overcollateralization, subordination, and the use of credit derivatives or insurance. Structured finance has gained popularity over the years due to its ability to efficiently allocate risks and maximize the value of underlying assets. It has been widely used in various sectors, such as real estate, infrastructure, corporate finance, and consumer finance. In summary, structured finance is a specialized area of financial management that involves the creation, securitization, and trading of customized financial instruments, allowing for efficient risk allocation and increased access to capital for issuers and investors.

Subordinated Debt

Subordinated debt refers to a type of debt that ranks below other debts in the event of bankruptcy or liquidation. It is also known as junior debt or subordinated debentures. In financial management, subordinated debt plays a crucial role in determining the capital structure of a company. Unlike senior debt, which has a higher priority, subordinated debt holders have a lower claim on the company's assets. In the event of bankruptcy or liquidation, senior debt holders are paid first, followed by subordinated debt holders. This means that subordinated debt holders have a higher risk of not being fully repaid compared to senior debt holders. Subordinated debt typically offers higher interest rates to compensate for the increased risk.

This makes it an attractive option for investors seeking higher returns. However, it is important for investors to carefully assess the creditworthiness of the company issuing the subordinated debt before investing, as the risk of default is higher. From the company's perspective, subordinated debt can be a valuable tool for raising capital. It allows companies to access additional funding while maintaining the seniority of existing debt. This can be particularly beneficial for companies with limited collateral or weaker credit ratings. Subordinated debt can also provide flexibility in capital structure management. By incorporating subordinated debt into their capital structure, companies can optimize the mix of debt and equity to achieve their desired level of financial leverage. In conclusion, subordinated debt is a type of debt that ranks below other debts in terms of priority. It carries a higher risk for investors but can offer attractive returns. For companies, subordinated debt is a useful tool for raising capital and managing their capital structure. However, it is important to carefully evaluate the creditworthiness of the issuer before investing in subordinated debt.

Supply Chain Finance

Supply Chain Finance refers to the financial management practice of optimizing the flow of capital throughout the supply chain to enhance efficiency and mitigate risks. It involves collaboration between suppliers, manufacturers, distributors, and customers to effectively manage the financial aspects of the supply chain. The primary objective of Supply Chain Finance is to provide working capital for suppliers and optimize cash flow for all stakeholders in the supply chain. By improving cash flow, it allows for quick and efficient completion of transactions, reduces the need for excessive inventory, and minimizes financial risks associated with payment delays or defaults.

Swap Rate

The swap rate, in the context of financial management, refers to the fixed rate of interest that is exchanged between two parties in a swap agreement. A swap is a financial contract between two parties, typically banks or corporations, in which they agree to exchange cash flows or financial instruments. In the case of an interest rate swap, the two parties agree to exchange interest payments based on a predetermined reference rate, such as LIBOR (London Interbank Offered Rate). The swap rate is the fixed interest rate that one party agrees to pay the other party for the duration of the swap. It is usually determined at the inception of the swap based on the prevailing market rates. The swap rate is often quoted as an annual percentage rate (APR). The swap rate serves as a benchmark for calculating the interest rate payments in a swap agreement. For example, if Party A agrees to pay a fixed swap rate of 5% and Party B agrees to pay a variable interest rate based on LIBOR, the actual interest payment made by Party A will depend on the difference between the swap rate and the prevailing LIBOR rate. The swap rate is influenced by various factors, including the creditworthiness of the parties involved, the term of the swap agreement, and macroeconomic conditions. Market expectations about future interest rate movements also play a role in determining the swap rate. If market participants expect interest rates to increase in the future, the swap rate may be higher to compensate for this perceived risk. Swap rates are widely used in financial markets for hedging purposes. They allow parties to manage interest rate risk by converting variable-rate debt into fixed-rate debt or vice versa. By entering into a swap agreement, a party can effectively control their exposure to interest rate fluctuations and stabilize their cash flows. In summary, the swap rate is the fixed interest rate exchanged between parties in an interest rate swap. It serves as a reference rate for calculating interest payments and is influenced by various factors such as creditworthiness, term, and market expectations. Swap agreements and their associated swap rates are an essential tool for managing interest rate risk in financial management.

Systematic Investment Plan (SIP)

A Systematic Investment Plan (SIP) is a financial management strategy that allows individuals to regularly invest a fixed amount of money in mutual funds or other financial instruments. It is a disciplined approach to investing, where a predetermined amount is deducted from the investor's bank account at fixed intervals, such as monthly or quarterly, and invested in the chosen scheme. The main objective of a SIP is to inculcate a habit of regular saving and investment, regardless of market conditions or the investor's financial situation. By investing a fixed amount regularly, investors can take advantage of the power of compounding and benefit from the

210

volatility of the markets. SIPs are particularly useful for individuals who may not have a large lump sum to invest but still want to participate in the financial markets. One of the key advantages of SIPs is that they help mitigate the risk of market timing. Since investments are made at regular intervals, investors do not have to worry about the timing of the market. They benefit from a strategy known as rupee-cost averaging, where they buy more units when prices are low and fewer units when prices are high. This ensures that the investor's average cost per unit is lower over time, reducing the impact of market fluctuations. SIPs are known to instill discipline in investors by encouraging regular savings and investment. It helps individuals overcome the emotional biases associated with investing, such as trying to time the market or panicking during market downturns. By automating the investment process, individuals are less likely to succumb to impulsive decisions, which can negatively impact their long-term investment goals. Furthermore, SIPs offer flexibility to investors by allowing them to increase or decrease the investment amount as per their financial capability. They can also choose to stop the SIP anytime without any penalty, providing them with liquidity when needed. SIPs are available in various mutual funds and other financial instruments, catering to different risk profiles and investment objectives. In summary, a Systematic Investment Plan (SIP) is a disciplined and regular investment strategy that allows individuals to invest a fixed amount at regular intervals. It helps individuals overcome the challenges of market timing, instills discipline in saving and investment, and offers flexibility to investors to meet their financial goals.

Systematic Risk

The term systematic risk, also known as market risk or undiversifiable risk, refers to the portion of overall risk that cannot be eliminated by diversification. It is a fundamental concept in financial management that measures the uncertainty or volatility of an investment's returns due to factors that affect the overall market or economy. Systematic risk is inherent in every investment and is caused by macroeconomic factors such as interest rates, inflation changes in government regulations, geopolitical events, and overall market conditions. Unlike idiosyncratic risk, which is specific to a particular company or industry and can be mitigated through diversification, systematic risk affects the entire market and cannot be diversified away. Investors are exposed to systematic risk regardless of the specific investment they choose. It is a risk that is beyond the control of individual investors or companies and is considered to be the minimum level of risk that every investor must bear. As a result, it is widely regarded as a crucial consideration when making investment decisions and portfolio management strategies. One of the most common measures of systematic risk is beta, which is calculated by comparing the returns of an investment to the returns of a benchmark, such as the overall market or a market index. A beta of 1 indicates that the investment's returns move in tandem with the benchmark, while a beta greater than 1 implies that the investment is more volatile than the benchmark. Conversely, a beta less than 1 suggests that the investment is less volatile than the benchmark. Understanding and managing systematic risk is essential for financial managers and investors. By diversifying across different asset classes, industries, and geographic regions, investors can reduce the impact of systematic risk on their investment portfolios. However, it is important to note that systematic risk can never be completely eliminated. Therefore, financial managers must carefully evaluate and assess the potential impact of systematic risk on investment decisions and regularly monitor market conditions to ensure the alignment of investment strategies with overall risk tolerance and objectives.

Tax Deduction

A tax deduction is a financial benefit allowed by the government that reduces the taxable income of an individual or business entity. It is an expense or reduction in income that can be used to lower the total amount of tax owed to the government. Tax deductions are implemented as incentives to encourage certain behaviors or support specific industries or activities. They are designed to reduce the tax burden on individuals and businesses and promote economic growth. There are various types of tax deductions available, including deductions for medical expenses, mortgage interest, charitable contributions, education expenses, business expenses, and retirement contributions. These deductions can be claimed by taxpayers if they meet certain eligibility criteria and follow the appropriate procedures. For individuals, tax deductions are often claimed on the annual tax return form, such as Form 1040 in the United States. The total amount of deductions claimed directly reduces the individual's taxable income, resulting in a lower tax liability. This means that individuals with more deductions will pay less in taxes.

Businesses also have the opportunity to claim various deductions to reduce their taxable income. These may include deductions for expenses related to operating the business, such as rent, utilities, salaries, and advertising. Businesses can also deduct expenses related to investments, research and development, and environmental initiatives. It is important to note that tax deductions are not the same as tax credits. While deductions reduce the taxable income, tax credits directly reduce the amount of tax owed. Tax credits are generally more valuable than deductions as they provide a dollar-for-dollar reduction in the tax liability. In conclusion, a tax deduction is a provision in the tax code that allows individuals and businesses to reduce their taxable income, thereby reducing the amount of tax owed. By taking advantage of eligible deductions, taxpayers can effectively lower their overall tax burden and potentially save money.

Tax Deferred

Tax deferred refers to a financial management strategy where individuals or businesses can postpone paying taxes on their income or investments until a later date, typically during retirement. This allows them to take advantage of potential tax savings by deferring the tax liability to a future period when their income or tax rate may be lower. One common example of tax deferral is through the use of retirement accounts, such as 401(k) plans or Individual Retirement Accounts (IRAs). Contributions made to these accounts are generally tax-deductible, meaning they reduce the individual's taxable income in the year of contribution. The investment earnings within the account also grow tax-free, without incurring any annual taxes on dividends, interest, or capital gains. While the individual or business does not pay taxes on the contributed amount and the investment earnings right away, they will be eventually taxed when they withdraw the money from the retirement account. Withdrawals from retirement accounts are typically treated as ordinary income and are subject to income tax at the individual's or business's applicable tax rate at that time. However, by deferring the taxes, individuals or businesses may benefit from a lower tax rate during retirement when their overall income may be lower than during their working years. Besides retirement accounts, other forms of tax-deferred investments include annuities, certain insurance policies, and certain types of real estate investments. These investments allow individuals or businesses to delay paying taxes on the growth or income from these investments until a future date. It is important to note that while tax deferral offers potential tax advantages, it does not eliminate or reduce the overall tax liability. It simply postpones the payment of taxes to a later time. Therefore, individuals or businesses must carefully consider the tax implications and evaluate whether tax deferral aligns with their long-term financial goals and objectives.

Tax Efficiency

Tax efficiency refers to the ability of a financial management strategy or investment to minimize the impact of taxes on returns. It involves making decisions that can help reduce the tax liability, maximizing after-tax returns, and optimizing wealth accumulation. Efficient tax management is crucial in financial management as taxes can significantly erode investment returns and affect the overall profitability of a business or individual. By implementing tax-efficient strategies, such as tax planning, tax-efficient investing, and utilizing tax advantages, individuals and businesses can minimize tax expenses and increase net income or wealth.

Tax Evasion

Tax evasion is a fraudulent practice of intentionally avoiding the payment of taxes owed to taxing authorities by illegally manipulating or misrepresenting financial information. It involves the deliberate concealment of income, profits, assets, or the inflation of expenses to reduce the tax liability. Individuals, businesses, or organizations engage in tax evasion with the intention of unlawfully reducing their tax liability or completely escaping their tax obligations. This illegal activity is often carried out through various means such as underreporting income, making false deductions and expenses, hiding assets, or using offshore accounts to avoid detection.

Tax Haven

A tax haven refers to a country or jurisdiction that offers individuals or businesses a variety of financial benefits, typically in the form of lower tax rates or a lack of certain taxes. These tax benefits are enticing to individuals and corporations seeking to minimize their tax liability and maximize their profits. Tax havens typically have relaxed regulations and opaque financial systems, which allow individuals and businesses to easily conceal their income or assets from tax authorities. Tax havens attract both legitimate businesses and individuals looking for legitimate tax planning opportunities, as well as those engaging in illegal activities such as tax evasion, money laundering, or hiding illicitly obtained wealth. The specific benefits offered by tax havens may include low or zero income tax rates, no or minimal capital gains taxes, no inheritance or wealth taxes, and privacy and confidentiality laws that protect the identities and transactions of individuals and corporations.

Tax Shield

Tax Shield refers to a reduction in taxable income due to the use of various tax deductions, credits, and exemptions provided by the tax code. It represents a financial advantage for companies and individuals as it enables them to lower their tax liability, resulting in increased after-tax cash flows. The concept of tax shield is rooted in the principle that taxes are based on taxable income, which considers both gross income and allowable deductions. By strategically utilizing tax deductions and credits, taxpayers can reduce their taxable income and consequently pay less in taxes. In the context of financial management, tax shield plays a crucial role in determining the net present value (NPV) of a project or investment. The NPV reflects the difference between the present value of cash inflows (such as revenues and tax savings) and the present value of cash outflows (such as expenses and investments). Tax shield affects the cash inflow component of the NPV calculation by reducing the amount of taxes paid, thus increasing the after-tax cash flows. One of the most common forms of tax shield is the deduction of interest expenses on debt financing. Companies that borrow money to finance their operations or investments can deduct the interest paid on the loans from their taxable income. This deduction decreases the amount of income subject to tax, resulting in a tax shield. Similarly, individuals can often claim deductions for mortgage interest payments on their primary residences, leading to a tax shield. Moreover, depreciation is another significant tax shield for businesses. Depreciation allows companies to deduct the cost of their fixed assets over their useful life, recognizing the gradual decline in value and wear and tear. This deduction reduces taxable income and generates a tax shield for the company.

Technical Analysis

Technical analysis is a method used in financial management to forecast the future price movements of financial instruments, such as stocks, bonds, and commodities, based on historical market data. It relies on the belief that historical price patterns can provide insight into future market trends. Technical analysts use various tools and techniques to analyze past market data, including charts, graphs, and mathematical indicators. These tools help them identify trends, patterns, and other statistical relationships that may indicate potential future price movements. By studying these patterns and trends, technical analysts attempt to make predictions about future price movements and to identify buying or selling opportunities.

Technical Default

A technical default in financial management refers to a situation where a borrower fails to meet the specific terms and conditions outlined in a loan agreement or bond contract. This occurs when the borrower is unable to make timely payments of principal and interest, violates a covenant or provision in the agreement, or breaches any other requirement specified in the contract. When a borrower is in technical default, it does not mean that they have completely stopped making payments or have defaulted on the entire amount owed. Instead, it signifies that they have violated certain terms of the agreement, often resulting in penalties or adverse consequences.

Terminal Value

Terminal value, in the context of financial management, refers to the estimated future value of an investment or a business at the end of a specific period. It is often used in valuation techniques such as discounted cash flow (DCF) analysis to determine the overall worth of an investment or project. The terminal value is based on the assumption that the investment or business will continue to generate cash flows beyond the explicit forecast period. It represents the present value of all future cash flows that occur after the forecast period, typically using a perpetual growth rate.

Thin Market

A thin market in the context of financial management refers to a market with low trading activity, low liquidity, and a limited number of buyers and sellers. In a thin market, there is a scarcity of buyers and sellers for a particular financial instrument, leading to wider bid-ask spreads and increased price volatility. Thin markets can occur for various reasons, including limited investor interest, low trading volumes, or lack of information or transparency. For example, a thinly traded stock may have a small number of outstanding shares and a limited number of investors actively trading the stock. In contrast, a heavily traded stock would have a large number of shares outstanding and a high level of investor participation.

Time Deposit

A Time Deposit, also known as a Fixed Deposit or Certificate of Deposit, is a financial instrument that allows individuals or businesses to deposit a specific amount of money with a bank or financial institution for a predetermined period of time. When making a Time Deposit, the depositor agrees to keep the money in the account for the agreed-upon term, which can vary from a few months to several years. In return for this commitment, the bank pays the depositor a predetermined interest rate on the deposited amount. Time Deposits are considered to be low-risk investments since they offer a guaranteed return and are typically insured by government deposit insurance schemes. Unlike regular savings accounts, Time Deposits have a fixed maturity date, and withdrawing the funds before this date may result in penalties or loss of interest. Time Deposits are commonly used by individuals and businesses as a means to save money, earn interest, and achieve financial goals. They are suitable for individuals who have excess funds and want to earn a higher rate of interest than a regular savings account can offer. Time Deposits are also used by businesses to preserve capital and meet short-term cash flow needs. Key features of Time Deposits include a fixed interest rate, a fixed term, and automatic renewal options. The interest rate offered on a Time Deposit is typically higher than that of a savings account or a checking account, making it an attractive option for individuals seeking higher returns on their savings. At the end of the Time Deposit term, the depositor has the option to roll over the deposit for a new term or withdraw the funds along with the accrued interest. If the depositor chooses to withdraw the funds, they can either receive a check or request a direct transfer to their bank account. In conclusion, Time Deposits are financial instruments that offer individuals and businesses the opportunity to earn a guaranteed return on their savings over a fixed period of time. They provide a secure and low-risk investment option, and the interest earned can be an additional source of income or used to accomplish financial objectives.

Time Horizon

The time horizon in financial management refers to the duration of time that an investor or a company plans to hold an investment or a project. It is an essential concept in financial decision-making as it directly influences the risk and return characteristics of the investment. The time horizon can be short-term, medium-term, or long-term, and it varies depending on the financial objectives, investment goals, and the nature of the investment. Short-term time horizons typically range from a few months to a year, medium-term time horizons can be several years, and long-term time horizons can extend over decades.

Time Value Of Money (TVM)

The Time Value of Money (TVM) is a fundamental concept in financial management that states that the value of money today is worth more than the same amount of money in the future. This concept is based on the premise that money has the potential to earn interest or generate returns over time. According to the TVM concept, a dollar today is worth more than a dollar tomorrow because of the potential to invest that dollar and earn a return. This is because money has the ability to grow or appreciate over time due to factors such as inflation, interest rates, and investment opportunities.

Time-Weighted Rate Of Return (TWR)

The Time-Weighted Rate of Return (TWR) is a measure used in financial management to calculate the performance of an investment portfolio over a specific time period. It is a geometric method that accounts for the impact of external cash flows and provides an unbiased assessment of the investment manager's performance. TWR is calculated by dividing the ending value of the portfolio by the beginning value and applying the appropriate geometric formula. The resulting rate of return is time-weighted because it takes into consideration the timing and size of cash flows into and out of the portfolio. By eliminating the distortion caused by cash flows, TWR allows for the comparison of different portfolios and investment managers. TWR is particularly useful in evaluating the performance of mutual funds, pension funds, and other investment portfolios that experience frequent cash inflows and outflows. It provides a more accurate measure of investment performance compared to other methods, such as the simple rate of return or the money-weighted rate of return, which can be influenced by the timing and magnitude of cash flows. One of the key advantages of TWR is that it enables investors to focus on the investment manager's skill and ability to generate returns, rather than being influenced by the timing of their own contributions or withdrawals. It is also a fair measure when comparing the performance of two investment managers with different investment styles or strategies. It is important to note that TWR does not take into consideration the impact of taxes or transaction costs. These factors can affect the actual return that investors receive and should be considered when assessing the overall performance of an investment portfolio. Additionally, TWR may not accurately reflect an individual investor's return if they do not hold the investment for the entire time period used in the calculation.

Time-Weighted Rate Of Return

The time-weighted rate of return is a measure used in financial management to assess the performance of an investment portfolio. It takes into account the different amounts of time that the investor's capital is invested in various assets. The time-weighted rate of return is calculated by determining the rate of return for each sub period and then combining these sub-period returns to get the overall rate of return for the entire period. This calculation method helps to eliminate the bias that can be introduced by changes in the amount of capital invested in the portfolio over time. By using the time-weighted rate of return, investors can evaluate the performance of their portfolio without being influenced by their own investment decisions. This metric is particularly useful for comparing the performance of different investment managers or strategies. For example, let's say an investor has a portfolio of stocks and bonds. The investor decides to invest $10,000 in stocks for the first six months of the year and then adds an additional $5,000 to the portfolio for the remaining six months, but this time in bonds. The time-weighted rate of return would calculate the rate of return for the stocks for the first six months and the rate of return for the bonds for the second six months separately, and then combine these two rates to get the overall rate of return for the year. In conclusion, the time-weighted rate of return is a useful tool in financial management for evaluating the performance of an investment portfolio. By considering the different time periods and their respective rates of return, this metric provides a more accurate assessment of portfolio performance and allows for fair comparisons between different investment strategies.

Total Asset Turnover Ratio

Total Asset Turnover Ratio is a financial ratio that measures the efficiency with which a company utilizes its assets to generate revenue. It is a key indicator of the company's operational performance and its ability to generate sales from its investments in assets. The Total Asset Turnover Ratio is calculated by dividing the company's net sales or revenue by its average total assets. Net sales or revenue represents the total amount of money generated by the company from its normal business operations, while average total assets represent the average value of all the assets owned by the company during a specific period. The formula for calculating the Total Asset Turnover Ratio is as follows: Total Asset Turnover Ratio = Net Sales / Average Total Assets A high Total Asset Turnover Ratio indicates that the company is effectively utilizing its assets to generate revenue, which implies that it is operating efficiently. On the other hand, a low Total Asset Turnover Ratio suggests that the company is not generating enough sales from its investments in assets, indicating inefficiency in its operations. The Total Asset Turnover Ratio is particularly useful for comparing the operational performance of companies within the same industry. It helps investors and analysts assess how well a company is utilizing its assets compared to its competitors. A higher ratio indicates that a company is generating more revenue per unit of assets, which can be a favorable sign for investors. However, it is important to note that the interpretation of the Total Asset Turnover Ratio may vary depending on the nature of the industry. Some industries, such as retail or manufacturing, typically have higher asset turnover ratios due to the nature of their business operations, while others, such as utilities or real estate, may have lower ratios. In conclusion, the Total Asset Turnover Ratio is a key metric in financial management that measures how efficiently a company utilizes its assets to generate sales. It provides valuable insights into the company's operational performance and its ability to generate revenue from its investments in assets.

Total Return

Total Return is a financial performance measure that takes into account both capital appreciation (or depreciation) and income generated from an investment. It calculates the overall return on an investment by including all forms of return, such as interest, dividends, and changes in the asset's value over a given time period. In finance, the return on an investment is a crucial factor in assessing its profitability and performance. However, it is not sufficient to only consider the capital gains or losses of an investment. By including all sources of return, the total return provides a more comprehensive picture of the investment's performance.

Total Shareholder Return (TSR)

Total Shareholder Return (TSR) is a financial metric used in the field of financial management to measure the performance of an investment over a specific period. TSR takes into account both capital appreciation (or depreciation) and dividends received by shareholders. TSR is calculated by dividing the difference between the ending value of an investment and the beginning value, including any dividends, by the beginning value. The result is then expressed as a percentage. This metric allows investors to assess the overall return they have received from their investment, taking into account both the change in share price and any income received in the form of dividends. TSR is a useful tool for evaluating the performance of an investment because it provides a comprehensive measure of the return achieved by shareholders. It takes into account both the income generated from dividends and the increase (or decrease) in the value of the investment. By considering both these factors, TSR provides a more complete picture of the return achieved by shareholders compared to just looking at capital appreciation alone. TSR can be used by investors to compare the performance of different investments and make informed decisions about where to allocate their capital. It allows investors to assess the total return they can expect to receive from an investment, taking into account both capital gains and any income generated. By considering the total shareholder return, investors can evaluate the overall performance of their investment and determine whether it has met their expectations. Furthermore, TSR can also be useful for evaluating the performance of company management. By comparing TSR with the performance of other companies in the same industry or sector, investors can assess whether the management team has been successful in creating value for shareholders. A positive TSR indicates that the investment has outperformed the market or industry average, while a negative TSR suggests that the investment has underperformed. In conclusion, Total Shareholder Return is a financial metric used in financial management to measure the performance of an investment. It takes into account both capital appreciation (or depreciation) and dividends received by shareholders, and is expressed as a percentage. TSR allows investors to evaluate the overall return achieved from an investment, considering both capital gains and income generated. It can be used to compare different investments and evaluate the performance of company management.

Trade Credit

Trade credit is a financial arrangement in which a supplier allows a customer to purchase goods or services on credit terms, allowing the customer to defer payment for a specified period of time. In other words, it is a form of short-term credit extended by one company to another company in a business-to-business transaction. The terms of trade credit typically include a specified period, known as the credit period, during which the customer can delay payment without incurring any interest or penalties. The credit period can vary depending on the agreement between the supplier and the customer, but it is typically 30 days or less. This allows the customer to receive and use the goods or services before having to pay for them, providing a source of liquidity and working capital for the customer. Trade credit provides several benefits to both the supplier and the customer. For the supplier, offering trade credit can help attract and retain customers, increase sales volume, and improve cash flow. It can also provide a competitive advantage by offering more flexible payment terms than competitors. For the customer, trade credit allows for easier cash flow management, as it provides a source of short-term financing without having to secure external loans or use existing cash reserves. It can also help improve the customer's credit rating, as timely payment of trade credit obligations can demonstrate financial responsibility. However, trade credit also carries risks for both parties. For the supplier, there is a risk of non-payment or delayed payment, which can negatively impact cash flow and profitability. To mitigate this risk, suppliers often conduct credit checks on potential customers and set credit limits to manage their exposure. For the customer, the risk lies in potential penalties or interest charges for late payment, which can strain liquidity and harm the business relationship with the supplier. Thus, it is important for both parties to carefully manage and monitor their trade credit arrangements.

Trailing Twelve Months (TTM)

Trailing Twelve Months (TTM) is a financial metric used in financial management to analyze the performance and financial health of a company. It refers to the most recent 12-month period for which financial data is available, starting from the last day of the previous month. TTM is commonly used in various financial ratios and calculations to provide a more accurate and up-to-date assessment of a company's financial performance, as it takes into account the most recent financial data. It allows analysts, investors, and stakeholders to evaluate a company's revenue, earnings, and other financial metrics over a specific period.

Tranche

A tranche is a term commonly used in financial management to refer to a specific portion or slice of a debt or investment instrument that has been divided into multiple parts. These parts, or tranches, are typically created with the goal of providing different levels of risk and return to investors or creditors. Tranches are commonly used in the context of structured financial products, such as collateralized debt obligations (CDOs) or mortgage-backed securities (MBS). In these cases, a pool of assets, such as a collection of loans or mortgages, is divided into different tranches based on various criteria, such as credit quality, maturity, or cash flow characteristics. Each tranche has its own set of terms and conditions, including its own interest rate, payment schedule, and priority of repayment. The tranches are structured in a way that allows investors or creditors to choose the tranche that best matches their risk appetite and investment goals. The senior tranche, or the tranche with the highest priority of repayment, is usually considered the least risky and offers lower interest rates compared to other tranches. It is the first to receive payments from the underlying assets and provides investors with a more secure stream of income. On the other hand, mezzanine or subordinated tranches carry higher levels of risk and typically offer higher interest rates to compensate for this risk. These tranches are subordinate to the senior tranche and are only paid after the senior tranche has been fully repaid. As a result, they are considered riskier but offer the potential for higher returns. Tranches can also be structured to include equity-like features, where investors receive a share of the profits or losses generated by the underlying assets. These equity tranches may have higher risk and return profiles compared to other tranches. In summary, a tranche is a specific portion or slice of a debt or investment instrument that has been divided into multiple parts. Tranches are used to provide different levels of risk and return to investors or creditors, allowing them to choose the tranche that best matches their investment goals and risk appetite.

Transaction Cost

Transaction cost refers to the expenses incurred in the process of purchasing or selling an asset or security. It includes various direct and indirect costs that are associated with executing a transaction in the financial markets. Direct transaction costs are explicit expenses that are directly payable to a broker or financial institution for the execution of a trade. These costs typically include brokerage fees, commissions, exchange fees, and regulatory charges. They are considered as part of the transaction cost because they reduce the overall profitability of the investment or trade. Indirect transaction costs, on the other hand, are the hidden costs that are not explicitly paid but can have a significant impact on the investment returns. These costs are associated with factors such as bid-ask spreads, market impact, and liquidity risk. Bid-ask spreads are the difference between the price at which a security can be bought and sold, and they represent the profit margin for market makers or intermediaries. Market impact refers to the effect of a large transaction on the market price of a security, which can result in unfavorable prices for subsequent trades. Liquidity risk arises when a security is illiquid or difficult to sell, leading to additional costs in executing the transaction. Transaction costs play a crucial role in financial management as they directly affect the overall profitability and performance of investment portfolios. High transaction costs can erode the returns on investments, especially for frequent traders or those with smaller investment amounts. Therefore, it is important for investors and fund managers to consider transaction costs while making investment decisions and designing trading strategies. Reducing transaction costs can be achieved through various strategies, such as negotiating lower brokerage fees, using online trading platforms with competitive commission rates, optimizing trade execution to minimize market impact, and selecting highly liquid securities to minimize liquidity risk. By managing transaction costs effectively, investors can enhance their investment returns and improve the efficiency of their portfolio management.

Transfer Pricing

Transfer pricing is a financial management concept that refers to the method used by companies to determine the price at which goods, services, or intangible assets are transferred between subsidiaries, branches, or divisions within the same organization. It involves the allocation of costs and revenues associated with these transactions in order to establish a fair and reasonable price for the transfer. The purpose of transfer pricing is to ensure that transactions between related entities are conducted in a manner that reflects the true economic value of the goods or services being exchanged. This is especially important in multinational companies where different subsidiaries or divisions may operate in different tax jurisdictions or have different cost structures. Transfer pricing plays a crucial role in financial management as it can impact a company's tax liability, profitability, and financial performance. By setting transfer prices that are consistent with market conditions and arm's length principles, companies can minimize the risk of tax audits, penalties, and disputes with tax authorities. To determine transfer prices, companies may use various methods such as comparable uncontrolled price (CUP), resale price method (RPM), cost plus method (CPM), or transactional net margin method (TNMM). These methods involve analyzing external market data and internal cost structures to establish a price that is reasonable and justifiable. Effective transfer pricing requires careful documentation, analysis, and monitoring to comply with both domestic and international tax regulations. Companies must maintain comprehensive records of the methodologies used, comparables analyzed, and assumptions made to support their transfer pricing decisions. Overall, transfer pricing is an essential tool in financial management that enables companies to allocate costs and revenues accurately among different entities within the organization. It ensures fairness, compliance with tax regulations, and optimal financial performance.

Treasury Bills (T-Bills)

Treasury Bills, also known as T-Bills, are short-term debt instruments issued by the government to finance its short-term requirements. They are considered one of the safest forms of investment since they are backed by the full faith and credit of the government. T-Bills are typically issued with maturities ranging from a few days to one year. They are sold in denominations of $1,000 or multiples thereof, and are sold at a discount from their face value. For example, a T-Bill with a face value of $1,000 may be sold at a price of $990, which represents a discount of $10.

Treasury Bond (T-Bond)

A Treasury Bond, also known as a T-Bond, is a type of debt instrument that is issued by the United States government to finance its borrowing needs. It is a long-term bond with a maturity period of 10 years or more. Treasury Bonds are considered to be one of the safest investment options available in the financial market as they are backed by the full faith and credit of the U.S. government. They are considered to be risk-free since the government has the power to tax its citizens to repay the debt.

Treasury Inflation-Protected Securities (TIPS)

Treasury Inflation-Protected Securities (TIPS) are a type of government bond that provides investors with protection against inflation. They are issued by the U.S. Department of the Treasury and are backed by the full faith and credit of the U.S. government. TIPS are designed to help investors preserve the purchasing power of their money. They offer a fixed interest rate and the principal value of the bond is adjusted to reflect changes in the Consumer Price Index (CPI), which measures the average price level of goods and services consumed by households. As inflation increases, the principal value of TIPS increases, providing investors with a return that keeps pace with inflation.

Treasury Stock

Treasury stock refers to the shares of a company's own stock that it has repurchased from the shareholders. These repurchased shares are held by the company itself and are not considered to be outstanding or available for sale to the public. When a company repurchases its own stock, the shares are typically kept in the company's treasury, hence the name "treasury stock." The repurchase of shares may be done for various reasons, such as to increase the company's earnings per share, to have shares available for employee stock option plans, or to have shares available for future acquisitions.

Turnkey Project

A turnkey project is a type of project management approach that involves the handing over of a fully completed project to the client at the end of the contract or agreement. Under this approach, the project contractor takes on the responsibility for the entire project, from design and planning to construction and installation. The client simply receives the finished project and assumes ownership and operation. In the context of financial management, a turnkey project is typically associated with large-scale infrastructure or construction projects, such as the development of power plants, industrial facilities, or transportation systems. These projects can involve significant investments and complex financial arrangements that require specialized expertise in project planning and financing. The key characteristic of a turnkey project in financial management is the transfer of risk and responsibility from the client to the contractor. The contractor assumes the financial risk associated with the project, including cost overruns, delays, and performance guarantees. This allows the client to focus on their core business activities without having to worry about the intricacies of project management and financing. From a financial perspective, turnkey projects often involve long-term financing arrangements, as the costs of the project may be spread out over several years. The contractor may secure financing from various sources, such as banks, private investors, or government agencies. The financial management of a turnkey project involves careful budgeting, cash flow management, and risk assessment to ensure the project's financial viability. In addition to financial management, turnkey projects also require effective project management to ensure the successful delivery of the project. This includes coordinating various stakeholders, managing timelines, and overseeing quality control. The project management aspect of turnkey projects is closely linked to financial management, as cost control and financial reporting are essential for monitoring and evaluating project progress.

Turnover Ratio

The turnover ratio is a financial metric used in the field of financial management to assess the efficiency and effectiveness of a company's operation in converting its assets into revenues. It measures the number of times a specific asset is converted into sales or revenue within a given period. The turnover ratio is calculated by dividing the net sales or revenue generated from a specific asset by the average value of that asset during a particular period. The result indicates how quickly the company is utilizing its assets to generate revenue. A higher turnover ratio suggests that the company is efficiently using its assets to generate sales, while a lower ratio indicates inefficiency in asset utilization. The turnover ratio is commonly used to analyze the efficiency of different assets within a company, such as inventory, accounts receivable, and fixed assets. By calculating the turnover ratio for each asset category, financial managers can identify areas of improvement or inefficiency within the company's operations. For example, a high turnover ratio for inventory indicates that the company is effectively selling its goods and minimizing excess inventory. This can lead to lower holding costs and improved cash flow. Conversely, a low turnover ratio for inventory suggests slow sales or excessive stockpiling, which can result in higher holding costs and reduced profitability. Similarly, analyzing the turnover ratio for accounts receivable can provide insights into the effectiveness of the company's credit and collection policies. A high turnover ratio indicates that the company is collecting payments from customers promptly, improving cash flow. On the other hand, a low turnover ratio suggests delayed collections and potential issues with credit management. Financial managers use the turnover ratio as a tool to assess the company's overall operational efficiency and profitability. By monitoring and improving the turnover ratio for different assets, companies can optimize their resource allocation, reduce costs, and enhance revenue generation.

Undercapitalization

Undercapitalization in the context of financial management refers to a situation where a company or business has insufficient capital or funding to support its operations, growth, and investment needs. It occurs when the capital structure of the business does not adequately meet its financial requirements. Undercapitalization can negatively impact the financial health and performance of a business in several ways. Firstly, it limits the company's ability to make necessary investments in machinery, equipment, technology, or research and development, hindering its competitiveness in the market. This lack of investment can result in outdated infrastructure, reduced productivity, and limited innovation capabilities. Secondly, undercapitalization may lead to liquidity problems as the business struggles to maintain sufficient cash flow to meet its day-to-day operational expenses and financial obligations. This can result in delayed payments to suppliers, inability to take advantage of trade discounts, or even defaulting on loans or obligations, which can damage the company's reputation and creditworthiness. Furthermore, undercapitalization can limit a business's ability to attract external financing or investment. Lenders and investors typically assess a company's capital structure and financial stability before providing funding. If a business is undercapitalized, it may be perceived as high-risk, making it difficult to secure loans or equity investments at favorable terms or interest rates. Undercapitalization can also hinder a company's growth potential. Without sufficient capital, the business may struggle to expand its operations, enter new markets, or develop new products or services. This can lead to missed opportunities for revenue growth and market share, allowing competitors to gain an advantage. It is important for businesses to properly assess their capital needs and ensure they have sufficient capital to support their financial requirements. This may involve raising additional funds through debt or equity financing, optimizing internal cash flow management, or revisiting the company's cost structure and financial planning.

Underwriting

Underwriting in the context of financial management refers to the process of evaluating and assessing the potential risks associated with providing financial support or insurance to individuals or organizations. It involves determining the level of risk involved, setting the terms and conditions of the financial agreement, and deciding the premium or interest rate charged. During the underwriting process, the financial institution or insurance company analyzes various factors to make an informed decision. These factors include the individual or organization's financial stability, credit history, income, existing debt, and the purpose of the financial support or insurance. The goal is to assess the likelihood of the borrower's or insured party's ability to meet their financial obligations. Underwriting is essential for managing financial risk and ensuring the financial institution's or insurance company's profitability. By carefully evaluating the risk factors, underwriters can protect against potential losses and determine the appropriate terms and conditions for the financial agreement. This helps the institution or company make informed decisions about who to provide financial support to or insure. Underwriting is commonly used in various financial activities, including lending, insurance, and securities issuance. In lending, underwriters assess the borrower's creditworthiness and determine the interest rate, loan amount, and repayment terms. For insurance, underwriters determine the coverage amount, deductible, and premium based on the insured party's risk profile. In securities issuance, underwriters evaluate the issuer's financial health and market conditions to set the terms and price of the securities being offered. The underwriting process typically involves collecting and analyzing financial documents, conducting thorough research, and applying industry-standard practices and guidelines. Underwriters use their expertise and judgment to assess the risk levels objectively and accurately. They may collaborate with other professionals, such as analysts, appraisers, and legal advisors, to gather necessary information and ensure a comprehensive evaluation. In conclusion, underwriting plays a crucial role in financial management by evaluating risks, setting terms and conditions, and determining the premium or interest rate. It helps financial institutions and insurance companies manage risk, ensure profitability, and make informed decisions about providing financial support or insurance to individuals or organizations.

Unleveraged Beta

The unleveraged beta is a measure of a company's systematic risk or volatility of returns in relation to the overall market. It is an important concept in financial management as it helps investors and financial analysts assess the risk and return characteristics of a specific investment or portfolio. In simple terms, beta measures the sensitivity of an asset's returns to changes in the market. It indicates how much an investment is likely to move, on average, for each unit change in the market index. A beta value of 1 indicates that the investment moves in line with the market, while a beta greater than 1 suggests higher volatility, and a beta less than 1 indicates lower volatility. The unleveraged beta specifically focuses on the risk of the asset or investment itself, without considering the impact of debt financing on the company's overall risk. It is calculated by regressing the asset's returns against the market returns, where the market returns serve as the independent variable and the asset returns as the dependent variable. The slope of the regression line represents the unleveraged beta. Unleveraged beta provides a measure of the asset's systematic risk, which cannot be diversified away through portfolio diversification. It is particularly useful for comparing the risk profiles of different investments or assets, as it allows for a standardized assessment of risk across different markets and industries. Investors and financial analysts use unleveraged beta to make informed investment decisions and construct diversified portfolios. By understanding the asset's risk characteristics, they can assess the potential returns and risks associated with the investment. Additionally, unleveraged beta is often used as a key input in various financial models, such as the capital asset pricing model (CAPM), to estimate the required rate of return on an investment. Overall, the unleveraged beta is a fundamental concept in financial management that helps in understanding the systematic risk of an investment or asset. It enables investors and financial analysts to make informed decisions, manage risk, and construct optimal portfolios.

Unsecured Loan

An unsecured loan, in the context of financial management, refers to a type of loan that is not secured by any form of collateral. In other words, it is a loan that is solely based on the borrower's creditworthiness and promise to repay the loan according to the agreed terms. Unlike secured loans, which are backed by assets such as real estate or vehicles, unsecured loans do not require the borrower to pledge any specific asset as collateral. This lack of collateral makes unsecured loans riskier for lenders, as they have no guarantee of recovering their funds in the event of default. As a result, unsecured loans generally have higher interest rates compared to secured loans.

Unsystematic Risk

Unsystematic risk, also known as specific risk or diversifiable risk, refers to the risk that is inherent to a specific investment or asset and can be mitigated through diversification. This type of risk is unique to a particular company, industry, or sector and is not related to overall market movements. Unsystematic risk arises due to factors that are specific to the individual investment and can be classified into two main categories: business risk and financial risk. Business risk is associated with the operations and performance of a particular company, such as changes in consumer demand, competition, or regulatory changes. Financial risk, on the other hand, relates to the company's financial structure, including its capital structure, liquidity, and leverage. Factors such as changes in interest rates, credit ratings, or access to financing can contribute to financial risk. Unlike systematic risk, which affects the overall market and cannot be diversified away, unsystematic risk can be reduced through diversification. Diversification involves spreading investments across different assets, sectors, or geographic regions to minimize the impact of any individual investment's performance. By holding a diversified portfolio, investors can reduce their exposure to unsystematic risk and potentially enhance their risk-adjusted returns. Furthermore, investors can also employ other risk management techniques to mitigate unsystematic risk. These techniques include conducting thorough research and analysis on individual investments, monitoring the performance and financial health of companies, and staying informed about industry trends and developments. By staying diligent and proactive in their investment decisions, investors can effectively manage and reduce unsystematic risk.

Utility Theory

Utility theory is a concept in financial management that involves analyzing and evaluating the preferences and decision-making behavior of investors and managers. It provides a framework for understanding how individuals make choices based on their subjective preferences and attitudes towards risk and uncertainty. At its core, utility theory posits that individuals make decisions by maximizing their overall satisfaction or well-being, referred to as utility. This utility is derived from the expected benefits, or returns, received from different financial instruments or investment opportunities. Utility theory assumes that individuals are rational decision-makers who aim to maximize their utility, given their available resources and constraints. It also considers that individuals have different risk attitudes, implying that their utility may vary depending on their tolerance for risk and uncertainty. In the context of financial management, utility theory helps explain investors' decisions when faced with different investment alternatives. It recognizes that investors must weigh the potential benefits against the associated risks and costs to make informed choices. Utility theory enables investors to evaluate investment opportunities and select those that offer the highest expected utility. One key concept within utility theory is the notion of indifference curves, which represent different combinations of risk and return that provide the same level of utility or satisfaction to an investor. These curves illustrate an investor's risk tolerance and preference for return, highlighting their trade-offs between risk and reward. Utility theory also considers the concept of expected utility, which combines an individual's subjective evaluation with the objective probabilities of different outcomes. By estimating the expected utility, investors can quantify the potential benefits and risks associated with different investment alternatives.

Valuation Ratios

Valuation ratios are financial metrics used to assess the value of a company or its securities. These ratios provide information about the attractiveness of an investment opportunity by comparing the market price of a company's stock or its financial performance to relevant financial variables. One commonly used valuation ratio is the price-to-earnings (P/E) ratio, which compares the market price per share to the earnings per share of a company. The P/E ratio is calculated by dividing the market price per share by the earnings per share. This ratio indicates the amount that investors are willing to pay for each dollar of earnings the company generates. A higher P/E ratio suggests that investors have high expectations for the company's future earnings growth. Another widely used valuation ratio is the price-to-book (P/B) ratio, which compares the market price per share to the book value per share of a company. The P/B ratio is calculated by dividing the market price per share by the book value per share. This ratio provides insight into whether the market price of a company's stock is overvalued or undervalued based on its net asset value. A P/B ratio below 1 suggests that the market price is lower than the company's book value. The price-to-sales (P/S) ratio is yet another valuation ratio that compares the market price per share to the revenue per share of a company. The P/S ratio is calculated by dividing the market price per share by the revenue per share. This ratio measures the market's valuation of a company's sales performance. A lower P/S ratio may indicate that the market is undervaluing the company's sales potential. Valuation ratios are useful tools for investors and analysts in evaluating investment opportunities. By comparing a company's financial metrics to the market price of its securities, valuation ratios provide insights into the expected future performance and value of a company. However, it is important to consider other factors and use valuation ratios in conjunction with other financial analysis techniques to make informed investment decisions.

Value Investing

Value investing is a financial management strategy that involves identifying and investing in undervalued stocks or assets. It is based on the principle that market prices do not always reflect the true intrinsic value of a company or asset, and that eventually the market will recognize and correct these mispricings. The goal of value investing is to find stocks or assets that are trading at a price lower than their intrinsic value. This is done by analyzing various indicators such as financial ratios, earnings, cash flow, and book value. Value investors believe that over the long term, the market will recognize and correctly price these assets, resulting in capital gains for the investor.

Value At Risk (VaR)

Value at Risk (VaR) is a widely used risk measurement technique in the field of financial management. It is a statistical measure that quantifies the potential loss that an investment or a portfolio of investments may incur within a certain time horizon, with a given level of confidence. VaR is based on the concept that financial markets are inherently volatile, and that the future returns of investments are uncertain. By calculating the VaR, financial managers can estimate the maximum loss that an investment or portfolio is likely to experience over a given time period.

Variable Cost

Variable cost is a financial term used in financial management to describe the expenses that change in direct proportion to the level of production or sales. It represents the cost of producing or providing additional units of a product or service. Variable costs are typically associated with the direct costs of labor, materials, and other inputs that are required to produce a product or provide a service. These costs fluctuate based on the quantity of output or sales volume. As production or sales increase, variable costs also increase proportionally, and vice versa.

Variable Interest Rate

A variable interest rate, also known as a floating interest rate, is a type of interest rate that can change over time. Unlike a fixed interest rate, which remains the same throughout the entire loan or investment term, a variable interest rate fluctuates based on certain factors, such as market conditions or changes in the underlying benchmark rate. In the context of financial management, variable interest rates are commonly used in various financial products, such as loans, mortgages, and credit cards. These rates are typically tied to a specific benchmark, such as the prime rate or the London Interbank Offered Rate (LIBOR), plus a margin determined by the lender or financial institution. One of the main advantages of a variable interest rate is its potential to decrease over time. If the benchmark or underlying rate decreases, the variable interest rate will also decrease, resulting in lower interest payments and potentially saving the borrower or investor money. However, it is important to note that variable interest rates can also increase, which can result in higher interest payments and potentially more expensive borrowing costs. Changes in variable interest rates are often determined by economic factors, such as inflation rates, central bank policies, and market demand for credit. For example, if the central bank decides to increase interest rates to control inflation, variable interest rates are likely to rise. On the other hand, if the central bank cuts interest rates to stimulate economic growth, variable interest rates may decrease. Financial management involves careful consideration of variable interest rates when making borrowing or investment decisions. It is important for individuals and businesses to assess their risk tolerance and financial stability before opting for a variable interest rate. Additionally, borrowers should closely monitor market conditions and economic indicators to anticipate potential changes in variable interest rates.

Variance Analysis

Variance analysis, in the context of financial management, refers to the process of comparing the expected or planned financial performance of a company with its actual performance in order to identify and analyze differences. It involves examining the discrepancies between budgeted or forecasted figures and the corresponding actual results, with the aim of understanding the reasons behind any variations. This analysis plays a crucial role in financial management as it allows businesses to evaluate their financial performance, identify areas of concern, and take appropriate management actions. By comparing the budgeted figures (which represent the desired or expected performance) with the actual results, variance analysis provides insights into how well a company has performed in meeting its financial goals or objectives. There are different types of variances that are commonly analyzed in financial management, including revenue variances, cost variances, and profit variances. Revenue variances focus on differences between the budgeted and actual sales or revenue figures, highlighting factors such as changes in pricing, volume, or product mix. Cost variances, on the other hand, examine discrepancies between budgeted and actual expenses, providing insights into factors such as increased costs of inputs, changes in production methods, or inefficiencies. Lastly, profit variances are calculated by comparing budgeted and actual profits, shedding light on the overall financial performance of the business. Variance analysis is an essential tool for financial managers and business owners to understand the reasons behind deviations from planned performance. By identifying and analyzing these differences, financial managers can make informed decisions to address any issues or inefficiencies, improve financial performance, and adjust future budgets and forecasts accordingly. It enables businesses to track progress, evaluate performance against goals, and take necessary actions to ensure profitability and long-term success.

Venture Capital Financing

Venture Capital Financing is a form of funding provided by investors, known as venture capitalists, to early-stage and high-potential companies with the aim of generating significant returns on their investment. This type of financing is typically sought by startups or small businesses that have limited access to traditional bank loans or other sources of capital. Venture capitalists are typically institutional investors, such as banks, pension funds, or specialized venture capital firms. They provide capital to these companies in exchange for equity ownership or a stake in the business. Unlike traditional loans, venture capital financing is considered a high-risk investment as most startup businesses have a high failure rate.

Venture Capital

Venture capital refers to the provision of financing to start-up or early-stage companies that have high growth potential but may lack the necessary funds to develop and expand their business. It involves investment in the form of equity or equity-related securities by venture capital firms or individuals, commonly known as venture capitalists. The primary objective of venture capital is to support innovative and promising business ideas that have the potential to generate substantial returns on investment. Venture capitalists typically invest in industries that are characterized by rapid technological advancements, such as technology, biotechnology, and clean energy, among others. Venture capital firms raise funds from various sources, including high-net-worth individuals, institutional investors, and pension funds, to create a pool of capital for investment. These firms employ a rigorous selection process to evaluate and identify companies with significant growth prospects. They often conduct extensive due diligence on the company's underlying business model, market potential, management team, and competitive landscape before making an investment decision. Once a venture capital firm invests in a company, it typically becomes actively involved in the strategic decision-making process. This may involve providing guidance and mentoring to the management team, leveraging industry contacts to facilitate business development opportunities, and assisting in the recruitment of key personnel. By doing so, venture capitalists not only provide financial capital but also contribute valuable expertise and resources to the growth and success of the investee company. As venture capital investments involve higher risks compared to traditional financing options, venture capitalists expect higher returns commensurate with the level of risk taken. They typically seek an exit strategy, such as an initial public offering (IPO) or acquisition, within a few years to realize their investment gains. The success of venture capital investments depends on the ability of the investee company to achieve significant growth and profitability.

Venture Capitalist

A venture capitalist is an individual or entity that provides financial backing to early-stage or high-potential companies in exchange for equity or ownership stakes in the business. These individuals or firms are typically experienced investors who seek to invest in start-up or emerging companies with the potential for significant growth and profitability. The primary role of a venture capitalist is to identify and invest in promising companies with high growth potential. They often invest in industries such as technology, healthcare, biotechnology, and social media, where there is a high level of innovation and potential for disruptive business models. They provide capital to these companies, which allows them to finance their operations, expand their market presence, and develop their products or services. Unlike traditional lenders, venture capitalists take on a higher level of risk by investing in companies that are in the early stages of development and may not have a proven track record or stable revenue streams. They understand that a significant portion of their investments may not yield favorable returns or could result in a complete loss of capital. However, they are willing to take this risk in exchange for the potential for substantial returns when the invested companies are successful. Aside from providing financial capital, venture capitalists also bring valuable expertise, industry knowledge, and connections to the companies they invest in. They often play an active role in the management and strategic decision-making of their portfolio companies, leveraging their experience and network to help drive growth and enhance the chances of success. Additionally, venture capitalists often have extensive networks of other investors, potential customers, and business partners, which can further benefit their portfolio companies. Once the invested companies reach a certain level of maturity or achieve specific milestones, venture capitalists may then exit their investments through methods such as a merger, acquisition, initial public offering (IPO), or secondary market sale. These exits allow the venture capitalists to realize their returns on investment and generate profits. In some cases, venture capitalists may also choose to provide follow-on funding to their portfolio companies to support their continued growth and expansion. In summary, venture capitalists are important players in the world of finance and entrepreneurship. They provide critical funding and support to start-up and early-stage companies, taking on higher risks in the hopes of substantial rewards. Their involvement goes beyond capital, as they actively participate in the growth and development of the companies they invest in, leveraging their expertise, connections, and resources to enhance the chances of success.

Volatility Index (VIX)

The Volatility Index (VIX) is a comprehensive measure of market volatility and investor sentiment in the financial markets. It is often referred to as the "fear index" as it reflects the level of uncertainty and fear among investors. The VIX is calculated based on the implied volatility of options on the S&P 500 index, which is the benchmark for the US stock market. The VIX is used as a gauge to assess the level of risk and market stability. It is measured on a scale from 0 to 100, with higher values indicating higher volatility and greater investor anxiety. A low VIX indicates that the market is relatively stable, while a high VIX suggests that investors are anticipating significant price swings and uncertainty in the market. The VIX is widely used by investors, traders, and analysts to manage their portfolios and make informed investment decisions. It provides valuable insights into market sentiment and helps investors gauge the level of risk in the market. By monitoring changes in the VIX, investors can adjust their investment strategies and take appropriate actions to protect their portfolios. One of the key applications of the VIX is in hedging strategies. Investors can use VIX futures and options to hedge against market volatility and protect their portfolios from potential losses. For example, if an investor expects the market to become more volatile in the future, they can purchase VIX futures or options to offset any potential losses in their stock portfolio. In addition, the VIX is also used as a benchmark to compare the performance of other asset classes. It can be used to assess the risk and return trade-off of different investment strategies and asset classes. For instance, if the VIX is significantly higher than historical levels, it may suggest that the market is experiencing a heightened level of risk, and investors may need to adjust their allocation to riskier assets. In conclusion, the Volatility Index (VIX) is a widely followed measure of market volatility and investor sentiment. It is used by investors, traders, and analysts to assess risk, manage portfolios, and make informed investment decisions.

Volatility Skew

Volatility skew, in the context of financial management, refers to the asymmetric curve or pattern that can be observed when plotting the implied volatilities of options with different strike prices but the same expiration date. It is a graphical representation of the market's perception of the potential risk and future movements of the underlying asset. The volatility skew is primarily observed in equity options and is commonly used by traders and investors to gain insights into market sentiment and directional biases. It is often depicted on a chart with the strike prices on the horizontal axis and the implied volatilities on the vertical axis. The presence of a volatility skew suggests that market participants have a different perception of the risk associated with different strike prices. In general, the skew appears in one of two ways: a positive skew or a negative skew. A positive volatility skew, also known as a "left skew," occurs when the implied volatilities increase as the strike prices decrease. This indicates that the market is pricing in a higher potential for downward movements in the underlying asset. It suggests that market participants are more concerned about a significant decline in the price of the asset and are therefore willing to pay higher premiums for put options with lower strike prices. Conversely, a negative volatility skew, or a "right skew," occurs when the implied volatilities increase as the strike prices increase. This suggests that the market is pricing in a higher potential for upward movements in the underlying asset. Market participants are more concerned about a significant increase in the price of the asset and are willing to pay higher premiums for call options with higher strike prices. The volatility skew can provide valuable insights for option traders and investors. It can help them identify opportunities to implement strategies such as buying or selling options to take advantage of perceived market mispricing or to hedge against specific risks. In conclusion, the volatility skew is a graphical representation of the market's perception of risk and future movements in the underlying asset. By analyzing the skew, traders and investors can gain insights into market sentiment and potentially exploit opportunities in the options market.

Volatility Smile

A volatility smile refers to a graphical representation of the implied volatility of options with the same underlying asset and expiration date, but different strike prices. It is named so because of its distinctive shape, which resembles a smile. The implied volatility is a measure of the market's perception of the likelihood of price movements in the underlying asset. It reflects the expected level of volatility that investors anticipate during the option's lifespan. Generally, the higher the implied volatility, the greater the expected price swings in the market. The volatility smile arises due to the market's perception of potential risks associated with certain strike prices. In the options market, strike prices that are close to the current market price of the underlying asset are considered at-the-money options. Strikes that are lower than the current market price are known as in-the-money options, while those higher are called out-of-the-money options. Typically, a volatility smile depicts a higher implied volatility for out-of-the-money options compared to at-the-money options. This is because investors perceive higher risks and potential price movements for options that are either deeply in or out of the money. The smile shape is a result of investors demanding a higher premium to compensate for the perceived risks. There are several possible reasons for the existence of a volatility smile. Firstly, it can be attributed to the skewness in the distribution of the underlying asset's returns. In many financial markets, returns have a tendency to exhibit negative skewness, meaning that extreme negative returns occur more frequently than extreme positive returns. This skewness contributes to the higher implied volatility on out-of-the-money options. Additionally, the volatility smile can be influenced by supply and demand dynamics in the options market. Market participants, especially institutional investors, may have specific trading strategies that involve buying or selling options at particular strike prices. Their actions impact the prices of these options, leading to deviations in implied volatility and the formation of the volatility smile.

Warrant

A warrant, in the context of financial management, refers to a financial instrument that gives the holder the right, but not the obligation, to buy a specified number of underlying securities (such as stocks, bonds, or commodities) at a predetermined price within a specific time period. Warrants are typically issued by corporations as a way to raise additional capital. They can be thought of as a type of derivative security, as their value is derived from the value of the underlying assets. However, unlike options, which are also derivative instruments, warrants are issued by the underlying company itself rather than by a separate financial institution.

Wash Sale

A wash sale is a transaction that occurs when an investor sells a security for a loss and buys the same or a substantially identical security within a certain period of time, typically within 30 days before or after the sale. The purpose of a wash sale is to create a tax loss that can be used to offset capital gains, thereby reducing the investor's overall tax liability. However, the Internal Revenue Service (IRS) has specific rules regarding wash sales to prevent investors from artificially creating losses for tax purposes. According to these rules, if an investor engages in a wash sale, they cannot claim the tax loss on the sale. Instead, the cost basis of the newly purchased security is adjusted to account for the disallowed loss. This means that the investor's tax basis in the new security will be the same as it was in the original security that was sold.

Weighted Average Cost Of Capital (WACC)

The Weighted Average Cost of Capital (WACC) is a financial metric used in the field of financial management to calculate the overall cost of capital for a company. It represents the average rate of return that a company must generate in order to satisfy its investors, both debt and equity holders.WACC takes into account the proportion of debt and equity capital used in the company's capital structure, as well as the respective costs of each type of capital. It is calculated by taking the weighted average of the cost of debt and the cost of equity, based on their proportion in the capital structure. The calculation of WACC involves several steps. Firstly, the cost of debt is determined by considering the interest rate paid on the company's debt obligations. This cost may also include any other expenses associated with obtaining and maintaining debt, such as fees and commissions. The proportion of debt in the capital structure is then multiplied by the cost of debt to obtain the weighted cost of debt. Secondly, the cost of equity is calculated by using the capital asset pricing model (CAPM) or other appropriate methods. This method takes into account the systematic risk of the company's equity, often represented by the beta coefficient. The proportion of equity in the capital structure is multiplied by the cost of equity to obtain the weighted cost of equity. Finally, the weighted cost of debt and the weighted cost of equity are added together to obtain the WACC. This metric represents the average rate of return that the company needs to generate in order to meet the expectations of its investors and maintain the value of the business. It is commonly used in investment decision-making processes, such as determining the feasibility of capital investment projects or assessing the value of companies. In summary, the WACC is a financial metric that calculates the weighted average cost of capital for a company, based on the proportion and cost of debt and equity in its capital structure. It helps determine the minimum rate of return that a company must achieve in order to satisfy its investors and is widely used in financial management for decision-making purposes.

Weighted Average Maturity (WAM)

Weighted Average Maturity (WAM) is a financial management indicator that measures the average time until a portfolio's debt obligations are expected to be repaid. It is calculated by taking the sum of the product of each debt instrument's outstanding amount and its respective maturity date, divided by the total outstanding amount of the portfolio. The WAM provides insights into the maturity structure and risk profile of a debt portfolio, enabling investors and managers to assess the timing and potential cash flow variations associated with their holdings. It is a commonly used metric in fixed-income investments, such as bonds, loans, or mortgage-backed securities.

Working Capital Management

Working capital management refers to the process of managing a company's current assets and liabilities in order to optimize its liquidity and operational efficiency. It involves monitoring and controlling the company's cash, inventory, accounts receivable, and accounts payable to ensure that the business has enough working capital to meet its short-term financial obligations and support its day-to-day operations. Effective working capital management is crucial for the financial health and stability of a company. By efficiently managing its working capital, a company can improve its cash flow, enhance its profitability, and minimize the risk of insolvency. It allows the company to take advantage of business opportunities, negotiate better terms with suppliers and customers, and maintain a favorable credit standing with lenders and investors. The main components of working capital management include managing the cash conversion cycle, optimizing inventory management, and monitoring accounts receivable and accounts payable. The cash conversion cycle measures the time it takes for a company to convert its investments in inventory and other resources into cash flow from sales. By reducing the cash conversion cycle, a company can free up cash and improve its liquidity. Inventory management involves balancing the costs of carrying inventory against the risk of stockouts and lost sales. It includes forecasting demand, setting optimal inventory levels, and implementing efficient ordering and production processes. Accounts receivable management focuses on collecting customer payments in a timely manner, while accounts payable management entails managing supplier payments to maintain good relationships and take advantage of payment discounts.

227

There are several strategies and techniques that companies can use to improve their working capital management. These include implementing effective cash flow forecasting and budgeting, negotiating favorable payment terms with vendors, optimizing the credit terms offered to customers, and implementing efficient inventory control systems. Additionally, companies can improve their working capital management by streamlining their processes, adopting technology solutions, and implementing robust internal controls to prevent fraud and other financial risks. In conclusion, working capital management is a critical aspect of financial management that involves managing a company's current assets and liabilities to ensure that it has enough liquidity to support its operations. By effectively managing its working capital, a company can enhance its profitability, improve its cash flow, and reduce the risk of financial distress.

Working Capital Ratio

The working capital ratio is a financial metric used in financial management to assess a company's ability to cover its short-term obligations with its current assets. It is also known as the current ratio or the working capital position ratio. The formula for calculating the working capital ratio is: Working Capital Ratio = Current Assets / Current Liabilities The current assets consist of cash, accounts receivable, inventory, and other assets that are expected to be converted into cash within the next 12 months. The current liabilities include accounts payable, short-term debt, and other obligations that are due within the next 12 months. A working capital ratio above 1 indicates that a company has more current assets than current liabilities, which suggests that it has a strong liquidity position. This means that the company has sufficient resources to meet its short-term obligations and fund its operations. On the other hand, a working capital ratio below 1 indicates that a company may have difficulty in meeting its short-term obligations, which may raise concerns about its financial health and ability to operate effectively. The working capital ratio is an important tool for financial managers as it helps them assess a company's ability to manage its working capital efficiently. By comparing the working capital ratio of a company with industry benchmarks or competitors, financial managers can gain insights into the company's liquidity position and identify areas for improvement. They can also use the working capital ratio to evaluate the impact of different financial decisions, such as changes in inventory levels or payment terms, on the company's short-term liquidity. In conclusion, the working capital ratio is a key financial metric used in financial management to evaluate a company's ability to cover its short-term obligations. It provides valuable insights into a company's liquidity position and helps financial managers make informed decisions regarding working capital management.

Working Capital Turnover Ratio

The working capital turnover ratio is a financial metric used by businesses to measure their efficiency in utilizing their working capital to generate sales revenue. It is a ratio that indicates how many times a company's working capital is converted into sales revenue over a specific period of time, usually a year. The formula for calculating the working capital turnover ratio is: Working Capital Turnover Ratio = Net Sales / Average Working Capital Net sales represents the total revenue generated by a company after deducting any sales returns, allowances, and discounts. Average working capital is the average amount of working capital a company has during a specific time period. Working capital is the difference between a company's current assets (such as cash, accounts receivable, and inventory) and its current liabilities (such as accounts payable and short-term debt). The working capital turnover ratio is used by financial managers and investors to assess how efficiently a company is using its working capital to generate sales. A higher ratio indicates that a company is able to generate more sales revenue with a given amount of working capital, which suggests better efficiency and profitability. On the other hand, a lower ratio may indicate that a company is not effectively using its working capital to generate sales, which may be a sign of poor financial management or operational inefficiencies. It is important to note that the ideal working capital turnover ratio varies by industry, and it is crucial to compare a company's ratio with its industry peers for meaningful analysis.

Working Capital Turnover

Working Capital Turnover is a financial ratio that measures the efficiency and effectiveness of a company's utilization of its working capital. It determines how well a company generates sales

228

revenue from its working capital investment. Working capital is the difference between a company's current assets and current liabilities. It represents the funds available to cover day-to-day operations and is an essential component for a company's growth and survival. The efficient management of working capital is crucial for maintaining a healthy cash flow and meeting short-term obligations. The Working Capital Turnover ratio is calculated by dividing the net sales of a company by its average working capital. Net sales represent the total revenue generated from the sale of goods or services after deducting any returns and allowances. Average working capital is calculated by adding the beginning and ending working capital amounts and dividing the sum by two. A higher working capital turnover ratio indicates that a company is effectively utilizing its working capital to generate sales revenue. This implies that the company is efficiently managing its current assets and liabilities, maintaining an optimal level of working capital to support its operations. It also suggests that the company has a high level of operational efficiency, as it can generate a significant amount of sales revenue from a relatively smaller investment in working capital. On the other hand, a lower working capital turnover ratio implies that a company is not utilizing its working capital efficiently to generate sales revenue. This may indicate that the company has excessive or inadequate levels of current assets or liabilities, leading to inefficiencies in its operations. It may also suggest that the company is experiencing difficulties in converting its working capital into sales revenue, possibly due to issues such as ineffective inventory management, slow collection of accounts receivable, or inefficient utilization of short-term financing. In summary, the working capital turnover ratio is a crucial financial metric that measures how effectively a company utilizes its working capital to generate sales revenue. It provides insights into the efficiency of a company's working capital management and operational performance, enabling businesses to identify areas for improvement and make informed decisions to enhance profitability and sustainability.

Working Capital

Working capital refers to the financial resources that a company has readily available to meet its daily operational needs and obligations. It represents the difference between a company's current assets and its current liabilities. In simple terms, working capital is the amount of money a company has to pay its short-term expenses and obligations, such as purchasing raw materials, paying utility bills, or covering payroll costs. It is a vital measure of a company's financial health and its ability to manage its day-to-day operations effectively. Working capital is calculated by subtracting a company's current liabilities from its current assets. Current assets include cash, accounts receivable, inventory, and any other assets that can be easily converted into cash within a year. Current liabilities, on the other hand, include accounts payable, accrued expenses, short-term loans, and other obligations that need to be paid within a year. A positive working capital indicates that a company has enough liquid resources to cover its short-term obligations. This allows the company to continue its operations smoothly without experiencing interruptions due to a lack of funds. On the other hand, a negative working capital suggests that a company may be facing financial difficulties and could struggle to meet its short-term obligations. Managing working capital efficiently is crucial for businesses of all sizes. It requires careful monitoring and control of cash flow, inventory levels, accounts receivable, and accounts payable. By optimizing these components, a company can maintain a healthy working capital position and improve its overall financial performance. Having a strong working capital position is especially important during times of economic uncertainty or when facing unexpected expenses. It provides a cushion to absorb financial shocks and allows a company to seize new opportunities or invest in growth initiatives.

Yield Curve Control (YCC)

Yield Curve Control (YCC) is a monetary policy tool employed by central banks to influence interest rates and market expectations by targeting the yield curve of government bonds. Under YCC, central banks set a target for specific bond yields along the yield curve, typically by purchasing or selling government securities in the open market. The goal is to keep borrowing costs low and maintain stability in financial markets. YCC operates by exerting control over the shape and level of the yield curve. The yield curve represents the relationship between bond yields and their respective maturities. In a normal yield curve, longer-term bonds have higher yields compared to shorter-term bonds to compensate investors for the added risk and uncertainty over longer periods. However, in the case of YCC, the central bank aims to normalize or flatten the yield curve by targeting specific bond yields. When implementing YCC, the central bank typically focuses on a specific maturity range, often the short or medium-term part of the curve. By purchasing or selling government bonds with these maturities, the central bank can influence their prices and yields. When the central bank wants to lower interest rates, it buys government bonds, which increases their prices and reduces their yields. Conversely, when the central bank wants to raise interest rates, it sells government bonds, which decreases their prices and increases their yields. YCC is often used as a complement to other monetary policy tools, such as adjusting the benchmark interest rate or quantitative easing. It provides central banks with additional flexibility to stimulate economic growth, control inflation, and stabilize financial markets. In conclusion, Yield Curve Control is a monetary policy strategy where central banks target specific bond yields along the yield curve to influence interest rates and market expectations. By purchasing or selling government bonds, central banks can shape the yield curve and maintain stability in financial markets. YCC is a valuable tool in the arsenal of central banks to manage economic conditions and promote sustainable growth.

Yield Curve

The yield curve is a graphical representation of the interest rates of fixed-income securities plotted against their respective maturities. It is a crucial tool in financial management as it provides insight into market expectations regarding future interest rates and economic conditions. The yield curve depicts the relationship between the interest rate (yield) and the time remaining until maturity for a range of fixed-income instruments, such as government bonds, corporate bonds, and treasury bills. Typically, the yield curve displays the yields for different maturities, ranging from short-term (e.g., 1 month) to long-term (e.g., 30 years). The shape of the yield curve is influenced by various factors, including monetary policy, inflation expectations, and market supply and demand dynamics. In a healthy economic environment, the yield curve tends to exhibit a normal or upward-sloping shape, where longer-term maturities offer higher yields compared to shorter-term maturities. This reflects the expectation that investors require higher compensation (yield) for tying up their capital for an extended period. Conversely, an inverted yield curve occurs when shorter-term maturities bear higher yields than longer-term maturities. This phenomenon is often associated with an economic slowdown or recession, as investors anticipate future interest rate cuts and lower inflation in response to worsening economic conditions. Financial managers closely monitor the yield curve as it provides crucial information for various financial decisions. For instance, analyzing the yield curve helps in determining an optimal debt structure, as it reveals the relationship between short-term and long-term borrowing costs. Additionally, the yield curve aids in assessing investment opportunities and managing risk. By analyzing the slope and shape of the curve, financial managers can make informed decisions regarding asset allocation and portfolio management strategies.

Yield To Call (YTC)

The Yield to Call (YTC) is a financial measure used in the field of financial management. It represents the annual return an investor would receive if a bond is called by the issuer before its maturity date. Bonds often have call provisions that allow the issuer to redeem the bond before its full duration. When a bond is called, it means that the issuer buys back the bond from the investors, usually at a premium to the face value or par value of the bond. The YTC takes into consideration the price paid to purchase the bond, the coupon payments received until the call date, and the call price at which the bond will be redeemed. It is calculated using a discounted cash flow (DCF) analysis, taking into account the time value of money. The YTC is expressed as an annual percentage rate (APR) and is used by investors to assess the potential return on an investment if the bond is called prior to its maturity.

Yield To Maturity (YTM)

Yield to Maturity (YTM) is a financial concept used in the field of investment and financial management to calculate the anticipated return an investor would receive from a fixed-income security, such as a bond, if it is held until its maturity date. YTM is expressed as an annual percentage rate. YTM takes into account several factors to determine the total return a bondholder would earn if they held the bond until maturity and received all the periodic interest payments and the face value of the bond at maturity. These factors include the coupon rate, the bond's market price, the time to maturity, and the reinvestment rate for the interest payments received. When calculating the YTM, the coupon rate is compared to the bond's current market price. If the bond is trading at a premium or a discount, the YTM will be higher or lower than the coupon rate, respectively. This is because the YTM accounts for the capital gain or loss that an investor would experience if the bond is held until maturity. The time to maturity is also an essential factor in calculating the YTM. The longer the time to maturity, the higher the YTM, assuming all other factors remain constant. This is because the longer-term bonds typically offer higher coupon rates to compensate investors for the risk associated with holding the investment for an extended period. Finally, the reinvestment rate for the periodic interest payments is considered when calculating the YTM. It assumes that the interest payments received from the bondholder will be reinvested at a rate equal to the YTM. The YTM accounts for the compounding effect of reinvesting the interest payments over the life of the bond. In summary, Yield to Maturity (YTM) is a crucial financial concept used to estimate the annualized return an investor would earn if they hold a fixed-income security until its maturity date. It considers factors such as the coupon rate, current market price, time to maturity, and reinvestment rate to determine the total return. By calculating the YTM, investors can assess the attractiveness of a bond investment and compare it to other investment opportunities.

Yield

Yield refers to the return on investment (ROI) received from an investment, typically expressed as a percentage. In the context of financial management, yield is an important measure that helps assess the profitability and performance of an investment. The yield can be calculated in different ways depending on the type of investment. One commonly used measure is the yield to maturity (YTM) for fixed-income securities such as bonds. YTM represents the total return an investor will receive if the bond is held until its maturity date and includes both the periodic interest payments and any capital gains or losses. It takes into account the bond's current market price, the face value of the bond, the coupon rate, and the time left until maturity. Another measure of yield is the dividend yield, which is relevant for stocks. It is calculated by dividing the annual dividend per share by the stock's current market price. Dividend yield indicates how much cash flow an investor can expect to receive from owning a particular stock in relation to the price paid for it. Yield can also be used to evaluate the performance of mutual funds and other investment vehicles. Total yield for a mutual fund includes both income generated from dividends and interest, as well as any capital appreciation or depreciation. This measure allows investors to compare the performance of different funds and understand the overall return on their investment. When comparing investment options, it is essential to consider the risk associated with each investment alongside the potential yield. Generally, higher-yielding investments tend to carry higher risk. Therefore, financial managers must assess the risk-to-yield ratio to determine if an investment aligns with their risk tolerance and investment objectives. In summary, yield is a crucial concept in financial management that measures the return on investment. It can be calculated in various ways, depending on the type of investment, and provides valuable insights into the profitability and performance of an investment.

Zero Coupon Bond (Zero Coupon)

A zero coupon bond, also known as a zero coupon or simply a discount bond, is a type of fixed-income security that does not pay any periodic interest payments. Instead, it is sold at a discount to its face value and pays the full face value to the bondholder at maturity. Zero coupon bonds are typically issued with a long maturity period, sometimes ranging from 10 to 30 years. During this period, the bondholder does not receive any interest payments. However, they have the potential to earn a return by purchasing the bond at a discount and receiving the full face value at maturity.

Zero Coupon Bond

A zero-coupon bond is a type of fixed-income investment that does not pay periodic interest payments to bondholders. Instead, it is sold at a discount to its face value and matures at its face value at a predetermined future date. This means that the investor will receive a lump sum payment equal to the bond's face value when it reaches its maturity. Unlike traditional bonds, zero-coupon bonds do not generate regular income for investors in the form of coupon payments. Instead, the return on investment comes from the difference between the purchase price and the face value of the bond. This difference is commonly referred to as the bond's discount, and it represents the implied interest that the investor will earn over the life of the bond.

Zero Growth Rate

A zero growth rate, in the context of financial management, refers to a situation where a company's sales, profits, and assets remain steady over time without any increase or decrease. It indicates that the business is maintaining a stable performance without any growth or decline in its operations.In financial terms, zero growth rate can be represented by a constant rate of return on investment (ROI) or earnings per share (EPS) over multiple accounting periods. This means that the company is neither expanding nor contracting, but instead maintaining a consistent level of financial performance.

Zero-Coupon Bond

A zero-coupon bond is a type of bond that does not pay any periodic interest payments to the bondholder. Instead, it is sold at a discounted rate and the bondholder receives a fixed amount at maturity, which is typically the face value of the bond. The difference between the discounted purchase price and the face value is the return that the bondholder earns. Zero-coupon bonds are also known as discount bonds or deep discount bonds. They are typically issued by governments, municipalities, and corporations as a way to raise capital. These bonds are particularly attractive to investors who are seeking a predictable return on their investment, as the fixed amount at maturity is known in advance. Since zero-coupon bonds do not pay interest during their term, they are sold at a significant discount to their face value. The discount is calculated by considering factors such as the prevailing interest rates, the term to maturity, and the creditworthiness of the issuer. The bondholder purchases the bond at the discounted price and holds it until maturity when they receive the full face value. One of the key advantages of zero-coupon bonds is that they have a fixed maturity date. This allows investors to plan for a specific future cash flow and can be beneficial for financing long-term financial goals or obligations. Additionally, the fixed return offered by these bonds can act as a hedge against inflation, as the purchasing power of the fixed amount at maturity is preserved regardless of changes in the general price level. However, there are also some risks associated with zero-coupon bonds. One of the most significant risks is interest rate risk. Since the price of the bond is heavily influenced by prevailing interest rates, changes in interest rates can impact the market value of the bond. If interest rates rise, the price of the bond may decline, resulting in a potential capital loss for the bondholder. In summary, zero-coupon bonds are a type of bond that does not pay periodic interest payments. They are sold at a discount to their face value and the bondholder receives the full face value at maturity. These bonds offer a fixed return and can be attractive to investors seeking a predictable cash flow. However, they also carry interest rate risk and may not be suitable for all investors.

Zero-Sum Game

A zero-sum game in the context of financial management refers to a situation where the gains and losses of participants involved in a transaction or investment are balanced out. In other words, the total benefits and losses of all the parties involved sum up to zero. Typically, in financial management, a zero-sum game arises when there is a fixed amount of wealth or resources involved, and any gain made by one party is offset by an equivalent loss incurred by another party. This means that the total value remains constant throughout the game or transaction.

www.ingramcontent.com/pod-product-compliance
Lightning Source LLC
LaVergne TN
LVHW041204050326
832903LV00020B/445

* 9 7 9 8 8 6 2 3 3 9 1 5 4 *